ZEW Economic Studies

Publication Series of the Centre for European Economic Research (ZEW), Mannheim, Germany

AF771828

ZEW Economic Studies

Further volumes of this series can be found at our homepage:
springeronline.com/series/4041

Vol. 9: O. Bürgel
The Internationalization of British Start-up Companies in High-Technology Industries
2000. XIV, 230 pp. ISBN 3-7908-1292-7

Vol. 10: J. Hemmelskamp et al. (Eds.)
Innovation-Oriented Environmental Regulation
Theoretical Approaches and Empirical Analysis
2000. VI, 348 pp. ISBN 3-7908-1313-3

Vol. 11: K.L. Brockmann, M. Stronzik (Eds.)
Flexible Mechanisms for an Efficient Climate Policy
Cost Saving Policies and Business Opportunities
2000. VIII, 130 pp. ISBN 3-7908-1314-1

Vol. 12: W. Smolny
Endogenous Innovations and Knowledge Spillovers
A Theoretical and Empirical Analysis
2000. VIII, 277 pp. ISBN 3-7908-1320-6

Vol. 13: M. Lechner, F. Pfeiffer (Eds.)
Econometric Evaluation of Labour Market Policies
2001. X, 242 pp. ISBN 3-7908-1372-9

Vol. 14: M. Beise
Lead Markets
Country-Specific Success Factors of the Global Diffusion of Innovations
2001. XVI, 305 pp. ISBN 3-7908-1430-X

Vol. 15: O.H. Jacobs, C. Spengel
Effective Tax Burden in Europe
Current Situation, Past Developments and Simulations of Reforms
2002. X, 131 pp. ISBN 3-7908-1470-9

Vol. 16: U. Kaiser
Innovation, Employment, and Firm Performance in the German Service Sector
2002. X, 164 pp. ISBN 3-7908-1481-4

Vol. 17: J. Köke
Corporate Governance in Germany
An Empirical Investigation
2002. VIII, 184 pp. ISBN 3-7908-1511-X

Vol. 18: E. Wolf
What Hampers Part-Time Work?
An Empirical Analysis of Wages, Hours Restrictions and Employment from a Dutch-German Perspective
2003. X, 174 pp. ISBN 3-7908-0006-6

Vol. 19: P. Cecchini et al. (Eds.)
The Incomplete European Market for Financial Services
2003. XII, 255 pp. ISBN 3-7908-0013-9

Vol. 20: C. Böhringer, A. Löschel (Eds.)
Empirical Modeling of the Economy and the Environment
2003. VI, 326 pp. ISBN 3-7908-0078-3

Vol. 21: K. Rennings, T. Zwick (Eds.)
Employment Impacts of Cleaner Production
2003. VIII, 322 pp. ISBN 3-7908-0093-7

Vol. 22: O. Bürgel, A. Fier, G. Licht, G. Murray
The Internationalisation of Young High-Tech Firms
An Empirical Analysis in Germany and the United Kingdom
2003. XII, 291 pp. ISBN 3-7908-0120-8

Vol. 23: F. Hüfner
Foreign Exchange Intervention as a Monetary Policy Instrument
Evidence for Inflation Targeting Countries
2004. X, 175 pp. ISBN 3-7908-0128-3

Vol. 24: E. Lüders
Economic Foundation of Asset Price Processes
2004. XII, 121 pp. ISBN 3-7908-0149-6

Vol. 25: F. Reize
Leaving Unemployment for Self-Employment
An Empirical Study
2004. XII, 241 pp. ISBN 3-7908-0168-2

Vol. 26: Ch. Böhringer, A. Löschel (Eds.)
Climate Change Policy and Global Trade
2004. VIII, 381 pp. ISBN 3-7908-0171-2

Lothar Lammersen · Robert Schwager

The Effective Tax Burden of Companies in European Regions

An International Comparison

With 48 Figures
and 36 Tables

Physica-Verlag
A Springer Company

ZEW
Zentrum für Europäische
Wirtschaftsforschung GmbH
Centre for European
Economic Research

Series Editor
Prof. Dr. Dr. h.c. mult. Wolfgang Franz

Authors
Lothar Lammersen
Centre for European Economic Research (ZEW)
L 7,1
68161 Mannheim
lammersen@zew.de

Professor Dr. Robert Schwager
Georg-August-Universität Göttingen
Wirtschaftswissenschaftliche Fakultät
Platz der Göttinger Sieben 3
37073 Göttingen
Germany
rschwag@gwdg.de

Cataloging-in-Publication Data
Library of Congress Control Number: 2004113687

ISBN 3-7908-1562-4 Physica-Verlag Heidelberg New York

This work is subject to copyright. All rights are reserved, whether the whole or part of the material is concerned, specifically the rights of translation, reprinting, reuse of illustrations, recitation, broadcasting, reproduction on microfilm or in any other way, and storage in data banks. Duplication of this publication or parts thereof is permitted only under the provisions of the German Copyright Law of September 9, 1965, in its current version, and permission for use must always be obtained from Physica-Verlag. Violations are liable for prosecution under the German Copyright Law.

Physica-Verlag is a part of Springer Science+Business Media

springeronline.com

© Physica-Verlag Heidelberg 2005
Printed in Germany

The use of general descriptive names, registered names, trademarks, etc. in this publication does not imply, even in the absence of a specific statement, that such names are exempt from the relevant protective laws and regulations and therefore free for general use.

Cover design: Erich Dichiser, ZEW, Mannheim

SPIN 11324652 43/3130-5 4 3 2 1 0 – Printed on acid-free paper

Preface

This book is the result of a research project commissioned by the «IBC BAK International Benchmark Club»®, an initiative by BAK Basel Economics, and carried out by Zentrum für Europäische Wirtschaftsforschung (ZEW – Centre for European Economic Research), Mannheim. It contributes to the IBC's effort to evaluate and compare economic performance and location factors across European regions. The report provides the background to the headline figures presented at the International Benchmark Forum on June 11th and 12th, 2003, in Basel, as well as a large number of additional results.

This work has benefited from the help of many institutions and individuals. Above all, we are indebted to the sponsors for financing the project in times of limited fiscal resources. We also would like to thank the members of the Steering Committee of the IBC module on taxation for their enduring support. Special thanks go to Kurt Dütschler of the Swiss Federal Tax Administration who was always ready to provide information on detailed aspects of the Swiss tax system. We are grateful to Christoph Koellreuter and Martin Eichler from BAK Basel for organising and promoting research on taxation inside the IBC. Our colleagues Christina Elschner and Gerd Gutekunst, ZEW, gave many detailed and very helpful comments. Finally, we owe thanks to Ulrike Nicolaus and Monika Jackmann who provided able help in preparing the final draft of this report. Of course, all remaining errors are our sole responsibility.

Mannheim and Göttingen, June 2004
Lothar Lammersen and Robert Schwager

Sponsors of the IBC module 'Taxation':

- Eidgenössische Steuerverwaltung, Bern;
- Wirtschaftsministerium Baden-Württemberg, Stuttgart; and
- Tax and Finance Departments of the cantons of Basel-Landschaft, Basel-Stadt, Bern, Schwyz, St. Gallen, Ticino, Valais, and Zug.

Contents

List of Abbreviations

A	Austria
App.	appendix
B	Belgium
CH	Switzerland
D	Germany
DB	declining balance
DE	debt
DK	Denmark
E	Spain
EATR	effective average tax rate
Ed.	editor
Eds.	editors
e.g.	for example
EMTR	effective marginal tax rate
et al.	and others
EU	European Union
F	France
f./ff.	following
FIFO	First-In-First-Out
fig.	figure
FIN	Finland
GB	United Kingdom
GR	Greece
I	Italy
IBC	International Benchmark Club®
ICI	imposta comunale immobiliare
i.e.	that is
IR	Ireland
IRAP	imposta regionale sulle attività produttive
IRPEF	imposta sul reddito delle persone fisiche
IRPEG	imposta sul reddito delle persone giuridiche
L	Luxembourg
LIFO	Last-In-First-Out
Max	maximum
Med	median
Min	minimum
NE	new equity
NL	The Netherlands
No.	number
OECD	Organisation for Economic Co-operation and Development
p.	page
pp.	pages
P	Portugal
q.sh.	qualified shareholder
RE	retained earnings
Rk	ranking
S	Sweden
SL	straight line
sh.	shareholder
StHG	Steuerharmonisierungsgesetz
ufd	until fully depreciated
UK	United Kingdom
U.S./US	United States
ZEW	Zentrum für Europäische Wirtschaftsforschung GmbH

List of Symbols

$EATR$	effective average tax rate
$EMTR$	effective marginal tax rate
i	nominal interest rate
m^i	personal income tax rate on interest income
p	pre-tax real rate of return
$\tilde{p}$	cost of capital
p_s	post-tax real rate of return
R	post-tax net present value
R^*	pre-tax net present value
r	real interest rate
s	marginal post-tax rate of return
w	tax wedge
w_c	corporate tax wedge
w_p	personal tax wedge
π	rate of inflation
τ	combined statutory corporate tax rate

Executive Summary

Companies pay taxes on profits and capital. Also, under competitive labour markets for highly skilled employees, companies have to compensate these employees for international differences in labour tax burdens. Both elements thus constitute a tax burden on companies and influence the attractiveness of a particular region as a location for investment.

This study presents estimates of the effective tax burden of companies located in 143 regions of eight European countries and the United States. It accompanies a study on the effective tax burden on highly qualified employees, which follows the same spirit.

The study was prepared for the «IBC BAK International Benchmark Club»® of BAK Basel Economics, which evaluates and compares economic performance and location factors across European regions. The headline figures of this report represent the IBC Taxation Index (see table 0.1.). This Index will be updated regularly in the future so as to illustrate trends in the effective tax burdens of companies and on highly qualified employees. The scope of the study is threefold:

- First, due to a great number of relevant tax rules, effective tax burdens may differ significantly from statutory tax burdens. Therefore, the analysis comprises meaningful quantitative estimates of effective tax burdens. These estimates take into account the most important rules of all the relevant taxes. The main part of the study focuses on taxation at the corporate level. A supplementary chapter also considers shareholder taxation.
- Second, taxation is considered to be an important location factor. In order to compare the attractiveness of different locations from a tax perspective, the study compares effective tax burdens inter-regionally and internationally.
- Third, an effective tax rate is always the result of each particular case. To identify the general context, and to find out the most relevant tax provisions in different economic constellations, the so-called tax drivers, the study examines the impact of important tax provisions on effective tax burdens.

In order to quantify and compare effective company tax burdens, we calculate effective average tax rates (EATRs), effective marginal tax rates (EMTRs), and costs of capital based on the approach developed by Devereux and Griffith. This approach builds on and extends the approach by King and Fullerton, which Gutekunst and Schwager (2002) applied for the study on company taxation presented at the International Benchmark Forum in 2001. Despite its novelty, a number of international tax burden comparisons have already used the approach by Devereux and Griffith. These comparisons include studies by the Bertelsmann-Stiftung, the European Commission, and the German Council of Economic Experts (*Sachverständigenrat zur Begutachtung der gesamtwirtschaftlichen Entwicklung*).

In the base case, which defines the IBC Taxation Index for companies, we refer to a corporation in the manufacturing sector. That corporation undertakes a particular mix of investments and uses a particular combination of sources of finance. The types of investment considered are intangibles, industrial buildings, machinery, financial assets, and inventories. The sources of finance are new equity capital, retained earnings, and debt. We vary the parameters defining the base case to check the sensitivity of the results.

The tax rates computed for each region comprise taxes levied at the national, the state and the municipal level. In compliance with the structure of the International Benchmark Report, the study uses as geographical units all nine Austrian states, 19 French departments, 63 German labour office districts, 33 provinces of Northern Italy, four Dutch cities, twelve cantons in Switzerland, and one municipality of each Ireland, Massachusetts (United States), and the United Kingdom. In order to have a measure for the taxes levied by municipalities, we choose one major city in each of these geographical units.

The main part of the study focuses on the effective tax burden at the corporate level, which is especially relevant for the choice of location of international corporations. Therefore, taxes on corporate income and capital are included. The provided estimates include the corporation tax with surcharges, other profit related taxes, real estate taxes, and specific taxes based on capital. The calculations consider the statutory tax rates of these taxes as well as the interaction of different kinds of taxes and the most important rules for the definition of the tax base, e.g. differences in depreciation allowances and inventory valuation.

We express the headline results and thus the IBC Taxation Index for companies by EATRs. EATRs indicate the effective tax burden on a very profitable investment; they are an important indicator for the attractiveness of a location for international companies.

The results indicate that there is considerable dispersion of the EATRs between the countries of the Extended Alpine Space (see table 0.1. and, in more detail, table 5.1., p. 54 f.). The EATRs range over 23.5 percentage points, from 13.8 per cent in Zug, Switzerland, to 37.3 per cent in Frankfurt, Germany. Whereas Ireland and Switzerland display comparatively low effective tax burdens, locations in France, Germany, and the United States show the highest EATRs. This finding suggests that the attractiveness of particular locations from a tax perspective differs dramatically, with Switzerland and Ireland as especially attractive countries.

Statutory profit tax rates are deemed important tax drivers for profitable investments. However, tax burdens always depend on the individual characteristics of each investment, thus special rules regarding the tax base or non-profit taxes may be very relevant in particular cases. French corporations carry an extra tax burden in form of the French trade tax, the *taxe professionnelle*, whereas Italian corporations take advantage of a comparatively favourable definition of the corporate tax base. Although the combined statutory profit tax rate in Italy (38.25 per cent) is significantly higher than the one in France (35.43 per cent), effective tax burdens are lower in Italy than in France. In Austria, corporations can take advantage of a dual income tax regime that provides a reduced tax rate on part of the profits if equity is added to the company. Furthermore, Austria grants an incremental investment tax credit (*Investitionszuwachsprämie*) for additional investments. If Austrian companies can take full advantage of these measures, they reduce effective average tax burdens by about four percentage points.

The study examines not only the international variation of effective tax burdens, but also inter-regional differences within each country. There is great inter-regional variation among the assessed Swiss cantons, with the cantons of Zug, Nidwalden, and Schwyz ahead of the others. Whereas the EATR for Zug is 13.8 per cent, it is 22.8 per cent for Basel-Landschaft. Moderate inter-regional variation exists in Germany, where the levels of the trade tax (*Gewerbesteuer*) and the real estate tax (*Grundsteuer*) vary between municipalities. Effective tax burdens range from 32.9 per cent in Weilheim to 37.3 per cent in Frankfurt. We find a smaller degree of inter-regional variation in France (32.1 per cent, Paris, to 35.7 per cent, Isère). In Austria (30.4 per cent), Italy (31.6 per cent to 31.8 per cent), and the Netherlands (30.2 per cent to 30.3 per cent), inter-regional variation is not, or almost not, relevant, as regional and local governments do not have autonomy over important corporate taxes, or do not make use of it. In general, however, the study finds that – with the exception of Switzerland – national tax legislation dominates the size of effective tax burdens.

We express a second set of results in terms of the EMTR. Although EMTRs are less relevant than EATRs for international location decisions, these figures provide some useful supplementary information on effective tax burdens of companies. In contrast to EATRs, EMTRs indicate the effective tax burden on an investment that is marginal in an economic sense, i.e. an investment that earns a net present value of zero. Such an investment limits the profitable investment opportunities of a company. The lower the EMTR at the corporate level, the larger the theoretically optimal level of investment. Moreover, a firm that faces a lower EMTR on its investment is deemed to have a competitive advantage over its competitors who face greater EMTRs.

The dispersion of effective marginal tax rates between the assessed regions is even greater than the dispersion of effective average tax rates. It ranges over almost 33 percentage points from 3.3 per cent in Austria in the case where the incentives fully apply up to 36.2 per cent in Isère, France (see table C.1., pp. 119 ff.). These results suggest that the optimal level of investment and the competitiveness of companies located in different regions also differ dramatically from a tax perspective. The impact of local and regional taxes – which are non-profit taxes in most cases – on the EMTRs is generally stronger than their impact on EATRs. There is also a strong impact of targeted measures like investment tax credits or the dual income tax. Therefore, Austrian companies that can take full advantage of such measures display a very low EMTR. On the other side, there is a disadvantage for companies that have to pay substantial non-profit taxes. Non-profit taxes weigh especially heavily on investments with a low rate of return. Consequently, the attractiveness of France as expressed by the EMTR is even lower than the one expressed by the EATR.

The headline figures of the study present effective tax burdens as of 2003. For all regions, we also calculate measures of the effective tax burden for the tax rules as effective in 2001 and 2002. Among those countries that display comparatively high effective tax burdens, Germany temporarily increased tax burdens in 2003, whereas France has reduced its tax burden in 2002, thus closing the gap that previously existed between both countries. In addition, there were significant changes in the Italian tax system during that period. At the lower end of the scale, Ireland has slightly increased the tax burden for manufacturing companies, thereby closing the gap between Ireland and the most favourable Swiss location, the canton of Zug.

Sensitivity analyses reveal some interesting mechanics of the impact of taxation on effective tax burdens. E.g., the impact of French non-profit taxes heavily depends on the relative importance of fixed assets in the investment mix. French regions significantly improve their position compared with German regions when corporations are considered which hardly invest in buildings and machinery, as e.g. in the service sector. However, although some notable changes in the rankings occur, these changes are not strong enough to challenge the main conclusions from the base case fundamentally. With respect to EMTRs, the impact of the economic assumptions on the ranking is stronger than with respect to EATRs: Compared with the weight of the statutory profit tax rate, the weight of various other tax drivers increases. Specific tax rules, e.g. the generosity of depreciation allowances, play a more prominent role, and the particular features of each individual investment become more important in determining the most tax efficient location.

A supplementary chapter also considers shareholder taxation, i.e. the personal income tax on dividends, interest payments, and capital gains on the disposal of shares, the surcharges on the personal income tax, and individual net wealth taxes on shareholding and lending. We assume that the owners of a company are domestic resident shareholders who reside at the location of the company. The objective of this investigation is to evaluate the impact of shareholder taxation on the effective tax burdens presented above. The estimates provide valuable insights into the distortionary effects of domestic personal tax systems, especially with respect to financing decisions. Their meaning for the attractiveness of a location for an investment is very limited, however.

In that constellation, effective marginal tax burdens are much more important than effective average tax rates. Consequently, we focus on the calculation of effective marginal tax burdens, which we express in terms of the cost of capital and the EMTR. In this setting, costs of capital are indicators for the optimal level of domestic investment and the competitiveness of companies. EMTRs indicate the proportion of the pre-tax rate of return of the marginal investment that is taken by taxation; they mix information on the distortion of investment and financing decisions and information on the distortion of the saving decision of households; therefore, they have to be interpreted with great care.

Our results suggest that effective tax burdens at the overall level heavily depend on the tax status of the relevant shareholder. Whereas for zero-rate shareholders there is often a bias in favour of debt financing, top-rate shareholders frequently prefer to finance an investment with retained earnings. For zero-rate shareholders, the effective tax burden at the corporate level remains the single most important factor in determining the size of the tax burden. For top-rate shareholders, also the tax treatment of capital gains and interest payments is very important in our calculations.

For all types of shareholders, there is a considerable correlation between effective marginal tax rates at the corporate level and at the overall level. Although we cannot conclude straightforwardly from these results that locations that impose a low level of corporate taxes also impose a low level of personal taxes, we find that in most cases personal taxes on capital income at least do not compensate the tax burdens at the corporate level. However, there are substantial exceptions to this finding: Especially those Swiss cantons which impose relatively high top personal income tax and net wealth tax rates display comparatively low corporate-level EMTRs but high overall-level EMTRs in an international comparison.

Another way to explore the correlation between corporate and personal tax burdens is to compare the headline figures of this study with those from the aforementioned study on the taxation of highly qualified employees, which are expressed in terms of the IBC Taxation Index for highly qualified employees. Due to a number of conceptual differences, we cannot compare the IBC Taxation Index for companies directly with the IBC Taxation Index for highly qualified employees. Especially, both concepts of effective tax burdens do not permit straightforward conclusions on distributional issues. Nevertheless, we can compare the rankings and the relative differences in effective tax burdens between both studies.

With the exception of Switzerland, the tax burden on highly skilled employees does not – or almost not – vary at the regional level in most countries. Therefore, the IBC Taxation Index for highly skilled employees has been calculated on a regional basis for the twelve Swiss cantons and on a national basis for the eight other countries included in the present study, adding up to twenty different geographical entities. Based on the situation in 2003, fig. 0.1. combines those results with the IBC Taxation Index for companies. In addition to the results for Switzerland, that figure includes the median regional values for those countries where the present study assesses more than one region. To make sure that one can compare the results, we divide the effective tax burdens by the average of the included Swiss cantons. By definition, this average corresponds to an indexed effective tax burden of 100. We add a trend line which is based on the 20 observations included in order to illustrate the correlation between the tax burden on capital and on highly skilled employees. Table 0.1. finally compares the headline results of both studies. To give an impression on the inter-regional variation of company tax burdens, that table additionally presents the figures for the region that displays the lowest tax burden and the region that displays the highest tax burden out of all the regions that have been assessed for each country.

Indeed, it is striking that effective tax burdens appear to be closely correlated for most locations. This suggests that countries that impose large corporate tax burdens usually also impose large tax burdens on comparatively high personal incomes. A notable exception to these findings is the United States (Massachusetts). There, the tax burden on companies is among the highest of all regions considered, while qualified employees are taxed quite moderately. On the other hand,

Ireland displays almost the lowest corporate tax burden of all regions together with a rather high tax burden on qualified employees. Despite these exceptions, however, from the point of view of a company, large corporate tax burdens usually are not compensated by small tax burdens on highly qualified employees, and vice versa. Therefore, those locations that already exhibit a competitive edge with respect to company taxation even improve their advantage when both types of taxes are considered.

Fig. 0.1. Correlation of the tax burdens on companies and on highly qualified employees

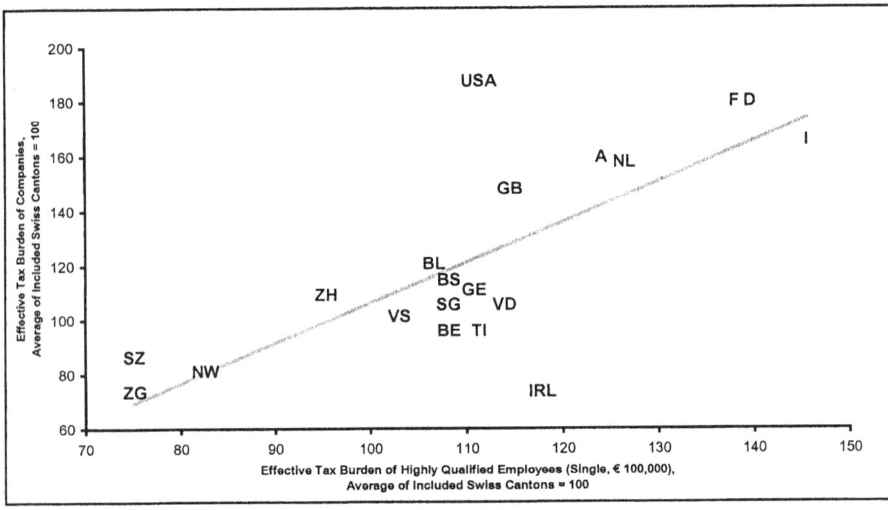

Table 0.1. IBC Taxation Index for companies and highly qualified employees, 2003

			Companies			Highly qualified employees		
	b)	Region	IBC Taxation Index (EATR, %)	% of Swiss [a] average	Rank (out of 143)	IBC Taxation Index (EATR, %)	% of Swiss [a] average	Rank (out of 20)
CH	–	Zug	13.8	71.8	1	25.9	75.7	2
IR	–	Dublin	14.0	72.9	2	40.3	117.8	15
CH	–	Nidwalden	15.4	80.2	3	28.3	82.8	3
CH	–	Schwyz	16.5	85.9	4	25.7	75.1	1
CH	–	Ticino	18.5	96.0	5	38.2	111.6	11
CH	–	Bern	18.6	96.6	6	36.8	107.8	8
CH	–	Valais	19.7	102.5	7	35.4	103.6	5
CH	–	St. Gallen	20.3	105.5	8	36.8	107.5	7
CH	–	Vaud	20.5	106.7	9	39.3	114.9	14
CH	–	Zürich	21.0	109.6	10	32.6	95.2	4
CH	–	Genève	21.4	111.4	11	37.9	110.9	10
CH	–	Basel-Stadt	22.1	115.0	12	36.9	108.0	9
CH	–	Basel-Land.	22.8	118.9	13	36.6	106.9	6
GB	–	London	28.1	146.3	14	39.2	114.7	13
NL	Min	Amsterdam	30.2	–	15	42.9	–	–
NL	Med	Utrecht	30.2	157.4	16	42.9	125.5	17
NL	Max	Rotterdam	30.3	–	18	42.9	–	–
A	All State Capitals		30.4	158.2	19	41.7	122.0	16
I	Min	V. d'Aosta	31.6	–	28	49.8	–	–
I	Med	Cremona	31.8	165.5	44	49.8	145.6	20
I	Max	Venezia	31.8	–	54	49.8	–	–
F	Min	Paris	32.1	–	61	47.3	–	–
D	Min	Weilheim	32.9	–	62	47.6	–	–
F	Med	Doubs	34.5	179.5	99	47.3	138.2	18
D	Med	Bayreuth	34.6	180.1	103	47.6	139.3	19
F	Max	Isère	35.7	–	128	47.3	–	–
US	–	Boston	36.0	187.3	133	38.2	111.6	12
D	Max	Frankfurt	37.3	–	143	47.6	–	–

Remarks:

a) Average of the twelve cantons that have been included; these columns provide the values used in fig. 0.1.

b) Min/Med/Max → Region that displays the lowest/median/highest EATR for companies out of each country's assessed regions.

1 Introduction

The tax burden on investment is an important factor for the attractiveness of a country or a region as a location for investment. This report presents effective tax burdens on domestic investment in nine different countries, with an emphasis on regional differences in taxation in the countries of the Extended Alpine Space.

The report extends and updates an earlier study by Gutekunst and Schwager (2002) into three important directions: First, as a *methodological* extension, we calculate effective average tax burdens in addition to effective marginal tax burdens. Whereas effective marginal tax burdens consider investments that are marginal in an economic sense, i.e., that earn a net present value of zero, effective average tax burdens consider investments that earn an economic rent and thus more than the minimum return required. Second, as a *geographical* extension, we investigate a number of additional countries and regions. These include Ireland, Austria, and Northern Italy. Third, we present a short *time series* by computing effective tax rates for 2001, 2002 and 2003.

Moreover, the present study should be seen in the context of another study (Elschner and Schwager, 2004) which considers the effective tax burden on highly qualified employees as a location factor. Both studies supplement each other, as they provide a more complete picture of taxes as a location factor for companies than one of the studies alone could do.

In order to present costs of capital, effective marginal tax rates (EMTRs), and effective average tax rates (EATRs), we apply the approach for measuring forward-looking effective tax burdens that Devereux and Griffith (1999 and 2003) have developed. Although the main part of the study focuses on taxes on corporations, a supplementary chapter presents estimates of effective tax rates that include personal taxes on capital income.

The structure of the study is as follows: Chapter 2 discusses the methodology, the basic assumptions, and the meaning of the measures of effective tax burdens. Chapter 3 summarises the structure of the tax rules that are taken into account for the calculations. Chapter 4 presents country-by-country estimates of the effective tax burdens and explains the potential impact of particular tax rules on the regional dispersion of effective tax burdens and on the favourability of particular sources of finance and types of assets. Chapter 5 compares these results internationally in order to establish whether one can rank a particular country or region as a rather favourable or unfavourable location for an investment. Sensitivity analyses and a comparison with the results and conclusions of related studies indicate the impact of different assumptions on the ranking. A synthesis with the headline results of the study on the effective tax burden on highly qualified employees adds insights into effective tax burdens from another important perspective. As a supplement to the main part of the study, chapter 6 investigates the impact of personal taxes on effective tax burdens. Chapter 7 summarises the most important results and concludes. Various appendices present the detailed tax data we apply (App. A), additional tables and figures (App. B), additional rankings (App. C), and the detailed results (App. D).

2 Methodology and Coverage of the Study

2.1 Methodology

2.1.1 Classification of the Approach

For measuring effective tax burdens, a number of different instruments exist. This study relies on a forward-looking approach developed by Devereux and Griffith (1999 and 2003). In contrast to backward-looking approaches, which divide tax payments from national or firm accounts by some measure of profit or operating surplus reported by companies, forward-looking approaches consider a hypothetical investment and estimate tax payments associated with a particular decision. Thus forward-looking measures, in contrast to backward-looking measures, are potentially suited for estimating the effects of taxation on business decision-making (see in detail Jacobs and Spengel, 2000; OECD, 2001; Gutekunst, Hermann, and Lammersen, 2003).

The Devereux-Griffith approach is similar to the framework developed by King and Fullerton (1984), which has been applied in a number of extensive international tax burden comparisons (see, e.g., OECD, 1991; European Commission, 1992; Baker & McKenzie, 1999 and 2001; Winner, 2000), including the former study on company taxation in the Extended Alpine Space (Gutekunst and Schwager, 2002). Devereux and Griffith (1999, 2003) have revised the King-Fullerton approach to account also for the calculation of effective average tax rates. This new methodology has already been applied in a number of international studies (see Bond and Chennells, 2000; Sachverständigenrat zur Begutachtung der gesamtwirtschaftlichen Entwicklung, 2001 and 2003; Spengel, 2003), including a major study commissioned by the European Commission (see Devereux, Lammersen, and Spengel, 2000 and 2001; European Commission, 2002).

In the present study, we will not discuss technical details of the Devereux-Griffith model as far as they are not relevant for the interpretation of the effective tax burden measures. A comprehensive technical presentation of the model is delivered by European Commission (2002: 519-533), Schreiber, Spengel, and Lammersen (2002), Devereux (2003), and Devereux and Griffith (2003).

2.1.2 Assumptions

For the calculations, an incremental, hypothetical corporate investment is considered. The investment consists of five different types of assets (intangibles, industrial buildings, machinery, financial assets[1], and inventories). We take three different sources of finance into account: retained earnings, new equity, and debt. The hypothetical investment takes place at the beginning of a period and generates a return at the end. Thus, we suppose a one-period perturbation of the capital stock. We measure the cash flows connected with this investment and compute various measures of effective tax rates.

For the base case, we suppose that the corporation is in the manufacturing sector and that all assets are weighted equally. The sources of finance are weighted according to empirical data that earlier studies have already applied (see table 2.1.). In addition, we undertake a sensitivity analysis considering weights for the assets and sources of finance of a typical service sector company.

Against the background of a neoclassical economic framework, the model considers several important economic parameters: the unique market interest rate, the rate of inflation, geometrically declining economic depreciation of intangibles, industrial buildings and machinery, and the pre-tax rate of return on the investment. Except for the calculation of the pre-tax rate of return of a marginal investment, these economic parameters are exogenous, i.e., their parameter values are supposed to be equal for all investments regardless of their location. Consequently, real and nominal interest rates are equal across all the locations and regardless of the level of profitability of an investment. Some sensitivity analyses rely on different sets of economic parameters, but again the parameter values are the same for all the calculations of each single sensitivity analysis. By proceeding this way, we can isolate the effects of taxation from other economic effects.

The calculations take into account the most important rules with respect to the taxation of the profit and capital of corporations. These include headline statutory corporate profit tax rates as well as surcharges and some special rates for particular types of income and expenditures. We generally assume that the company possesses sufficient profits and capital in order for the top-bracket statutory tax rates to apply. Moreover, we consider depreciation allowances and the most relevant rules for the taxation of financial assets and the valuation of inventories. The model assumes immediate loss compensation, i.e., any excess deductions generated by the incremental investment are supposed to be deductible from other corporate profits which are taxed at the headline corporate tax rate. We consider effective tax burdens on current investment. Therefore, we generally do not consider special, occasional investment incentives. We take into account the most important features of taxes on capital and net wealth of corporations as well as real estate taxes. In addition, some important generally available investment incentives are included in the calculations.

The main part of the study considers taxes at the corporate level only. A supplementary chapter, however, additionally considers personal taxes.

Fig. 2.1. illustrates the structure of the model investment, table 2.1. summarises the most important assumptions. We describe the tax data in detail in chapter 3 and App. A.

---

[1] For the interpretation of the results it should be noted that, due to the inclusion of financial assets, we do not suppose a pure real investment.

Fig. 2.1. Structure of the supposed investment

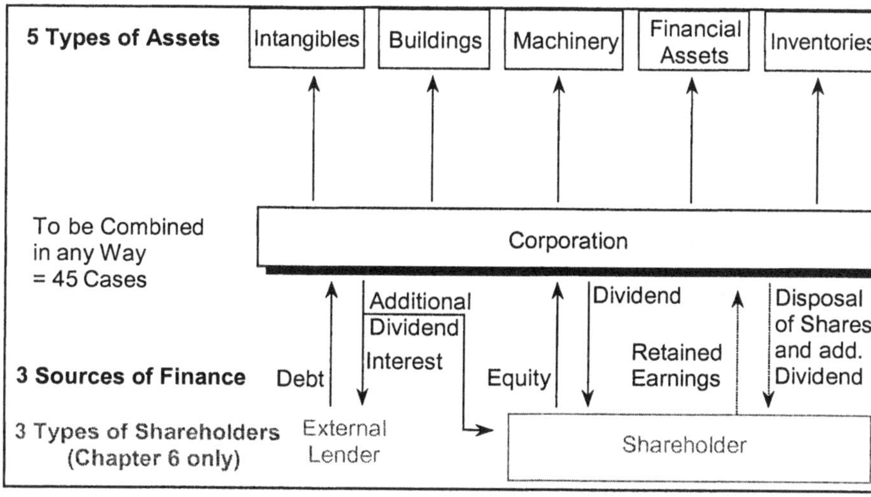

Table 2.1. Summary of the most important assumptions (base case)

Assumption on ...	Value	
Legal form	Corporation	
Industry	Manufacturing Sector	
Assets	Intangibles, industrial buildings, machinery, financial assets, inventories (at equal weights)	
Sources of finance	Retained earnings (55 %), new equity (10 %), debt (35 %)	
True economic depreciation	Intangibles	– 12.5 years
	Industrial buildings	– 53 years
	Machinery	– 11 years
Real interest rate	5 %	
Pre-tax real rate of return (for calculation of EATR)	20 %	
Inflation rate	2 %	

2.1.3 Measures of Effective Tax Burdens and Their Interpretation

A number of economic issues are related to the size of the effective tax burden. In an international and inter-regional economic context, especially two issues should be considered: location and competition (see, also for the following, Devereux, Lammersen and Spengel, 2000; European Commission, 2002: 129-173; Lammersen, 2002). Taxation might distort the choice of location of a new investment. This is the case when a firm is attracted by low effective tax burdens. In addition, firms located in different countries might compete in the same market for goods. Differences in effective tax burdens then might distort competition in these markets.

To analyse these issues, we present measures of the effective tax burdens that we express in terms of the cost of capital, the EMTR, and the EATR.

We calculate the *cost of capital* as the minimum pre-tax rate of return the hypothetical corporate investment has to earn in order to compete with a financial asset that yields the market interest rate. In this case, the investment displays a net present value of zero, i.e., the investor considers it just worthwhile to be undertaken.

The model assumes that only those investment projects are realised that earn at least their cost of capital. The further taxation increases the cost of capital above the real market interest rate, the more investment theoretically is depressed. The overall level of the cost of capital thus indicates the theoretical impact of taxation on the level of investment activity. The spread and the variability of the cost of capital indicate economic distortions between different assets, sources of finance, types of shareholders, locations etc. and therefore suggest losses in economic efficiency caused by taxation. Capital might be employed in sectors or locations where the pre-tax rate of return is lower than it would be if the capital were invested elsewhere.

The cost of capital also might serve as an indicator for competitiveness. If we assume the price a firm can demand to be the parameter for competition, the cost of capital indicates competitiveness inasmuch as the rate of profitability depends on the selling price. If the competitor with the lowest potential price serves the market with the products of one incremental unit of investment, greater cost of capital indicates lower competitiveness. Ceteris paribus, a company facing a cost of capital of three per cent might offer its products at a lower price than a company that faces a cost of capital of four per cent. This effect is not a proof, but an indicator that with differential tax treatment a firm that was less competitive before taxes were taken into account drives a more competitive one out of the market, causing a welfare loss.

The *EMTR* is defined as the percentage difference between the cost of capital, denoted by $\tilde{p}$, and the post-tax real rate of return, denoted by s:

$$EMTR = \frac{\tilde{p} - s}{\tilde{p}}. \tag{2.1}$$

As an example, suppose that an investment competes with a financial asset that yields a post-tax real rate of return of 4.5 per cent, and suppose that due to taxation the said investment has to earn a pre-tax real rate of return of 6 per cent. In that case, the EMTR is 25 per cent, as taxation takes away 25 per cent of the real rate of return of the investment.

If we consider only corporate taxes, the EMTR contains the same information as the cost of capital, only expressed in a different way. As under these assumptions the post-tax real rate of return s is equal to the real market interest rate r, the EMTR is a strictly monotonously increasing transformation of the cost of capital. Equal EMTRs indicate equal costs of capital, higher (lower) EMTRs indicate higher (lower) costs of capital. The most relevant advantage of expressing effective marginal tax burdens in terms of the EMTR is that they are easier to communicate and to compare with other concepts of tax rates: We can compare an EMTR with an EATR and, under particular assumptions, we can also compare EMTRs with the statutory profit tax rate τ. This particular feature might permit conclusions on whether investments that are more profitable trigger a greater percentage tax burden than investments that are less profitable, and whether taxation deters or promotes an investment in general (see Schneider, 1992: 239-251).

EMTRs might be negative: In case only corporate taxes are considered and the real interest rate is fixed at a particular, positive level, the EMTR is negative if the cost of capital is below the real market interest rate, but above zero (see also fig. 2.2.):

$$0 < \tilde{p} < r \Rightarrow EMTR < 0. \tag{2.2}$$

In that case, taxation increases the rate of return of an investment: The post-tax rate of return is greater than the corresponding pre-tax rate of return, but the investment still has to earn a positive return.

Fig. 2.2. Relation between the cost of capital and the EMTR

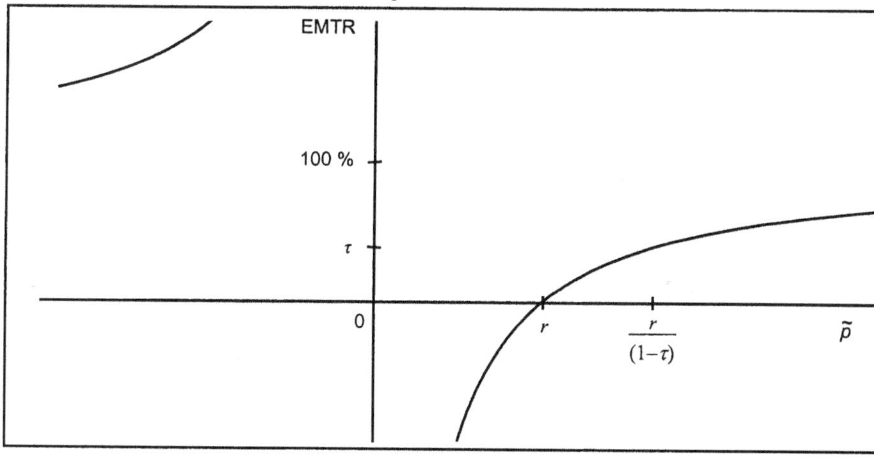

Note: Fig. 2.2. shows that as long as the cost of capital is positive, the EMTR increases with an increasing cost of capital. The EMTR equals the statutory tax rate τ if the cost of capital is $\tilde{p} = r/(1-\tau)$. As the cost of capital tends towards infinity, the EMTR approaches 100 per cent.

Moreover, EMTRs might exceed 100 per cent: In case the cost of capital is negative, there is such a strong subsidy by the tax system that the investment before taxes even may earn a negative rate of return, i.e. may lose its value without compensation from the market, in order to earn the real market interest rate after taxes. Algebraically, the EMTR then is positive and above 100 per cent:[2]

$$\tilde{p} < 0 \Rightarrow \tilde{p} - r < \tilde{p} < 0 \Rightarrow EMTR > 100\%. \tag{2.3}$$

[2] The denominator of equation (2.1) is negative in that case, the numerator is negative and below the value of the denominator, thus the fraction is positive and above 100 per cent.

EMTRs like that cannot provide intuitive insights into the effects of taxation on investment. However, costs of capital still provide an intuitive measure in that case.

The *EATR* indicates the extent to which taxation reduces the net present value of a profitable, inframarginal investment project. In case a company chooses between two or more mutually exclusive projects, profit-maximising behaviour requires that it chooses the alternative that generates the greatest post-tax profit. Under the assumptions of the model, this most favourable alternative is the one that exhibits the lowest EATR (Devereux and Griffith, 1999 and 2003). The most important decision of this type is the decision where to locate an investment. High EATRs might prevent companies from investing in a location (see Devereux and Griffith, 1998; Richter, Seitz, and Wiegard, 1996: 19). As with the EMTR and the cost of capital, the extent of the spread and the variability of the EATRs indicate economic distortions and thus losses in economic efficiency.

The EATR is defined as the difference between the pre-tax net present value R^* and the post-tax net present value R of the particular investment the Devereux-Griffith approach considers, divided by the present value of the income stream p in the absence of taxation:

$$EATR = \frac{R^* - R}{p/(1+r)}. \tag{2.4}$$

If we consider only corporate taxes, this expression is equal to the percentage difference between the pre-tax rate of return p and the post-tax rate of return p_s of a profitable investment under some basic assumptions:[3]

$$EATR = \frac{p - p_s}{p}. \tag{2.5}$$

Typically, such an EATR is positive and between zero and 100 per cent, as the post-tax real rate of return of a very profitable investment will be greater than zero and below the pre-tax real rate of return of such an investment in most cases:

$$0 < p_S < p \Rightarrow 0 < EATR < 100\%. \tag{2.6}$$

Consequently, with respect to its interpretation, the EATR is a less complicated measure than the EMTR.

2.1.4 The Impact of Tax Rules on Effective Tax Burdens

A great number of tax rules potentially have an impact on effective tax burdens. At the corporate level, we can group these rules into

---

[3] For details, see Schreiber, Spengel and Lammersen (2002).

1. the level of (combined) statutory profit tax rates,
2. the definition of the profit tax base, and
3. the level of non-profit taxes.

The weights of these items in the determination of the effective marginal versus the effective average tax burden differ. All three items mentioned affect the effective marginal tax burden strongly, whereas for the calculation of effective average tax burdens the level of tax rates dominates over the other factors.

We can explain this effect by considering a particular relationship between the cost of capital, the EMTR, and the EATR. In fact, Devereux and Griffith (1999) have pointed out that under particular conditions[4] the EATR of the marginal investment is equal to its EMTR. For highly profitable investments, the EATR tends towards the statutory tax rate on profits. Furthermore, the EATR as defined above has been shown to be a weighted average of the EMTR and the combined effective statutory corporate tax rate, denoted by τ (for similar formulations, see Spengel and Lammersen, 2001: 227-228; Schreiber, Spengel and Lammersen, 2002: 13-16; Devereux and Griffith, 2003: 112-113):

$$EATR = \frac{\tilde{p}}{p} \cdot EMTR + \frac{p - \tilde{p}}{p} \cdot \tau . \tag{2.7}$$

The weights are determined by the fraction of the financial return p that is covered by the cost of capital (for the EMTR) and the fraction that is not covered (for the combined tax rate). For a pre-tax rate of return equal to the cost of capital, the EATR equals the EMTR. With an increasing rate of return, the measure approaches the combined effective statutory corporate tax rate.

A marginal investment only earns its cost of capital, i.e., the lowest sufficient rate of return to be worthwhile for the investor. The receipts exceed the expenses only by little; therefore, the treatment of these expenses for purposes of taxation – especially the path of tax depreciation allowances – is relatively important. Also, property and net wealth taxes take away a comparatively large fraction of the return.

On the contrary, the calculation of the EATR supposes a rather profitable investment. Compared to a marginal investment, a higher level of receipts now accompanies the same level of expenses. The additional receipts regularly are taxed at the statutory tax rate without triggering additional allowances. The relative weight of these allowances in the determination of the effective tax burden thus declines with an increasing level of profitability. Moreover, property and net wealth taxes usually are based on historic cost. Thus, their absolute amount does not differ between marginal and profitable investments which display the same initial cost but different levels of return. Consequently, property and net wealth taxes take away a lower fraction of the return of a more profitable investment.

[4] These particular assumptions include the conditions that one omits personal taxes on interest payments and capital gains and that the sum of depreciation allowances is based on the initial cost of the investment. The said conditions are satisfied for all the estimations of EATRs for the corporate level in this study.

An example: Suppose that investment A earns a real rate of return of 20 per cent, and investment B earns a real rate of return of 5 per cent. We ignore inflation. Non-profit taxes, which are not deductible for purposes of calculating the base of profit taxes, are imposed at a rate of one per cent of the initial cost of each investment. The statutory profit tax rate is 40 per cent. In that case, investment A's post-tax real rate of return is $20 \cdot (1 - 0.4) - 1 = 11$ per cent, resulting in an EATR of $(20 - 11)/20 = 45$ per cent, whereas investment B's post-tax real rate of return is $5 \cdot (1 - 0.4) - 1 = 2$ per cent, resulting in an EATR of $(5 - 2)/5 = 60$ per cent. Non-profit taxes thus impose a relatively heavier burden on the return of comparatively low-yielding investments.

An additional note: These issues also hint at notable exceptions to the rule that the definition of the profit tax base and the level of non-profit taxes have a comparatively small impact on the EATR and a comparatively stronger impact on the cost of capital and the EMTR. There might be rules on the definition of the tax base that do not refer to the initial cost of the investment, but to the profits earned by the investment. One example for such a rule is the opportunity of a company to dedicate a defined fraction of its profits to a tax-exempt reserve, which might have to be resolved only after a number of consecutive years. A rule of this kind exists e.g. in Sweden. Such a rule would have the same effect as a reduction in the statutory profit tax rate. For other rules, e.g. the Italian dual income tax regime (see section 3.1.3), it might be hard to decide whether they should be characterised as a rule defining the taxable base or as a rule setting the statutory tax rate.

When interpreting effective tax rates one always has to keep in mind that – independently from the approach used – these measures always depend on the assumptions of each particular case and thus cannot be generalised arbitrarily. Nevertheless, standardised comparisons of effective tax rates – like the one undertaken here – can provide a good impression of the magnitudes of effective tax burdens and help to identify the most important tax drivers.

2.1.5 Comparison with the Former Study

As the Devereux-Griffith approach conceptually builds on the approach that King and Fullerton (1984) have developed and that was applied in the former study on effective tax burdens in the Extended Alpine space, both approaches are very similar. However, some important differences exist, which we have to keep in mind when we compare the results of different studies that are based on different approaches.[5]

Conceptually, both approaches rely on neoclassical investment theory and compute effective marginal tax burdens, which one can express as costs of capital or as EMTRs. Moreover, both approaches consider one hypothetical unit of an incremental investment of a company. Both do not calculate the tax burden on a whole company, as e.g. the European Tax Analyzer model developed by the ZEW and the University of Mannheim does (see e.g. Jacobs and Spengel, 2000; Jacobs and Spengel, 2002). However, whereas the King-Fullerton approach supposes an infinite extension of the capital stock by one unit, the Devereux-Griffith model as-

[5] For a comparison between a major study based on the Devereux-Griffith approach and various important earlier studies based on the King-Fullerton framework, see European Commission (2002: 270-285).

sumes a one-period perturbation of the firm's capital stock only. After that period, the increment to the capital stock is reversed again, and the corporation distributes all the investment's proceedings to its shareholders. This modification to the model secures the consistency and the simplicity of the assumptions in order to calculate – in contrast to the King-Fullerton approach – also EATRs.[6]

Both approaches model a great number of tax details in the same or at least in a very similar way, for example the depreciation for tax purposes. However, due to conceptual differences, the numerical results are exactly equal under both approaches only for a very limited number of base cases, even if both models use the same tax and non-tax parameters (for an example, see Lammersen, 2002: 19 and 34).

Compared with the study by Gutekunst and Schwager (2002), besides these conceptual differences between the approaches, we have also changed some assumptions of the model:

- Gutekunst and Schwager (2002) applied the so-called fixed-p case for calculating EMTRs. This means that their model supposed a given pre-tax real rate of return p of an investment and calculated the corresponding post-tax rates of return (see Gutekunst and Schwager, 2002: 23-28). In the present study, we apply the so-called fixed-r case for computing EMTRs. We fix the real market interest rate r at a level of five per cent and calculate the pre-tax real rate of return that the investment has to earn in order to display a zero net present value. I.e., whereas the former study fixed the cost of capital for all investments at a level of ten per cent, the present study treats the cost of capital as endogenous, and consequently that measure differs between alternative investments.
  An important reason for changing this assumption is to guarantee consistency between the measures of the EATR and the EMTR. For computing the EATR, the real market interest rate is fixed at a level below the pre-tax rate of return in order to design an investment that earns an economic rent. Thus for both measures, the same real market interest rate and the same economic conditions are applied.
  This assumption obviously has an impact on the results. Where the cost of capital based on the Devereux-Griffith approach is below ten per cent – which occurs quite frequently –, according to the explanations in section 2.1.4, the present study ascribes a greater weight to the level of non-profit taxation than the former study. However, as we present also EATRs calculated for a pre-tax rate of return of 20 per cent in the base case, the present study can explore the impact of different components of the tax system in more detail than before.
- A second significant modification concerns the structure of the investment that we consider for our investigations. The types of assets, their economic depreciation rates, and the rate of inflation are the same as in the former study. How-

[6] For a detailed discussion of the conceptual problems inherent in the measurement of EATRs, especially in the definition of a consistent standard measure, see Schneider (1992: 243-244); Schreiber, Spengel and Lammersen (2002: 4-5). Moreover, Oldenburg (1998), Knirsch (2002), and Ruf (2002) have undertaken approaches to solve these problems.

ever, in the base case we apply equal weights to the five assets, whereas the former study used different weights which were based on empirical data (see Gutekunst and Schwager, 2002: 28-30).

We make this modification mainly in order to guarantee the comparability with the results of the extensive study on effective tax burdens commissioned by the European Commission (2002), which also applied equal weights to the different assets. The actual weights applied for different sources of finance, however, are almost the same as in the former study.

This assumption also has a significant impact on the results of the study. The weight of intangibles now strongly increases from 1.43 per cent to 20 per cent. In contrast, the weight of financial assets decreases from 38.25 per cent to also 20 per cent. Thus, countries that, e.g., grant a very generous tax treatment for intangibles will display a comparatively lower effective tax burden. The relative weight of the statutory tax rate, which is the most important factor in the taxation of financial assets, consequently decreases. To capture the effects of this assumption, we conduct a sensitivity analysis that considers the formerly applied weights (see section 5.3.1, App. C, and App. D.2).

- A third important modification concerns the range of tax rules included in the present study. At the corporate level, the former study in addition to taxes on the production factor capital also considered the payroll component of the French trade tax, the *taxe professionnelle* as well as other taxes levied on the basis of the payroll. For the present study, we only consider taxes on capital; consequently, we do not consider the payroll component.

  In general, models for measuring the effective tax burden on capital that are based on neoclassical investment theory assume that taxes on other factors of production have to be borne by those who supply these production factors. Thus, the payroll component of the French trade tax would reduce income from wages, not income from capital. This assumption is a very strong one, which probably holds partly, but not completely in reality, especially if the elasticity of labour supply strongly exceeds the elasticity of labour demand. The assumption that payroll taxes have to be borne by companies is used by the study on the effective tax burden on highly qualified employees as a location factor, which is carried out in parallel to the present study. That study assumes that skilled employees are very mobile at the inter-regional level and thus can shift taxes on payroll and wages onto their employers. The accompanying study therefore considers the effective tax burden of these taxes, considering it here would mean a double count of them. Moreover, note that also the abovementioned study by the European Commission included only taxes on capital, thus the approach presented here is comparable to the one of that study.

  Compared with the former study, this modification especially has an impact on the relative position of France; the relative weight of French non-profit taxes in the computation of effective tax burdens is lower in the present study. In the periods assessed here (2001–2003), also Austria and Italy – which were not included in the former study – raised similar taxes that also included at least a payroll component.[7] With effect from 2003, Italy and France have abolished the payroll component of these taxes.

2.2 Geographical Coverage and Time Horizon

This study covers 143 regions from nine countries:

- *Austria*: The present study covers all nine Austrian states; none of which were included in the former study.
- *France*: In addition to the six departments of the regions Alsace and Lorraine, which the former study considered, we include twelve more departments of the regions Franche-Comté and Rhône-Alpes, and we add Paris (Ile-de-France). In total, we assess the effective level of taxation at 19 different French locations.
- *Germany*: The former study considered cities in all 53 labour office districts of the states of Bayern and Baden-Württemberg; now, the cities of Berlin and Hamburg, two additional regions from Hessen, three from Nordrhein-Westfalen, and another three from Rheinland-Pfalz are included. In total, we assess 63 German locations.
- *Italy*: The present study covers all 33 provinces from the regions Friuli-Venezia Giulia, Lombardia, Piemonte, Trentino-Alto Adige (which consists of the two autonomous provinces of Bolzano and Trento), Valle d'Aosta, and Veneto. The former study considered none of these regions.
- *Ireland*: We assess the effective level of taxation for companies located in Dublin; Ireland was not included in the former study.
- *The Netherlands*: Whereas the former study considered the Netherlands without a regional assessment, we now analyse effective tax burdens separately for the four cities of Amsterdam, Den Haag, Rotterdam and Utrecht.
- *Switzerland*: As in the former study, we cover the cantons of Basel-Landschaft, Basel-Stadt, Bern, Genève, Nidwalden, Schwyz, St. Gallen, Vaud, Zug and Zürich. We drop the canton of Aargau from the sample, and we additionally include the cantons of Valais and Ticino. Thus, we cover twelve out of the 26 Swiss cantons.
- *United Kingdom*: As in the former study, we consider the situation in London.
- *United States*: Whereas the former study assessed the situation in the state of California, we now consider the situation in Boston (Massachusetts).

A number of taxes – especially real estate taxes – vary at a sub-regional level. For these taxes, we consider the local level of taxation that exists in a major municipality of the region. For the Swiss cantons, we assess taxes at the cantonal capitals. The municipalities chosen for each region of the other countries are indicated in the tables of the appendices. In contrast to the former study, we no longer differentiate between regions from the Extended Alpine Space and benchmark re-

---

[7] The taxes mentioned are the payroll tax (*Kommunalsteuer*) in Austria and the regional tax on productive activities (*Imposta regionale sulle attività produttive*, IRAP) in Italy. For more details, see section 3.1.

gions. Furthermore, for the present study, we focus on domestic investment, i.e., we do not calculate effective tax burdens that take into account particular tax rules for cross-border investment.[8]

The time horizon of this study covers the tax years 2001, 2002, and 2003. We consider the situation on January 1st of each of these years. However, some restrictions have to be mentioned: In some cases, local governments are authorised to change local tax coefficients even during the tax year.[9] Furthermore, in some cases, local tax rates on a year's profit are fixed in later years, or they are not generally available earlier.[10] To cope with these issues and to obtain a consistent time series, as for the former study, which covered the tax year 2001, we consider some local taxes with a one-period time lag.[11]

---

8 However, previous studies have shown that estimates of domestic effective tax burdens at the corporate level often capture the tax rules that are most relevant for a location's attractiveness also for cross-border investment. See European Commission (2002: 213-214); Gutekunst and Schwager (2002: 17-18 and 105-111).

9 For example, the German municipal parliaments are authorized by law to increase the tax coefficients of the trade tax by June 30th of each tax year; they may pass reductions even later, see § 16 section 3 of the German Trade Tax Code (*Gewerbesteuergesetz*).

10 For example, the French trade tax (*taxe professionnelle*) of a particular tax year is based on the profits of earlier tax years; see Willenborg (2003: 1354).

11 For details, see App. A. This time lag can also be justified if we consider the situation of a particular investor, who might have to rely on historic local tax data when choosing a location.

3 Characteristics and Development of the Tax Systems

This chapter provides a survey of the relevant tax rules for corporations in the assessed regions. It follows the treatment of the former study (see Gutekunst and Schwager, 2002: 31-49), supplementing it with information on countries and regions that the said study did not cover (section 3.1). Moreover, it considers important changes that have occurred in the meantime, i.e. between 2001 and 2003 (section 3.1). The scope of this chapter is to present the most important structural features of the tax systems. The detailed rates and provisions concerning the tax bases are summarised in App. A.1 and App. A.2.

3.1 Tax Systems

3.1.1 Austria

Austrian corporations are obliged to pay corporate income tax (*Körperschaftsteuer*) and real estate tax (*Grundsteuer*). A corporate payroll tax exists (*Kommunalsteuer*), which we do not consider for this study, as we do not deem it a tax on profits or capital.[12]

The corporate income tax is imposed at a standard rate of 34 per cent; it does not vary at the regional or local level. The municipalities are authorised to fix local multipliers (*Hebesatz*) for the real estate tax; these multipliers may not exceed an upper ceiling of 500 per cent. All regional capitals that we assess here have imposed their real estate tax at this upper ceiling between 2001 and 2003, thus effectively there is no variation.[13]

An unconventional measure of the Austrian tax system is the dual income tax. The Austrian corporate dual income tax system taxes a part of the profits at a reduced corporate income tax rate of 25 per cent. The said part of the profits is determined by applying a statutory rate of return, which is deduced from market interest rates, on any addition to the equity of the tax year. As only the additional equity qualifies for such an incentive, the effect of this measure is very limited for most companies. However, companies that plan extensive additional investments

[12] See the explanations in section 2.1.5, pp. 18 ff.

[13] See table A.10. on p. 98. There may, of course, be smaller municipalities which, however, apply rates below that upper ceiling.

might take advantage of this measure. For this study, we take into account both situations: One scenario where the corporation cannot exploit this rule and, for the calculations of the base case, one scenario where the corporation can take optimal advantage of the dual income tax.

Another unconventional measure of the Austrian tax system is the incremental investment tax credit (*Investitionszuwachsprämie*). As with the dual income tax, this tax credit – which comes at a rate of ten per cent of the initial cost of the investment – only applies to additional investments, i.e., the difference between the investment of one period and the average investment of the periods before. Therefore, the impact of this measure also depends on the particular situation of each firm. As with the dual income tax, we assume the case where the company cannot take advantage of this measure and the case where it can optimally exploit this measure.

3.1.2 France

In addition to the corporate income tax (*impôt sur les sociétés*) with surcharges, French companies are subject to a large number of taxes and charges which are not based on profit. Among these, only the trade tax (*taxe professionnelle*) and the real estate tax (*impôt foncier*) are relevant for the purpose of the present study. The other non profit related taxes[14] are not taken into account since they are levied on the payroll and hence are not considered to be a tax on capital investment.[15]

The statutory rate of the corporate income tax is 33.33 per cent. On top of this, two surcharges are due: a general surcharge of 3 per cent and a social contribution (*contribution sociale sur les bénéfices*) amounting to 3.3 per cent of the corporate income tax bill. Both the tax base and the rates of the corporate income tax including surcharges are fixed nationally, implying that there is no inter-regional variation.

The trade tax and the real estate taxes serve as a source of revenue for the subnational layers of government (municipalities, *départments*, regions, and possibly other public entities). The base of the trade tax, defined by national law, is composed of the rental value of buildings and machinery. The lower level jurisdictions which are entitled to a share of the revenue apply autonomously determined rates to this base. Similarly, the real estate tax is levied on a nationally defined base consisting of land and buildings, with locally determined rates. Consequently, one observes a non-negligible variation in the effective rates of the trade and real estate taxes between French locations.[16]

---

[14] These taxes are: *taxe d'apprentissage, taxe sur les salaires, contribution des entreprises à la formation professionnelle continue, participation à l'effort de construction.* The payroll component of the *taxe professionnelle* has been abolished in 2003.

[15] See the discussion in section 2.1.5 on pp. 18 ff.

[16] See table A.11. on p. 99 for the rates of the *taxe professionnelle* and table A.12. on p. 100 for the rates of the real estate tax applicable in the sample of locations considered.

3.1.3 Germany

The tax burden of companies located in Germany is determined by the corporate income tax (*Körperschaftsteuer*) including solidarity surcharge (*Solidaritätszuschlag*) and the trade tax (*Gewerbesteuer*), as well as the real estate tax (*Grundsteuer*).

The rate of the corporate income tax was temporarily increased in 2003 to 26.5 per cent. It is due to return to its previous level of 25 per cent in 2004. The solidarity surcharge amounts to 5.5 per cent of the corporate income tax. The base of the trade tax is obtained by modifying the profit as assessed for the purpose of the corporate income tax in several ways. The most important modification consists of adding half of the interest paid on long-term debt to the taxable income. Thus, interest payments reduce the base of the trade tax only by half. Moreover, the trade tax and the real estate tax are deductible as a business expense when calculating profits and hence reduce both the bases of the corporate income tax and the trade tax itself.

The base of the real estate tax is the value of land and buildings owned by the company. Due to a valuation below market prices based on historical values (*Einheitswerte*) effective tax rates are substantially below nominal rates.

The base and the rate of the corporate income tax as well as the solidarity surcharge are determined by federal law. The same holds for the bases and the basic rates (*Steuermesszahlen*) of the trade and the real estate taxes. Since both the trade and the real estate taxes are designed to provide an autonomous source of revenue for the municipalities, the latter are entitled to choose a multiplier (*Hebesatz*) for each of these taxes. This is then multiplied with the product of the tax base and the basic rate so as to yield the tax liability.[17]

3.1.4 Ireland

For corporations located in Ireland, we consider the corporate income tax (*corporation tax*) and the real estate tax (*business rates*).

The corporate income tax, which currently is imposed at a statutory rate of 12.5 per cent, does not vary regionally or locally; the real estate tax does: Whereas the tax base is regulated centrally, the municipalities (cities and townships) may set their own tax rates. As we only consider the situation for companies located in Dublin, this regional variation does not show up in our study.

The so-called 'manufacturing relief' is an important unconventional Irish tax measure, which is highly relevant for this study. Under the manufacturing relief, corporations in the manufacturing sector have access to a reduced corporate income tax rate of ten per cent for the fraction of their profits which results from manufacturing activities.

---

[17] See table A.3. on p. 91 f for the trade tax and table A.13. on p. 101 f for the real estate tax.

3.1.5 Italy

For Italian corporations, we take into account corporate income tax (*imposta sul reddito delle persone giuridiche*, IRPEG), the regional tax on productive activities (*imposta regionale sulle attività produttive*, IRAP), and real estate tax (*imposta comunale immobiliare*, ICI).

The corporate income tax, which is imposed at a statutory rate of currently 34 per cent, does not vary regionally or locally. Italian regions may vary the standard rate of the IRAP, which is 4.25 per cent, by one percentage point. However, during 2001–2003, none of the regions assessed here have changed that standard rate. The tax base of the real estate tax is regulated centrally. The municipalities may fix tax rates within a range of 0.4 to 0.7 percentage points.[18]

Between 2001 and 2003, Italy has applied a number of unconventional tax measures:

- Under the Italian dual income tax, a part of the profits may be taxed at a lower corporate income tax rate. This part is determined by applying a statutory imputed interest rate to qualifying equity, which consists of equity that was added between 1996 and 2001. The qualifying equity is multiplied by 1.4 in case the overall equity of the company meets some particular conditions. In contrast to the Austrian version of the dual income tax, increments of equity thus qualify for the dual income tax for a number of consecutive years, not only for one year.
- We take into account one additional, generally available unconventional measure: the Tremonti incentive. Under that incentive, additional investments in defined assets or increases in equity capital qualify for an additional deduction of up to 50 per cent of the initial cost of the investment for purposes of calculating the corporate income tax base. As the Tremonti incentive is granted only for increments of investment or equity and thus depends on the investment history of the corporation, as with Austria we undertake analyses for companies that cannot take advantage of these rules and companies where the rules are fully effective.[19]
- Two more unconventional measures are worth mentioning here as they might – in some very particular cases – significantly lower corporate tax burdens. However, as these measures primarily apply to old capital, not to new one as assumed for this study, we have not considered them for the computations. The first one is a one-time opportunity to revalue particular assets that was available in 2001. A voluntary step-up of asset values reverses former depreciation allowances but creates additional future allowances. As the revaluation gain was taxed at a reduced corporate income tax rate of 19 per cent, whereas later depreciation allowances can be deducted from profits taxed at ordinary rates, this measure potentially decreases tax burdens for Italian corporations. The second measure mentioned is the tax amnesty in 2003, which included corporate tax-

[18] The rates of the real estate tax in Italy are shown in table A.14. on p. 103 f.

[19] We do not take into account another, similar incentive, the Visco incentive, which was available for some companies in 2001.

payers. These taxpayers could arrange previously evaded taxes by paying a comparatively small fee.

Due to these unconventional measures, we note that general conclusions on effective tax burdens in Italy are very hard to draw. One should keep this restriction in the interpretation of the results in mind when looking at the results for this country.

3.1.6 The Netherlands

Corporations located in the Netherlands are liable to pay two taxes only, the corporate income tax (*Vennootschapsbelasting*) and the real estate tax (*Onroerend-belasting*).

The base and the rate of the corporate income tax are determined at the national level. The rate has been reduced in 2003 from 35 to 34.5 per cent. The real estate tax is based on the value of land and buildings. It is a local tax with tax rates determined by the municipalities, inducing a moderate variation in effective statutory real estate tax rates among the four cities examined.[20]

3.1.7 Switzerland

The Swiss tax system is characterised by the federal structure of that country. Thus, the profit of a corporation is taxed at the three layers of the state (confederation, cantons, and municipalities) and sometimes also by the church. In addition, all cantons levy a capital tax, and some of them also tax real estate of corporations.

The corporate income tax (*Direkte Bundessteuer*) of the Swiss confederation is due at a rate of 8.5 per cent. The bases of the cantonal profit taxes (*Gewinnsteuern*), although regulated in separate cantonal laws, are largely harmonised and essentially coincide with the base of the federal profit tax. Profit tax payments can be deducted from the bases of both the federal and the cantonal profit tax.

The cantonal and municipal profit tax is computed by multiplying the headline cantonal tax (*einfache Staatssteuer*) with the sum of the annual multiples (*Steuerfüsse*) chosen by the canton, the municipality, and, where applicable, the church. As the cantons make substantial use of their tax autonomy, the resulting effective profit tax rates differ markedly between the Swiss locations examined in the present study.[21]

To determine the headline cantonal tax, some cantons apply proportional tax schedules while the majority uses progressive tax schedules where the rates increase either with the level of profits or the rate of return on equity. Among the cantons with a tax schedule relating to the return on equity, only St. Gallen applies

---

[20] See table A.15. on p. 104.

[21] See table A.4. on p. 93.

this schedule without a cap[22] on the average statutory tax rate. In this case, the addition of equity is rewarded by the tax code since the amount of profit eligible for a lower tax rate is increased. In that respect, this schedule resembles a dual income tax system as encountered in Austria and Italy.

The capital tax (*Kapitalsteuer*) of the cantons is based on the taxable equity of the firm. As in the case of the profit tax, the capital tax payment is obtained by multiplying the headline cantonal tax by annual multiples chosen by canton, municipality, and possibly church. Some cantons in addition impose a real estate tax (*Liegenschaftssteuer*). These two taxes also vary considerably among the locations assessed.[23]

3.1.8 United Kingdom

Similarly to Ireland and the Netherlands, the United Kingdom imposes only two kinds of taxes on companies, the corporate income tax (*corporation tax*) and the real estate tax (*rates*).

The corporate income tax is regulated at the national level. Its current rate is 30 per cent. Although the revenue of the real estate tax accrues to the local jurisdictions, the rate is fixed annually by the national Parliament. Thus, the tax rates computed for London in this study also apply for other locations in the United Kingdom.

3.1.9 United States (Boston)

In the United States, only Boston, Massachusetts is considered. For companies located there, the relevant taxes are the federal corporate income tax and the state profit tax (*corporate excise tax*) as well as the property tax (*franchise tax*) imposed by the state on corporations in the manufacturing sector.

The rate of the federal corporate income tax is 35 per cent. The state profit tax, which is levied at a rate of 9.5 per cent, is deductible from the federal corporate income tax. A special tax credit of 3 per cent is granted by the state of Massachusetts for particular investment outlays of companies in the manufacturing sector.

The property tax amounts to 0.26 per cent of the corporation's tangible property and is deductible from the federal corporate income tax.

---

[22] In our sample, the cantons of Basel-Landschaft, Basel-Stadt, and Zürich apply rate-of-return dependent profit tax schedules with a cap on the average tax rate. See also section 4.1.7 on pp. 46 ff.

[23] See tables A.16. on p. 105 and A.17. on p. 106.

3.2 Important Developments 2001–2003 and Beyond

Over the time horizon of this study, some important changes in the tax systems have developed. As far as these changes are relevant for the results of the present study, we briefly present them in the following:

- *Austria*: In September 2002, the Austrian parliament passed the rules for the incremental investment tax credit mentioned above. This tax credit thus is available for the tax years 2002 and 2003.
- *France*: From 2001 to 2003, the French central government reduced the surcharge on the corporate income tax from six per cent in 2001 to three per cent in 2003 and beyond. Additionally, a number of local tax authorities changed the rates of the trade tax and the real estate tax.
- *Germany*: Some municipalities varied the tax coefficients for the trade tax and the real estate tax. In addition, the central government of Germany raised the corporate income tax rate because of the flood in southern and eastern Germany in autumn 2002 for the tax year 2003 from 25 per cent to 26.5 per cent.
- *Ireland*: The standard statutory tax rate of the corporate income tax has been reduced from 20 per cent (2001) to 16 per cent (2002) and 12.5 per cent in 2003 and beyond. The manufacturing relief, i.e. the reduced corporate income tax rate of ten per cent, is no longer available for companies that were not already eligible for this rule on 23 July 1998 as from 2003 on. Depreciation allowances for machinery were loosened in 2001, when a five-year straight-line depreciation replaced the former 15 per cent-straight line depreciation schedule. In 2003, this depreciation rate has been tightened again; machinery now is depreciated over eight years. In addition, the local rates of the real estate tax have been altered.
- *Italy*: Italy has reduced the statutory corporate income tax rate from 36 per cent to 34 per cent in 2003. The government has announced plans to reduce that rate to 33 per cent in the long run. It also has announced plans to abolish IRAP; however, until 2003 only the payroll component of that tax – which has no impact on the results of this study – has been abolished. Some municipalities have changed real estate tax rates, mostly upwards. The dual income tax regime is no longer available for increases in equity after 30 June 2001. The Tremonti incentive was available in 2001 and 2002.
- *The Netherlands*: The Netherlands reduced their 35 per cent corporate income tax rate for the years 2002 and later to 34.5 per cent. The four municipalities assessed here slightly changed their local real estate tax rates between 2001 and 2003.
- *Switzerland*: Corporate income tax at the federal level was not changed between 2001 and 2003, although there were discussions on a reduction from 8.5 per cent down to eight per cent. Some of the cantons and municipalities have slightly changed their tax coefficients, with an impact on effective corporate income tax and capital tax burdens. In the canton of Basel-Landschaft, a small reform of the cantonal and municipal capital tax slightly increased the effective statutory profit tax rate. The canton of Bern reduced the statutory capital tax

rate from 0.5 per cent to 0.3 per cent for 2003 and beyond, for the same periods the canton of Ticino reduced that rate from 0.2 per cent to 0.15 per cent.

Note: The canton of Zürich has passed the long-awaited reform of the corporate income tax schedule in 2003. A proportional corporate income tax schedule with a rate of eight per cent will replace the current tax schedule, which depends on the rate of return of the investment and contains a tax rate ceiling at ten per cent, in 2005. That reform also will halve the capital tax rate from 0.15 per cent to 0.075 per cent.

- *United Kingdom*: From 2001–2003, the only change that affects this study is the periodical adjustment of the real estate tax.
- *United States*: In late 2001, the U.S. government introduced a 30 per cent immediate depreciation allowance for particular assets in the light of the economic impact of the New York terror attacks.

4 The Effective Tax Burdens in the Assessed Countries

In this chapter, we present country-by-country figures for the variation of the EATR and the EMTR over different assets, different sources of finance, and different regions in the years 2001–2003 (section 4.1). We take the example of Austria in order to explain the meaning of the results and to discuss some interesting patterns that also show up for other countries. Subsequently, we briefly assess effective tax burdens in the other eight countries. At the end of this chapter, we compare the patterns that emerged between these countries (section 4.2). Yet, we do not compare the overall levels of effective tax burdens, which will be the subject of the following chapter.

4.1 Results for Each Country

4.1.1 Austria

Table 4.1. provides the detailed results (costs of capital, EMTRs and EATRs) for each combination of one of the five types of assets and one of the three sources of finance considered for the location of Wien in 2003. In addition, it presents weighted averages of these figures

- for each type of asset, weighted over all three sources of finance,
- for each source of finance, weighted over all five types of assets, and
- over all sources of finance and all types of assets.

A technical note: We calculate the weighted average of the EMTRs as the weighted average tax wedge, i.e. the weighted average difference between the cost of capital and the post-tax rate of return of five per cent. Due to non-linearity of the EMTR, this is not precisely the same as taking an average of different EMTRs. See also European Commission (2002: 145).

For Austria, we first assume that the investment qualifies neither for the dual income tax treatment[24] nor for the incremental investment tax credit. Later on, we will relax this assumption.

---

[24] The Austrian type of dual income tax is deemed not to be very effective, see Wurmsdobler (2002: 149-152) and the explanation on the draft of § 11a of the Austrian income tax code from 28 March 2003 by the Austrian ministry of finance, code Zl. 040010/7-Pr.4/03, available at http://www.parlinkom.gv.at/archiv/XXII.pdf/ME/00/00/000021e.pdf.

Table 4.1. Effective tax burdens at the corporate level for Wien, 2003

Cost of capital EMTR EATR (%)	Intangibles	Industrial buildings	Machinery	Financial assets	Inventories	Mean
Retained earnings	7.6 34.5 34.2	7.7 35.4 34.5	7.1 29.2 32.3	8.6 41.8 37.3	7.6 34.0 34.0	7.7 35.2 34.5
New equity	7.6 34.5 34.2	7.7 35.4 34.5	7.1 29.2 32.3	8.6 41.8 37.3	7.6 34.0 34.0	7.7 35.2 34.5
Debt	4.2 -19.9 22.8	4.2 -19.5 22.8	3.7 -36.8 21.1	5.0 0.0 25.5	4.0 -25.3 22.2	4.2 -19.1 22.9
Mean	6.4 22.1 30.2	6.5 23.0 30.4	5.9 14.9 28.4	7.3 31.8 33.2	6.3 20.9 29.9	6.5 22.9 30.4

The rows labelled "Retained earnings" and "New equity" in table 4.1. present effective tax burdens of an equity-financed investment. These figures do not differ in case the corporate tax system treats both sources of finance equally at the corporate level, which is the standard case for most tax systems, and which is true for the Austrian tax system. These figures would differ in case a country operated a split-rate corporate tax system.

An example: The former German split-rate tax system led to different effective tax burdens at the corporate level on an investment financed with retained earnings or financed with new equity. This was because distributed profits were taxed differently from retained profits. Up to the year 2000, retained profits were subject to a corporate income tax rate of 40 per cent, whereas distributed profits were taxed at 30 per cent. For the impact of such a split-rate corporate tax system on effective tax burdens, with a focus on Germany's 2001 corporate tax reform, see e.g. Sachverständigenrat zur Begutachtung der gesamtwirtschaftlichen Entwicklung (2001: 296-316); European Commission (2002: 165-171).

For an equity-financed investment, a comparison with the statutory profit tax rate unveils whether an investment is favoured or deterred by the tax system, compared with an investment that bears only a profit tax which displays some basic neutrality properties. Here, neutrality means that taxation does not have an impact on corporate decision-making, i.e., taxation does not influence the relative attractiveness of particular types of assets, sources of finance, or the overall level of investment.

A technical note: With respect to marginal investments, a neutral income tax system supposes that the present value of tax depreciation allowances equals the present value of the economic depreciation path of an asset. Johansson (1961 and 1969) and Samuelson (1964) showed that taxation does not affect the valuation of an investment in case depreciation for tax purposes is equal to true economic depreciation. This requires that in the case of an inframarginal investment the sum of depreciation allowances is greater than the initial cost of the investment: In addition to the initial cost, the net present value of the investment is written down for tax purposes. Consequently, a tax system that leaves valuations unchanged would result in an EATR of zero, as it would imply that the numerator in equation (2.4) would always be zero.

Under the assumptions applied here, a tax system where the depreciation rate for tax purposes is equal to the true economic depreciation rate of the investment, but which restricts the sum of tax depreciation allowances to the initial cost of the investment – as it is the standard case in most real world income tax systems –, displays an EMTR and an EATR which is equal to the statutory tax rate. Such a tax system nevertheless is not neutral in the sense of Johansson's and Samuelson's findings, as it taxes positive net present values. For further details on the behaviour of EATRs and EMTRs under neutral tax systems, see Devereux and Griffith (1999 and 2003); Lammersen (2002); Schreiber, Spengel and Lammersen (2002).

An effective tax rate on an equity-financed investment that exceeds the statutory profit tax rate might especially result from non-profit taxes, or from an unfavourable definition of the profit tax base. The profit tax base might provide rates of tax depreciation allowances that are below economic depreciation rates; also, it might not adjust appropriately for the taxation of inflationary gains.

In the case of Wien, the EMTR on financial assets financed with equity is 41.8 per cent. Due to the taxation of inflationary gains, it is greater than the statutory profit tax rate of 34 per cent. In contrast, under the LIFO method for inventory valuation, which is applicable in Austria, inflationary gains are not taxed, and consequently the EMTR on inventories is equal to the statutory profit tax rate. If inventories were valued at the FIFO method, inflationary gains would fully be taxed, and the EMTR on inventories would also be 41.8 per cent. For a marginal investment, the taxation of inflationary gains thus is equal to an increase in the statutory tax rate of 7.8 percentage points under a tax system that perfectly adjusts profits for inflation.

For machinery, we obtain an EMTR below the statutory profit tax rate, which results from a tax depreciation schedule that is favourable compared with the assumed true economic depreciation rate. For industrial buildings, the real estate tax imposes an extra tax burden, and the EMTR of industrial buildings is above the statutory profit tax rate. We find that EATRs of an equity-financed investment in general are relatively close to EMTRs, which illustrates the limited impact of non-profit taxes and the definition of the profit tax base on effective tax rates in this case.

As in Austria, effective marginal tax rates on debt-financed investment often are negative (see table 4.1.). In that case, the cost of capital is below the real market interest rate (see again section 2.1.3, pp. 13 ff.). This indicates that there is an indirect tax subsidy on the investment, which drives the post-tax rate of return above the pre-tax rate of return. We can explain this effect by looking at the effective marginal tax burden of an investment in financial assets: In Austria, interest payments in general are completely deductible for purposes of profit taxation. Moreover, there are no non-profit taxes on an investment in financial assets. Thus, the EMTR for debt-financed financial assets simply is zero, and the cost of capital is equal to the real market interest rate. The corporation pays out all the proceedings of the investment as interest payments, which are completely deductible from the profit tax base, leaving a zero net present value of taxable profits and tax payments. Nominal deductibility of interest payments eliminates the taxation of inflationary gains in this case. Consequently, for debt-financed inventories valued at LIFO, there is a double relief from inflationary gains, forcing the EMTR below zero and the cost of capital below the market interest rate. For depreciable assets, similar effects occur, and especially because of the combination of complete deductibility of nominal interest payments and relatively favourable tax depreciation schedules, negative marginal tax burdens result.

The EATR on debt-financed assets generally is positive: the more profitable an investment, the relatively less important the deductibility of interest payments at the market interest rate. Such an investment generates positive taxable profits, which are subject to taxation at the effective statutory tax rate.

As we only regard taxes at the corporate level, we cannot compare the effective tax rate on debt-financed investments appropriately with the statutory corporate profit tax rate in order to identify tax subsidies.

An example: Suppose we abstract from inflation and depreciation allowances. An investment of 1,000 generates a pre-tax rate of return of $p = 20$ per cent and thus a profit before the deduction of taxes or interest payments of 200. Moreover, suppose that the investment is financed with debt, and that the market interest rate is five per cent, then the taxable profit amounts to 150. The corporate profit tax rate is 34 per cent, thus the profit tax due is 51. According to equation (2.5), the tax wedge is divided by a pre-tax measure of profitability that can be characterised as a rate of return on assets, not as a rate of return on equity. From the point of view of the economy as a whole, the rate of return on assets is especially relevant for identifying economic inefficiencies, therefore the Devereux-Griffith approach bases effective tax rates on that measure. The EATR in that case is 25.5 per cent, whereas the investor pays exactly 34 per cent profit tax out of his part of the return.

Fig. 4.1. Effective tax rates for Austria (all nine states), 2001–2003

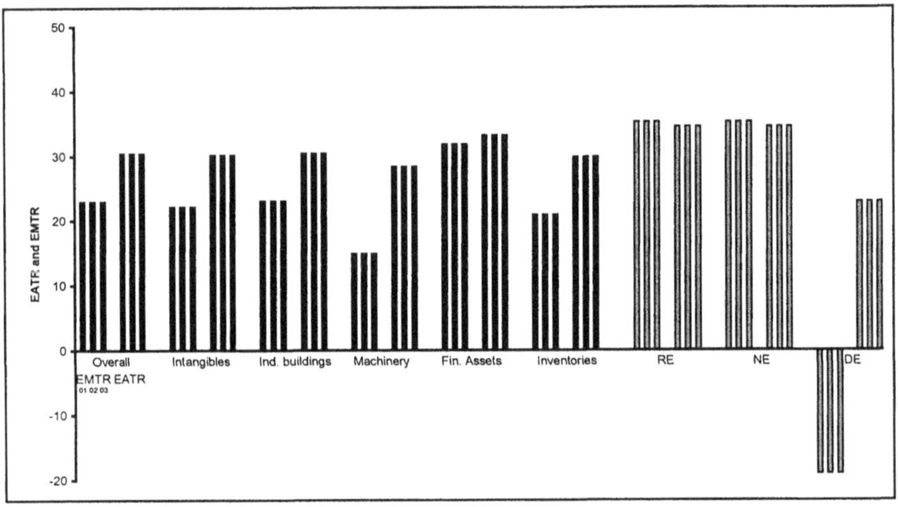

For the same reason, weighted averages that include effective tax rates from debt-financed investments carry a downward bias. Thus, one cannot compare them directly with the statutory profit tax rate.

As we will see, the standard Austrian case as illustrated by table 4.1. provides a picture of the structure of effective tax burdens on different investments that is also very common in other countries.

Fig. 4.1. illustrates the weighted averages from table 4.1. for the EMTR and the EATR for 2001, 2002, and 2003. Metaphorically speaking, fig. 4.1. x-rays the effective tax burdens and unveils a number of particular features and developments of a tax system. Subsequently, we will present such a figure for the median location of each country; App. D provides the accompanying tables that contain the detailed results.

- If, for example, the real estate tax was increased or the rules for the depreciation of buildings were tightened from one period to another, this would especially be reflected by an increase of the bars for the EMTR of buildings.
- An increase in net wealth taxes or in capital taxes would especially be reflected by an increase of the bars for equity financing, i.e., retained earnings (RE) and new equity (NE), whereas there would be no impact as far as an investment is financed with debt (DE).
- Increasing statutory profit tax rates would be reflected by an increase of all of the EMTR- and EATR-bars in most cases, with the notable exception of debt-financed investments, where an increase in statutory tax rates often might decrease effective marginal tax burdens: As deductions dominate over proceedings, an increased tax rate raises the value of deductions from the taxable base.[25]

Note: We do not present the cost of capital: We express the measures of the EMTR and the EATR both as effective tax rates. Thus, we can compare them easily, whereas the costs of capital are expressed as a rate of return, which cannot be compared directly with an effective tax rate. However, in the absence of personal taxes, an EMTR is an uncomplicated transformation of the cost of capital, thus both measures carry the same information. See section 2.1.3 above, pp. 13 ff.

In Austria, we obtain a very untypical picture, as in the standard case there are no changes between 2001 and 2003. In case an Austrian corporation can take maximum advantage of the dual income tax and the incremental investment tax credit, we observe two effects:[26]

- The dual income tax system reduces the effective tax burden of investments financed with equity. The tax reduction triggered by one unit of additional equity is equal to the imputed interest rate (which is set at 0.8 per cent above the market interest rate) times the tax rate differential of nine percentage points be-

[25] In that case, we obtain a case of the so-called 'tax paradox': an increase in the statutory tax rate effectively increases the net present value of an investment, which is counterintuitive at first sight. For some cases of the 'tax paradox', see e.g. Sinn (1987); Schneider (1992: 246-250).

[26] For a discussion of the impact of tax systems that grant such an 'allowance for corporate equity' on investment decisions, see, e.g., Lammersen (1999 and 2003).

tween the standard and the reduced corporate income tax rate. As this tax reduction only depends on the amount of equity added and not on the level of profitability, the reduction in effective tax rates is strongest for low-yielding investments; the relative impact of this measure decreases with a higher level of profitability.

- Under the incremental investment tax credit, additional new fixed tangible assets – with the notable exception of buildings – qualify for a ten per cent tax credit. For purposes of this study, only machinery meets all the legal requirements and consequently qualifies for the tax credit. As this measure bases on the initial cost of the investment and not on the level of profitability, its effect on effective tax rates also is strongest for low-yield investments but declines for more profitable investments.

If both measures are taken together and both unfold their maximum effect, the marginal investments assumed for this investigation are effectively almost tax exempt; the EMTR decreases from 22.9 to 3.3 per cent. Profitable investments, however, still carry a tax burden of 26.1 per cent, which is just 4.3 percentage points below the EATR in the standard case of 30.4 per cent (see also App. D.1).

4.1.2 France

Fig. 4.2. presents the median effective tax rates for France. These median rates describe the median of all effective tax rates for each combination, i.e., the bars do not necessarily represent the effective tax rates at one single location. If, e.g., the municipality that displays the median overall effective tax burden imposes a comparatively high real estate tax but a comparatively low trade tax, another municipality might be the median location an investment in machinery and buildings.

In France, a relatively high level of non-profit taxes (trade tax and real estate tax) on industrial buildings and machinery raises the EMTR for these assets above the statutory profit tax rate of 35.43 per cent. For investments financed with debt, the weighted average EMTR is only slightly negative (in 2001) or even positive (in 2002 and 2003): Debt financing shields marginal investments from the French corporate income tax and its surcharges, but not from the trade tax. The reduction of corporate income taxes shows up in fig. 4.2. as described above. Furthermore, the tax burden on industrial buildings has increased between 2001 and 2003 due to increases in the effective burdens of local tax rates; the median real estate tax rate has been quite constant over these years, whereas the median statutory trade tax rate increased from 25.90 to 26.83 per cent.

Fig. 4.2. Median effective tax rates for France (19 departments), 2001–2003

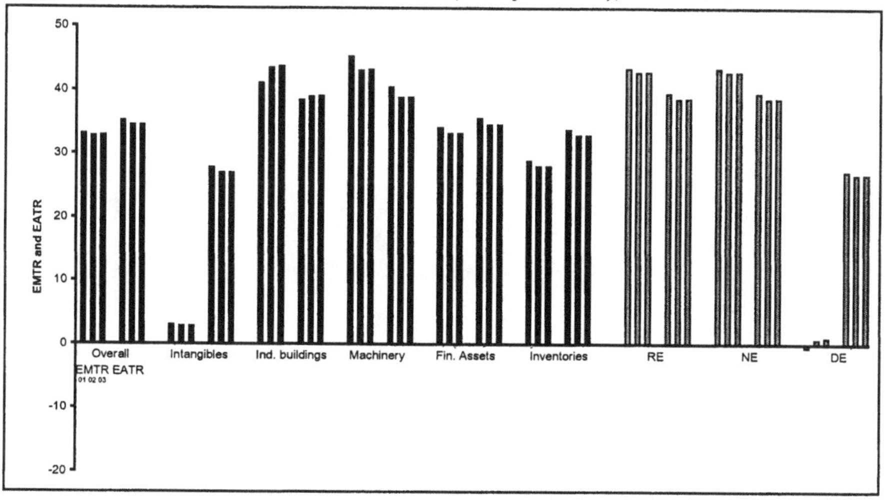

See p. 35 for further explanation.

Fig. 4.3. Regional variation of EATRs in France, 2003

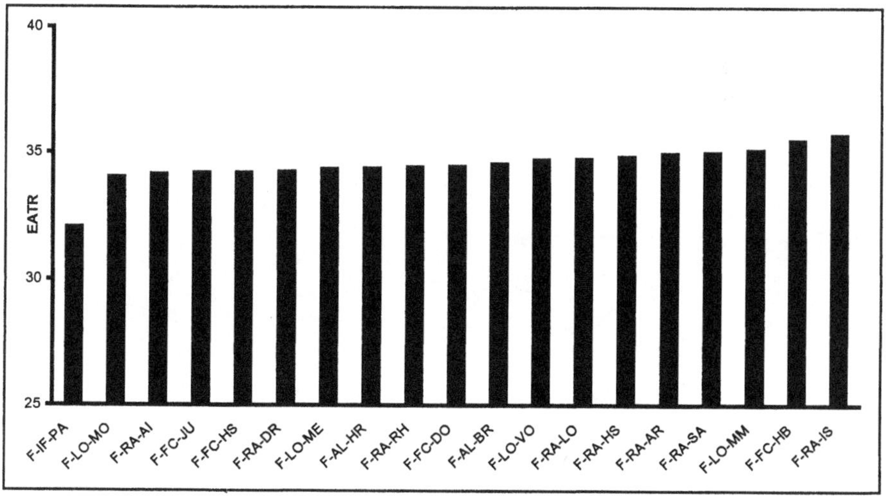

See table B.1. on pp. 111 f. for a list of the assessed regions.

Fig. 4.4. Regional variation of EMTRs in France (19 departments), 2003

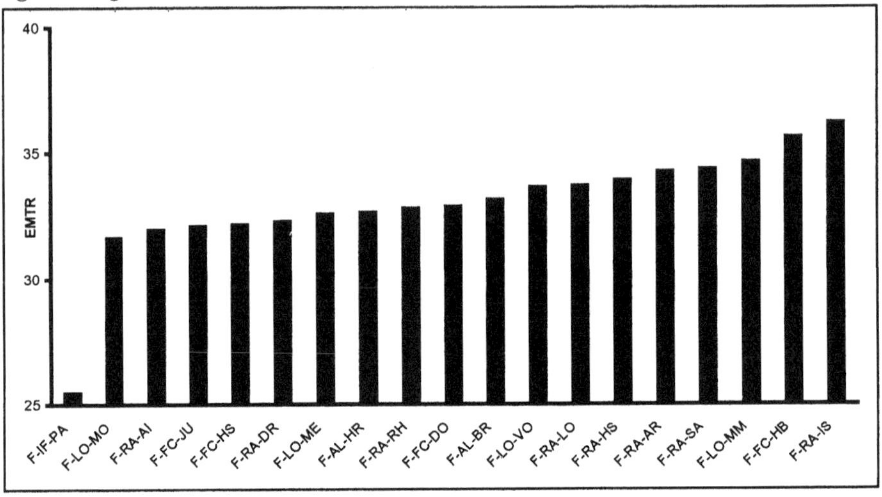

See table B.1. on pp. 111 f. for a list of the assessed regions.

Fig. 4.3. illustrates the inter-regional variation of EATRs, fig. 4.4. illustrates the inter-regional variation of EMTRs in 2003 between the 19 French regions that have been included here.[27] As only non-profit taxes (trade tax and real estate tax) vary locally, inter-regional variation is more developed for marginal investments (10.7 percentage points) than for profitable investments (3.6 percentage points). We can trace a great part of the variation back to the extraordinarily low level of local tax rates in Paris, which displays by far the lowest effective tax burdens. However, note that due to the non-linearity of EMTRs and the different denominators of both measures comparisons between differences in EMTRs and EATRs must be regarded with some caution.

4.1.3 Germany

In Germany, comparatively generous depreciation allowances and a low level of non-profit taxes, combined with a relatively high combined statutory profit tax rate, result in EMTRs that in general are below the EATRs. Only half of the interest payments are deductible from the base of the trade tax; therefore, as an exception to the general rule, debt-financed financial assets carry a positive EMTR.[28]

---

[27] We have chosen the regional codes for the different locations as follows: The first letter indicates the country code (F for France, I for Italy, etc.); the two following letters represent the code of the entity at the first regional level; the final two letters represent the code of the entity at the second regional level, i.e., the particular location. In most cases, each two-letter code consists of the first two letters of the regional denomination or, in case the denomination combines two places, of the first letters of these places. App. B.1 provides a detailed list of the assessed regions.

[28] For the detailed results, see App. D.

From 2001 to 2003, the median municipal multiplier of the real estate tax has been constant at 360 per cent, whereas the median municipal multiplier of the trade tax has slightly decreased from 375 to 370 per cent. Furthermore, fig. 4.5. clearly illustrates the temporary increase in the statutory rate or the corporate income tax from 25 per cent up to 26.5 per cent in 2003. The EMTR for debt-financed investments decreases because of that measure.

We find comparatively strong regional variation, which is slightly more developed for the EMTR (2003: 4.8 percentage points, fig. 4.7.) than it is for the EATR (2003: 4.4 percentage points, fig. 4.6.). This is because the real estate tax, as a non-profit tax, and the trade tax vary regionally. As a tendency, rather rural regions impose lower municipal multipliers than metropolitan regions; consequently, Hamburg, Köln, München, and Frankfurt occupy four out of the last six positions.

Fig. 4.5. Median effective tax rates for Germany (63 municipalities), 2001– 2003

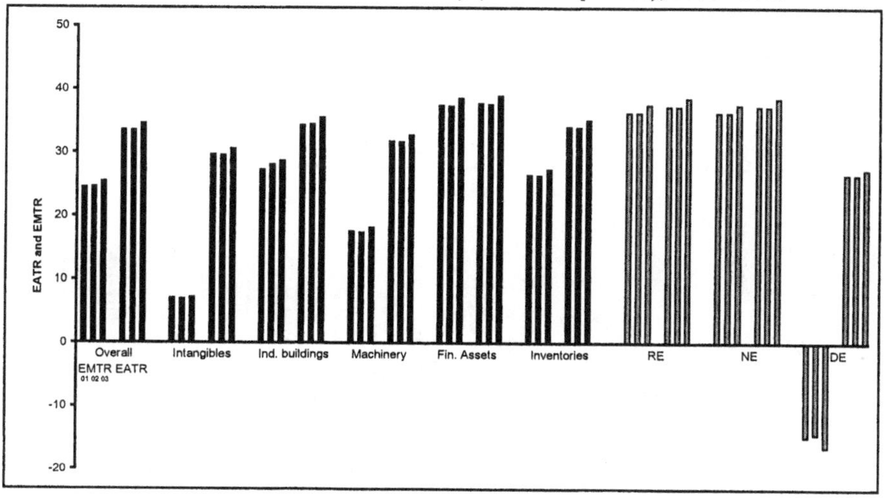

See p. 35 for further explanation.

Fig. 4.6. Regional variation of EATRs in Germany, 2003[29]

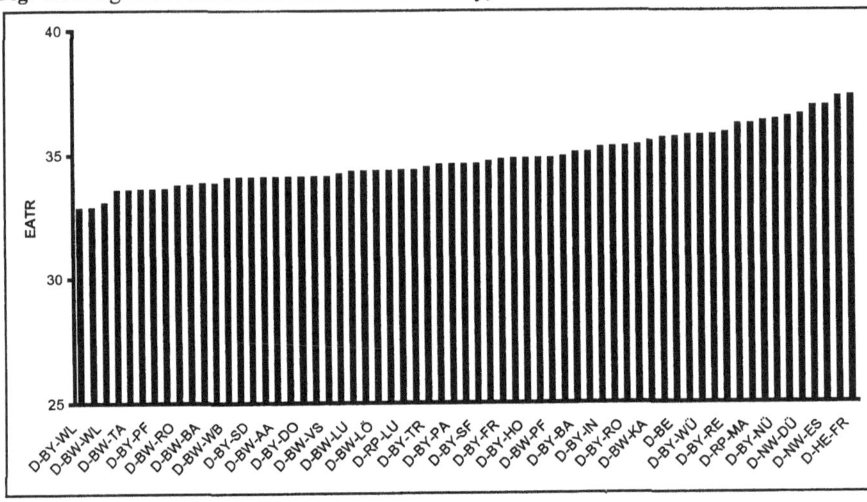

See table B.1. on pp. 111 f. for a list of the assessed regions.

Fig. 4.7. Regional variation of EMTRs in Germany, 2003[30]

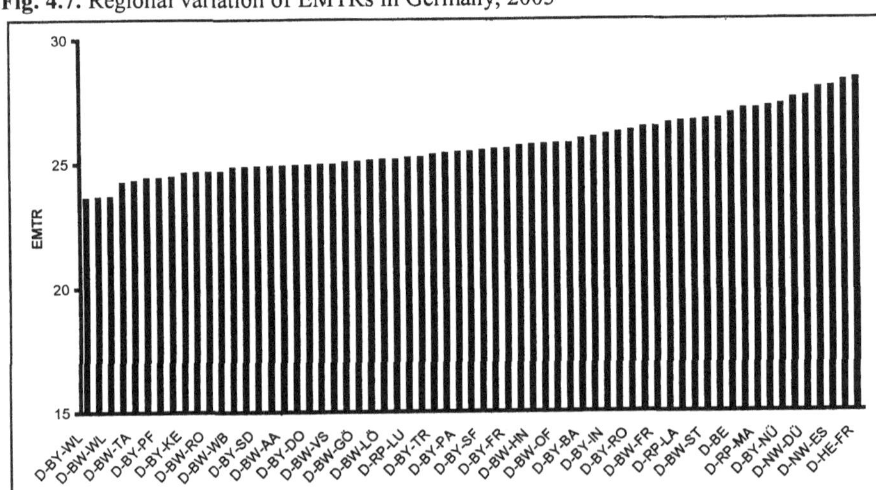

See table B.1. on pp. 111 f. for a list of the assessed regions.

---

[29] Due to the limited available space, figures 4.6. and 4.7. contain 63 bars each, but only every second bar is denominated by the name of the corresponding region. For a complete list of results, see table 5.1. on pp. 54 f.

[30] See footnote 29 above. For a complete list of results, see table C.1. on pp. 119 ff.

4.1.4 Ireland

In Ireland, investments in manufacturing corporations carry a comparatively low effective tax burden, which is especially due to a very low corporate profit tax. However, financial assets are taxed as non-trading income at a higher rate of 25 per cent, which is illustrated by fig. 4.8. With the beginning of 2003, the manufacturing relief is no longer available, which means an increase in the profit tax rate for trading income of 2.5 percentage points and which clearly shows up in fig. 4.8. Additionally, fig. 4.8. illustrates that depreciation rates for machinery have been tightened in 2003.

Fig. 4.8. Effective tax rates for Ireland (Dublin), 2001–2003

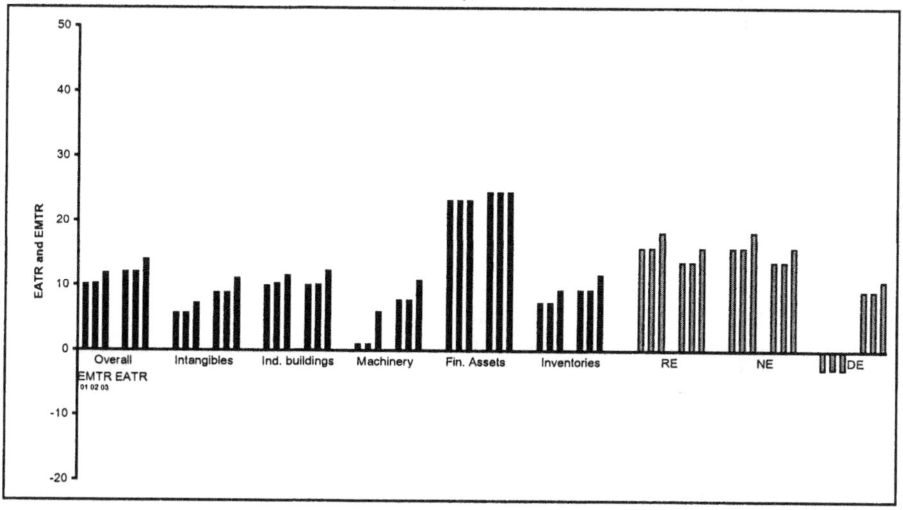

See p. 35 for further explanation.

4.1.5 Italy

As already mentioned above, the Italian tax system has gone through many significant changes in recent years, which have included some special, one-time opportunities to avoid or reduce corporate tax payments. One should keep this fact in mind when looking at the following results.

The Italian tax system grants relatively favourable depreciation allowances, especially for intangibles. Real estate taxes are low. Consequently, comparatively low EMTRs result. On the other hand, the combined corporate profit tax rate is rather high, thus there is a large gap between EMTRs and EATRs (see fig. 4.9.).

Fig. 4.9. Median effective tax rates for Italy (33 provinces), 2001–2003

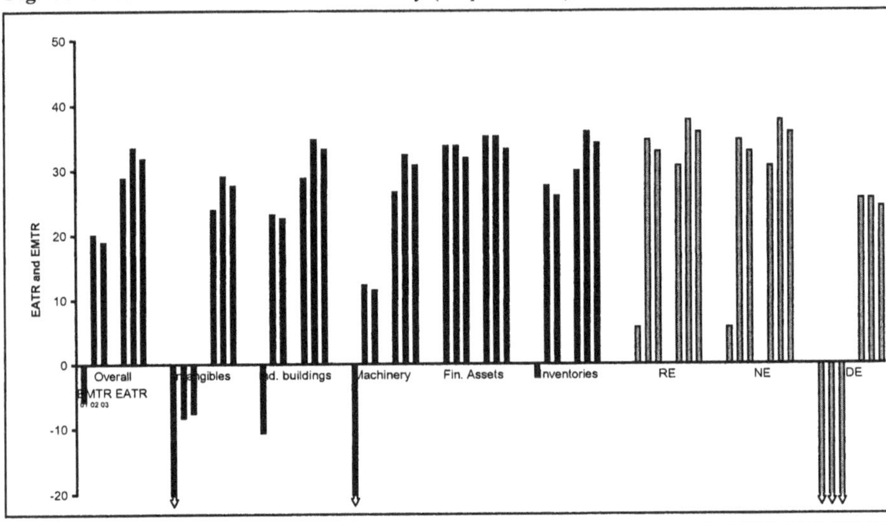

See p. 35 for further explanation.

In 2001, equity-financed investments benefited strongly from the Italian type of dual income tax. As in the case of Austria, the effect of this measure reduces effective tax rates especially for marginal investments. However, the impact of the Italian dual income tax system was much stronger than the one that results from the present Austrian dual income tax system, which had various reasons:

- The difference between the reduced profit tax rate (23.25 per cent including IRAP) and the standard profit tax rate (40.25 per cent including IRAP) was much greater in Italy (17 percentage points) than it is in Austria (nine percentage points).
- In 2001, an Italian corporation that had sufficient old equity, i.e. equity that was added before the end of the tax year current on 30 September 1996, could benefit from the application of a factor of 140 per cent on equity added after that date for purposes of the determination of the allowance for corporate equity.
- Finally, in Italy each Euro of equity added permanently qualified for the dual income tax, whereas in Austria in fact additional equity qualifies for one period only.

As another potential difference, the rules for the definition of the imputed interest rate in Italy were more favourable in the past than those in Austria, as the Italian government in general was entitled to consider a greater risk premium. However, in 2001, according to tax law both countries fixed their imputed interest rate at a level of approximately 0.8 percentage points above the market interest rate. Thus for that particular tax year we have considered no difference between the imputed interest rates of both countries.

Note: The imputed interest rate of the Italian dual income tax regime was designed to be fixed with reference to the market interest rate, which could be increased by a risk premium of up to three percentage points (Bordignon, Giannini and Panteghini, 2000: 339). The rate was fixed at a level of seven per cent until 2000. A ministerial decree from 30 March 2001 reduced that rate to six per cent. Based on Italian market interest rates, we assume that the risk component of that rate for 2001 was 0.8 percentage points. The Austrian dual income tax regime fixes the imputed interest rate at 0.8 percentage points above the market interest rate (§ 11 section 1 no. 6 of the Austrian income tax code). Consequently, we add 0.8 percentage points to the market interest rate in both cases in order to obtain imputed interest rates for Austria and Italy in 2001.

In 2002, Italy abolished the dual income tax regime for new investments. Consequently, as fig. 4.9. illustrates, the tax burden on new investments financed with equity rose sharply. For companies which could take maximum advantage of the Tremonti-rules, effective marginal tax burdens in 2002 were conserved at a very low level (for details, see App. D.1). In 2003, the Tremonti rules no longer apply, but there has been a reduction in the statutory corporate income tax rate of two percentage points.

Regional variation of effective tax burdens in Northern Italy is very low in the case assessed here. Although the sample includes regions that choose the lowest permissible real estate tax rate and regions that choose the highest permissible real estate tax rate, the span of EMTRs is only 0.6 percentage points (see fig. 4.11.), and the span of the EATRs is even as low as 0.2 percentage points (see fig. 4.10.).

Fig. 4.10. Regional variation of EATRs in Italy, 2003

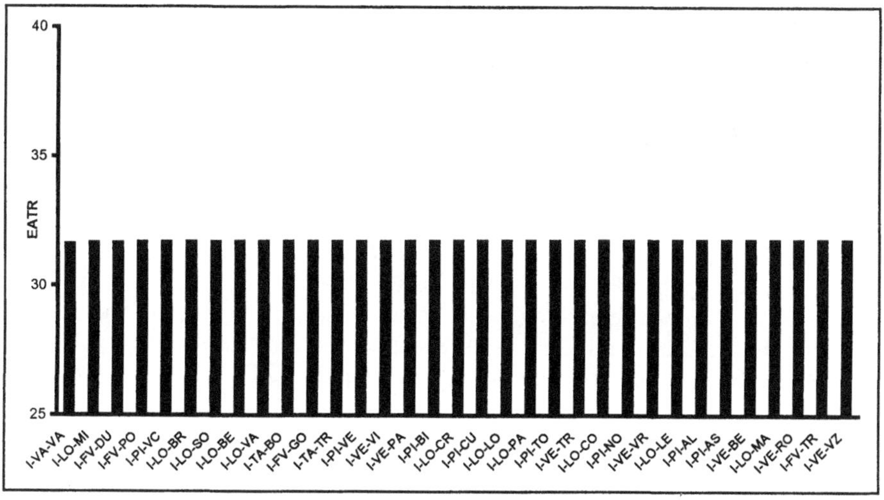

See table B.1. on pp. 111 f. for a list of the assessed regions.

Fig. 4.11. Regional variation of EMTRs in Italy, 2003

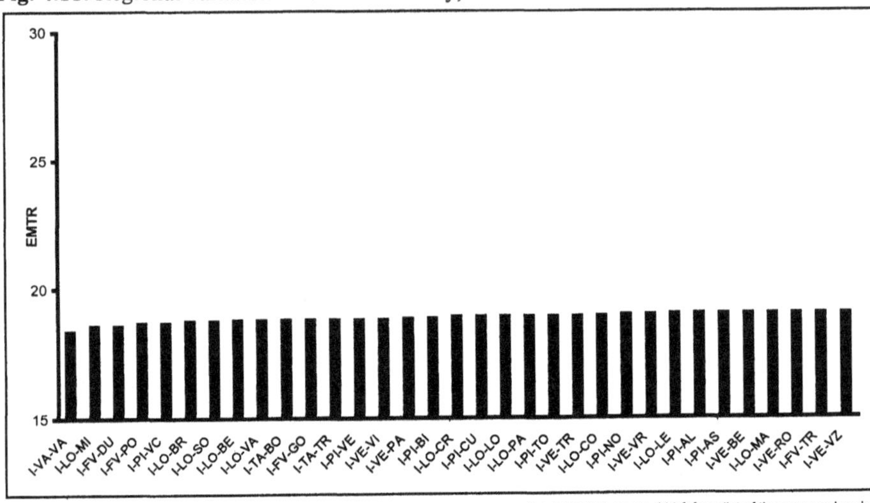

See table B.1. on pp. 111 f. for a list of the assessed regions.

4.1.6 The Netherlands

In the Netherlands, low non-profit taxes and complete deductibility of interest payments combined with a relatively high statutory corporate income tax rate induce a large gap between effective marginal and effective average tax burdens, especially for debt-financed investments (see fig. 4.12.).[31] The corporate profit tax reduction in 2002 has a negligible effect on effective tax burdens; little variation results from changes in local real estate taxes.

Only the – comparatively low – real estate tax varies regionally, thus regional variation for the four municipalities assessed here is very low (see fig. 4.13.). For the EATR, the span is 0.1 percentage points, for the EMTR, it is 0.8 percentage points.

[31] For each bar, we choose the lower of the two centre values as the median for the Netherlands in order to avoid averaging effective tax burdens of two regions.

Fig. 4.12. Median effective tax rates for the Netherlands (four municipalities), 2001–2003

See p. 35 for further explanation.

Fig. 4.13. Regional variation of EATRs and EMTRs in the Netherlands, 2003

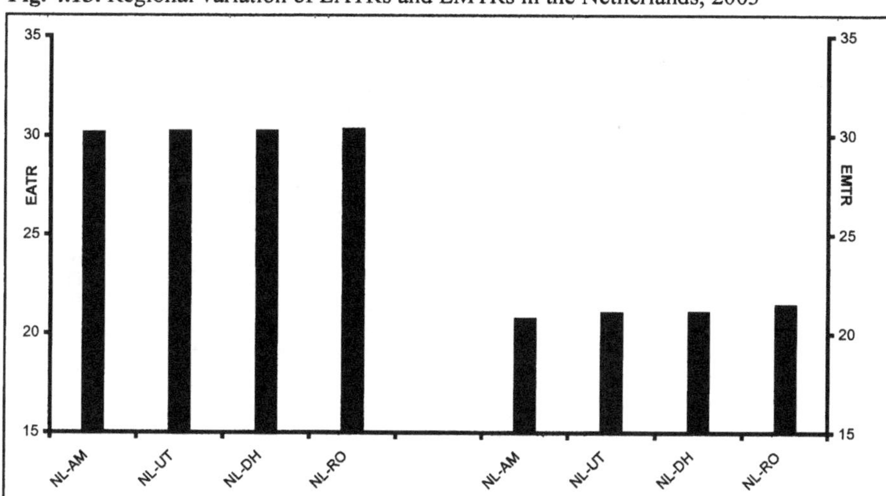

See table B.1. on pp. 111 f. for a list of the assessed regions.

4.1.7 Switzerland

In Switzerland, we find favourable depreciation allowances that virtually eliminate the marginal tax burden on intangibles financed with the assumed mix of debt and equity for our model investment (see fig. 4.14.).[32]

On the other side, there are perceptible real estate taxes in a few cantons, and there are capital taxes, which burden on equity-financed investments and which can be avoided by relying on debt financing. Some cantons – in our sample only the canton of St. Gallen – apply corporate income tax schedules that depend on the rate of return of an investment without being capped[33] at a particular level. In some respect, we can compare these schedules with dual income tax regimes: If equity is added to the company, corporate tax payments are reduced as the amount of profits eligible for the reduced corporate profit tax rate increases, reducing the hurdle rate an equity-financed investment has to earn in order to be worthwhile.

Fig. 4.14. Median effective tax rates for Switzerland (twelve cantons), 2001–2003

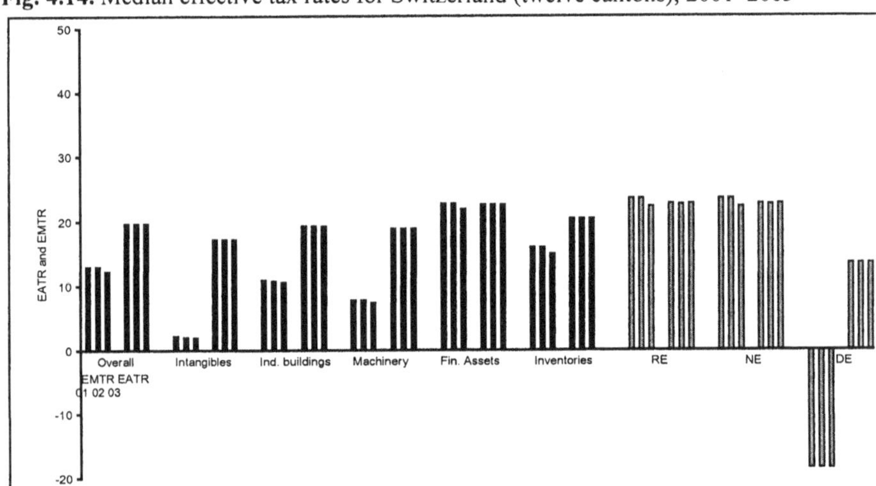

See p. 35 for further explanation.

Variation over time is relatively limited, what might be because a number of cantons reformed their tax systems as a reaction to the Federal Tax Harmonisation Act (*Steuerharmonisierungsgesetz*, StHG) just in 2001. Main effects result from changes in the tax coefficients, notably in the canton of Schwyz, and changes in the statutory tax rates of capital taxes in the cantons of Bern and Ticino.

---

[32] For each bar, we chose the lower of the two centre values as the median for Switzerland in order to avoid averaging effective tax burdens of two cantons.

[33] With respect to the cantons assessed here, such a cap exists in Basel-Landschaft, Basel-Stadt, and Zürich. In case a corporation does not reach that cap and the marginal statutory tax rate is above the one for the lowest tax bracket, these systems consequently also work partly like the dual income tax systems mentioned above.

Fig. 4.15. Regional variation of EATRs in Switzerland, 2003

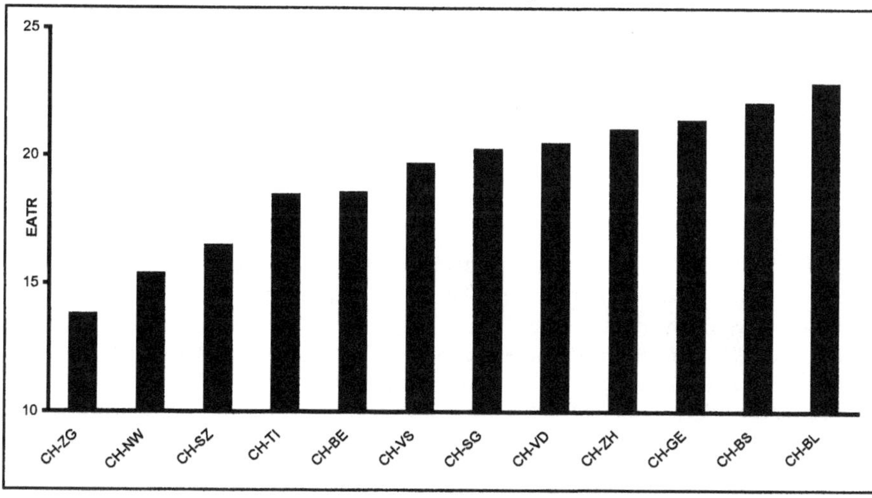

See table B.1. on pp. 111 f. for a list of the assessed regions.

Fig. 4.16. Regional variation of EMTRs in Switzerland, 2003

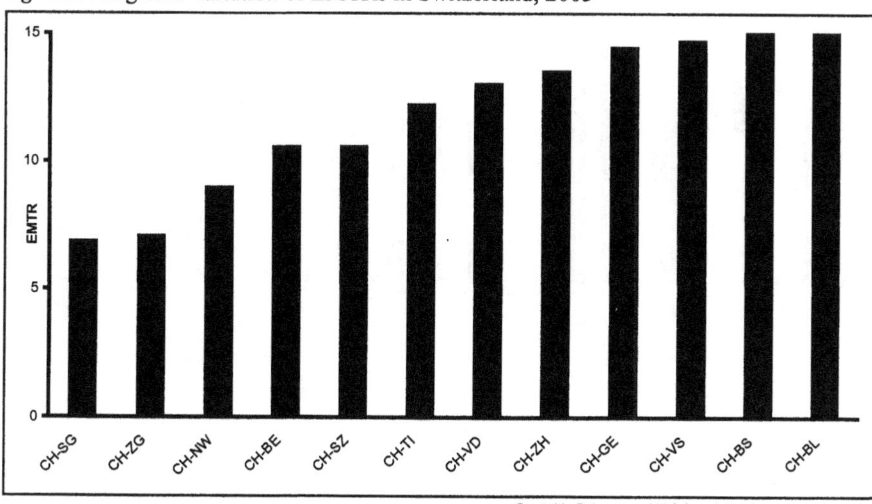

See table B.1. on pp. 111 f. for a list of the assessed regions.

Due to their far-reaching fiscal autonomy, regional variation between the Swiss cantons assessed here is very strong (EMTR: 9.2 percentage points, EATR: 9 percentage points), with Zug, Schwyz, Nidwalden, and Bern at the lower end of the scale and Zürich, Genève, Basel-Stadt and Basel-Landschaft at the upper end (see figures 4.15. and 4.16.). The latter four cantons display especially large headline profit tax rates; however, note that effective tax burdens might be lower in case progressive tax rates apply and a company does not expect to be in the top-profit tax bracket.

4.1.8 United Kingdom

In the United Kingdom, depreciation allowances are slightly more favourable compared with the economic lifetime of the assets assumed here, and interest payments are completely deductible, which drives the EMTRs a good way below the EATRs. The EMTR on an investment in buildings displays a heavy real estate tax burden; the EMTR on inventories equals the one on financial assets, indicating the taxation of inflationary gains due to the use of the FIFO method (see fig. 4.17.).

Between 2001 and 2003, no significant changes in the tax system that affect our model investment have taken place. The only variation results from an increase in the statutory rates of the real estate tax.

Note: According to tax law, these increases in the rate of the real estate tax simply should mirror an adjustment for price increases between 2001 and 2003. As we abstracted from particular price effects between 2001 and 2003, which in fact are minor, these changes in the effective tax rates in fact represent the nominal increase in the real estate tax burden.

Fig. 4.17. Effective tax rates for the United Kingdom (London), 2001–2003

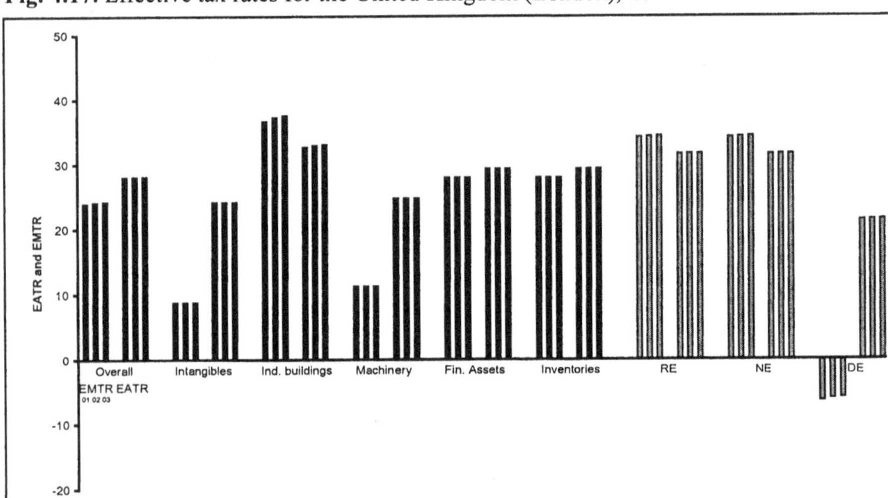

See p. 35 for further explanation.

4.1.9 United States (Boston)

In the United States, depreciation allowances are especially favourable for investments in machinery, which additionally take advantage of the accelerated depreciation regime in 2002 and 2003 (see fig. 4.18.). Perceptible state property taxes on tangible capital affect especially the EMTR of investments in these assets. On the other hand, the Massachusetts tax credit induces a countervailing impact on EMTRs. A comparatively high statutory profit tax rate and complete interest deductibility result in a large gap between the EMTR and the EATR of debt-financed investments.

Fig. 4.18. Effective tax rates for the United States (Boston), 2001–2003

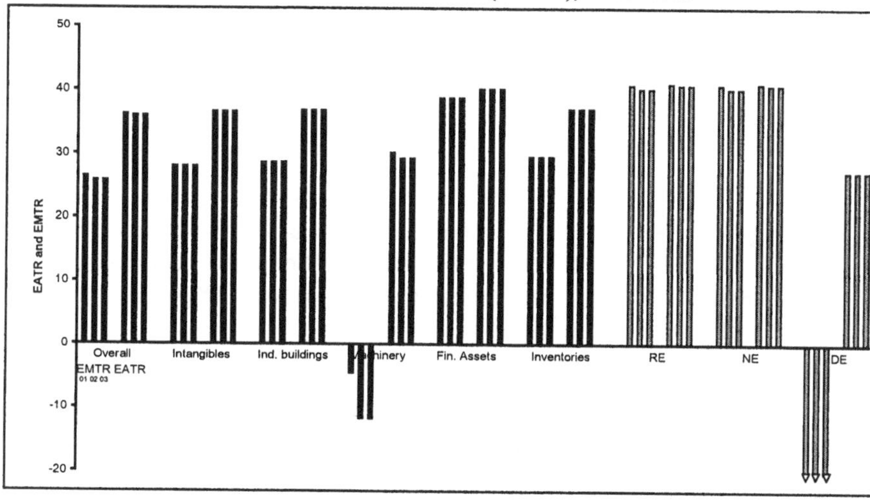

See p. 35 for further explanation.

Overall, the effect of the tax reduction that the special depreciation regime delivers does not appear to be very strong. It reduces the overall EMTR by 0.7 percentage points and the overall EATR by only 0.2 percentage points.

4.2 Comparison of Patterns in Effective Tax Burdens

To sum up, we find some interesting patterns in the results presented here:

- *Inter-asset-variation*: Intangibles, industrial buildings and machinery can be depreciated for tax purposes, i.e., the cost of the assets can gradually be set against taxable earnings during the lifetime of the asset. The more generous these depreciation allowances are, the lower especially the effective marginal tax burden is. Financial assets and inventories cannot be depreciated. The return of both assets in general is subject to taxation at the statutory profit tax rate. Thus for financial assets and for inventories that are not valued using the LIFO method, in addition to the real gain also an inflationary gain is taxed, which might drive effective tax rates above the statutory tax rate. Industrial buildings usually have to carry an additional tax burden imposed by real estate taxes. This additional tax burden becomes especially obvious when we assess effective marginal tax burdens. Although a general conclusion on the ranking of these assets shows up – the tax burden on intangibles and machinery often is lower than the tax burden on industrial buildings, financial assets, and inventories –, we have to keep in mind that this particular result, of course, depends to a large degree on the assumptions of the model, particularly on the assumed economic lifetimes of the assets.
- *Variation over different sources of finance*: At the corporate level, effective tax burdens on investment financed with retained earnings in general equal those

on investment financed with new equity. One important reason for this effect is that the assessed tax systems do not differ in the treatment of retained and distributed profits. As interest payments are completely or at least partially deductible at the corporate level, investment financed with debt is relieved from corporate taxes. Nominal interest payments are deductible, thus already in cases where only real gains are taxed at the statutory rate and interest payments are completely deductible – e.g. debt-financed inventories valued under the LIFO method – negative EMTRs result. For inframarginal investment, earnings exceed interest payments, which are limited to the market interest rate. As these additional earnings are subject to corporate taxation without triggering additional deductions, the EATR on debt-financed investment generally is positive.

- *Variation caused by unconventional tax measures*: The Austrian, Italian, and Massachusetts investment incentives significantly reduce the effective marginal tax burden of the assets and sources of finance that qualify for these special rules. They also reduce the EATR, but the reduction is less obvious: For very profitable investments, comparatively high statutory tax rates significantly reduce the advantage that results from such measures.
- *Level of profitability*: EMTRs that are weighted over all three sources of finance usually display lower values than weighted average EATRs. This effect primarily results from the inclusion of debt financing and its above-mentioned impact on effective tax burdens. For equity-financed investments, the difference between the EMTR and the EATR shows some general tendencies of the tax systems. We distinguish between three main cases: (1) The EMTR is lower than the EATR: Such a system takes relatively less from investments that demonstrate low profitability than from those that demonstrate high profitability. This effect usually results from generous depreciation allowances and/or special investment incentives, e.g. tax credits, special immediate allowances or the Italian or Austrian type of dual income tax, combined with a low level of non-profit taxes. Consequently, the results indicate that the Italian and – for the incentive cases – the Austrian tax systems display this property. (2) The EMTR is very close to the EATR: In this case, we expect (a) a tax system that imposes a very low level of non-profit taxes and – compared to our assumptions of the economic lifetime – relatively neutral depreciation allowances. Alternatively, (b) a tax system that imposes a great non-profit tax burden and provides for relatively generous depreciation allowances would produce such a result. Our results indicate such behaviour of effective tax rates for Switzerland, Germany, the Netherlands, and the United States. Especially for the United States, generous depreciation allowances in addition to an investment tax credit neutralise a perceptible level of non-profit taxes. (3) An EMTR above the EATR indicates tight depreciation allowances and/or high non-profit taxes. Our results suggest that France, Ireland, and the United Kingdom operate corporate tax systems of this type. However, it should be borne in mind that the results strongly depend on the assumptions of this tax burden comparison. Thus these classifications can show some tendencies for the cases assessed here, but one should be careful not to generalize these findings arbitrarily.

- *Inter-regional variation within the assessed countries*: According to the size of inter-regional variation, we can distinguish between four groups of countries: Inter-regional variation in effective tax burdens markedly shows up between the Swiss cantons. Less, but still significant variation shows up in France and Germany. There is little variation in Italy and in the Netherlands, and – for our sample – no variation in Austria. In these three countries, regional and local governments do not have autonomy over important corporate taxes, or they do not make great use of it. We have not assessed the remaining three countries with respect to inter-regional variation of effective tax burdens.
- *Variation over the assessment period*: Relatively strong variation between 2001 and 2003 shows up for France, Ireland, and Italy. In Germany, in the Netherlands, in the United States, and in some Swiss cantons, tax changes over that period have had comparatively small effects. With respect to the tax rules assessed here, the tax systems of the United Kingdom, a number of Swiss cantons, and Austria (disregarding the incremental investment tax credit) have shown a large degree of continuity between 2001 and 2003.

5 International Comparison of Effective Tax Burdens

This chapter broadens the perspective of chapter 4 by comparing the size of effective tax burdens internationally (section 5.1). An assessment of the sensitivity of the results supplements the comparison of tax burdens in the base case (section 5.2). Section 5.3 provides a comparison of the results with those provided by the study of the European Commission (2002), which relied on a similar methodology, and Gutekunst and Schwager (2002), who computed effective tax burdens for a subset of the regions covered by this study. Moreover, that section draws common conclusions from the present analysis and the accompanying study by Elschner and Schwager (2004), who assess the effective level of taxation on highly qualified employees.

5.1 Effective Tax Rates in the Base Case

Table 5.1. ranks the EATRs of all the regions assessed for this study. Fig. 5.1. summarises the EATRs of all countries for 2003.

Note: For countries where there is no regional variation, or where regional variation has not been assessed, only a single bar has been included (Austria, Ireland, United Kingdom, United States). We include three bars for each country where numerous regions have been assessed (France, Germany, Italy) and for the four Dutch municipalities, which demonstrate only small regional variation. These three bars mark the locations that display the minimum, the median, and the maximum effective tax burden in each country. Finally, we include all of the assessed Swiss cantons, as in the case of Switzerland a comparatively small sample of regions shows noteworthy regional variation.

Table 5.1. Ranking of regions 2003

Rk		Region	EATR	Rk		Region	EATR
1	CH	Zug	13.8	44	I	Pavia	31.8
2	IR	Dublin	14.0	44	I	Torino	31.8
3	CH	Nidwalden	15.4	44	I	Treviso	31.8
4	CH	Schwyz	16.5	50	I	Como	31.8
5	CH	Ticino	18.5	51	I	Novara	31.8
6	CH	Bern	18.6	51	I	Verona	31.8
7	CH	Valais	19.7	53	I	Lecco	31.8
8	CH	St. Gallen	20.3	54	I	Alessandria	31.8
9	CH	Vaud	20.5	54	I	Asti	31.8
10	CH	Zürich	21.0	54	I	Belluno	31.8
11	CH	Genève	21.4	54	I	Mantova	31.8
12	CH	Basel-Stadt	22.1	54	I	Rovigo	31.8
13	CH	Basel-Landschaft	22.8	54	I	Trieste	31.8
14	GB	London	28.1	54	I	Venezia	31.8
15	NL	Amsterdam	30.2	61	F	Paris	32.1
16	NL	Utrecht	30.2	62	D	Weilheim	32.9
17	NL	Den Haag	30.3	63	D	Coburg	32.9
18	NL	Rotterdam	30.3	64	D	Walldorf b. Heidelberg	33.1
19	A	Burgenland	30.4 [a)]	65	D	Landkreis Mannheim	33.6
19	A	Kärnten	30.4 [a)]	66	D	Tauberbischofsheim	33.6
19	A	Niederösterreich	30.4 [a)]	67	D	Memmingen	33.6
19	A	Oberösterreich	30.4 [a)]	67	D	Pfarrkirchen	33.6
19	A	Salzburg	30.4 [a)]	69	D	Ravensburg	33.6
19	A	Steiermark	30.4 [a)]	70	D	Rottweil	33.8
19	A	Tirol	30.4 [a)]	71	D	Kempten	33.8
19	A	Vorarlberg	30.4 [a)]	72	D	Balingen	33.9
19	A	Wien	30.4 [a)]	73	D	Weißenburg i. Bayern	33.9
28	I	Valle d'Aosta	31.6	74	F	Moselle	34.1
29	I	Milano	31.7	75	D	Waiblingen	34.1
29	I	Udine	31.7	76	D	Weiden	34.1
31	I	Pordenone	31.7	77	D	Schwandorf	34.1
31	I	Verb.-Cusio-Ossola	31.7	78	D	Reutlingen	34.1
33	I	Brescia	31.7	79	D	Aalen	34.1
33	I	Sondrio	31.7	80	D	Deggendorf	34.1
35	I	Bergamo	31.7	81	D	Donauwörth	34.1
35	I	Varese	31.7	82	D	Nagold	34.1
37	I	Bolzano	31.7	82	D	Vill.-Schwenningen	34.1
37	I	Gorizia	31.7	84	F	Ain	34.2
37	I	Trento	31.7	85	F	Jura	34.2
37	I	Vercelli	31.7	86	D	Göppingen	34.2
37	I	Vicenza	31.7	87	F	Haute-Saône	34.2
42	I	Padova	31.7	88	F	Drôme	34.3
43	I	Biella	31.7	89	D	Ludwigsburg	34.3
44	I	Cremona	31.8	90	D	Konstanz	34.3
44	I	Cuneo	31.8	91	D	Ansbach	34.3
44	I	Lodi	31.8	91	D	Lörrach	34.3

Table 5.1. continued

Rk		Region	EATR	Rk		Region	EATR
93	D	Ludwigshafen	34.4	119	F	Meurthe-et-Moselle	35.1
94	D	Ulm	34.4	120	D	Ingolstadt	35.3
95	F	Meuse	34.4	121	D	Landshut	35.3
96	F	Haut-Rhin	34.4	122	D	Rosenheim	35.3
97	F	Rhône	34.5	123	D	Freiburg	35.4
98	D	Traunstein	34.5	124	F	Territoire-de-Belfort	35.5
99	F	Doubs	34.5	125	D	Karlsruhe	35.5
100	D	Rastatt	34.6	126	D	Mannheim	35.7
101	F	Bas-Rhin	34.6	127	D	Berlin	35.7
102	D	Passau	34.6	128	F	Isère	35.7
103	D	Bayreuth	34.6	129	D	Landau	35.8
104	D	Schweinfurt	34.6	130	D	Würzburg	35.8
105	D	Schwäbisch-Hall	34.7	131	D	Stuttgart	35.8
106	F	Vosges	34.8	132	D	Regensburg	35.9
107	F	Loire	34.8	133	US	Boston	36.0
108	D	Freising	34.8	134	D	Mainz	36.2
109	D	Heilbronn	34.8	134	D	Offenbach	36.2
110	D	Hof	34.8	136	D	Augsburg	36.3
111	D	Offenburg	34.8	137	D	Nürnberg	36.4
111	D	Pforzheim	34.8	138	D	Köln	36.5
113	F	Haute-Savoie	34.9	139	D	Düsseldorf	36.6
114	D	Aschaffenburg	34.9	140	D	Hamburg	36.9
115	F	Ardèche	35.0	141	D	Essen	36.9
116	F	Savoie	35.0	142	D	München	37.3
117	D	Bamberg	35.1	143	D	Frankfurt	37.3
118	D	Heidelberg	35.1				

[a] The Austrian EATR is 26.1 per cent in case the incentives fully apply.

Fig. 5.1. International variation of EATRs, 2003

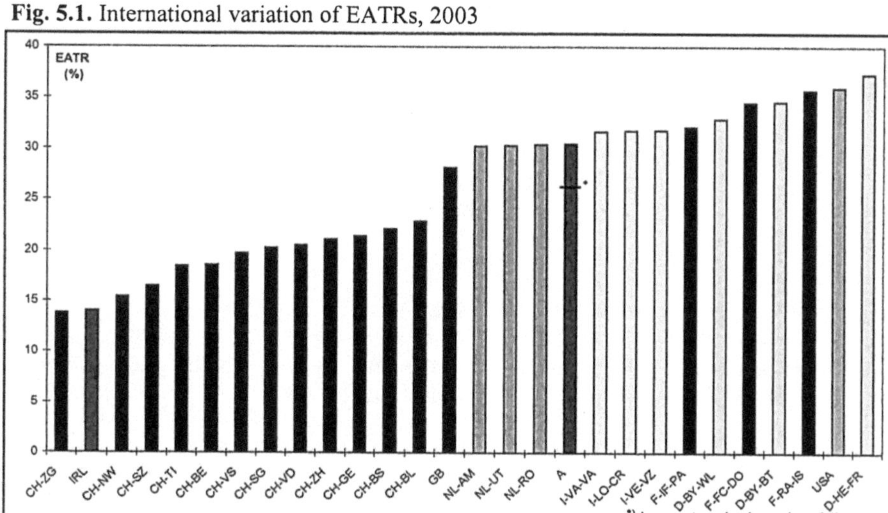

We can summarise the main findings from table 5.1. and fig. 5.1. as follows:

1. First, we find a great dispersion of effective tax rates in the assessed countries, which range over 23.5 percentage points between 13.8 per cent in the canton of Zug, Switzerland, and 37.3 per cent in Frankfurt, Germany. This result suggests that the attractiveness of particular locations from a tax perspective differs dramatically. Taxation might strongly influence the locational decisions of corporations. However, to conclude on the true magnitude of tax-induced economic distortions of the locational decision, studies on the empirical behaviour of companies are necessary.
2. Second, the EATRs of the model investment are determined largely by nationwide tax rules. In general, the level of regional and local tax autonomy which local governments currently make use of cannot improve a location's attractiveness compared to regions of other countries. Nevertheless, Swiss cantons compete with Ireland, and German and French regions compete with each other and with the U.S. city of Boston.
3. The model investment assessed here bears a comparatively low effective average tax burden in Ireland and in Switzerland. Company taxation in Austria, the Netherlands, the U.K., and in Italy can be deemed moderate, whereas Germany, France, and the United States can be classified as countries imposing a relatively heavy tax burden on corporate investment.
4. Largely, this ranking is driven by combined statutory profit tax rates. However, in some cases the definition of the tax base (e.g. in Italy), special provisions (like the Austrian incentives), and the level of non-profit taxes (especially in the case of France) also play an important role in determining the effective tax burden of investments that earn an economic rent.

In the same manner as fig. 5.1. does for the EATRs, fig. 5.2. displays the ranking of EMTRs.[34] We obtain the following main findings:

1. The dispersion of EMTRs between the assessed regions is even larger than the dispersion of EATRs. It ranges over almost 33 percentage points from 3.3 per cent in Austria in case the incentives fully apply up to 36.3 per cent in Isère, France. This result suggests that – in addition to the attractiveness as a location for an investment that earns an economic rent – also the optimal level of investment and the competitiveness of companies located in different regions differ dramatically from a tax perspective.
2. The impact of local and regional taxes – which are non-profit taxes in most cases – on the EMTRs is generally stronger than their impact on EATRs. Nevertheless, the finding from above which concluded that local governments can hardly improve the international standing of their region by varying their local tax rates at current levels is not challenged by the results. The exceptions mentioned above still prevail, however, and the change in the ranking between Weilheim, Germany and London, United Kingdom suggests that there are more exceptions to this rule for the EMTR than for the EATR.

[34] For a table that provides the ranking of all the assessed regions with respect to EMTRs, see table C.1., pp. 119 ff.

Germany have levelled out Germany's obvious advantage, which was a result of the 2001 German corporate tax reform.[39] However, in 2004, Germany's statutory corporate income tax rate will return down to its 2002 level. This does not mean, however, that France necessarily will fall behind again: There are plans for a comprehensive corporate tax reform in France for the time beyond 2003. EATRs in Italy have significantly changed between 2001 and 2003. In 2002, if an Italian investment did not qualify for an incentive, e.g. the Tremonti incentive, the EATR on such an investment easily reached the EATR on a German investment. Taking the Tremonti incentive into account, however, the Italian EATR in 2002 would be about nine percentage points and the Italian EATR in 2001 would be about four percentage points lower than fig. 5.4. indicates. With its 2003 tax reduction, Italy again displays an advantage over Germany and France.

Fig. 5.4. EATRs in France, Germany, and Italy, 2001–2003

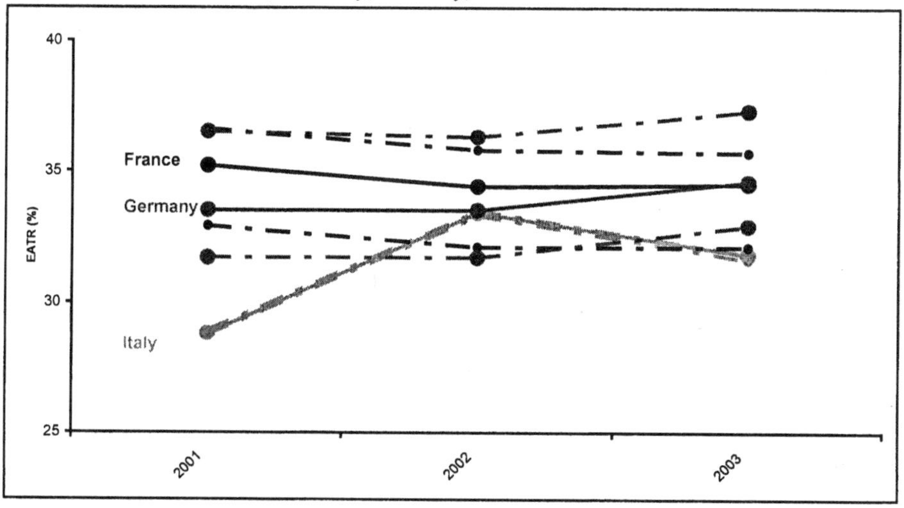

5.2 Sensitivity Analyses

In this section, we present results of four sensitivity analyses. These analyses should meet two separate goals:

- First, we assess whether the basic conclusions remain the same if we vary some basic economic conditions, which are represented by the basic economic parameters of the model. Obviously, one has to bear in mind that such a sensitivity analysis cannot cover all potentially relevant cases, and that such an analysis is still bound by the restrictive assumptions of the model.

[39] For the situation before that reform, see the results for 1999 from section 5.3.2, pp. 64 ff.

- Second, we try to single out the tax drivers for particular economic circumstances in order to illuminate how the different components of the tax system influence the level and the distribution of effective tax burdens.

Therefore, we recalculate effective tax burdens for the 143 regions under four additional parameter sets. These sets include a variation of the pre-tax rate of return of the profitable investment, a variation of the real interest rate, and two variations using different weights for the assets and the sources of finance. Tables C.1. and C.3. on pp. 119 ff. and 127 ff. present the detailed results.[40] Here, we focus again on the most important issues.

By increasing the *real rate of profitability* for purposes of the calculation of the EATR from 20 per cent up to 40 per cent, the EATRs come closer to the combined statutory profit tax rate.[41] This effect corresponds to the mechanisms mentioned in section 2.1.4, pp. 16 ff. We find some changes in the ranking as investments in Switzerland, which take advantage of comparatively favourable tax depreciation schedules, fall behind of those in Ireland, which are taxed at a lower profit tax rate. French locations improve their position, largely at the cost of German locations. This is due to the different weights of non-profit taxes and profit taxes in both countries. Also, the United States becomes slightly less favourable.[42]

An increase in the *real interest rate* from five per cent up to ten per cent decreases the relative weight of non-profit taxes in the measures of the effective marginal tax burdens. Also, as the discount factor changes, the present value of depreciation allowances is influenced: the net present values of depreciation allowances as a whole decreases, and the relative advantage of a fast depreciation schedule over a slow one increases. Increasing the real interest rate to ten per cent reduces the pre-tax economic rent of the profitable investment, i.e. the difference between the profitable rate of return and the market interest rate, from 15 per cent to ten per cent in real terms. Interest deductions increase. Therefore, EMTRs and EATRs are closer to each other than in the base case. With respect to the EATR, changes in the ranking are quite limited. French locations and Boston slightly improve their position.[43] With respect to the EMTR, changes are more significant, but still not dramatic.

As a third simulation, we use the *weights for the assets and sources of finance* that Gutekunst and Schwager (2002) applied.

Note: The weights Gutekunst and Schwager (2002: 29-30) applied and that we use for this sensitivity analysis are 1.43 per cent for intangibles, 12.99 per cent for industrial buildings, 17.49 per cent for machinery, 38.25 per cent for financial assets, 29.84 per cent for inventories, 55.45 per cent for retained earnings, 10.08 per cent for new equity, and 34.47 per cent for debt. For the weights we apply in the base case of the present study, see table 2.1., p. 13.

---

[40] For more detailed figures, see also App. D.2.

[41] Note that for Ireland the combined effective profit tax rate on the mix of assets is greater than the headline tax rate of 12.5 per cent: remember that financial assets are taxed at the non-trading corporate income tax rate of 25 per cent, see section 3.1.4, p. 25.

[42] See the results in table C.1., pp. 119 ff., and App. D.2.

[43] See the results in table C.3., pp. 127 ff., and App. D.2.

Only on the asset side of the balance sheet, these weights differ notably from those applied in the base case: We increase the weights of financial assets and inventories at the cost of the weights of fixed assets, especially intangibles.

Due to these changes, we obtain significantly increased EMTRs and slightly increased EATRs in most cases.[44] This is because fixed, depreciable assets often display a lower tax burden than financial assets and inventories do under our assumptions. Regional variation of effective tax burdens decreases as the weights of those assets that are especially hit by local taxes – industrial buildings and in France also machinery – decrease. With respect to the ranking of the EATRs, French regions slightly improve their positions, but there are no really substantial changes. Again, the impact on the ranking of locations according to EMTRs is stronger than according to the EATRs.

Finally, we apply typical *weights for a company in the service sector*. These parameters attach an even greater importance to financial assets and to debt than those of the sensitivity analysis above.

Note: We use the service sector weights from European Commission (2002: 178); these parameters base on information from the European Commission's BACH database. The weights are 3.2 per cent for intangibles, 12.3 per cent for industrial buildings, 11.9 per cent for machinery, 54.2 per cent for financial assets, 8.4 per cent for inventories, 21.6 per cent for retained earnings, 19.4 per cent for new equity, and 59.0 per cent for debt. For the weights applied in the base case, see table 2.1., p. 13.

For the purpose of these calculations, those special tax rules which are only available for companies in the manufacturing sector have been eliminated or modified.[45] Although the weight of financial assets increases, effective tax rates decrease.[46] This effect is due to the increased level of debt financing, which leads to greater interest deductions. However, the effective tax burden on equity-financed investments increases as expected. Because of the different levels of debt financing, we cannot draw a meaningful comparison of the magnitude of effective tax burdens between the base case and under this sensitivity analysis. Instead, we can draw some interesting and meaningful conclusions from changes in the ranking of the EATR in 2003: Due to the special tax treatment of financial assets in Ireland, that country now falls behind the canton of Schwyz. For 2001 and 2002, Ireland fares much worse than in 2003 as the corporate tax rate for companies in the service sector was 20 per cent (2001) and 16 per cent (2002). French regions strongly improve their position, as the weights of buildings and machinery, which bear the French trade tax, are very low. Additionally, interest payments are completely deductible for companies in France, whereas in Germany a trade tax burden remains, which might be relevant for investments of highly leveraged corporations; both effects of course are even stronger for marginal investments than they are for very profitable investments.

---

[44] See the results in table C.3., pp. 127 ff., and App. D.2.

[45] Changes concern the manufacturing relief in Ireland for the years 2001 and 2002, some rules on state and municipal property taxes in Massachusetts, USA, and the Massachusetts investment tax credit. For details, see section 3.1, pp. 23 ff., and table A.9., p. 97.

[46] See the results in table C.3., pp. 127 ff., and App. D.2.

To conclude, the sensitivity analyses have revealed a part of the interesting mechanics of the impact of taxation on effective tax burdens. With respect to the EATR, some notable changes in the rankings occur. These changes, however, are not strong enough to challenge the basic conclusions on effective tax burdens from the base case fundamentally. With respect to EMTRs, the impact of the economic assumptions on the ranking is stronger than with respect to EATRs: As the weight of various tax drivers increases, different tax structures play a more prominent role, and the most tax efficient location depends more heavily on the particular features of an investment.

5.3 Comparison with the Results of Other Studies

5.3.1 Gutekunst and Schwager (2002)

As this study is a follow-up and update to the one by Gutekunst and Schwager (2002), and as that study already covered a great number of regions included here, we expect that a comparison of the results provides valuable additional insights. We have already presented and discussed the most important differences in the models and the assumptions between both studies above.[47] Because of these differences, we cannot compare the numerical results of both studies directly, whereas we can do so with respect to the rankings and the conclusions. Fig. 5.5. presents the headline ranking of countries and regions that was calculated by Gutekunst and Schwager.[48]

We can summarise the main findings of Gutekunst and Schwager with respect to company taxation at the corporate level as follows:[49]

1. Switzerland clearly is a low-tax country. On the other end of the scale, France consistently displays high effective tax rates.
2. Variation in inter-regional effective tax burdens in Germany and in France is low, whereas in Switzerland it is notable.
3. With respect to inter-regional tax competition, national tax legislation dominates. Thus, German and French regions do not have the power to compete with neighbouring foreign regions on their own, i.e. without the support of the central government.
4. The extent of the tax advantage conferred by a Swiss location varies considerably between cantons, with the most attractive cantons located in Central Switzerland.
5. Mainly two reasons explain the differences in EMTRs: First, profit tax rates are lower in Switzerland as compared to Germany and France. Second, the tax structure differs between these three countries. In Switzerland and Germany, profit taxes dominate, whereas in France, there are substantial non-profit taxes.

[47] See section 2.1.5, pp. 18 ff.

[48] See Gutekunst and Schwager (2002: 75 and 87).

[49] See Gutekunst and Schwager (2002: 12-18 and 113).

6. Recent tax reforms in Germany and France, while reducing the tax burden, fell short of substantially improving the position of those countries in the international competition for investment. Effective tax burdens in France and Germany approached those in the United States, whereas the reforms could not nearly close the gap between those countries and the Netherlands, the United Kingdom, and especially Switzerland.

Fig. 5.5. Headline ranking by Gutekunst and Schwager (2002)

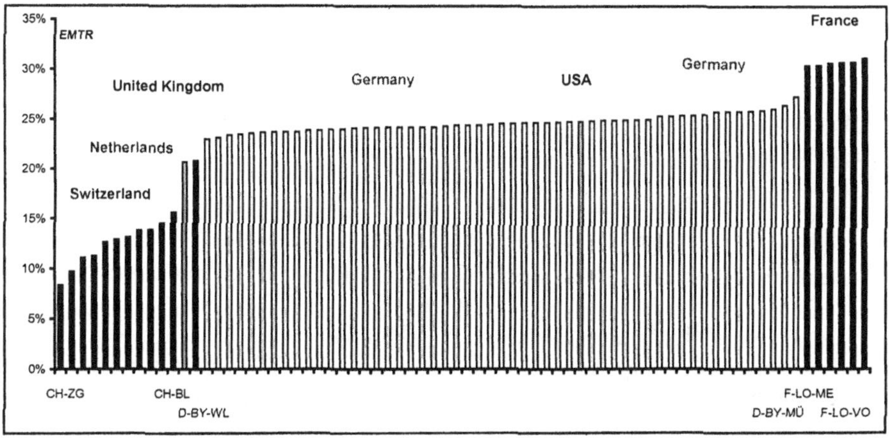

We see that most of the former conclusions still hold. However, a closer look is necessary with respect to conclusions 1 and 3. Gutekunst and Schwager stated, "sorting the regions according to the EMTR at the company level, the three countries [Switzerland, Germany and France, *author's note*] are neatly separated"[50], with the Swiss cantons at the low end of the scale and the French departments at the high end. In today's study, effective tax burdens for Germany's and France's regions are mixed even for the year 2001, which is due to different reasons:

- The combined statutory profit tax rate has a greater influence on the EATR than on the EMTR; this effect works in favour of France, which imposes a lower combined statutory profit tax rate than Germany.
- Moreover, the elimination of the payroll component of the French trade tax in the calculation of the effective tax burden on capital reduces effective tax rates. Elschner and Schwager (2004) consider this tax component in their study as part of the effective tax burden on highly qualified employees.[51]

If we include the countries that the earlier study did not address, we find that Ireland accompanies Switzerland as a low tax country now; in the marginal case, also the Austrian and Italian regions can compete with Switzerland if their dual income tax system and the Austrian incremental tax credit fully apply.

The Netherlands now display a lower EMTR and a greater EATR than the United Kingdom, whereas in the former study both countries displayed almost the

[50] See Gutekunst and Schwager (2001: 2); in German: Gutekunst and Schwager (2002: 13).

[51] See section 2.1.5, pp. 18 ff.

same EMTR. By separating between the two measures, we now obtain a more complete picture of the tax drivers for particular investments in these countries.[52]

Overall, the results of the present study confirm the general conclusions taken by Gutekunst and Schwager, although the enlarged geographic range, the expanded time horizon, and the additional calculation of effective average tax rates permit a more detailed picture of the magnitude and the driving forces of effective tax burdens on investment.

5.3.2 European Commission (2002)

Apart from some minor differences, the study conducted by the European Commission (2002) basically relies on the same approach and the same assumptions as the present study does. That study assessed effective tax burdens for an average level of regional taxes for each of the 15 EU countries in 1999 and 2001.

Fig. 5.6. adds EATRs as provided by European Commission (2002) for those EU-countries that the present study does not address, based on the tax rules in 2001.[53]

Compared with the present study, two additional issues are of interest: The enlarged geographic range, and the additional period (1999), which especially illustrates the impact of two important tax reforms in Germany and France.

- The Scandinavian countries fare quite well. Especially corporate tax burdens in Sweden are relatively close to those in Switzerland. The results for 2001 hide, however, that in Belgium, Luxembourg, and Portugal substantial tax reforms have come into force after that year, which have reduced combined statutory profit tax rates.[54] These countries, which displayed comparatively high EATRs in 2001, can be supposed to have reduced their effective average tax burdens significantly by now.
- The 1999 results provided by European Commission (2002: 157 and 159) show the magnitude of Germany and France's tax reforms of that time. Consequently, they supplement the time series displayed in fig. 5.4.: Germany reduced its EATR from 39.1 per cent in 1999 to 34.9 per cent in 2001; France went down from 37.5 per cent to 34.7 per cent. Whereas France kept on reducing effective corporate tax burdens between 2001 and 2003, Germany has left its path of reducing taxes on corporate investment in 2003.

---

[52] In the former study, the United Kingdom improved its position compared with the Netherlands already in the sensitivity analysis that supposed an increased pre-tax rate of return. See Gutekunst and Schwager (2002), p. 96, who, however, still supposed a marginal investment.

[53] The results for the countries included are regional tax burdens or median values of regional tax burdens, thus they are slightly different from those provided by the EU Commission study.

[54] Between 2001 and 2003, the combined statutory tax rate in Belgium went down from 40.17 to 33.99 per cent; in Luxembourg, it was reduced from 37.45 to 30.38 per cent, and in Portugal it was reduced from 35.2 to 33 per cent.

Fig. 5.6. EATRs 2001, present study combined with European Commission (2002: 269)

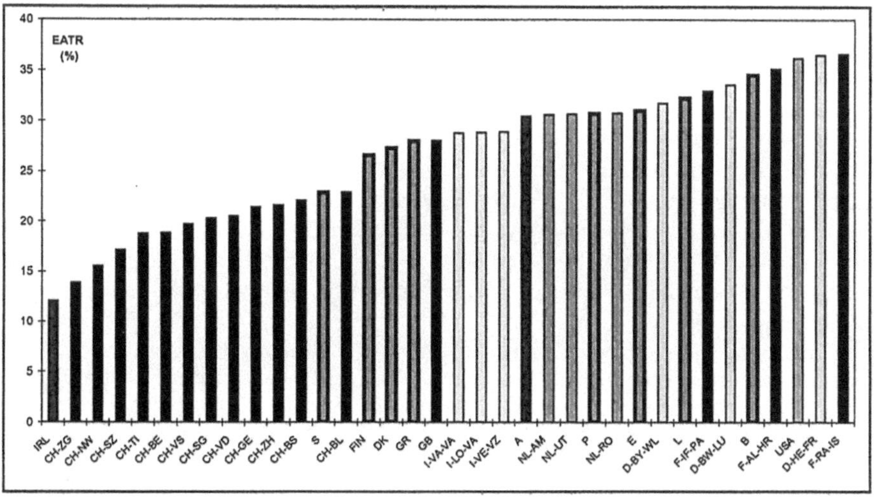

5.3.3 Elschner and Schwager (2004)

As mentioned above, an analysis of the effective tax burden on highly qualified employees as a location factor (Elschner and Schwager, 2004) accompanies the present study. As a theoretical starting point of that study, Elschner and Schwager assume that skilled employees are very mobile at the inter-regional level. Therefore, they can shift taxes on payroll and on wages onto their employers. Companies have to compensate those employees for differences in personal taxation. Under these premises, personal taxes of highly skilled employees also constitute a tax burden on companies. Therefore, they influence the attractiveness of a particular region as a location for investment.

Elschner and Schwager fix the income an employee demands after taxes and calculate an effective average tax rate[55] on an employee's total remuneration – i.e. the remuneration that the company must pay in order to reach the fixed post-tax income – under the tax rules of each location. The considered tax burden contains taxes on personal income, tax-like social security contributions, and payroll taxes paid by the company. The study takes a great number of different types of employees (married, single), different categories of remuneration (cash, perquisites, stock options, old-age contributions), and different levels of disposable income into account. However, for the comparison of fig. 5.7. and table 5.2., we only focus on the headline figures provided by that report. Therefore, we must stress that our conclusions have to be interpreted very cautiously: Effective tax burdens always are a result of each particular case's circumstances. A simple comparison of

[55] Note that this effective *average* tax rate now considers the whole income of a person, i.e., not an additional source of income, as the EATR calculated by the Devereux-Griffith approach does.

headline figures conceals considerable variation in the results, which makes it hard to draw general conclusions from these figures. The purpose of this comparison thus is to illustrate the correlation of effective tax burdens for one particular, but relevant case, not to present general conclusions.

The figures chosen as headline figures represent the effective tax burden of a single-earner employee who obtains a disposable income of 100.000 € per year. To make sure that we can compare the results, we index effective tax burdens based on the average of the included Swiss cantons. By definition, this average corresponds to an indexed effective tax burden of 100. We add a trend line which is based on the 20 observations included in fig. 5.7. in order to illustrate the correlation between the tax burden on the production factor capital and on highly skilled employees.

Note: Although the study by Elschner and Schwager also provides effective average tax rates, we cannot compare the numerical results of that study with those provided by the present study due to a number of conceptual differences. Especially, note that both concepts of effective tax burdens do not permit straightforward conclusions on distributional issues.

Fig. 5.7. Correlation of headline figures, taxation of companies and highly qual. employees

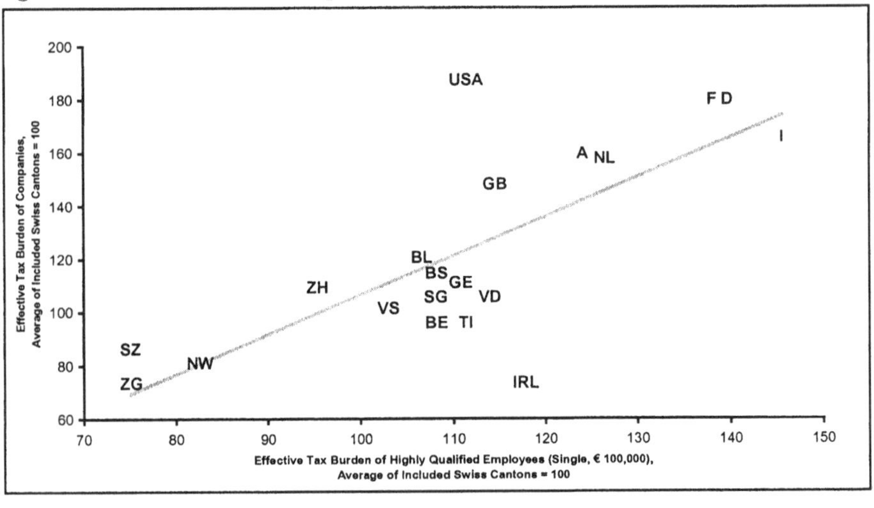

It is striking that effective tax burdens appear to be closely correlated for most locations. This suggests that – with the notable exceptions of Ireland and the United States – countries which impose large (small) corporate tax burdens also impose large (small) tax burdens on comparatively high personal incomes. Thus, from the point of view of a company, in most cases small (large) individual income tax burdens do not compensate large (small) corporate tax burdens. Therefore, those locations that already exhibit a competitive edge with respect to company taxation even improve their advantages when we consider both types of taxes.

Table 5.2. Indices of the headline results, taxation of companies and highly qualified employees (% of average of twelve included Swiss cantons)

	Region	Companies	Highly qualified employees
CH	Zug	71.8	75.7
IR	Dublin	72.9	117.8
CH	Nidwalden	80.2	82.8
CH	Schwyz	85.9	75.1
CH	Ticino	96.0	111.6
CH	Bern	96.6	107.8
CH	Valais	102.5	103.6
CH	St. Gallen	105.5	107.5
CH	Vaud	106.7	114.9
CH	Zürich	109.6	95.2
CH	Genève	111.4	110.9
CH	Basel-Stadt	115.0	108.0
CH	Basel-Land.	118.9	106.9
GB	London	146.3	114.7
NL	Med	157.4	125.5
A	Med	158.2	122.0
I	Med	165.5	145.6
F	Med	179.5	138.2
D	Med	180.1	139.3
US	Boston	187.3	111.6

6 Supplement: The Impact of Shareholder Taxation

6.1 Scope, Methodology, and Coverage

This supplementary chapter presents estimates of the effective level of taxation that take into account not only taxes at the corporate level, but also the impact of personal taxation, i.e. taxation of the marginal shareholder of a company. The marginal shareholder occupies a key role in the valuation of the firm: His tax position determines the value of the firm and therefore should theoretically be taken into account for corporate decision-making. For the main part of the study, we assume that corporations do not explicitly take into account the tax position of their marginal shareholder. Ignoring personal taxation is adequate in case managers do not know the tax position of the marginal shareholder of their company; especially under substantial international capital mobility, domestic personal taxes do not affect corporate investment decisions (for a discussion of these issues, see OECD, 1991: 124; Devereux, Lammersen and Spengel, 2000: 6; European Commission, 2002: 142 f.). Also, it is not misleading in case personal tax systems are designed in a way such that corporate decision-making can omit personal taxation without promoting inefficiencies.[56]

We can identify a number of situations where shareholder taxation is relevant for corporate decision-making, but we find these situations more frequently within a pure domestic economic setting than in a setting where companies conduct international operations. These companies often rely on international capital markets, thus there is not necessarily a connection between their home country and the home country of their shareholders or lenders.

In the present chapter, we assume that the owners of a company are domestic resident shareholders. These shareholders reside at the location of the company, e.g., the shareholders of a company located in Zürich also are residents of that city. The scope of this investigation is to evaluate the impact of shareholder taxation on the effective tax burdens presented above. The estimates provide valuable insights into the distortionary effects of domestic personal tax systems. Their meaning for the attractiveness of a location for an investment is very limited, however, since under this approach changing the location of the firm would necessarily imply a parallel move by or change of the shareholder.

---

[56] One example for such a situation is a situation where the marginal shareholder of a company does not pay taxes, e.g. because the shares are held by a tax-exempt pension fund.

The approach we apply, the basic assumptions on the model investment, and the basic assumptions on the economic framework are the same as those used in the main part of the study. With respect to the tax environment, we now consider additional tax parameters that describe the personal tax system: These include personal income tax rates on dividends, on capital gains on the disposal of shares, and on interest payments. Moreover, we take personal net wealth taxes on shares and bonds into account. We consider the particular situation of three different types of shareholders: a zero-rate shareholder, a shareholder in the top-income tax bracket who holds a qualified participation, and a shareholder in the top-income tax bracket who holds a non-qualified participation. We assume that all of these shareholders are individuals, i.e., we do not consider the tax situation of financial intermediaries holding shares in our model company.

The estimates of effective tax rates we present are relevant for tracing distortions created by domestic corporate tax systems, especially distortions between different sources of finance for small and medium sized companies and distortions of the optimal level of investment and the competitiveness of these firms. Furthermore, with some limitations which are explained below, the size of effective marginal tax rates illustrates the size of the tax wedge and – to the extent that personal taxation reduces post-tax marginal rates of return – indicates incentives or disincentives to save. In an international setting, the indicators are relevant in a scenario where domestic companies resident in different countries and owned by domestic shareholders compete in the same market by exporting. In that case, a company facing a lower cost of capital theoretically has a competitive advantage (see Devereux, Lammersen and Spengel, 2000: 15-16).

To evaluate these issues, effective marginal tax burdens are relevant. On the contrary, the main focus of the calculations of the effective average tax burdens is on the choice of location. The implicit underlying assumption in this case is that capital is mobile internationally, and consequently that firms can raise capital on international capital markets. In such a setting, it is difficult to justify the relevance of personal taxes of domestic individuals (see European Commission, 2002: 142-143). Therefore, we only present measures of effective marginal tax burdens in this chapter.

According to equation (2.1),[57] the effective marginal tax rate scales the difference between the cost of capital $\tilde{p}$ and the post-tax marginal rate of return to the shareholder s by the cost of capital. If we consider only corporate taxes, the post-tax marginal rate of return s always equals the real interest rate r. If we consider personal taxes, however, the value of s depends on the tax position of the marginal shareholder. The model assumes that the alternative use of funds of the marginal shareholder is lending. The taxation of interest payments thus reduces the post-tax marginal rate of return s on lending. Considering personal income taxes on nominal interest i at the rate m^i and inflation at the rate π, we obtain

$$s = \frac{\left(1 - m^i\right) \cdot i - \pi}{1 + \pi}. \tag{6.1}$$

[57] See section 2.1.3, p. 14.

Allowing for different personal income tax rates on interest payments, the EMTR is no longer a strictly monotonously increasing transformation of the cost of capital. Indeed, the tax wedge

$$w = \tilde{p} - s \tag{6.2}$$

between the cost of capital and the post-tax rate of return to the shareholder can be split up into two different components:

- a component w_C, the corporate tax wedge, that drives the minimum required rate of return of corporate investment above the market interest rate and thus deters investment and weakens corporate competitiveness compared with the non-tax case,

$$w_C = \tilde{p} - r\,. \tag{6.3}$$

- and a component w_P, the personal tax wedge, that drives the post-tax rate of return below the market interest rate and thus deters saving,

$$w_P = r - s\,, \tag{6.4}$$

with

$$w = w_C + w_P\,, \tag{6.5}$$

i.e., the sum of both components is equal to the overall tax wedge.

Indeed, a high cost of capital might come with a low EMTR in case interest is lightly taxed, and vice versa. In addition, a greater tax wedge does not necessarily imply a greater EMTR. Therefore, we will present both measures of effective tax burdens in order to obtain a more complete picture of the impact of personal taxes on economic decision-making.

In chapter 2, we separated between three groups of tax rules at the corporate level according to their impact on effective tax rates.[58] When we consider personal taxes, another set of rules becomes relevant: the type of tax system, i.e. the different taxation of dividends and interest payments and the integration of corporate taxation into personal taxation. In the following, we will briefly explain the impact of the personal tax parameters on effective marginal tax burdens (see also Devereux, Lammersen and Spengel, 2000: 13-15; Schreiber, Spengel and Lammersen, 2002: 12-13). In turn, we will discuss the income tax on dividends, the income tax on interest payments, the income tax on capital gains on the disposal of shares, and the personal net wealth tax as the most relevant non-profit tax here.

- The income taxation of *dividends* consists of the personal tax rate on corporate profit distributions and – in case the corporate tax system is designed as an imputation system – the tax credit that is connected with a dividend payment. For a marginal investment financed by retained earnings, the taxation of dividends has no impact on the effective tax burden: Shareholders save dividend taxes when the company retains funds, but these taxes become due later upon the distribution of dividends. This result is in line with the so-called 'new view' of

[58] See section 2.1.4, p. 16.

dividend taxation (see Sinn, 1991: 34; Zodrow, 1991: 498-501; Sørensen, 1995: 282-283). The taxation of dividends is also not relevant in the case of a debt-financed marginal investment. In this instance, the investment earns just enough to service the debt, and the present value of dividends is zero. In contrast, the taxation of dividends always has an impact on effective tax burdens when the firm finances the investment with new equity.

- The income taxation of *interest payments* affects the discount rate of the shareholder and – as shown above – the marginal post-tax rate of return. For all assets, the investor demands a rate of return that equals at least the post-tax rate of return on financial assets that yield the market interest rate. Raising personal taxes on interest income therefore theoretically favours real investment: Once the alternative use of funds is taxed more heavily, real investments may yield a lower rate of return to compete. If we consider debt-financed marginal investments, an increase in tax rates on interest payments in general does not have a strong impact on the cost of capital, but the EMTR increases.
  We can explain this outcome if we consider the different components of the tax wedge discussed above: An increase in taxes on interest payments raises the personal tax wedge w_P. In case of an equity-financed investment, the overall tax wedge w is almost left unchanged; the corporate tax wedge w_C declines correspondingly, and the cost of capital falls. In case of a debt-financed marginal investment, a corporate tax wedge might exist, which often occurs because interest payments are not completely deductible for purposes of the calculation of the profit tax base, because of a non-neutral tax depreciation schedule, or because of corporate non-profit taxes. In that case, an increase in taxes on interest payments usually has a negligible impact on that component of the overall tax wedge; consequently, such an increase leaves the cost of capital almost unchanged. However, the personal tax wedge rises, and the overall tax wedge increases correspondingly.
- The personal income tax on *capital gains* when investors sell shares has an impact on share values and thus its own tax base. In the model, there are two different situations where share values increase: the case where a company retains earnings and the case where the company expects to earn an economic rent on an investment. If a company retains earnings, these earnings add to the value of the shares until they are distributed. Consequently, they increase the effective burden of capital gains taxes. When the company distributes the funds, the value of the shares falls and there is some relief from capital gains taxation. In the model, the corporation retains some earnings and makes some distributions regardless of the source of finance of the investment, but the greatest impact of this tax obviously occurs when a company finances an investment completely with retained earnings. Personal income taxes on capital gains also weigh on economic rents and reduce positive net present values generated by profitable investments, which increase share values. However, our focus is on marginal investments, which generate a net present value of zero. Thus this component of the capital gains tax is not relevant here.
- The *personal non-profit taxes* relevant here usually are designed as net wealth taxes. These taxes reduce the marginal post-tax rate of return. In case they dif-

fer between funds invested as equity and funds lent, they also affect the relative favourability of different sources of finance and thus the cost of capital: If investing in equity were tax-favoured over lending, an equity-financed investment would have to yield less in order to compete, which would reduce the cost of capital of an equity-financed investment. If, on the contrary, both uses of funds were taxed equally, the cost of capital would not be affected by personal non-profit taxes, whereas the EMTR would be.

To conclude: The taxation of dividends raises the cost of capital and the EMTR of an investment financed with new equity. The most important impact of the taxation of capital gains is that it raises the cost of capital and the EMTR of an investment that is financed with retained earnings. The taxation of interest payments primarily raises the EMTR but lowers the cost of capital for an equity-financed investment, whereas it raises the EMTR and leaves the cost of capital almost unchanged under debt financing. Neutrally designed net wealth taxes leave the cost of capital unchanged but increase the EMTR.

In addition to corporate level-EMTRs, also Gutekunst and Schwager (2002) presented measures of the EMTR that considered the impact of personal taxes. Section 2.1.5 already explains the most important differences between that study and the present investigation. With respect to personal taxation, we additionally include a zero-rate shareholder, and we calculate weighted averages of effective tax burdens over the three types of taxpayers in order to obtain summary measures of the impact of personal taxation. However, one should keep in mind that relying on these averages is difficult to justify in case only one type of shareholder can be deemed the marginal shareholder.

The investigation of personal taxes covers the same countries and the same years as the investigation in the main part of the present study. In order to keep the number of results manageable and to take into account the limited meaning of these figures for the main subject of this study, which focuses on the attractiveness of a location for investment, we reduce the number of locations that we assess. Out of the countries that we assess with respect to regional variation of effective tax burdens, only in Switzerland there is considerable variation of taxes at the individual level.[59] Consequently, we focus on the calculation of overall level effective tax burdens at three different locations from Germany, France, and Italy. More precisely, we include the locations that display the minimum, the median, and the maximum effective corporate tax burden in each of these countries in each of the three years. We include one location each from Austria, Ireland, the Netherlands, the United States, and the United Kingdom. As we expect considerable variation in effective tax burdens in Switzerland, we include all twelve Swiss cantons, adding up to 26 different locations. To focus on the most relevant features, we do neither perform additional sensitivity analyses nor include special incentive cases.

[59] In Italy, the personal income tax varies regionally and between municipalities; nevertheless, the range of these variations is relatively low.

6.2 Characteristics and Development of the Tax Systems

In the following, we describe the basic features of the personal tax systems – as far as they are relevant for our study – of the countries assessed. Moreover, we present important developments that have taken place between 2001 and 2003. App. A.3 summarises the detailed tax data.

6.2.1 Tax Systems

- *Austria*: Austrian shareholders pay federal personal income tax (*Einkommensteuer*) on their income. There are neither local personal income taxes nor taxes on net wealth. The top income tax rate is 50 per cent; however, that rate is not relevant for our study as Austria taxes most types of capital income at a reduced rate of 25 per cent or half the personal income tax rate. The corporate income tax system is designed as a shareholder relief system (half-rate system).
- *France*: The taxes relevant for a shareholder residing in France are the personal income tax (*impôt sur le revenu*) including various surcharges (*contribution sociale généralisée*, *prélèvement social*, *contribution pour le remboursement de la dette sociale*) and the wealth tax (*impôt de solidarité sur la fortune*). These taxes are determined at the national level. For dividends, a full imputation system is used such that the corporate income tax is credited against the personal income tax liability. While dividends are subject to the general income tax schedule with a top marginal rate, including surcharges, of 56.69 per cent, there are special reduced rates of 25 and 26 per cent for interest income and capital gains, respectively. The wealth tax is levied at a top rate of 1.8 per cent.
- *Germany*: In Germany there is no net wealth tax. Thus shareholders are only subject to the personal income tax (*Einkommensteuer*) plus solidarity surcharge (*Solidaritätszuschlag*), with a combined top rate in 2003 of 51.17 per cent. Interest income is fully taxed according to the income tax schedule. Dividends are also subject to the income tax, but only half of the dividend enters the income tax base. The taxation of capital gains depends on whether they accrue to a qualified or a non-qualified shareholder. In the case of a qualified shareholder, half of the capital gain is subject to income tax. Capital gains obtained by a non-qualified shareholder are tax free if the shareholder has owned the shares for more than one year.
- *Ireland*: Ireland levies personal income taxes at a top-bracket rate of 42 per cent. There is no net wealth tax. Particular types of investment income, including interest payments and capital gains on the disposal of shares, are taxed at a reduced rate of 20 per cent. Ireland operates a classical corporate tax system, i.e., the dividend paid is taxed at the full personal income tax rate, without any reduction.
- *Italy*: Italy levies no net wealth taxes, but personal income taxes at three different levels of government: the central government collects the lion's share at a top rate of 45 per cent; the regions may impose an addition to that tax at a rate

between 0.9 and 1.4 percentage points. Municipalities may add up to 0.5 percentage points to that measure. For our assessment, we ignore regional variation; in accordance with the study by Elschner and Schwager (2004), we suppose that the 2003 local tax level at the capital of Rome, which is 1.1 per cent, is relevant for all locations. As with Ireland and Austria, most types of investment income are not subject to personal income tax (*imposta sul reddito delle persone fisiche*, IRPEF); instead, they are subject to a special, reduced substitute tax, which is levied at flat rates of 12.5 or 27 per cent.[60] Up to the beginning of 2001, Italy taxed capital gains of non-qualified shareholders on the disposal of shares based on a deemed accrual system. In case of increasing share values and delayed disposal of the shares, the effective tax burden of a capital gains tax based on accruals is greater than the effective tax burden of a realisation-based capital gains tax at the same statutory tax rate. This effect takes place because in the latter case, the shareholder succeeds in deferring tax payments. In mid-2001, however, the Italian capital gains tax system was ruled unconstitutional and abolished (for details, see Alworth et al., 2001); consequently, we apply a realisation-based capital gains tax regime in all three years. Italy's corporate income tax system is basically designed as a full imputation system. However, non-qualified shareholders are subject to the reduced substitute tax, which works as a shareholder relief system. Nevertheless, these shareholders may opt for being taxed according to the imputation system.

Note: Like most imputation systems, the Italian imputation system refuses the tax credit in a number of cases where the company's distributions have not been subject to a sufficient extent to Italian corporate income taxes. For purposes of this analysis, we ignore this restriction, i.e., we assume that the company possesses enough sufficiently taxed reserves. The impact of a binding restriction obviously would be immense in particular situations; however, due to our choice of the sources of finance and the types of shareholders, such a restriction in the Italian tax regime for dividend payments would play only a minor role in our assessment: It would only be relevant for a top-rate qualified shareholder who finances the investment with new equity.

As for the corporate level, Italy has recently introduced various tax amnesty measures at the personal level, which make a straightforward assessment and interpretation of effective tax burdens in Italy difficult to undertake.

- *The Netherlands*: For purposes of the income tax (*Inkomstenbelasting*) in the Netherlands, every source of income is assigned to one of three boxes, each of which has its own schedule. A qualified shareholder's dividends and capital gains are part of box two where a rate of 25 per cent applies. There is no imputation credit for dividends. However, as this rate is less than half the top rate in box one relevant for labour income, the tax system in the Netherlands can be characterised as a form of shareholder relief. Box three contains both interest income and the dividends and capital gains obtained by non-qualified shareholders. In that box, instead of the actual income, a normalised return of four per cent is taxed at a rate of 30 per cent. The tax due on income in box three is therefore equivalent to a wealth tax at the rate of 1.2 per cent.

[60] See tables A.19. and A.20., p. 107.

- *Switzerland*: Swiss shareholders pay income tax at the federal (*Direkte Bundessteuer*) and cantonal (*Einkommenssteuer*) level. In addition, all cantons levy a wealth tax (*Vermögenssteuer*). The federal income tax is progressive with a rate of 11.5 per cent in the top-income tax bracket. The cantonal taxes are obtained by multiplying the headline cantonal tax (*einfache Staatssteuer*) with the sum of the annual multiples (*Steuerfüsse*) decided by the canton, the municipality, and the church. The capital gains from the disposal of shares are tax exempt throughout. Interest income is subject to the regular federal and cantonal income tax schedules. The federation and, with one exception, all cantons in our sample tax dividend income according to the classical system, such that there is neither imputation credit nor shareholder relief. The exception is the canton of Nidwalden where only half of the dividends received by a qualified shareholder are subject to the cantonal income tax. Geographically, the effective statutory tax rates vary substantially, between 19.08 and 45.43 per cent. The wealth tax varies between 0.10 and 1.01 per cent, where, similarly to the income tax on dividends, the lowest value refers to a special treatment of shares owned by a qualified shareholder in Nidwalden.
- *United Kingdom*: The income tax schedule in the United Kingdom provides for a top rate of 40 per cent. This rate applies to interest income. Dividend income is taxed according to a shareholder relief system. The shareholder obtains a tax credit of 10 per cent of the gross dividend. Since the basic income tax rate for dividends is also 10 per cent, for shareholders in the lowest income bracket this amounts to a complete relief from income tax. For shareholders in the top bracket the tax rate on dividend income is 32.5 per cent of the gross dividend. Accounting for the tax credit, this is equivalent to an effective tax rate of 25 per cent on the cash dividend. Capital gains are taxed by the *capital gains tax* which is levied at the same rate as the income tax. However, depending on the holding period, the taxable gain is reduced by the *taper relief*; thus, the effective tax rate falls short of the statutory rate.
- *United States (Boston, Massachusetts)*: For the United States, we consider federal and state income taxes. The federal income tax is levied at a rate of 35 per cent, Massachusetts currently levies its tax on income at 5.3 per cent. State taxes are deductible from the tax base of the federal income tax. There are no net wealth taxes. The United States currently operates a shareholder relief corporate income tax system and taxes dividends and capital gains at a reduced maximum rate of 15 per cent in general.

6.2.2 Important Developments 2001–2003 and Beyond

Between 2001 and 2003, we note no relevant changes in the personal tax systems of *Austria*, *Germany*, and *the Netherlands*. In 2001, Germany decided to reduce the personal income tax rate in several steps. The top income-tax rate was scheduled to decrease from 48.5 per cent in 2001 to 47 per cent in 2003 and 42 per cent in 2005. On grounds of the flood in southern and eastern Germany in autumn 2002, the German parliament postponed the 2003 rate-reduction to 2004. Consequently, we expect personal tax rates to decrease significantly in Germany in the near future.

- *France*: France reduced the personal income tax liabilities in 2002 by 5 per cent and in 2003 by another one per cent.
- *Ireland*: From 2002, Ireland has reduced the top personal income tax rate and the flat tax rate on interest income by two percentage points to 42 and 20 per cent, respectively.
- *Italy*: According to the reduction in the statutory corporate income tax rate in 2003, the imputation credit attached to a dividend has been reduced. Moreover, the Italian government has announced further tax reforms in the future, which might abolish the Italian imputation system.
- *Switzerland*: As with corporate taxation, we note a number of changes in tax coefficients between 2001 and 2003; there have been only a few changes in statutory tax rates (see in detail tables A.21. and A.23., pp. 108 and 109).
- *United Kingdom*: In 2003, the UK has reduced the holding-periods of its so-called 'taper relief' regime for the taxation of capital gains (see Gutekunst and Schwager, 2002: 54 f. and 123). Thereupon, the maximum reduction in income from capital gains has been halved from 40 per cent to 20 per cent for non-qualified shareholders.
- *United States*: The federal top personal income tax rate was reduced from 39.6 per cent to 38.6 per cent in 2002; the state of Massachusetts reduced the top personal income tax rate from 5.6 per cent to 5.3 per cent at the same time. Moreover, federal capital gains taxes on the disposal of shares, especially on shares held for more than five years, were cut in 2002. In 2003, the U.S. Congress passed the '*Jobs and Growth Act*', which reduced the top statutory income tax rate to 35 per cent. The new headline capital gains tax rate is 15 per cent, which means a reduction in the standard capital gains tax rate but a tax increase of seven percentage points on the sale of shares held for more than five years. It applies for disposals of shares after 5 May 2003. Nevertheless, we already consider that measure in our calculations in order to suppose a more consistent tax system.[61] Whereas the United States conducted a classical corporate income tax system up to 2002, it switched over to a shareholder relief system in 2003. The changes with respect to the taxation of dividends and capital gains are scheduled to expire in 2008 in case they are not extended.

6.3 International Comparison of Effective Tax Burdens

Tables 6.1. to 6.4. present the most relevant figures for the cost of capital and the EMTR in the assessed locations. As the personal tax systems do not differentiate between different assets but between different sources of finance, the effective tax burdens of different sources of finance at the overall level are particularly inter-

[61] Remember that we rely on the tax rules as effective on 1 January of a year in the other cases, see section 2.2, pp. 21 ff.

esting. These figures show how the corporate tax system deters or promotes a particular source of finance from the perspective of different types of shareholders.

Table 6.1. Cost of capital for the shareholder mix and the zero-rate shareholder, 2003

		Shareholder Mix					Zero-rate shareholder				
	Region	Mean	Rk	RE	NE	Debt	Mean	Rk	RE	NE	Debt
A	All	5.8	*20*	6.5	7.8	4.2	6.5	*19*	7.7	7.7	4.2
F	Min	5.8	*19*	6.4	6.7	4.4	6.4	*18*	8.0	4.5	4.3
F	Med	6.5	*25*	7.2	7.5	5.2	7.1	*25*	8.7	5.3	5.0
F	Max	6.9	*26*	7.6	7.9	5.5	7.5	*26*	9.1	5.7	5.4
D	Min	4.7	*9*	4.7	5.5	4.4	6.5	*20*	7.8	7.8	4.3
D	Med	4.8	*13*	4.9	5.7	4.5	6.7	*22*	8.0	8.0	4.3
D	Max	5.0	*15*	5.1	6.0	4.6	7.0	*24*	8.4	8.4	4.3
IR	Dublin	5.3	*16*	5.1	7.6	4.9	4.6	*1*	4.5	4.5	4.9
I	Min	5.9	*21*	7.0	7.2	3.8	5.4	*2*	6.2	6.2	3.9
I	Med	5.9	*22*	7.0	7.3	3.8	5.4	*5*	6.2	6.2	3.9
I	Max	5.9	*23*	7.0	7.3	3.8	5.4	*6*	6.2	6.2	3.9
NL	Utrecht	6.3	*24*	7.5	8.0	4.0	6.3	*17*	7.6	7.6	4.0
CH	Basel-L.	4.7	*7*	4.5	7.1	4.2	6.0	*16*	7.0	7.0	4.1
CH	Basel-S.	4.7	*11*	4.6	7.0	4.2	5.9	*15*	6.9	6.9	4.1
CH	Bern	4.4	*2*	4.0	6.4	4.4	5.6	*8*	6.3	6.3	4.3
CH	Genève	4.5	*4*	4.2	6.9	4.3	5.8	*13*	6.7	6.7	4.2
CH	Nidw.	4.7	*8*	4.6	5.8	4.5	5.5	*7*	6.1	6.1	4.4
CH	Schwyz	4.9	*14*	5.0	6.3	4.4	5.6	*9*	6.2	6.2	4.4
CH	St. Gall.	4.3	*1*	4.0	6.1	4.2	5.4	*3*	6.0	6.0	4.1
CH	Ticino	4.5	*3*	4.1	6.5	4.4	5.7	*10*	6.4	6.4	4.3
CH	Vaud	4.5	*5*	4.2	6.7	4.3	5.8	*11*	6.6	6.6	4.2
CH	Valais	4.8	*12*	4.7	6.8	4.4	5.9	*14*	6.7	6.7	4.3
CH	Zug	4.7	*10*	4.6	5.9	4.5	5.4	*4*	5.9	5.9	4.5
CH	Zürich	4.6	*6*	4.4	6.8	4.3	5.8	*12*	6.7	6.7	4.2
GB	London	5.6	*18*	6.0	6.4	4.8	6.6	*21*	7.6	7.6	4.7
US	Boston	5.4	*17*	6.2	6.6	3.8	6.7	*23*	8.4	8.4	3.7

In addition, these tables present the weighted average cost of capital and EMTR over all assets and all sources of finance. Figures 6.1. to 6.4. present a ranking of these figures for the shareholder mix, i.e. an unweighted average of all three types of shareholders, and for the top-rate qualified shareholder. The baseline in fig. 6.1. and fig. 6.2. marks the real interest rate of five per cent. A cost of capital below that measure indicates that – in the case of our very particular calculation – an investment is advantaged compared with the case where no taxes were raised, whereas a cost of capital above five per cent shows that an investment is deterred. Note, however, that such a ranking is not as meaningful as an indicator for the attractiveness of a location from a tax perspective as the rankings in the main part of the study are: We only analyse an investment that is undertaken in a particular location by a resident of that particular location. App. D.3 presents more detailed time series for each location.

Table 6.2. Cost of capital for the two types of top-rate shareholders, 2003

		Top-rate non-qualified shareholder					Top-rate qualified shareholder				
	Region	Mean	Rk	RE	NE	Debt	Mean	Rk	RE	NE	Debt
A	All	5.1	*17*	5.2	7.8	4.3	5.9	*22*	6.7	7.7	4.2
F	Min	6.4	*24*	7.1	9.8	4.4	4.5	*15*	4.3	5.9	4.6
F	Med	7.1	*25*	7.8	10.6	5.1	5.3	*19*	5.0	6.6	5.3
F	Max	7.5	*26*	8.2	10.9	5.5	5.7	*21*	5.4	7.0	5.7
D	Min	3.5	*1*	2.6	4.4	4.6	4.1	*8*	3.7	4.3	4.5
D	Med	3.6	*2*	2.7	4.5	4.6	4.2	*10*	3.9	4.5	4.5
D	Max	3.7	*3*	2.9	4.8	4.7	4.3	*13*	4.1	4.7	4.6
IR	Dublin	5.6	*19*	5.4	9.2	4.9	5.6	*20*	5.4	9.2	4.9
I	Min	5.9	*20*	6.9	7.4	3.8	6.5	*24*	7.9	8.1	3.7
I	Med	5.9	*21*	6.9	7.5	3.8	6.5	*25*	7.9	8.2	3.8
I	Max	5.9	*22*	6.9	7.5	3.9	6.5	*26*	7.9	8.2	3.8
NL	Utrecht	6.3	*23*	7.6	7.6	4.0	6.4	*23*	7.4	8.7	4.0
CH	Basel-L.	4.0	*10*	3.3	7.1	4.3	4.0	*7*	3.3	7.1	4.3
CH	Basel-S.	4.1	*11*	3.5	7.0	4.3	4.1	*9*	3.5	7.0	4.3
CH	Bern	3.8	*5*	2.9	6.4	4.4	3.8	*2*	2.9	6.4	4.4
CH	Genève	3.8	*6*	2.9	6.9	4.3	3.8	*3*	2.9	6.9	4.3
CH	Nidw.	4.4	*13*	4.0	6.1	4.5	4.2	*12*	3.9	5.3	4.5
CH	Schwyz	4.6	*15*	4.3	6.3	4.4	4.6	*16*	4.3	6.3	4.4
CH	St. Gall.	3.7	*4*	2.9	6.2	4.3	3.7	*1*	2.9	6.2	4.3
CH	Ticino	3.9	*7*	3.0	6.6	4.5	3.9	*4*	3.0	6.6	4.5
CH	Vaud	3.9	*8*	3.1	6.7	4.4	3.9	*5*	3.1	6.7	4.4
CH	Valais	4.2	*12*	3.6	6.8	4.4	4.2	*11*	3.6	6.8	4.4
CH	Zug	4.4	*14*	4.0	5.9	4.5	4.4	*14*	4.0	5.9	4.5
CH	Zürich	4.0	*9*	3.2	6.8	4.3	4.0	*6*	3.2	6.8	4.3
GB	London	5.4	*18*	5.7	5.7	4.8	4.7	*17*	4.5	5.8	4.8
US	Boston	4.8	*16*	5.2	5.7	3.9	4.8	*18*	5.2	5.7	3.9

We will investigate the situation of the three different types of shareholders in the nine different countries in turn; subsequently, we will draw some common conclusions.

Starting with the situation of the *zero-rate shareholder*, we find that, from the perspective of such a person, the costs of capital and the EMTRs in different locations are quite similar to those that we calculate at the corporate level. Obviously, there is no additional tax layer for zero-rate shareholders in most countries. Due to the low level of corporate taxes, Switzerland displays comparatively low effective tax burdens for these shareholders. The advantage of debt financing over equity-financing remains: Interest payments generally are deductible for purposes of calculating the corporate income tax base; moreover, they are taxed at zero personal income tax rates at the shareholder level.

Table 6.3. EMTR for the shareholder mix and the zero-rate shareholder, 2003

		Shareholder Mix					Zero-rate shareholder				
	Region	Mean	Rk	RE	NE	Debt	Mean	Rk	RE	NE	Debt
A	All	34.3	*10*	41.2	50.5	9.3	22.9	*16*	35.2	35.2	-19.1
F	Min	54.2	*24*	59.0	60.9	40.4	21.4	*14*	37.5	-10.2	-15.8
F	Med	59.4	*25*	63.2	64.7	48.8	29.6	*25*	42.8	5.1	0.9
F	Max	61.7	*26*	65.1	66.5	52.4	33.3	*26*	45.3	11.5	7.9
D	Min	44.1	*18*	44.2	52.2	41.0	23.6	*19*	35.7	35.7	-17.3
D	Med	45.4	*20*	45.9	53.7	41.5	25.5	*22*	37.6	37.6	-16.5
D	Max	47.6	*22*	48.7	56.0	42.5	28.4	*24*	40.5	40.5	-15.2
IR	Dublin	31.7	*8*	29.6	52.8	25.9	22.0	*15*	19.7	19.7	26.0
I	Min	30.0	*4*	40.9	43.0	-8.7	23.1	*17*	33.1	33.1	-6.7
I	Med	30.4	*5*	41.2	43.3	-7.6	23.6	*18*	33.5	33.5	-5.6
I	Max	30.5	*6*	41.3	43.4	-7.3	23.7	*20*	33.6	33.6	-5.4
NL	Utrecht	33.8	*9*	44.3	47.2	-4.7	21.1	*13*	34.1	34.1	-24.7
CH	Basel-L.	46.2	*21*	44.5	64.6	40.3	16.3	*12*	28.4	28.4	-22.1
CH	Basel-S.	44.4	*19*	43.2	62.4	37.9	15.6	*11*	27.5	27.5	-21.0
CH	Bern	40.5	*12*	35.1	59.2	40.5	10.6	*4*	20.6	20.6	-16.6
CH	Genève	50.1	*23*	46.6	67.3	47.8	14.5	*9*	25.9	25.9	-19.7
CH	Nidw.	22.1	*1*	21.1	37.3	17.9	9.0	*3*	17.7	17.7	-13.3
CH	Schwyz	24.3	*3*	25.2	41.0	16.0	10.6	*5*	20.0	20.0	-14.2
CH	St. Gall.	30.8	*7*	25.5	51.7	30.1	6.9	*1*	17.1	17.1	-20.8
CH	Ticino	41.9	*15*	37.3	60.1	41.1	12.2	*6*	22.3	22.3	-15.4
CH	Vaud	43.6	*16*	40.0	61.8	41.0	13.1	*7*	24.0	24.0	-18.5
CH	Valais	40.2	*11*	38.7	57.9	34.9	14.7	*10*	25.4	25.4	-16.2
CH	Zug	22.3	*2*	21.0	37.9	18.6	7.1	*2*	14.8	14.8	-11.8
CH	Zürich	41.3	*14*	38.6	60.3	37.0	13.6	*8*	24.9	24.9	-20.1
GB	London	43.7	*17*	47.2	50.8	34.2	24.2	*21*	34.3	34.3	-6.0
US	Boston	40.7	*13*	48.5	51.3	15.7	25.8	*23*	40.2	40.2	-34.1

Some countries, e.g. Ireland and Italy, impose flat, final taxes on interest payments. Compared with the corporate-level case, these taxes reduce the cost of capital on equity-financed investments for zero-rate shareholders. Also, countries that operate imputation systems which give a refund on corporate taxes significantly reduce the cost of capital on investment financed with new equity. We find such a situation in the case of France. Nevertheless, according to the aspects mentioned above, recall from section 6.1 that the impact of dividend taxation on the overall cost of capital is much lower than one would intuitively expect; consequently, the tax burden on French investments from the perspective of a French zero-rate shareholder remains very high.

Table 6.4. EMTR for the two types of top-rate shareholders, 2003

		Top-rate non-qualified shareholder					Top-rate qualified shareholder				
	Region	Mean	Rk	RE	NE	Debt	Mean	Rk	RE	NE	Debt
A	All	36.5	*8*	37.3	58.2	23.6	45.0	*9*	51.1	57.9	22.9
F	Min	77.2	*23*	79.3	85.1	66.7	67.9	*22*	65.8	75.3	68.2
F	Med	79.5	*25*	81.3	86.2	71.4	72.3	*24*	70.8	78.0	72.6
F	Max	80.6	*26*	82.2	86.7	73.4	74.2	*25*	72.9	79.2	74.4
D	Min	58.6	*13*	44.5	67.3	68.6	64.6	*17*	61.5	66.7	68.0
D	Med	59.6	*15*	46.6	68.4	69.0	65.5	*19*	62.8	67.7	68.4
D	Max	61.2	*16*	49.7	70.1	69.6	66.8	*21*	64.8	69.4	68.9
IR	Dublin	35.7	*7*	33.7	60.9	25.8	35.7	*4*	33.7	60.9	25.8
I	Min	29.6	*1*	40.1	44.5	-8.5	36.0	*5*	47.7	49.2	-11.0
I	Med	30.1	*2*	40.4	44.8	-7.4	36.4	*6*	47.9	49.4	-9.8
I	Max	30.2	*3*	40.5	44.9	-7.1	36.5	*7*	48.0	49.5	-9.6
NL	Utrecht	40.0	*9*	49.9	49.9	5.2	40.4	*8*	49.0	56.4	5.4
CH	Basel-L.	68.5	*22*	61.6	82.3	70.3	68.5	*23*	61.6	82.3	70.3
CH	Basel-S.	65.1	*20*	58.8	79.5	66.3	65.1	*18*	58.8	79.5	66.3
CH	Bern	62.7	*18*	51.0	78.1	68.2	62.7	*15*	51.0	78.1	68.2
CH	Genève	77.5	*24*	70.5	87.6	80.2	77.5	*26*	70.5	87.6	80.2
CH	Nidw.	31.5	*4*	24.6	51.4	33.3	29.3	*1*	22.9	43.4	33.3
CH	Schwyz	32.7	*6*	29.0	51.4	30.9	32.7	*3*	29.0	51.4	30.9
CH	St. Gall.	48.1	*10*	34.0	68.6	54.7	48.1	*10*	34.0	68.6	54.7
CH	Ticino	63.8	*19*	53.3	78.6	68.6	63.8	*16*	53.3	78.6	68.6
CH	Vaud	66.1	*21*	57.1	80.4	69.8	66.1	*20*	57.1	80.4	69.8
CH	Valais	57.9	*12*	50.9	73.9	59.7	57.9	*13*	50.9	73.9	59.7
CH	Zug	31.7	*5*	25.5	49.4	33.7	31.7	*2*	25.5	49.4	33.7
CH	Zürich	61.5	*17*	52.8	77.6	64.6	61.5	*14*	52.8	77.6	64.6
GB	London	59.0	*14*	61.4	61.4	53.7	53.3	*12*	50.7	61.8	54.1
US	Boston	51.3	*11*	55.1	59.4	39.7	51.3	*11*	55.1	59.4	39.7

From the perspective of a *top-rate non-qualified shareholder*, effective tax burdens present themselves completely differently. In case interest payments and therefore the alternative use of funds are taxed at high progressive rates, the cost of capital decreases dramatically compared with the perspective of a zero-rate shareholder. Especially the figures for Germany, Switzerland, and the United States show such an effect; within Switzerland, the cantons of Genève and Vaud strongly improve their position.

On the contrary, locations that impose comparatively low effective tax burdens on interest payments – mostly because of flat, final taxes on that type of income – display large costs of capital and an advantage of debt financing over equity financing. Especially the case of a French investment that is financed with new equity is striking: Here, the cost of capital might easily exceed ten per cent; although the French corporate income tax system grants full imputation of the corporate income tax, it does not neutralise the French trade tax, and dividends are taxed at comparatively high progressive income tax rates.

In a number of locations, capital gains on the disposal of shares are tax exempt from the point of view of a non-qualified shareholder, whereas dividends are taxed. Consequently, we obtain a bias in favour of financing an investment with retained earnings over financing an investment with new equity in most locations, with the notable exceptions of the Netherlands and the United Kingdom.

The ranking of locations according to the EMTR is very different from the ranking according to the cost of capital. Recall from equations (2.1) and (6.2) to (6.5)[62] that under the assumptions of the model both figures have a completely different meaning. The EMTR at the overall level considers not only the part of capital taxation that theoretically deters investment, but also the part that drives a tax wedge between the real interest rate and the real post-tax rate of return. That part theoretically deters domestic saving. Accordingly, locations that tax interest payments heavily often display a low cost of capital but a large EMTR, and vice versa. As the cost of capital is the basis and thus the denominator for computing the EMTR, moreover, a low cost of capital amplifies the weight of non-profit taxes and the taxation of inflationary gains in calculating the EMTR. These effects explain the poor performance e.g. of the canton of Genève according to that measure. Moreover, it shows that such an EMTR has to be seen with great caution.

Finally, turning towards the *top-rate qualified shareholder*, things are very similar compared with a top-rate non-qualified shareholder in most locations. Ireland, most Swiss cantons, and the United States do not have any relevant tax rules that differentiate between both types of investors. Austria, Germany, and Italy tax qualified shareholders more heavily on their capital gains than non-qualified shareholders, thereby increasing the effective tax burden on investment financed with retained earnings. The bias in favour of financing an investment with retained earnings over financing it with new equity decreases in these locations, but to the extent that these shareholders are able to defer personal income taxes on their capital gains by delaying share disposals, there remains a substantial gap.

In some cases, the tax burden on equity-financed investments decreases: The canton of Nidwalden offers reduced income tax rates and net wealth tax rates for qualified shareholders. In the United Kingdom, these shareholders are taxed more favourably on their capital gains, and, under particular premises, France does not impose net wealth taxes on qualifying share values.

In the Netherlands, and partly in Italy, the corporate tax system that applies for qualified shareholders is very different from the one that applies for non-qualified shareholders, thus the level and the structure of effective tax burdens differs substantially between both types of shareholders.

[62] See section 2.1.3, p. 14, and section 6.1, p. 71.

Fig. 6.1. International variation of the cost of capital, shareholder mix, 2003

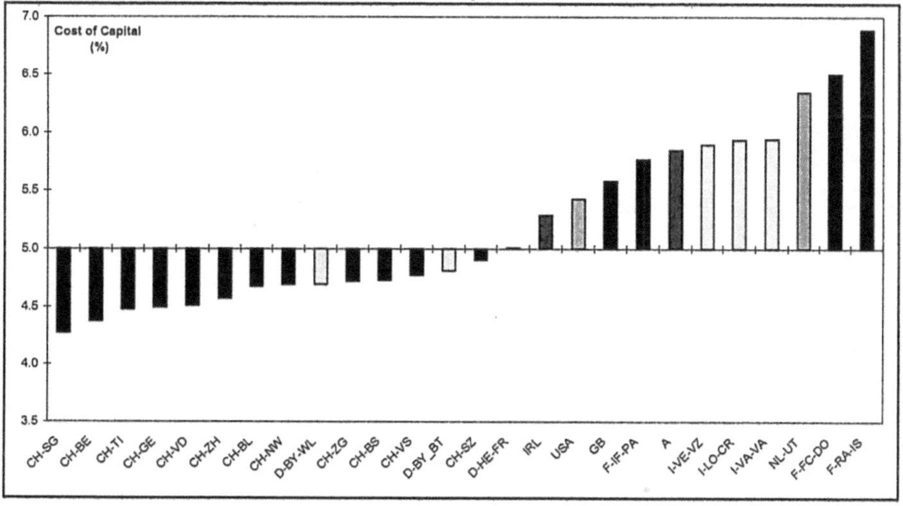

Fig. 6.2. International variation of the cost of capital, top-rate qualified shareholder, 2003

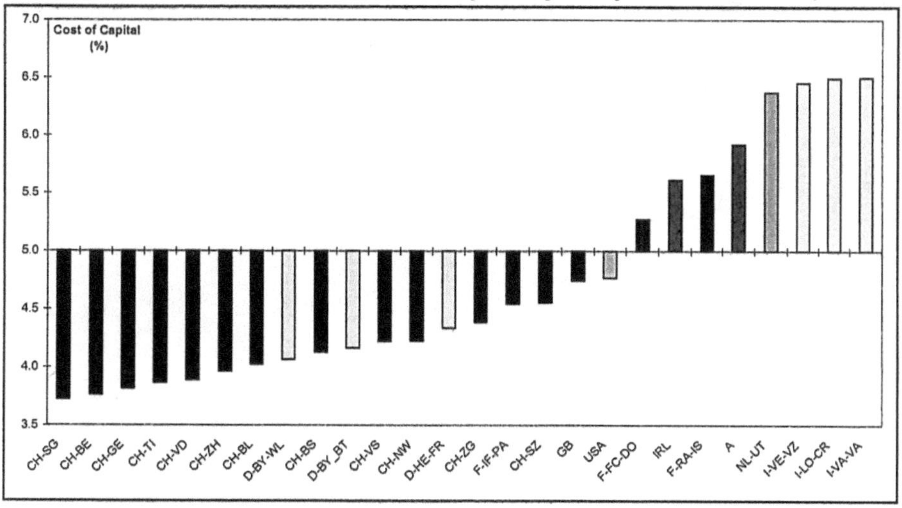

Fig. 6.3. International variation of EMTRs, shareholder mix, 2003

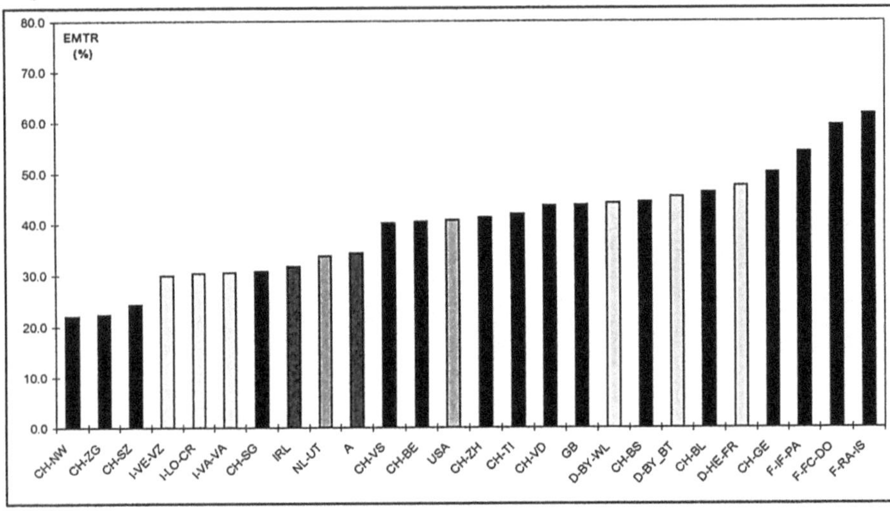

Fig. 6.4. International variation of EMTRs, top-rate qualified shareholder, 2003

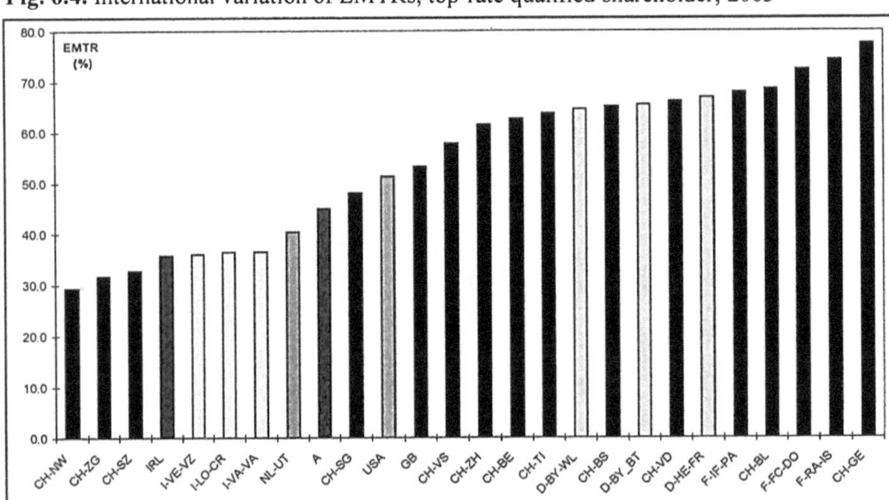

6.4 Conclusions

To conclude, our results suggest that effective tax burdens at the overall level heavily depend on the tax status of the relevant shareholder. Consequently, the results for the shareholder mix conceal substantial variation. Whereas for zero-rate shareholders there often is a bias in favour of debt financing, top-rate shareholders prefer financing an investment with retained earnings in most cases. For zero-rate shareholders, the effective tax burden at the corporate level remains the most important factor in determining the size of the tax burden. For top-rate shareholders, the tax treatment of capital gains and interest payments is very important in our calculations.[63] For these shareholders, there is a considerable correlation between effective marginal tax rates at the corporate level and at the overall level, as a comparison between fig. 6.4. and fig. 5.2. on p. 57 shows. Although we cannot conclude straightforwardly that locations that impose a low level of corporate taxes also impose a low level of personal taxes – which would mean that differences in effective tax burdens that exist at the corporate level were amplified by personal taxation[64] –, we find that in most cases personal taxes on capital income at least do not compensate the tax burdens at the corporate level. However, there are substantial exceptions to this finding: In an international comparison, especially those Swiss cantons which impose relatively high top personal income tax rates and high net wealth tax rates display comparatively low corporate-level EMTRs but high overall-level EMTRs.

Our findings are largely in line with those from Gutekunst and Schwager (2002), although the modified assumptions, especially the comparatively low marginal rates of return assumed in the present study, result in a greater spread of the Swiss canton's EMTRs and a greater weight of the Dutch investment income tax, which is based on deemed profits and thus works like a non-profit tax in most cases. In Gutekunst and Schwager's study, which focused on top-rate shareholders, Zug also displayed the lowest overall EMTR for non-qualified shareholders, Nidwalden also displayed the lowest overall-level EMTR for qualified shareholders, and Genève displayed the greatest overall-level EMTR in Switzerland. In that study, Genève was slightly in front of all the non-Swiss locations that were assessed, whereas it now ranks 23rd and 26th out of 26 locations. France is still far behind of Germany and most Swiss cantons; the United Kingdom and the United States are still very close to each other, with the United States in front today after the 2003 tax cuts.

[63] Note that in case an investment is financed predominantly with new equity and in case an investor expects inframarginal rates of return, dividend taxes are very important, too.

[64] Due to the non-linearity of EMTRs, we do not compare the absolute or relative differences in these measures between the corporate-level case and the overall-level case.

7 Summary and Conclusions

(1) The present study calculates and compares forward-looking effective tax burdens, expressed in terms of the effective average tax rate (EATR), effective marginal tax rate (EMTR), and the cost of capital for 143 locations from eight European countries and the United States for the years 2001–2003. The calculations are based on the methodology set out by Devereux and Griffith (1999 and 2003). The results depend on the particular assumptions of the approach and the calculations; thus they can provide an impression on comparative effective tax burdens in particular cases, but – as any calculation of that kind – they cannot be generalised arbitrarily. The main scope of the calculations is to evaluate the attractiveness of particular locations for an investment.

(2) The results indicate that there is considerable dispersion of the EATRs at the corporate level between the assessed countries. Whereas Ireland and Switzerland display comparatively low effective tax burdens, locations in France, Germany, and the United States show the highest EATRs. This finding suggests that the attractiveness of particular locations from a tax perspective differs dramatically, with Switzerland and Ireland being especially attractive countries.

(3) Statutory profit tax rates are deemed important tax drivers for profitable investments at the corporate level. However, tax burdens always depend on the individual characteristics of each investment, thus special rules regarding the tax base or non-profit taxes may be very relevant in particular cases, e.g. in France, where the trade tax (*taxe professionnelle*) as a non-profit tax has a considerable impact on the results.

(4) The study examines not only the international variation of effective tax burdens, but also inter-regional differences at the corporate level within each country. There is great inter-regional variation among the assessed Swiss cantons, with the cantons of Zug, Nidwalden, and Schwyz ahead of the others. Moderate inter-regional variation exists in Germany and, to a smaller degree, in France. In Austria, Italy, and the Netherlands, inter-regional variation is not, or almost not, relevant.

(5) For international location decisions, EMTRs are less relevant than EATRs; nevertheless, they provide some useful supplementary information on the impact of taxes on investment and financing decisions. The impact of local and regional taxes on the EMTRs at the corporate level is generally stronger than their impact on EATRs. There is also a strong impact of targeted measures like investment tax credits or the dual income tax. We find that the dis-

persion of effective marginal tax rates between the assessed regions is even greater than the dispersion of effective average tax rates.

(6) The time series from 2001–2003 gives an impression on recent tax reform activity in the assessed countries. Sensitivity analyses reveal some interesting mechanics of the impact of taxation on effective tax burdens; relative to EATRs, EMTRs are comparatively strongly affected by changes in the economic assumptions.

(7) Estimates that also take into account shareholder taxation provide valuable insights into the distortionary effects of domestic personal tax systems, especially with respect to financing decisions. Their meaning for the attractiveness of a location for an investment is very limited, however. Our results suggest that taxation substantially distorts financing decisions; the direction of the distortion heavily depends on the tax status of the shareholder, as does the overall level of effective tax burdens. With some notable exceptions, there is a considerable correlation between effective marginal tax rates at the corporate level and at the overall level.

App. A Description of the Relevant Tax Parameters

A.1 Taxation of Corporate Profits

A.1.1 Effective Statutory Profit Tax Rates

Table A.1. Summary of nominal and effective profit tax rates (%)

Country	Year	Nominal corporation tax rate (central)	Surcharge	Local profit tax rates (nominal)	Effective statutory profit tax rate
Austria	'01–'03	34.00	–	–	34.00
France	'01	33.33	9.3	–	36.43
	'02–'03	33.33	6.3	–	35.43
Germany	'01	25.00	5.5	13.04–20.00 [a]	35.98–41.10
	'02	25.00	5.5	13.04–19.68 [a]	35.98–40.86
	'03	26.50	5.5	13.04–19.68 [a]	37.35–42.13
Ireland	'01–'02	10.00 [b]	–	–	10.00
	'03	12.50	–	–	12.50
Italy	'01–'02	36.00	–	4.25	40.25
	'03	34.00	–	4.25	38.25
The Netherlands	'01	35.00	–	–	35.00
	'02–'03	34.50	–	–	34.50
Switzerland	'01	7.83 [c]	–	9.91–20.61 [d]	16.32–25.63
	'02	7.83 [c]	–	9.90–20.63 [d]	16.31–25.65
	'03	7.83 [c]	–	9.86–20.63 [d]	16.27–25.65
United Kingdom	'01–'03	30.00	–	–	30.00
United States	'01–'03	35.00	–	9.50	41.17

Remarks:

[a] See table A.3., pp. 91 ff.; considering deductibility of trade tax from its own base.

[b] Generally available tax rate for the manufacturing sector. See table A.2., p. 90.

[c] Considering deductibility of corporate income tax from its own base.

[d] See table A.4., p. 93; considering deductibility of corporate income tax from its own base.

Table A.2. Special profit tax treatment of particular categories of income

Country	Special rule
Austria	Dual income tax: Lower corporation tax rate (25 per cent) on part of the profits that does not exceed a deemed interest rate (0.8 percentage points above market interest rate) applied to additional equity. Tax credit on additional investment of 10 per cent for particular additional investments; here, machinery qualifies for this credit.
Germany	Only half of the interest payments are deductible from tax base of the local profit tax.
Ireland	General corporate income tax rate of 20 per cent ('01) and 16 per cent ('02) for companies not active in the manufacturing sector; corporate income tax rate of 25 per cent for non-trading income, especially income from financial assets.
Italy	Income from financial assets is exempt from local profit taxation (IRAP); interest payments are not deductible for purposes of the IRAP. Dual income tax: Reduced profit tax rate of effectively 23.25 per cent (in '01) on the part of the profits that does not exceed a deemed interest rate rate (assumption: 0.8 percentage points above market interest rate) applied to qualifying equity of the company.
Switzerland (St. Gallen)	Lower cantonal corporation tax rate (4.50 per cent) on the part of the profits that does not exceed 6 per cent of qualifying equity of the company.
United States	State tax credit of 3 per cent for an investment in particular goods for companies in the manufacturing sector; here, industrial buildings and machinery qualify for this credit.

Table A.3. Trade tax multipliers and effective profit tax rates for Germany (%)

	'01		'02		'03	
Municipality of ...	Multi-plier of trade tax	Effec-tive profit tax rate	Multi-plier of trade tax	Effec-tive profit tax rate	Multi-plier of trade tax	Effec-tive profit tax rate
Baden-Württemberg						
Aalen	350	37.34	350	37.34	350	38.69
Balingen	340	37.07	340	37.07	340	38.43
Freiburg	400	38.65	400	38.65	400	39.96
Göppingen	355	37.47	355	37.47	355	38.82
Heidelberg	390	38.39	390	38.39	390	39.71
Heilbronn	380	38.13	380	38.13	380	39.46
Karlsruhe	410	38.90	410	38.90	410	40.21
Konstanz	360	37.61	360	37.61	360	38.95
Lörrach	325	36.67	360	37.61	360	38.95
Landkreis Mannheim	320	36.53	330	36.80	330	38.16
Ludwigsburg	375	38.00	360	37.61	360	38.95
Mannheim	430	39.40	415	39.03	415	40.34
Nagold	350	37.34	350	37.34	350	38.69
Offenburg	380	38.13	380	38.13	380	39.46
Pforzheim	380	38.13	380	38.13	380	39.46
Rastatt	350	37.34	370	37.87	370	39.20
Ravensburg	330	36.80	330	36.80	330	38.16
Reutlingen	350	37.34	350	37.34	350	38.69
Rottweil	335	36.94	335	36.94	335	38.29
Schwäbisch-Hall	375	38.00	375	38.00	375	39.33
Stuttgart	420	39.15	420	39.15	420	40.46
Tauberbischofsheim	330	36.80	330	36.80	330	38.16
Ulm	360	37.61	360	37.61	360	38.95
Villingen-Schwenningen	350	37.34	350	37.34	350	38.69
Waiblingen	350	37.34	350	37.34	350	38.69
Walldorf bei Heidelberg	310	36.26	310	36.26	310	37.63
Bayern						
Ansbach	360	37.61	360	37.61	360	38.95
Aschaffenburg	385	38.26	385	38.26	385	39.59
Augsburg	420	39.15	445	39.78	445	41.07
Bamberg	380	38.13	390	38.39	390	39.71
Bayreuth	370	37.87	370	37.87	370	39.20
Coburg	360	37.61	360	37.61	300	37.35
Deggendorf	320	36.53	350	37.34	350	38.69
Donauwörth	350	37.34	350	37.34	350	38.69
Freising	380	38.13	380	38.13	380	39.46

Table A.3. continued

	'01		'02		'03	
Municipality of ...	Multi-plier of trade tax	Effec-tive profit tax rate	Multi-plier of trade tax	Effec-tive profit tax rate	Multi-plier of trade tax	Effective profit tax rate
Hof	380	38.13	380	38.13	380	39.46
Ingolstadt	400	38.65	400	38.65	400	39.96
Kempten	337	36.99	337	36.99	337	38.35
Landshut	400	38.65	400	38.65	400	39.96
Memmingen	330	36.80	330	36.80	330	38.16
München	490	40.86	490	40.86	490	42.13
Nürnberg	447	39.82	447	39.82	447	41.12
Passau	370	37.87	370	37.87	370	39.20
Pfarrkirchen	330	36.80	330	36.80	330	38.16
Regensburg	425	39.28	425	39.28	425	40.58
Rosenheim	400	38.65	400	38.65	400	39.96
Schwandorf	350	37.34	350	37.34	350	38.69
Schweinfurt	370	37.87	370	37.87	370	39.20
Traunstein	365	37.74	365	37.74	365	39.08
Weiden	367	37.79	350	37.34	350	38.69
Weilheim	300	35.98	300	35.98	300	37.35
Weißenburg i. Bayern	340	37.07	340	37.07	340	38.43
Würzburg	420	39.15	420	39.15	420	40.46
Berlin						
Berlin	410	38.90	410	38.90	410	40.21
Hamburg						
Hamburg	470	40.38	470	40.38	470	41.67
Hessen						
Frankfurt	500	41.10	490	40.86	490	42.13
Offenbach	440	39.65	440	39.65	440	40.95
Nordrhein-Westfalen						
Düsseldorf	460	40.14	455	40.02	455	41.31
Essen	470	40.38	470	40.38	470	41.67
Köln	450	39.90	450	39.90	450	41.19
Rheinland-Pfalz						
Landau	420	39.15	420	39.15	420	40.46
Ludwigshafen	390	38.39	390	38.39	360	38.95
Mainz	440	39.65	440	39.65	440	40.95

Remark: We apply the data with a lag. E.g., for calculating the tax burden in '01, we apply the multiplier from '00.

Table A.4. Statutory and effective corporate income tax rates for Switzerland (%)

Canton of ...	Year	Cantonal headline tax rate	Annual multiple (%) Canton	Munici-pality	Church	Sum	Combined effective profit tax rate
Basel-Land.	'01	20.00	100.00	24.78 [a)]	5.00	129.78	25.63
	'02–'03	20.00	100.00	25.00 [a)]	5.00	130.00	25.65
Basel-Stadt	'01–'03	24.50	100.00	–	–	100.00	24.81
Bern	'01	3.99	230.00	230.00	19.15	479.15	21.64
	'02–'03	3.99	306.00	154.00	19.15	479.15	21.64
Genève [b)]	'01–'03	10.00	189.50	45.40	–	234.90	24.26
Nidwalden	'01–'02	2.50	240.00	265.00	30.00	535.00	17.95
	'03	2.50	240.00	258.00	30.00	528.00	17.83
Schwyz	'01	4.00	120.00	245.00 [c)]	27.05	392.05	19.47
	'02	4.00	110.00	230.00 [c)]	27.05	367.05	18.82
	'03	4.00	110.00	230.00 [c)]	26.11	366.11	18.79
St. Gallen	'01	7.50	115.00	220.00 [d)]	– [d)]	335.00	25.16
	'02	7.50	112.00	220.00 [d)]	– [d)]	332.00	25.04
	'03	7.50	115.00	220.00 [d)]	– [d)]	335.00	25.16
Ticino	'01–'03	9.00	100.00	100.00 [e)]	–	200.00	20.95
Vaud	'01–'03	9.50	129.00	105.00	–	234.00	23.51
Valais	'01–'03	9.50	100.00	100.00	3.00	203.00	21.74
Zug	'01	7.00	82.00	65.00	10.22	157.22	16.32
	'02	7.00	82.00	65.00	10.00	157.00	16.31
	'03	7.00	82.00	65.00	9.22	156.22	16.27
Zürich	'01	10.00	105.00	126.00	12.01	243.01	24.70
	'02	10.00	105.00	122.00	11.02	238.02	24.42
	'03	10.00	100.00	122.00	10.52	232.52	24.10

Remarks:

a) The municipal tax rate is legally defined as a rate on the profit. For purposes of this comparison, we convert this measure into an annual multiple.

b) Includes *taxe professionnelle communale*, effective rate here 0.035 per cent.

c) Includes the annual multiples at the level of the municipality and the district.

d) Combined multiple for municipalities and church.

e) The municipal annual multiplier is determined at the end of each tax year. For 2003, we apply the value for the tax year 2002.

A.1.2 Definition of the Profit Tax Base

Table A.5. Capital allowances for intangibles

Country	Year	Kind of allowance	Allowance rate (%)	Length of period
Austria	'01–'03	SL	10.00	10
France	'01–'03	SL	20.00	5
Germany	'01–'03	SL	20.00	5
Ireland	'01–'03	SL	10.00	10
Italy	'01–'03	SL	33.33	3
The Netherlands	'01–'03	SL	20.00	5
Switzerland	'01–'03	DB	40.00	ufd
United Kingdom	'01–'03	DB	25.00	ufd
United States	'01–'03	SL	10.00	10

Remarks:
Specifically, we assume the purchase of a patent. The kind of capital allowances represents the most tax efficient possibility; other possibilities are ignored. If depreciation depends on the useful life of an asset and no period is specified in the national tax codes, a period of ten years is assumed for the calculation of the allowance rate.
DB = declining balance; SL = straight line; ufd = until fully depreciated.

Table A.6. Capital allowances for industrial buildings

Country	Year	Kind of allowance	Allowance rate (%)	Length of period
Austria	'01–'03	SL	3.00	ufd
France	'01–'03	SL	5.00	20
Germany	'01–'03	SL	3.00	ufd
Ireland	'01–'03	SL	4.00	25
Italy	'01–'03	SL	4.00	1
		SL	8.00	2
		SL	4.00	20
The Netherlands	'01–'03	SL	2.50	40
Switzerland	'01–'03	DB	8.00	ufd
United Kingdom	'01–'03	SL	4.00	25
United States	'01–'03	SL	2.46	1
		SL	2.56	ufd

Remarks:
The kind of capital allowances represents the most tax efficient possibility; other possibilities are ignored. If for one year multiple rates are given, these rates represent the development of depreciation allowances over the lifetime of the asset. E.g., in the United States in the first period of its lifetime, 2.46 per cent of the acquisition cost of an industrial building can be deducted; in subsequent periods, that rate is 2.56 per cent.
DB = declining balance; SL = straight line; ufd = until fully depreciated.

Table A.7. Capital allowances for machinery

Country	Year	Kind of allowance	Allowance rate (%)	Length of period
Austria	'01–'03	SL	14.29	7
France	'01–'03	DB	32.14	4
		SL	7.07	3
Germany	'01–'03	DB	20.00	2
		SL	12.80	5
Ireland	'01–'02	SL	20.00	5
	'03	SL	12.50	8
Italy	'01–'03	SL	12.50	1
		SL	25.00	2
		SL	12.50	3
The Netherlands	'01–'03	SL	14.29	7
Switzerland	'01–'03	DB	30.00	ufd
United Kingdom	'01–'03	DB	25.00	ufd
United States	'01	DB	20.00	1
		DB	40.00	2
		SL	11.52	ufd
	'02–'03	DB	44.00 a)	1
		DB	40.00	2
		SL	8.06	ufd

Remarks:
The kind of capital allowances represents the most tax efficient possibility; other possibilities are ignored. If depreciation depends on the useful life of an asset and no period is specified in the national tax codes, a period of seven years is assumed for the calculation of the allowance rate. If for one year multiple rates are given, these rates represent the development of depreciation allowances over the lifetime of the asset. E.g., machinery in France is depreciated according to the declining balance method for the first four years of its lifetime for tax purposes; for the remaining three years, it is depreciated according to the straight line method.

[a] Includes a 30 per cent special depreciation allowance, which is deductible for purposes of the federal corporate income tax, but which is not deductible for purposes of the Massachusetts tax on corporate income.

DB = declining balance; SL = straight line; ufd = until fully depreciated.

Table A.8. Tax treatment of inventories

Country	Year	Inventory valuation
Austria	'01–'03	LIFO
France	'01–'03	Weighted Average
Germany	'01–'03	LIFO
Ireland	'01–'03	Weighted Average
Italy	'01–'03	LIFO
The Netherlands	'01–'03	LIFO
Switzerland	'01–'03	LIFO
United Kingdom	'01–'03	FIFO
United States	'01–'03	LIFO

Remark:
Valuation of inventories represents the most tax-efficient possibility; other possibilities are ignored.
FIFO = First-In-First-Out method; LIFO = Last-In-First-Out method

A.2 Taxation of Corporate Capital and Real Estate

Table A.9. Summary of effective tax rates on capital and real estate (%)

Country	Year	Effective capital or net wealth tax rate	Effective real estate tax rate	See table(s) ..
Austria	'01–'03	–	0.17	A.10.
France	'01	0.57–2.93 [a]	0.20–1.15	A.11. and A.12.
	'02	0.58–2.93 [a]	0.21–1.17	A.11. and A.12.
	'03	0.58–2.98 [a]	0.21–1.17	A.11. and A.12.
Germany	'01–'02	–	0.12–0.32	A.13.
	'03	–	0.11–0.35	A.13.
Ireland	'01	–	0.31 [b]	–
	'02	–	0.33 [b]	–
	'03	–	0.34 [b]	–
Italy	'01–'03	–	0.38–0.67	A.14.
The Netherlands	'01	–	0.18–0.24	A.15.
	'02	–	0.18–0.25	A.15.
	'03	–	0.19–0.26	A.15.
Switzerland	'01	0.07–0.44	0.00–0.15	A.16. and A.17.
	'02–'03	0.07–0.41	0.00–0.15	A.16. and A.17.
United Kingdom	'01	–	1.46 [c]	–
	'02	–	1.51 [c]	–
	'03	–	1.53 [c]	–
United States	'01–'03	0.17 [d]	–	–

Remarks:

[a] Lower rate on buildings, higher rate on machinery.

[b] The annual rent of the building is assumed to amount to five per cent of the acquisition costs. The rental values are discounted back to 1988 levels, which are about 25 per cent of the market values. The rateable valuation is 63 per cent (the valuation coefficient for real estate located in Dublin) of that value. The rate in the pound (euro) is 43.99 ('01), 46.86 ('02), and 49.90 ('03).

[c] The annual rent of the building is assumed to amount to five per cent of the acquisition costs. The rate in the pound is 41.60 pence ('01), 43.00 pence ('02), and 43.70 pence ('03).

[d] The state of Massachusetts imposes a state franchise tax of 2.60 $ per 1,000 $ of tangible property of corporations in the manufacturing sector; other commercial corporations are subject to Boston real and personal property taxes at a rate of 3.017 ('01), 3.033 ('02), and 3.149 ('03) per cent.

Table A.10. Multipliers and effective real estate tax rates for Austria (%)

State of ...	Year	Multiplier of real estate tax	Effective tax rate
Burgenland (Eisenstadt)	'01–'03	500	0.17
Kärnten (Klagenfurt)	'01–'03	500	0.17
Niederösterreich (St. Pölten)	'01–'03	500	0.17
Oberösterreich (Linz)	'01–'03	500	0.17
Salzburg	'01–'03	500	0.17
Steiermark (Graz)	'01–'03	500	0.17
Tirol (Innsbruck)	'01–'03	500	0.17
Vorarlberg (Bregenz)	'01–'03	500	0.17
Wien	'01–'03	500	0.17

Remark: It is assumed that the tax base amounts to 25 per cent of the acquisition costs, which are equal to the market value.

Table A.11. Statutory and effective tax rates of the *taxe professionnelle* in France (%)

	'01		'02		'03	
Département (municipality) of ...	Sum of statutory tax rates	Effective rate (buildings/machinery)	Sum of statutory tax rates	Effective rate (buildings/machinery)	Sum of statutory tax rates	Effective rate (buildings/machinery)
Alsace						
Bas-Rhin (Strasbourg)	27.76	1.19/2.37	27.85	1.21/2.42	28.16	1.22/2.44
Haut-Rhin (Mulhouse)	25.90	1.11/2.21	25.92	1.12/2.25	26.31	1.14/2.28
Franche-Comté						
Doubs (Besançon)	25.58	1.09/2.19	25.49	1.11/2.21	25.64	1.11/2.22
Jura (Lons-le-Saunier)	21.51	0.92/1.84	21.45	0.93/1.86	22.01	0.95/1.91
Haute-Saône (Vésoul)	21.69	0.93/1.85	21.85	0.95/1.90	22.33	0.97/1.94
T.-de-Belfort (Belfort)	34.35	1.47/2.93	33.76	1.46/2.93	34.30	1.49/2.98
Ile-de-France						
Paris	13.36	0.57/1.14	13.37	0.58/1.16	13.37	0.58/1.16
Lorraine						
Meurthe-et-Moselle (Nancy)	32.61	1.39/2.79	32.13	1.39/2.79	31.59	1.37/2.74
Meuse (Verdun)	20.20	0.86/1.73	20.22	0.88/1.75	23.45	1.02/2.03
Moselle (Metz)	24.91	1.06/2.13	24.91	1.08/2.16	24.71	1.07/2.14
Vosges (Épinal)	26.47	1.13/2.26	26.48	1.15/2.30	26.83	1.16/2.33
Rhône-Alpes						
Ain (Bourg-en-Bresse)	25.05	1.07/2.14	24.77	1.07/2.15	24.68	1.07/2.14
Ardèche (Privas)	28.41	1.21/2.43	28.44	1.23/2.47	28.86	1.25/2.50
Drôme (Valence)	23.63	1.01/2.02	23.66	1.03/2.05	24.16	1.05/2.10
Isère (Grenoble)	33.39	1.43/2.85	33.17	1.44/2.88	32.85	1.43/2.85
Loire (Saint Etienne)	28.06	1.20/2.40	28.01	1.22/2.43	28.27	1.23/2.45
Rhône (Lyon)	25.81	1.10/2.21	25.85	1.12/2.24	27.86	1.21/2.42
Savoie (Chambéry)	29.16	1.25/2.49	29.05	1.26/2.52	29.69	1.29/2.58
Haute-Savoie (Annecy)	27.83	1.19/2.38	29.50	1.28/2.56	30.31	1.32/2.63

Remarks:
The sum of statutory tax rates includes taxes at different levels of government.
We apply the data with a lag. E.g., for calculating the tax burden in '01, we apply the tax rate from '00.

Table A.12. Statutory and effective tax rates of the real estate tax in France (%)

	'01		'02		'03	
Département (municipality) of ...	Sum of statutory tax rates	Effective rate of real estate tax	Sum of statutory tax rates	Effective rate of real estate tax	Sum of statutory tax rates	Effective rate of real estate tax
Alsace						
Bas-Rhin (Strasbourg)	25.43	0.65	25.51	0.66	25.86	0.67
Haut-Rhin (Mulhouse)	28.10	0.71	28.18	0.73	28.54	0.74
Franche-Comté						
Doubs (Besançon)	34.11	0.87	34.28	0.89	34.95	0.90
Jura (Lons-le-Saunier)	42.10	1.07	41.76	1.08	43.25	1.12
Haute-Saône (Vésoul)	41.37	1.05	41.55	1.07	42.43	1.10
T.-de-Belfort (Belfort)	28.96	0.74	29.13	0.75	29.60	0.76
Ile-de-France						
Paris	7.98	0.20	7.98	0.21	7.98	0.21
Lorraine						
Meurthe-et-Moselle (Nancy)	29.28	0.74	28.95	0.75	29.09	0.75
Meuse (Verdun)	37.17	0.95	37.20	0.96	42.13	1.09
Moselle (Metz)	23.71	0.60	23.73	0.61	23.73	0.61
Vosges (Épinal)	38.69	0.98	38.71	1.00	39.25	1.01
Rhône-Alpes						
Ain (Bourg-en-Bresse)	26.65	0.68	26.67	0.69	27.92	0.72
Ardèche (Privas)	37.07	0.94	37.09	0.96	37.55	0.97
Drôme (Valence)	34.06	0.87	34.07	0.88	34.61	0.89
Isère (Grenoble)	45.28	1.15	45.30	1.17	45.30	1.17
Loire (Saint Etienne)	32.48	0.83	32.05	0.83	32.64	0.84
Rhône (Lyon)	21.38	0.54	21.41	0.55	22.84	0.59
Savoie (Chambéry)	33.96	0.86	33.98	0.88	34.60	0.89
Haute-Savoie (Annecy)	21.25	0.54	22.46	0.58	25.33	0.65

Remarks:
The sum of statutory tax rates includes taxes at different levels of government.
We apply the data with a lag. E.g., for calculating the tax burden in '01, we apply the multiplier from '00.

Table A.13. Multipliers and effective real estate tax rates for Germany (%)

	'01		'02		'03	
Municipality of ...	Multiplier of real estate tax	Effective rate of real estate tax	Multiplier of real estate tax	Effective rate of real estate tax	Multiplier of real estate tax	Effective rate of real estate tax
Baden-Württemberg						
Aalen	305	0.17	305	0.17	325	0.17
Balingen	320	0.18	320	0.18	320	0.17
Freiburg	500	0.27	500	0.27	500	0.26
Göppingen	340	0.19	340	0.19	340	0.18
Heidelberg	410	0.22	410	0.22	410	0.22
Heilbronn	380	0.21	380	0.21	380	0.20
Karlsruhe	370	0.20	370	0.20	370	0.19
Konstanz	310	0.17	310	0.17	310	0.17
Lörrach	320	0.18	320	0.17	320	0.17
Landkreis Mannheim	220	0.12	250	0.14	250	0.14
Ludwigsburg	290	0.16	280	0.15	280	0.15
Mannheim	400	0.21	400	0.21	400	0.21
Nagold	350	0.19	350	0.19	350	0.19
Offenburg	400	0.22	400	0.22	400	0.21
Pforzheim	400	0.22	400	0.22	400	0.21
Rastatt	330	0.18	330	0.18	330	0.18
Ravensburg	350	0.19	350	0.19	350	0.19
Reutlingen	320	0.18	320	0.18	320	0.17
Rottweil	380	0.21	380	0.21	380	0.21
Schwäbisch-Hall	350	0.19	350	0.19	350	0.19
Stuttgart	445	0.24	420	0.22	420	0.22
Tauberbischofsheim	280	0.15	280	0.15	280	0.15
Ulm	375	0.20	375	0.20	375	0.20
Villingen-Schwenningen	350	0.19	350	0.19	350	0.19
Waiblingen	290	0.16	290	0.16	290	0.16
Walldorf bei Heidelberg	210	0.12	210	0.12	210	0.11
Bayern						
Ansbach	320	0.17	320	0.17	320	0.17
Aschaffenburg	300	0.16	300	0.16	300	0.16
Augsburg	390	0.21	390	0.21	390	0.20
Bamberg	365	0.20	375	0.20	375	0.20
Bayreuth	360	0.20	360	0.20	360	0.19
Coburg	320	0.17	320	0.17	320	0.18
Deggendorf	330	0.18	330	0.18	330	0.18
Donauwörth	340	0.19	340	0.19	340	0.18
Freising	300	0.16	300	0.16	300	0.16

Table A.13. continued

	'01		'02		'03	
Municipality of ...	Multiplier of real estate tax	Effective rate of real estate tax	Multiplier of real estate tax	Effective rate of real estate tax	Multiplier of real estate tax	Effective rate of real estate tax
Hof	390	0.21	390	0.21	390	0.21
Ingolstadt	350	0.19	350	0.19	350	0.18
Kempten	345	0.19	345	0.19	345	0.19
Landshut	350	0.19	370	0.20	390	0.20
Memmingen	330	0.18	330	0.18	330	0.18
München	400	0.21	400	0.21	400	0.20
Nürnberg	410	0.22	410	0.22	410	0.21
Passau	350	0.19	350	0.19	350	0.19
Pfarrkirchen	330	0.18	330	0.18	330	0.18
Regensburg	370	0.20	370	0.20	370	0.19
Rosenheim	420	0.23	420	0.23	420	0.22
Schwandorf	250	0.14	250	0.14	310	0.17
Schweinfurt	385	0.21	385	0.21	385	0.20
Traunstein	365	0.20	365	0.20	365	0.19
Weiden	310	0.17	300	0.16	300	0.16
Weilheim	300	0.17	300	0.17	300	0.16
Weißenburg i. Bayern	410	0.23	330	0.18	330	0.18
Würzburg	390	0.21	390	0.21	390	0.20
Berlin						
Berlin	600	0.32	600	0.32	660	0.35
Hamburg						
Hamburg	490	0.26	490	0.26	490	0.25
Hessen						
Frankfurt	510	0.26	460	0.24	460	0.23
Offenbach	400	0.21	400	0.21	400	0.21
Nordrhein-Westfalen						
Düsseldorf	490	0.26	480	0.25	475	0.24
Essen	490	0.26	490	0.26	510	0.26
Köln	500	0.26	500	0.26	500	0.26
Rheinland-Pfalz						
Landau	375	0.20	375	0.20	375	0.20
Ludwigshafen	370	0.20	370	0.20	370	0.20
Mainz	400	0.21	400	0.21	400	0.21

Remark: We apply the data with a lag. E.g., for calculating the tax burden in '01, we apply the multiplier from '00.

Table A.14. Statutory and effective real estate tax rates for Italy (%)

	'01		'02		'03	
Province (municipality) of ...	Statutory rate of real estate tax	Effective rate of real estate tax	Statutory rate of real estate tax	Effective rate of real estate tax	Statutory rate of real estate tax	Effective rate of real estate tax
Friuli-Venezia Giulia						
Gorizia (Gorizia)	0.60	0.57	0.60	0.57	0.60	0.57
Pordenone (Pordenone)	0.45	0.43	0.55	0.53	0.55	0.53
Trieste (Trieste)	0.60	0.57	0.70	0.67	0.70	0.67
Udine (Udine)	0.50	0.48	0.50	0.48	0.50	0.48
Lombardia						
Bergamo (Bergamo)	0.59	0.56	0.59	0.56	0.59	0.56
Brescia (Brescia)	0.58	0.56	0.58	0.56	0.58	0.56
Como (Como)	0.56	0.54	0.56	0.54	0.66	0.63
Cremona (Cremona)	0.57	0.54	0.65	0.62	0.65	0.62
Lecco (Lecco)	0.59	0.56	0.59	0.56	0.69	0.66
Lodi (Lodi)	0.65	0.62	0.65	0.62	0.65	0.62
Mantova (Mantova)	0.70	0.67	0.70	0.67	0.70	0.67
Milano (Milano)	0.50	0.48	0.50	0.48	0.50	0.48
Pavia (Pavia)	0.65	0.62	0.65	0.62	0.65	0.62
Sondrio (Sondrio)	0.58	0.56	0.58	0.56	0.58	0.56
Varese (Varese)	0.59	0.56	0.59	0.56	0.59	0.56
Piemonte						
Alessandria (Alessandria)	0.65	0.62	0.70	0.67	0.70	0.67
Asti (Asti)	0.65	0.62	0.65	0.62	0.70	0.67
Biella (Biella)	0.63	0.60	0.63	0.60	0.63	0.60
Cuneo (Cuneo)	0.65	0.62	0.65	0.62	0.65	0.62
Novara (Novara)	0.58	0.56	0.68	0.65	0.68	0.65
Torino (Torino)	0.60	0.57	0.65	0.62	0.65	0.62
Verbano-C.-O. (Verbania)	0.55	0.53	0.55	0.53	0.55	0.53
Vercelli (Vercelli)	0.50	0.48	0.60	0.57	0.60	0.57
Trentino-Alto Adige						
Bolzano (Bolzano)	0.60	0.57	0.60	0.57	0.60	0.57
Trento (Trento)	0.50	0.48	0.60	0.57	0.60	0.57
Valle d'Aosta						
Valle d'Aosta (Aosta)	0.40	0.38	0.40	0.38	0.40	0.38

Table A.14. continued

Province (municipality) of ...	'01 Statutory rate of real estate tax	'01 Effective rate of real estate tax	'02 Statutory rate of real estate tax	'02 Effective rate of real estate tax	'03 Statutory rate of real estate tax	'03 Effective rate of real estate tax
Veneto						
Belluno (Belluno)	0.70	0.67	0.70	0.67	0.70	0.67
Padova (Padova)	0.55	0.53	0.62	0.59	0.62	0.59
Rovigo (Rovigo)	0.70	0.67	0.70	0.67	0.70	0.67
Treviso (Treviso)	0.65	0.62	0.65	0.62	0.65	0.62
Venezia (Venezia)	0.70	0.67	0.70	0.67	0.70	0.67
Verona (Verona)	0.55	0.53	0.55	0.53	0.68	0.65
Vicenza (Vicenza)	0.60	0.57	0.60	0.57	0.60	0.57

Remark: The cadastral value applied is assumed to amount to 50 per cent of the acquisition costs.

Table A.15. Statutory and effective real estate tax rates for the Netherlands (%)

Municipality of ...	'01 Statutory rate of real estate tax	'01 Effective rate of real estate tax	'02 Statutory rate of real estate tax	'02 Effective rate of real estate tax	'03 Statutory rate of real estate tax	'03 Effective rate of real estate tax
Amsterdam	0.28	0.18	0.28	0.18	0.29	0.19
Den Haag	0.43	0.28	0.42	0.27	0.42	0.27
Rotterdam	0.50	0.32	0.52	0.34	0.55	0.36
Utrecht	0.37	0.24	0.38	0.25	0.40	0.26

Remark: It is assumed that the tax base amounts to 100 per cent of the acquisition costs.

Table A.16. Statutory and effective capital tax rates for Switzerland (%)

			Annual (%)	multiple			
Canton of ...	Year	Canto-nal tax rate	Canton	Munici-pality	Church	Sum	Combined eff. capital tax rate
Basel-Land.	'01	0.15	100.00	295.00 [a]	5.00	400.00	0.44
	'02	0.15	100.00	275.00 [a]	5.00	380.00	0.41
	'03	0.14	100.00	275.00 [a]	5.00	380.00	0.41
Basel-Stadt	'01–'03	0.53	100.00	–	–	100.00	0.39
Bern	'01	0.05	230.00	230.00	19.15	479.15	0.19
	'02	0.05	306.00	154.00	19.15	479.15	0.19
	'03	0.03	306.00	154.00	19.15	479.15	0.11
Genève	'01–'03	0.18	178.50	45.40	–	223.90	0.31
Nidwalden	'01–'02	0.04	240.00	265.00	30.00	535.00	0.15
	'03	0.04	240.00	258.00	30.00	528.00	0.15
Schwyz	'01	0.08	120.00	245.00 [b]	27.05	392.05	0.25
	'02	0.08	110.00	230.00 [b]	27.05	367.05	0.24
	'03	0.08	110.00	230.00 [b]	26.11	366.11	0.24
St. Gallen	'01	0.03	115.00	220.00 [c]	– [c]	335.00	0.08
	'02	0.03	112.00	220.00 [c]	– [c]	332.00	0.07
	'03	0.03	115.00	220.00 [c]	– [c]	335.00	0.08
Ticino	'01–'02	0.20	100.00	100.00	–	200.00	0.32
	'03	0.15	100.00	100.00 [d]	–	200.00	0.24
Vaud	'01–'03	0.12	129.00	105.00	–	234.00	0.21
Valais	'01–'03	0.25	100.00	100.00	3.00	203.00	0.40
Zug	'01	0.05	82.00	65.00	10.22	157.22	0.07
	'02	0.05	82.00	65.00	10.00	157.00	0.07
	'03	0.05	82.00	65.00	9.22	156.22	0.07
Zürich	'01	0.15	105.00	126.00	12.01	243.01	0.27
	'02	0.15	105.00	122.00	11.02	238.02	0.27
	'03	0.15	100.00	122.00	10.52	232.52	0.26

Remarks:

[a] The municipal tax rate is legally defined as a rate on the capital. For purposes of this comparison, it has been converted into an annual multiple.

[b] Includes the annual multiples at the level of the municipality and the district.

[c] Combined multiple for municipalities and church.

[d] The municipal annual multiple is determined at the end of each tax year. For 2003, the value for the tax year 2002 has been applied.

Table A.17. Statutory and effective real estate tax rates for Switzerland (%)

	'01		'02		'03	
Canton of ...	Statutory rate of real estate tax	Effective rate of real estate tax	Statutory rate of real estate tax	Effective rate of real estate tax	Statutory rate of real estate tax	Effective rate of real estate tax
Bern [a)]	0.15	0.08	0.15	0.08	0.15	0.08
Genève	0.10	0.08	0.10	0.08	0.10	0.08
St. Gallen	0.10	0.07	0.10	0.07	0.10	0.07
Ticino [b)]	0.30	0.15	0.30	0.15	0.30	0.15
Vaud	0.15	0.11	0.15	0.11	0.15	0.11
Valais [c)]	0.23	0.08	0.23	0.08	0.23	0.08

Remark: The taxable value of the building is assumed to amount to [a)] 70 per cent, [b)] 65 per cent, [c)] 48 per cent of the acquisition costs.

A.3 Personal Taxation of Income and Net Wealth

Table A.18. Personal income tax rates including surcharges (zero-rate shareholder, %)

Country	Year	Dividends	Imputation Credit	Interest	Capital gain (share disposal)
Austria	'01–'03	0.00	0.00	0.00	0.00
France	'01–'03	0.00	33.33	0.00	0.00
Germany	'01–'03	0.00	0.00	0.00	0.00
Ireland	'01	0.00	0.00	22.00	0.00
	'02–'03	0.00	0.00	20.00	0.00
Italy	'01–'03	0.00	0.00	12.50	0.00
The Netherlands	'01–'03	0.00	0.00	0.00	0.00
Switzerland	'01–'03	0.00	0.00	0.00	0.00
United Kingdom	'01–'03	10.00	10.00	0.00	0.00
United States	'01–'03	0.00	0.00	0.00	0.00

Table A.19. Personal income tax rates including surcharges (top-rate non-qual. shareh., %)

Country	Year	Dividends	Imputation Credit	Interest	Capital gain (share disposal)
Austria	'01–'03	25.00	0.00	25.00	0.00
France	'01	60.18	33.33	25.00	26.00
	'02	57.20	33.33	25.00	26.00
	'03	56.69	33.33	25.00	26.00
Germany	'01–'03	25.58	0.00	51.17	0.00
Ireland	'01	44.00	0.00	22.00	20.00
	'02–'03	42.00	0.00	20.00	20.00
Italy	'01–'03	12.50	0.00	12.50	12.50
The Netherlands	'01–'03	0.00	0.00	0.00	0.00
Switzerland [a]	'01–'03	23.42–45.43	0.00	23.42–45.43	0.00
United Kingdom	'01–'02	32.50	10.00	40.00	34.40 [b]
	'03	32.50	10.00	40.00	35.60 [b]
United States	'01	42.98	0.00	42.98	23.38
	'02	41.85	0.00	41.85	16.25 [b]
	'03	18.45	0.00	38.45	18.45

Remarks: [a] See table A.21., p. 108. [b] Relevant tax rate varies over holding period and is averaged over an assumed holding period of ten years.

Table A.20. Personal income tax rates including surcharges (top-rate qualified shareh., %)

Country	Year	Dividends	Imputation Credit	Interest	Capital gain (share disposal)
Austria	'01–'03	25.00	0.00	25.00	25.00
France	'01	60.18	33.33	25.00	26.00
	'02	57.20	33.33	25.00	26.00
	'03	56.69	33.33	25.00	26.00
Germany	'01–'03	25.58	0.00	51.17	25.58
Ireland	'01	44.00	0.00	22.00	20.00
	'02–'03	42.00	0.00	20.00	20.00
Italy	'01–'02	46.10 [a]	36.00	12.50	27.00
	'03	46.10	34.00	12.50	27.00
The Netherlands	'01–'03	25.00	0.00	0.00	25.00
Switzerland [b]	'01–'03	19.08–45.43	0.00	23.42–45.43	0.00
United Kingdom	'01–'02	32.50	10.00	40.00	18.50 [c]
	'03	32.50	10.00	40.00	14.00 [c]
United States	'01	42.98	0.00	42.98	23.38
	'02	41.85	0.00	41.85	11.25 [c]
	'03	18.45	0.00	38.45	18.45

Remarks: [a] Takes into account a regional and municipal tax level of 1.1 per cent. [b] See table A.21., p. 108. [c] Relevant tax rate varies over holding period and is averaged over an assumed holding period of ten years.

Table A.21. Statutory and effective personal top income tax rates for Switzerland (%)

Canton of ...	Year	Cantonal headline tax rate	Annual multiple (%) Canton	Munici-pality	Sum	Combined effective income tax rate
Basel-Land.	'01	18.62	100.00	67.26	167.26	42.64
	'02–'03	18.62	100.00	67.00	167.00	42.60
Basel-Stadt	'01–'02	29.00	100.00	–	100.00	40.50
	'03	29.00	97.00	–	97.00	39.63
Bern	'01	6.50	230.00	230.00	460.00	41.40
	'02–'03	6.50	306.00	154.00	460.00	41.40
Genève	'01–'03	19.00	130.80 [a)]	45.50	176.30 [a)]	45.00
Nidwalden	'01–'02	3.00/1.50 [b)]	240.00	265.00	505.00	26.65/19.08 [b)]
	'03	3.00/1.50 [b)]	240.00	258.00	498.00	26.44/18.97 [b)]
Schwyz	'01	3.65	120.00	245.00 [c)]	365.00	24.82
	'02–'03	3.65	110.00	230.00 [c)]	340.00	23.91
St. Gallen	'01	9.00	115.00	159.00	274.00	36.16
	'02	9.00	112.00	159.00	271.00	35.89
	'03	9.00	115.00	159.00	274.00	36.16
Ticino	'01–'02	16.15	100.00	100.00 [d)]	200.00	43.80
	'03	15.08	100.00	100.00 [d)]	200.00	41.65
Vaud	'01–'03	14.50	129.00	105.00	234.00	41.50 [e)]
Valais	'01–'03	14.00	100.00	82.14 [f)]	182.14 [f)]	37.00
Zug	'01–'03	8.00	82.00	67.00	149.00	23.42
Zürich	'01	13.00	105.00	126.00	231.00	41.53
	'02	13.00	105.00	122.00	227.00	41.01
	'03	13.00	100.00	122.00	222.00	40.36

Remarks:

a) The statutory cantonal annual multiple is 148.5 per cent; for purposes of calculating the income tax, that multiple is reduced by 12 per cent of 147.5 per cent.

b) Lower value considers special tax treatment of dividends received by a qualified shareholder.

c) Includes the annual multiples at the level of the municipality and the district.

d) The municipal annual multiple is determined at the end of each tax year. For 2003, the value for the tax year 2002 has been applied.

e) According to art. 8 of the law of municipal taxes, the municipal and the cantonal income tax together may not exceed the rate of 30 per cent; consequently, we use a top-bracket income tax rate of 41.5 per cent.

f) The top municipal tax rate is lower than the top cantonal tax rate. For purposes of this comparison, this reduced rate has been considered in the calculation of the (effective) annual multiple.

Table A.22. Marginal top tax rates of individual net wealth tax/non-profit tax (%)

Country	Year	Shareholding	Lending
Austria	'01–'03	0.00	0.00
France	'01–'03	0.00/1.80 [a)]	1.80
Germany	'01–'03	0.00	0.00
Ireland	'01–'03	0.00	0.00
Italy	'01–'03	0.00	0.00
The Netherlands [b)]	'01–'03	0.00/1.20 [a)]	1.20
Switzerland [c)]	'01–'02	0.10–1.01	0.18–1.01
	'03	0.10–1.01	0.17–1.01
United Kingdom	'01–'03	0.00	0.00
United States	'01–'03	0.00	0.00

Remarks:

a) Zero-rate considers special tax treatment of a qualified shareholder.

b) Technically, that tax is designed as an income tax; effectively, it works like a non-profit tax as it considers a deemed rate of return on the investment.

c) See table A.23., p. 109.

Table A.23. Statutory and effective individual net wealth tax rates for Switzerland (%)

			Annual multiple (%)			
Canton of ...	Year	Cantonal tax rate	Canton	Munici-pality	Sum	Combined effective net wealth tax
Basel-Land.	'01	0.46	100.00	67.26	167.26	0.77
	'02–'03	0.46	100.00	67.00	167.00	0.77
Basel-Stadt	'01–'02	0.90	100.00	–	100.00	0.90
	'03	0.80	100.00	–	100.00	0.80
Bern	'01	0.16	230.00	230.00	460.00	0.71
	'02–'03	0.16	306.00	154.00	460.00	0.71
Genève	'01–'03	0.45	148.50	45.50	194.00	1.01 [a)]
Nidwalden	'01–'02	0.04/0.02 [b)]	240.00	265.00	505.00	0.18/0.10 [b)]
	'03	0.04/0.02 [b)]	240.00	258.00	498.00	0.17/0.10 [b)]
Schwyz	'01	0.08	120.00	245.00	365.00	0.29
	'02–'03	0.08	110.00	230.00	340.00	0.27
St. Gallen	'01	0.20	115.00	159.00	274.00	0.55
	'02	0.20	112.00	159.00	271.00	0.54
	'03	0.20	115.00	159.00	274.00	0.55
Ticino	'01–'03	0.35	100.00	100.00	200.00	0.70
Vaud	'01–'03	0.34	129.00	105.00	234.00	0.79
Valais	'01–'03	0.30	100.00	115.00	215.00	0.65
Zug	'01–'03	0.25	82.00	67.00	149.00	0.37
Zürich	'01	0.30	105.00	126.00	231.00	0.69
	'02	0.30	105.00	122.00	227.00	0.68
	'03	0.30	100.00	122.00	222.00	0.67

Remark:

a) Includes a supplementary net wealth tax (*impôt supplémentaire sur la fortune*) at a rate of 0.135 per cent.

b) Lower value considers special tax treatment of shares held by a qualified shareholder.

App. B Supplementary Tables and Figures

B.1 Assessed Regions

Table B.1. Assessed regions

	Region		Region
Austria		D-BW-FR	Freiburg
A-BU	Burgenland	D-BW-GÖ	Göppingen
A-KÄ	Kärnten	D-BW-HD	Heidelberg
A-NI	Niederösterreich	D-BW-HN	Heilbronn
A-OB	Oberösterreich	D-BW-KA	Karlsruhe
A-SA	Salzburg	D-BW-KO	Konstanz
A-ST	Steiermark	D-BW-LÖ	Lörrach
A-TI	Tirol	D-BW-LM	Landkreis Mannheim
A-VO	Vorarlberg	D-BW-LU	Ludwigsburg
A-WI	Wien	D-BW-MA	Mannheim
		D-BW-NA	Nagold
France		D-BW-OF	Offenburg
F-AL-BR	Bas-Rhin	D-BW-PF	Pforzheim
F-AL-HR	Haut-Rhin	D-BW-RS	Rastatt
F-FC-DO	Doubs	D-BW-RV	Ravensburg
F-FC-JU	Jura	D-BW-RE	Reutlingen
F-FC-HS	Haute-Saône	D-BW-RO	Rottweil
F-FC-HB	Territoire-de-Belfort	D-BW-SH	Schwäbisch-Hall
F-IF-PA	Paris	D-BW-ST	Stuttgart
F-LO-MM	Meurthe-et-Moselle	D-BW-TA	Tauberbischofsheim
F-LO-ME	Meuse	D-BW-UL	Ulm
F-LO-MO	Moselle	D-BW-VS	Villingen-Schwenningen
F-LO-VO	Vosges	D-BW-WB	Waiblingen
F-RA-AI	Ain	D-BW-WL	Walldorf bei Heidelberg
F-RA-AR	Ardèche	D-BY-AN	Ansbach
F-RA-DR	Drôme	D-BY-AS	Aschaffenburg
F-RA-IS	Isère	D-BY-AU	Augsburg
F-RA-LO	Loire	D-BY-BA	Bamberg
F-RA-RH	Rhône	D-BY-BT	Bayreuth
F-RA-SA	Savoie	D-BY-CO	Coburg
F-RA-HS	Haute-Savoie	D-BY-DE	Deggendorf
		D-BY-DO	Donauwörth
Germany		D-BY-FR	Freising
D-BW-AA	Aalen	D-BY-HO	Hof
D-BW-BA	Balingen	D-BY-IN	Ingolstadt

Table B.1. continued

	Region		Region
D-BY-KE	Kempten	I-PI-AS	Asti
D-BY-LA	Landshut	I-PI-BI	Biella
D-BY-ME	Memmingen	I-PI-CU	Cuneo
D-BY-MÜ	München	I-PI-NO	Novara
D-BY-NÜ	Nürnberg	I-PI-TO	Torino
D-BY-PA	Passau	I-PI-VC	Verbano-Cusio-Ossola
D-BY-PF	Pfarrkirchen	I-PI-VE	Vercelli
D-BY-RE	Regensburg	I-TA-BO	Bolzano
D-BY-RO	Rosenheim	I-TA-TR	Trento
D-BY-SD	Schwandorf	I-VA-VA	Valle d'Aosta
D-BY-SF	Schweinfurt	I-VE-BE	Belluno
D-BY-TR	Traunstein	I-VE-PA	Padova
D-BY-WD	Weiden	I-VE-RO	Rovigo
D-BY-WL	Weilheim	I-VE-TR	Treviso
D-BY-WS	Weißenburg i. Bayern	I-VE-VZ	Venezia
D-BY-WÜ	Würzburg	I-VE-VR	Verona
D-BE	Berlin	I-VE-VI	Vicenza
D-HH	Hamburg		
D-HE-FR	Frankfurt	*The Netherlands*	
D-HE-OF	Offenbach	NL-AM	Amsterdam
D-NW-DÜ	Düsseldorf	NL-DH	Den Haag
D-NW-ES	Essen	NL-RO	Rotterdam
D-NW-KÖ	Köln	NL-UT	Utrecht
D-RP-LA	Landau		
D-RP-LU	Ludwigshafen	*Switzerland*	
D-RP-MA	Mainz	CH-BL	Basel-Landschaft
		CH-BS	Basel-Stadt
Ireland		CH-BE	Bern
IRL	Dublin	CH-GE	Genève
		CH-NW	Nidwalden
Italy		CH-SZ	Schwyz
I-FV-GO	Gorizia	CH-SG	St. Gallen
I-FV-PO	Pordenone	CH-TI	Ticino
I-FV-TR	Trieste	CH-VD	Vaud
I-FV-UD	Udine	CH-VS	Valais
I-LO-BE	Bergamo	CH-ZG	Zug
I-LO-BR	Brescia	CH-ZH	Zürich
I-LO-CO	Como		
I-LO-CR	Cremona	*United Kingdom*	
I-LO-LE	Lecco	GB	London
I-LO-LO	Lodi		
I-LO-MA	Mantova	*United States*	
I-LO-MI	Milano	USA	Boston
I-LO-PA	Pavia		
I-LO-SO	Sondrio		
I-LO-VA	Varese		
I-PI-AL	Alessandria		

B.2 Supplementary Cantonal Effective Tax Rates

See p. 34 for further explanation on the following figures.

Fig. B.1. Effective tax rates in the canton of Basel-Landschaft, 2001–2003

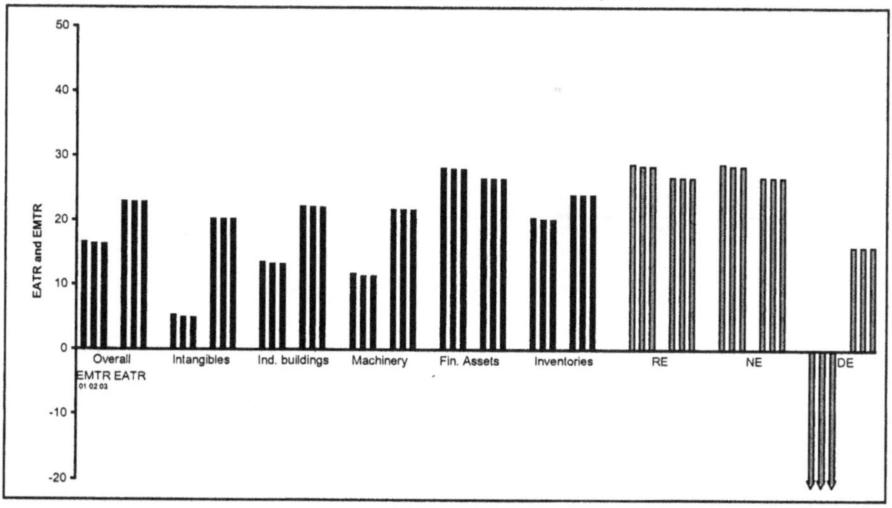

Fig. B.2. Effective tax rates in the canton of Basel-Stadt, 2001–2003

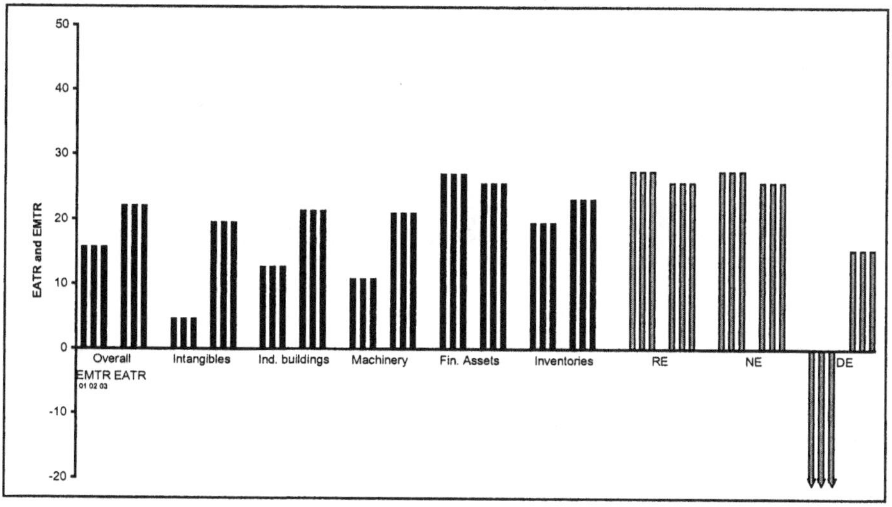

Fig. B.3. Effective tax rates in the canton of Bern, 2001–2003

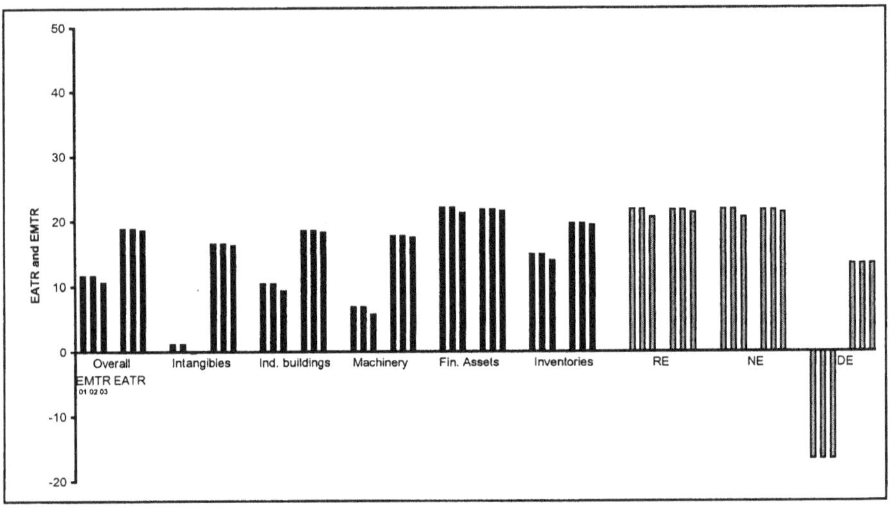

Fig. B.4. Effective tax rates in the canton of Genève, 2001–2003

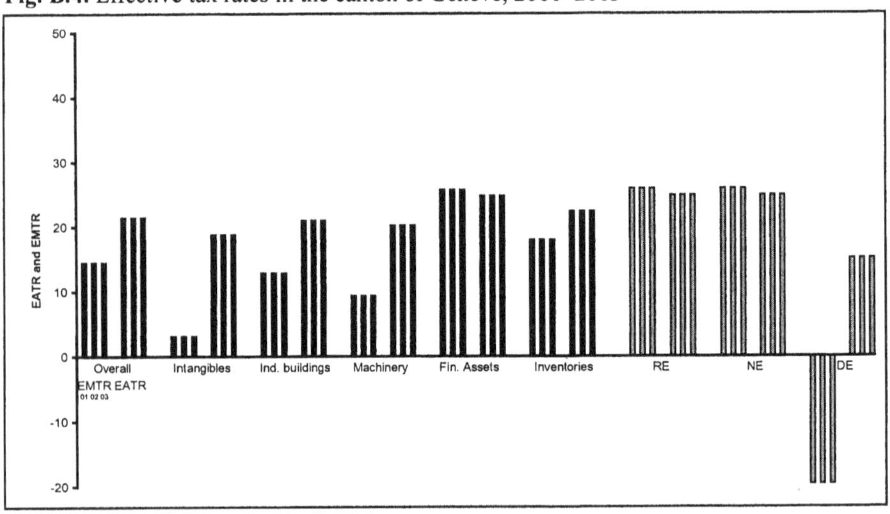

Fig. B.5. Effective tax rates in the canton of Nidwalden, 2001–2003

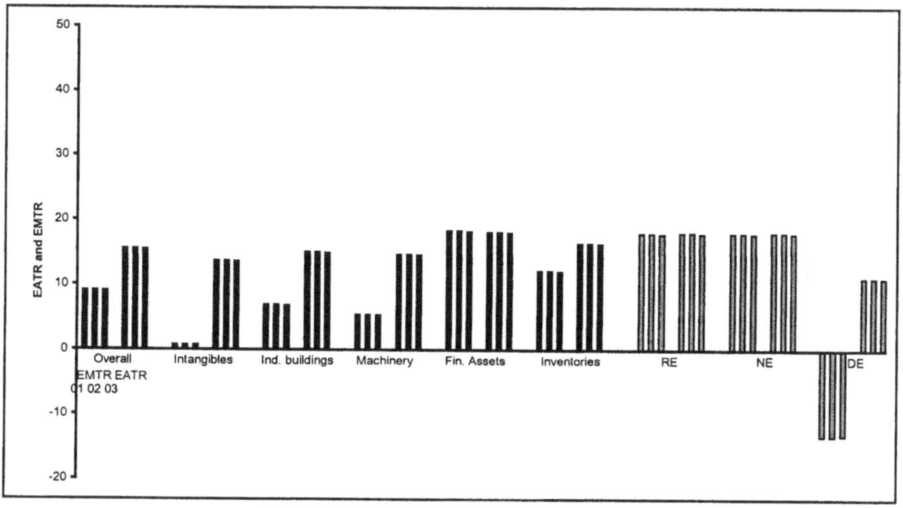

Fig. B.6. Effective tax rates in the canton of Schwyz, 2001–2003

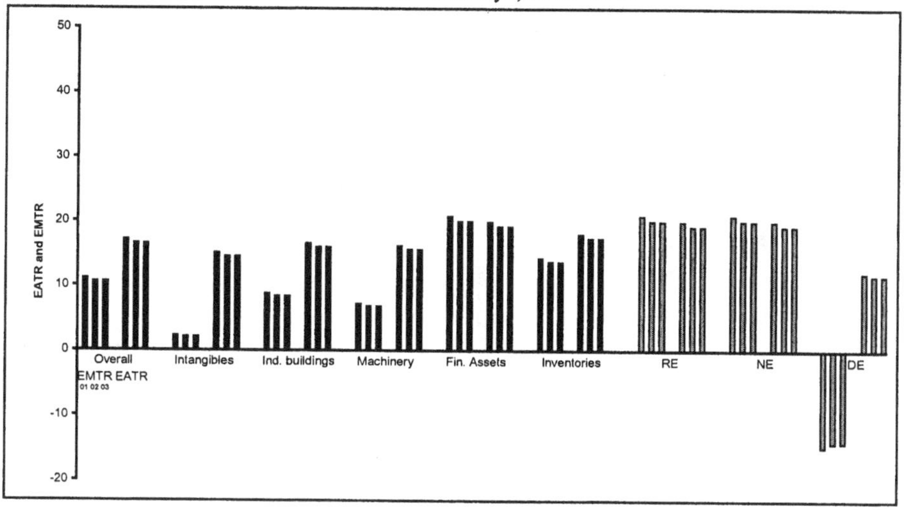

Fig. B.7. Effective tax rates in the canton of St. Gallen, 2001–2003

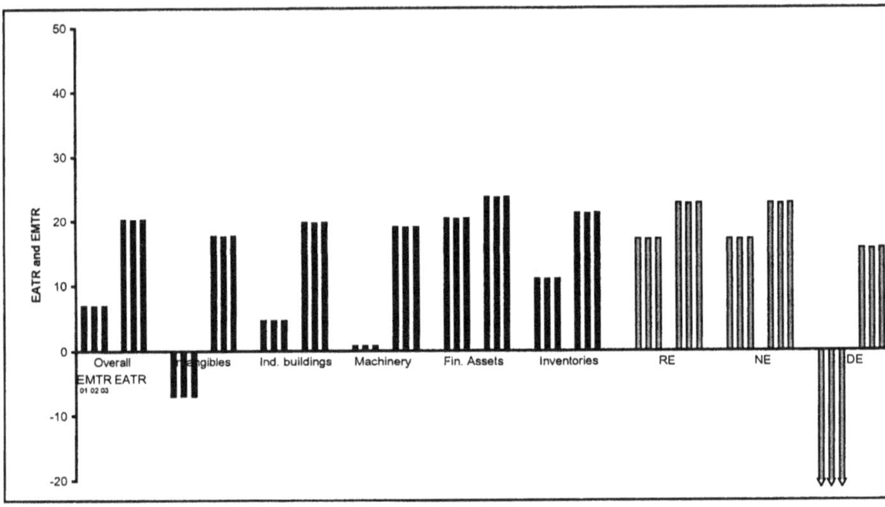

Fig. B.8. Effective tax rates in the canton of Ticino, 2001–2003

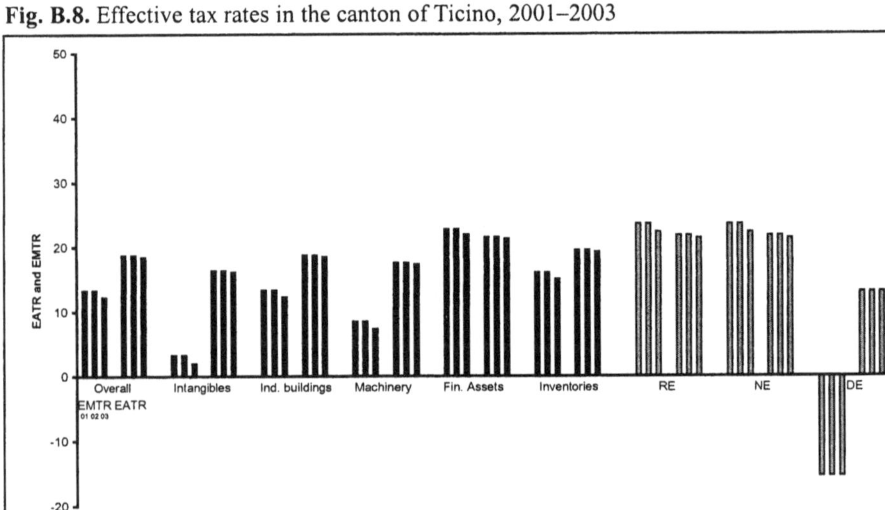

Fig. B.9. Effective tax rates in the canton of Vaud, 2001–2003

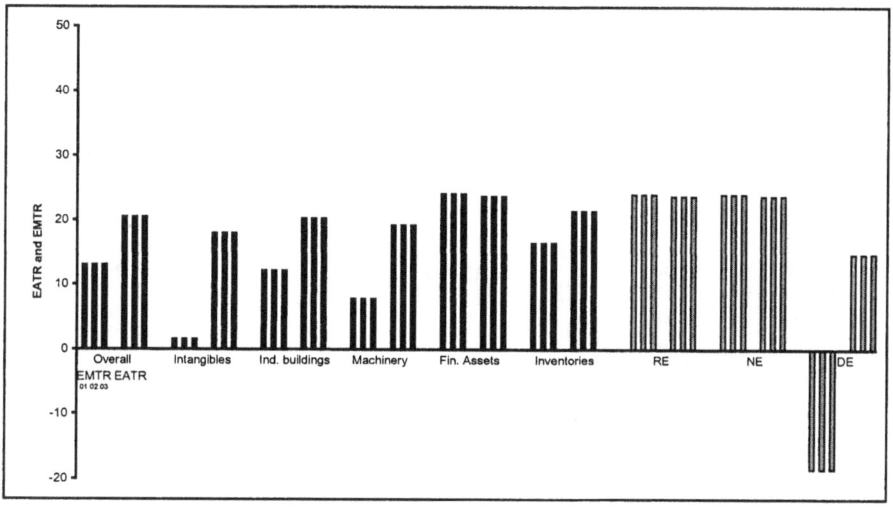

Fig. B.10. Effective tax rates in the canton of Valais, 2001–2003

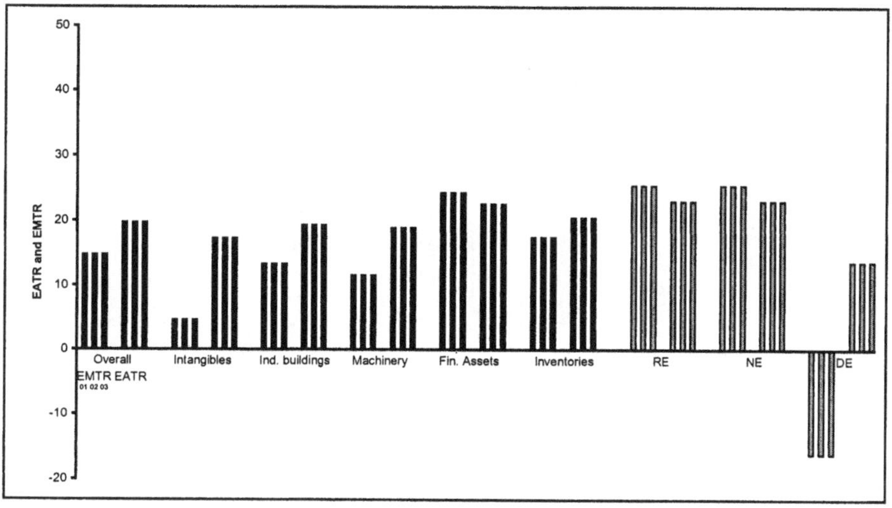

Fig. B.11. Effective tax rates in the canton of Zug, 2001–2003

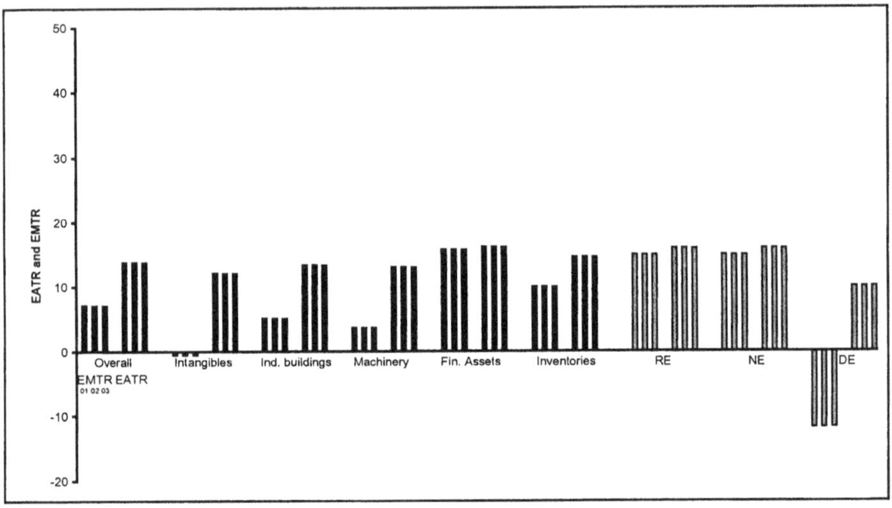

Fig. B.12. Effective tax rates in the canton of Zürich, 2001–2003

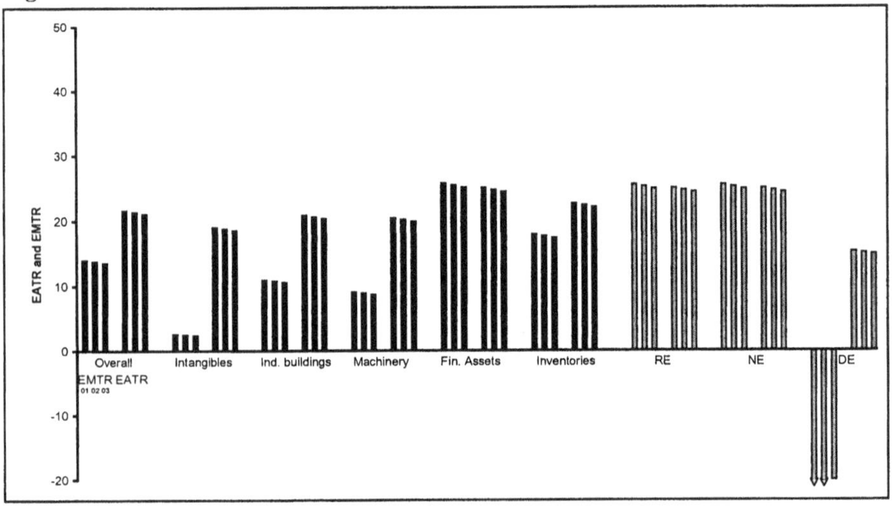

App. C Supplementary Rankings

C.1 Ranking Tables

Table C.1. Ranking of regions – levels of profitability 2003

Rk		Region	EATR 20	EMTR	Rk	EATR 40	Rk	Eff. Profit Tax Rate	Rk
1	CH	Zug	13.8	7.1	2	15.0	2	16.3	2
2	IR	Dublin	14.0	11.9	6	14.5	1	12.5	1
3	CH	Nidwalden	15.4	9.0	3	16.6	3	17.8	3
4	CH	Schwyz	16.5	10.6	5	17.6	4	18.8	4
5	CH	Ticino	18.5	12.2	7	19.7	5	20.9	5
6	CH	Bern	18.6	10.6	4	20.1	6	21.6	6
7	CH	Valais	19.7	14.7	11	20.7	7	21.7	7
8	CH	St. Gallen	20.3	6.9	1	22.7	10	25.2	12
9	CH	Vaud	20.5	13.1	8	22.0	8	23.5	8
10	CH	Zürich	21.0	13.6	9	22.6	9	24.1	9
11	CH	Genève	21.4	14.5	10	22.8	11	24.3	10
12	CH	Basel-Stadt	22.1	15.6	12	23.5	12	24.8	11
13	CH	Basel-Landschaft	22.8	16.3	13	24.2	13	25.7	13
14	GB	London	28.1	24.2	63	29.0	14	30.0	14
15	NL	Amsterdam	30.2	20.8	47	32.3	24	34.5	24
16	NL	Utrecht	30.2	21.1	48	32.4	25	34.5	24
17	NL	Den Haag	30.3	21.1	49	32.4	26	34.5	24
18	NL	Rotterdam	30.3	21.4	50	32.4	27	34.5	24
19	A	Burgenland	30.4 [a)]	22.9 [a)]	51	32.2	15	34.0	15
19	A	Kärnten	30.4 [a)]	22.9 [a)]	51	32.2	15	34.0	15
19	A	Niederösterreich	30.4 [a)]	22.9 [a)]	51	32.2	15	34.0	15
19	A	Oberösterreich	30.4 [a)]	22.9 [a)]	51	32.2	15	34.0	15
19	A	Salzburg	30.4 [a)]	22.9 [a)]	51	32.2	15	34.0	15
19	A	Steiermark	30.4 [a)]	22.9 [a)]	51	32.2	15	34.0	15
19	A	Tirol	30.4 [a)]	22.9 [a)]	51	32.2	15	34.0	15
19	A	Vorarlberg	30.4 [a)]	22.9 [a)]	51	32.2	15	34.0	15
19	A	Wien	30.4 [a)]	22.9 [a)]	51	32.2	15	34.0	15
28	I	Valle d'Aosta	31.6	18.4	14	34.5	29	38.3	55
29	I	Milano	31.7	18.6	15	34.5	30	38.3	55
29	I	Udine	31.7	18.6	15	34.5	30	38.3	55
31	I	Pordenone	31.7	18.7	17	34.6	32	38.3	55
31	I	Verbano-Cusio-Ossola	31.7	18.7	17	34.6	32	38.3	55

Table C.1. continued (1)

Rk		Region	EATR 20	EMTR	Rk	EATR 40	Rk	Eff. Profit Tax Rate	Rk
33	I	Brescia	31.7	18.8	19	34.6	34	38.3	55
33	I	Sondrio	31.7	18.8	19	34.6	34	38.3	55
35	I	Bergamo	31.7	18.8	21	34.6	36	38.3	55
35	I	Varese	31.7	18.8	21	34.6	36	38.3	55
37	I	Bolzano	31.7	18.8	23	34.6	38	38.3	55
37	I	Gorizia	31.7	18.8	23	34.6	38	38.3	55
37	I	Trento	31.7	18.8	23	34.6	38	38.3	55
37	I	Vercelli	31.7	18.8	23	34.6	38	38.3	55
37	I	Vicenza	31.7	18.8	23	34.6	38	38.3	55
42	I	Padova	31.7	18.9	28	34.6	43	38.3	55
43	I	Biella	31.7	18.9	29	34.6	44	38.3	55
44	I	Cremona	31.8	18.9	30	34.6	45	38.3	55
44	I	Cuneo	31.8	18.9	30	34.6	45	38.3	55
44	I	Lodi	31.8	18.9	30	34.6	45	38.3	55
44	I	Pavia	31.8	18.9	30	34.6	45	38.3	55
44	I	Torino	31.8	18.9	30	34.6	45	38.3	55
44	I	Treviso	31.8	18.9	30	34.6	45	38.3	55
50	I	Como	31.8	19.0	36	34.6	51	38.3	55
51	I	Novara	31.8	19.0	37	34.6	52	38.3	55
51	I	Verona	31.8	19.0	37	34.6	52	38.3	55
53	I	Lecco	31.8	19.0	39	34.6	54	38.3	55
54	I	Alessandria	31.8	19.0	40	34.6	55	38.3	55
54	I	Asti	31.8	19.0	40	34.6	55	38.3	55
54	I	Belluno	31.8	19.0	40	34.6	55	38.3	55
54	I	Mantova	31.8	19.0	40	34.6	55	38.3	55
54	I	Rovigo	31.8	19.0	40	34.6	55	38.3	55
54	I	Trieste	31.8	19.0	40	34.6	55	38.3	55
54	I	Venezia	31.8	19.0	40	34.6	55	38.3	55
61	F	Paris	32.1	25.5	93	33.8	28	35.4	28
62	D	Weilheim	32.9	23.6	60	35.1	74	37.4	47
63	D	Coburg	32.9	23.7	61	35.1	75	37.4	47
64	D	Walldorf b. Heidelberg	33.1	23.7	62	35.3	80	37.6	49
65	D	Landkreis Mannheim	33.6	24.3	64	35.9	83	38.2	50
66	D	Tauberbischofsheim	33.6	24.3	65	35.9	84	38.2	50
67	D	Memmingen	33.6	24.4	66	35.9	85	38.2	50
67	D	Pfarrkirchen	33.6	24.4	66	35.9	85	38.2	50
69	D	Ravensburg	33.6	24.5	68	35.9	87	38.2	50
70	D	Rottweil	33.8	24.7	71	36.0	88	38.3	88
71	D	Kempten	33.8	24.6	69	36.1	89	38.3	89
72	D	Balingen	33.9	24.7	70	36.1	90	38.4	90
73	D	Weißenburg i. Bayern	33.9	24.7	72	36.1	91	38.4	90
74	F	Moselle	34.1	31.7	126	34.7	62	35.4	28

Table C.1. continued (2)

Rk		Region	EATR 20	EMTR	Rk	EATR 40	Rk	Eff. Profit Tax Rate	Rk
75	D	Waiblingen	34.1	24.8	73	36.4	92	38.7	92
76	D	Weiden	34.1	24.9	74	36.4	93	38.7	92
77	D	Schwandorf	34.1	24.9	75	36.4	94	38.7	92
78	D	Reutlingen	34.1	24.9	76	36.4	95	38.7	92
79	D	Aalen	34.1	24.9	77	36.4	96	38.7	92
80	D	Deggendorf	34.1	24.9	78	36.4	97	38.7	92
81	D	Donauwörth	34.1	24.9	79	36.4	98	38.7	92
82	D	Nagold	34.1	25.0	80	36.4	99	38.7	92
82	D	Vill.-Schwenningen	34.1	25.0	80	36.4	99	38.7	92
84	F	Ain	34.2	32.0	127	34.8	63	35.4	28
85	F	Jura	34.2	32.1	128	34.8	64	35.4	28
86	D	Göppingen	34.2	25.1	83	36.5	101	38.8	101
87	F	Haute-Saône	34.2	32.2	129	34.8	65	35.4	28
88	F	Drôme	34.3	32.3	130	34.9	66	35.4	28
89	D	Ludwigsburg	34.3	25.1	82	36.6	102	38.9	102
90	D	Konstanz	34.3	25.1	84	36.6	103	38.9	102
91	D	Ansbach	34.3	25.1	85	36.6	104	38.9	102
91	D	Lörrach	34.3	25.1	85	36.6	104	38.9	102
93	D	Ludwigshafen	34.4	25.2	87	36.7	106	38.9	102
94	D	Ulm	34.4	25.2	88	36.7	107	38.9	102
95	F	Meuse	34.4	32.6	131	34.9	67	35.4	28
96	F	Haut-Rhin	34.4	32.7	132	34.9	68	35.4	28
97	F	Rhône	34.5	32.8	133	34.9	69	35.4	28
98	D	Traunstein	34.5	25.3	89	36.8	108	39.1	108
99	F	Doubs	34.5	32.9	134	35.0	70	35.4	28
100	D	Rastatt	34.6	25.4	90	36.9	109	39.2	109
101	F	Bas-Rhin	34.6	33.2	135	35.0	71	35.4	28
102	D	Passau	34.6	25.4	91	36.9	110	39.2	109
103	D	Bayreuth	34.6	25.5	92	36.9	111	39.2	109
104	D	Schweinfurt	34.6	25.5	94	36.9	112	39.2	109
105	D	Schwäbisch-Hall	34.7	25.6	95	37.0	113	39.3	113
106	F	Vosges	34.8	33.7	136	35.1	72	35.4	28
107	F	Loire	34.8	33.7	137	35.1	73	35.4	28
108	D	Freising	34.8	25.6	96	37.1	114	39.5	114
109	D	Heilbronn	34.8	25.7	98	37.1	115	39.5	114
110	D	Hof	34.8	25.7	99	37.2	116	39.5	114
111	D	Offenburg	34.8	25.8	100	37.2	117	39.5	114
111	D	Pforzheim	34.8	25.8	100	37.2	117	39.5	114
113	F	Haute-Savoie	34.9	33.9	138	35.1	76	35.4	28
114	D	Aschaffenburg	34.9	25.7	97	37.2	119	39.6	119
115	F	Ardèche	35.0	34.3	139	35.2	77	35.4	28
116	F	Savoie	35.0	34.4	140	35.2	78	35.4	28

Table C.1. continued (3)

Rk		Region	EATR 20	EMTR	Rk	EATR 40	Rk	Eff. Profit Tax Rate	Rk
117	D	Bamberg	35.1	26.0	103	37.4	120	39.7	120
118	D	Heidelberg	35.1	26.0	104	37.4	121	39.7	120
119	F	Meurthe-et-Moselle	35.1	34.7	141	35.3	79	35.4	28
120	D	Ingolstadt	35.3	26.1	105	37.6	122	40.0	122
121	D	Landshut	35.3	26.2	106	37.6	123	40.0	122
122	D	Rosenheim	35.3	26.3	107	37.6	124	40.0	122
123	D	Freiburg	35.4	26.4	109	37.7	125	40.0	122
124	F	Territoire-de-Belfort	35.5	35.7	142	35.5	81	35.4	28
125	D	Karlsruhe	35.5	26.4	108	37.9	126	40.2	126
126	D	Mannheim	35.7	26.6	110	38.0	128	40.3	128
127	D	Berlin	35.7	27.0	115	37.9	127	40.2	126
128	F	Isère	35.7	36.2	143	35.6	82	35.4	28
129	D	Landau	35.8	26.6	111	38.1	129	40.5	129
130	D	Würzburg	35.8	26.7	112	38.1	130	40.5	129
131	D	Stuttgart	35.8	26.7	113	38.1	131	40.5	129
132	D	Regensburg	35.9	26.7	114	38.2	132	40.6	132
133	US	Boston	36.0	25.8	102	38.6	135	41.2	137
134	D	Mainz	36.2	27.1	116	38.6	133	40.9	133
134	D	Offenbach	36.2	27.1	116	38.6	133	40.9	133
136	D	Augsburg	36.3	27.2	118	38.7	136	41.1	135
137	D	Nürnberg	36.4	27.3	119	38.7	137	41.1	136
138	D	Köln	36.5	27.6	120	38.8	138	41.2	138
139	D	Düsseldorf	36.6	27.6	121	38.9	139	41.3	139
140	D	Hamburg	36.9	28.0	122	39.3	140	41.7	140
141	D	Essen	36.9	28.0	123	39.3	141	41.7	140
142	D	München	37.3	28.3	124	39.7	142	42.1	142
143	D	Frankfurt	37.3	28.4	125	39.7	143	42.1	142

Remarks:
EATR 20 EATR calculated at a pre-tax rate of return of 20 per cent
EATR 40 EATR calculated at a pre-tax rate of return of 40 per cent
[a] The Austrian EATR 20 is 26.1 per cent in case the incentives fully apply, the corresponding EMTR is 3.3 per cent.

Table C.2. Ranking of regions – EATR 2001 to 2003

Rk		Region	EATR '03	EATR '02	Rk	EATR '01	Rk
1	CH	Zug	13.8	13.8	2	13.8	2
2	IR	Dublin	14.0	12.1	1	12.0	1
3	CH	Nidwalden	15.4	15.5	3	15.5	3
4	CH	Schwyz	16.5	16.5	4	17.1	4
5	CH	Ticino	18.5	18.7	5	18.7	5
6	CH	Bern	18.6	18.8	6	18.8	6
7	CH	Valais	19.7	19.7	7	19.7	7
8	CH	St. Gallen	20.3	20.2	8	20.3	8
9	CH	Vaud	20.5	20.5	9	20.5	9
10	CH	Zürich	21.0	21.3	10	21.6	11
11	CH	Genève	21.4	21.4	11	21.4	10
12	CH	Basel-Stadt	22.1	22.1	12	22.1	12
13	CH	Basel-Landschaft	22.8	22.9	13	22.9	13
14	GB	London	28.1	28.1	14	28.0	14
15	NL	Amsterdam	30.2	30.2	15	30.6	57
16	NL	Utrecht	30.2	30.2	16	30.7	58
17	NL	Den Haag	30.3	30.3	17	30.7	59
18	NL	Rotterdam	30.3	30.3	18	30.7	60
19	A	Burgenland	30.4	30.4	19	30.4	48
19	A	Kärnten	30.4	30.4	19	30.4	48
19	A	Niederösterreich	30.4	30.4	19	30.4	48
19	A	Oberösterreich	30.4	30.4	19	30.4	48
19	A	Salzburg	30.4	30.4	19	30.4	48
19	A	Steiermark	30.4	30.4	19	30.4	48
19	A	Tirol	30.4	30.4	19	30.4	48
19	A	Vorarlberg	30.4	30.4	19	30.4	48
19	A	Wien	30.4	30.4	19	30.4	48
28	I	Valle d'Aosta	31.6	33.3	56	28.7	15
29	I	Milano	31.7	33.4	58	28.8	17
29	I	Udine	31.7	33.4	58	28.8	17
31	I	Pordenone	31.7	33.4	60	28.8	16
31	I	Verbano-Cusio-Ossola	31.7	33.4	60	28.8	21
33	I	Brescia	31.7	33.4	64	28.8	26
33	I	Sondrio	31.7	33.4	64	28.8	26
35	I	Bergamo	31.7	33.4	66	28.8	29
35	I	Varese	31.7	33.4	66	28.8	29
37	I	Bolzano	31.7	33.4	69	28.8	32
37	I	Gorizia	31.7	33.4	69	28.8	32
37	I	Trento	31.7	33.4	69	28.8	17
37	I	Vercelli	31.7	33.4	69	28.8	17
37	I	Vicenza	31.7	33.4	69	28.8	32
42	I	Padova	31.7	33.4	74	28.8	21

Table C.2. continued (1)

Rk		Region	EATR '03	EATR '02	Rk	EATR '01	Rk
43	I	Biella	31.7	33.4	75	28.9	37
44	I	Cremona	31.8	33.4	76	28.8	25
44	I	Cuneo	31.8	33.4	76	28.9	38
44	I	Lodi	31.8	33.4	76	28.9	38
44	I	Pavia	31.8	33.4	76	28.9	38
44	I	Torino	31.8	33.4	76	28.8	32
44	I	Treviso	31.8	33.4	76	28.9	38
50	I	Como	31.8	33.4	63	28.8	24
51	I	Novara	31.8	33.4	84	28.8	26
51	I	Verona	31.8	33.4	60	28.8	21
53	I	Lecco	31.8	33.4	66	28.8	29
54	I	Alessandria	31.8	33.5	86	28.9	38
54	I	Asti	31.8	33.4	76	28.9	38
54	I	Belluno	31.8	33.5	86	28.9	44
54	I	Mantova	31.8	33.5	86	28.9	44
54	I	Rovigo	31.8	33.5	86	28.9	44
54	I	Trieste	31.8	33.5	86	28.8	32
54	I	Venezia	31.8	33.5	86	28.9	44
61	F	Paris	32.1	32.1	30	32.9	75
62	D	Weilheim	32.9	31.7	28	31.7	61
63	D	Coburg	32.9	33.2	52	33.2	85
64	D	Walldorf b. Heidelberg	33.1	31.9	29	31.9	62
65	D	Landkreis Mannheim	33.6	32.4	31	32.1	63
66	D	Tauberbischofsheim	33.6	32.4	32	32.4	66
67	D	Memmingen	33.6	32.5	33	32.5	67
67	D	Pfarrkirchen	33.6	32.5	33	32.5	67
69	D	Ravensburg	33.6	32.5	35	32.5	69
70	D	Rottweil	33.8	32.6	36	32.6	70
71	D	Kempten	33.8	32.6	37	32.6	71
72	D	Balingen	33.9	32.7	38	32.7	72
73	D	Weißenburg i. Bayern	33.9	32.7	39	32.8	73
74	F	Moselle	34.1	34.1	105	34.9	116
75	D	Waiblingen	34.1	32.9	41	32.9	76
76	D	Weiden	34.1	32.9	42	33.4	89
77	D	Schwandorf	34.1	32.9	40	32.9	74
78	D	Reutlingen	34.1	32.9	44	32.9	78
79	D	Aalen	34.1	32.9	43	32.9	77
80	D	Deggendorf	34.1	33.0	45	32.2	64
81	D	Donauwörth	34.1	33.0	46	33.0	80
82	D	Nagold	34.1	33.0	47	33.0	81
82	D	Vill.-Schwenningen	34.1	33.0	47	33.0	81
84	F	Ain	34.2	34.1	107	35.0	121

Table C.2. continued (2)

Rk		Region	EATR '03	EATR '02	Rk	EATR '01	Rk
85	F	Jura	34.2	34.1	106	34.9	118
86	D	Göppingen	34.2	33.1	49	33.1	83
87	F	Haute-Saône	34.2	34.2	108	34.9	119
88	F	Drôme	34.3	34.2	112	35.0	122
89	D	Ludwigsburg	34.3	33.2	50	33.5	93
90	D	Konstanz	34.3	33.2	51	33.2	84
91	D	Ansbach	34.3	33.2	52	33.2	85
91	D	Lörrach	34.3	33.2	52	32.3	65
93	D	Ludwigshafen	34.4	33.9	102	33.9	102
94	D	Ulm	34.4	33.2	55	33.2	87
95	F	Meuse	34.4	33.8	101	34.6	110
96	F	Haut-Rhin	34.4	34.3	115	35.1	125
97	F	Rhône	34.5	34.2	109	34.9	120
98	D	Traunstein	34.5	33.3	57	33.3	88
99	F	Doubs	34.5	34.4	117	35.2	127
100	D	Rastatt	34.6	33.4	83	33.0	79
101	F	Bas-Rhin	34.6	34.5	118	35.3	129
102	D	Passau	34.6	33.4	85	33.4	90
103	D	Bayreuth	34.6	33.5	92	33.5	91
104	D	Schweinfurt	34.6	33.5	93	33.5	92
105	D	Schwäbisch-Hall	34.7	33.6	94	33.6	94
106	F	Vosges	34.8	34.7	125	35.5	131
107	F	Loire	34.8	34.7	126	35.5	132
108	D	Freising	34.8	33.7	95	33.7	95
109	D	Heilbronn	34.8	33.7	96	33.7	97
110	D	Hof	34.8	33.7	97	33.7	98
111	D	Offenburg	34.8	33.7	98	33.7	99
111	D	Pforzheim	34.8	33.7	98	33.7	99
113	F	Haute-Savoie	34.9	34.7	124	35.2	126
114	D	Aschaffenburg	34.9	33.8	100	33.8	101
115	F	Ardèche	35.0	34.9	129	35.7	134
116	F	Savoie	35.0	34.9	128	35.7	135
117	D	Bamberg	35.1	33.9	103	33.7	96
118	D	Heidelberg	35.1	34.0	104	34.0	103
119	F	Meurthe-et-Moselle	35.1	35.2	132	36.1	138
120	D	Ingolstadt	35.3	34.2	110	34.2	104
121	D	Landshut	35.3	34.2	111	34.2	104
122	D	Rosenheim	35.3	34.2	113	34.2	106
123	D	Freiburg	35.4	34.2	114	34.2	107
124	F	Territoire-de-Belfort	35.5	35.4	136	36.3	141
125	D	Karlsruhe	35.5	34.4	116	34.4	108
126	D	Mannheim	35.7	34.5	120	34.9	117

Table C.2. continued (3)

Rk		Region	EATR '03	EATR '02	Rk	EATR '01	Rk
127	D	Berlin	35.7	34.5	119	34.5	109
128	F	Isère	35.7	35.8	138	36.6	143
129	D	Landau	35.8	34.6	121	34.6	111
130	D	Würzburg	35.8	34.6	122	34.6	112
131	D	Stuttgart	35.8	34.7	123	34.7	114
132	D	Regensburg	35.9	34.8	127	34.8	115
133	US	Boston	36.0	36.0	141	36.2	139
134	D	Mainz	36.2	35.1	130	35.1	123
134	D	Offenbach	36.2	35.1	130	35.1	123
136	D	Augsburg	36.3	35.2	133	34.6	112
137	D	Nürnberg	36.4	35.3	134	35.3	128
138	D	Köln	36.5	35.4	135	35.4	130
139	D	Düsseldorf	36.6	35.5	137	35.6	133
140	D	Hamburg	36.9	35.8	139	35.8	136
141	D	Essen	36.9	35.8	139	35.8	136
142	D	München	37.3	36.2	142	36.2	140
143	D	Frankfurt	37.3	36.3	143	36.5	142

Table C.3. Ranking of regions – EATR 2003 under different weights and interest rate

Rk		Region	EATR 20	Study '01	Rk	Service Sector	Rk	Real interest rate 10 %	Rk
1	CH	Zug	13.8	14.7	1	13.7	1	11.3	1
2	IR	Dublin	14.0	16.4	3	18.1	4	12.4	2
3	CH	Nidwalden	15.4	16.4	2	15.2	2	12.7	3
4	CH	Schwyz	16.5	17.5	4	16.2	3	13.6	4
5	CH	Ticino	18.5	19.6	5	18.1	5	15.3	6
6	CH	Bern	18.6	19.7	6	18.3	6	15.2	5
7	CH	Valais	19.7	20.8	7	19.1	7	16.4	8
8	CH	St. Gallen	20.3	21.6	8	20.5	9	16.4	7
9	CH	Vaud	20.5	21.7	9	20.1	8	16.9	9
10	CH	Zürich	21.0	22.4	10	20.7	10	17.4	10
11	CH	Genève	21.4	22.7	11	20.9	11	17.7	11
12	CH	Basel-Stadt	22.1	23.4	12	21.6	12	18.3	12
13	CH	Basel-Landschaft	22.8	24.2	13	22.3	13	19.0	13
14	GB	London	28.1	29.0	14	26.6	14	24.2	14
15	NL	Amsterdam	30.2	31.5	24	29.5	24	25.8	15
16	NL	Utrecht	30.2	31.6	25	29.5	25	25.9	16
17	NL	Den Haag	30.3	31.6	26	29.5	26	25.9	17
18	NL	Rotterdam	30.3	31.6	27	29.6	27	26.0	18
19	A	Burgenland	30.4	31.0	15	29.1	15	26.7	52
19	A	Kärnten	30.4	31.0	15	29.1	15	26.7	52
19	A	Niederösterreich	30.4	31.0	15	29.1	15	26.7	52
19	A	Oberösterreich	30.4	31.0	15	29.1	15	26.7	52
19	A	Salzburg	30.4	31.0	15	29.1	15	26.7	52
19	A	Steiermark	30.4	31.0	15	29.1	15	26.7	52
19	A	Tirol	30.4	31.0	15	29.1	15	26.7	52
19	A	Vorarlberg	30.4	31.0	15	29.1	15	26.7	52
19	A	Wien	30.4	31.0	15	29.1	15	26.7	52
28	I	Valle d'Aosta	31.6	32.9	28	29.9	28	26.2	19
29	I	Milano	31.7	33.0	29	29.9	29	26.3	20
29	I	Udine	31.7	33.0	29	29.9	29	26.3	20
31	I	Pordenone	31.7	33.0	31	30.0	31	26.3	22
31	I	Verbano-Cusio-Ossola	31.7	33.0	31	30.0	31	26.3	22
33	I	Brescia	31.7	33.0	33	30.0	33	26.3	24
33	I	Sondrio	31.7	33.0	33	30.0	33	26.3	24
35	I	Bergamo	31.7	33.0	35	30.0	35	26.3	26
35	I	Varese	31.7	33.0	35	30.0	35	26.3	26
37	I	Bolzano	31.7	33.0	37	30.0	37	26.3	28
37	I	Gorizia	31.7	33.0	37	30.0	37	26.3	28
37	I	Trento	31.7	33.0	37	30.0	37	26.3	28
37	I	Vercelli	31.7	33.0	37	30.0	37	26.3	28
37	I	Vicenza	31.7	33.0	37	30.0	37	26.3	28
42	I	Padova	31.7	33.0	42	30.0	42	26.3	33

Table C.3. continued (1)

Rk		Region	EATR 20	Study '01	Rk	Service Sector	Rk	Real interest rate 10 %	Rk
43	I	Biella	31.7	33.0	43	30.0	43	26.3	34
44	I	Cremona	31.8	33.0	44	30.0	44	26.3	35
44	I	Cuneo	31.8	33.0	44	30.0	44	26.3	35
44	I	Lodi	31.8	33.0	44	30.0	44	26.3	35
44	I	Pavia	31.8	33.0	44	30.0	44	26.3	35
44	I	Torino	31.8	33.0	44	30.0	44	26.3	35
44	I	Treviso	31.8	33.0	44	30.0	44	26.3	35
50	I	Como	31.8	33.0	50	30.0	50	26.3	41
51	I	Novara	31.8	33.0	51	30.0	51	26.3	42
51	I	Verona	31.8	33.0	51	30.0	51	26.3	42
53	I	Lecco	31.8	33.0	53	30.0	53	26.4	44
54	I	Alessandria	31.8	33.0	54	30.0	54	26.4	45
54	I	Asti	31.8	33.0	54	30.0	54	26.4	45
54	I	Belluno	31.8	33.0	54	30.0	54	26.4	45
54	I	Mantova	31.8	33.0	54	30.0	54	26.4	45
54	I	Rovigo	31.8	33.0	54	30.0	54	26.4	45
54	I	Trieste	31.8	33.0	54	30.0	54	26.4	45
54	I	Venezia	31.8	33.0	54	30.0	54	26.4	45
61	F	Paris	32.1	33.6	61	30.9	61	27.0	61
62	D	Weilheim	32.9	34.4	62	32.7	77	28.4	62
63	D	Coburg	32.9	34.4	63	32.7	78	28.4	63
64	D	Walldorf b. Heidelberg	33.1	34.7	64	32.9	80	28.5	64
65	D	Landkreis Mannheim	33.6	35.2	69	33.4	83	29.0	65
66	D	Tauberbischofsheim	33.6	35.2	70	33.4	84	29.0	66
67	D	Memmingen	33.6	35.2	72	33.4	85	29.1	67
67	D	Pfarrkirchen	33.6	35.2	72	33.4	85	29.1	67
69	D	Ravensburg	33.6	35.2	74	33.5	87	29.1	69
70	D	Rottweil	33.8	35.4	77	33.6	88	29.2	72
71	D	Kempten	33.8	35.4	80	33.6	89	29.2	73
72	D	Balingen	33.9	35.5	81	33.7	90	29.3	76
73	D	Weißenburg i. Bayern	33.9	35.5	82	33.7	91	29.3	77
74	F	Moselle	34.1	35.1	65	32.1	62	29.1	70
75	D	Waiblingen	34.1	35.7	87	33.9	92	29.5	81
76	D	Weiden	34.1	35.7	88	33.9	93	29.5	82
77	D	Schwandorf	34.1	35.7	89	33.9	94	29.5	83
78	D	Reutlingen	34.1	35.7	90	33.9	95	29.5	84
79	D	Aalen	34.1	35.7	91	33.9	96	29.5	86
80	D	Deggendorf	34.1	35.7	92	33.9	97	29.5	87
81	D	Donauwörth	34.1	35.7	93	33.9	98	29.5	88
82	D	Nagold	34.1	35.7	94	33.9	99	29.5	89
82	D	Vill.-Schwenningen	34.1	35.7	94	33.9	99	29.5	89
84	F	Ain	34.2	35.1	68	32.2	63	29.2	71

Table C.3. continued (2)

Rk		Region	EATR 20	Study '01	Rk	Service Sector	Rk	Real interest rate 10 %	Rk
85	F	Jura	34.2	35.1	66	32.2	64	29.2	74
86	D	Göppingen	34.2	35.8	98	34.1	101	29.6	92
87	F	Haute-Saône	34.2	35.1	67	32.2	65	29.3	75
88	F	Drôme	34.3	35.2	71	32.2	66	29.3	78
89	D	Ludwigsburg	34.3	35.9	100	34.2	102	29.7	94
90	D	Konstanz	34.3	36.0	101	34.2	103	29.7	95
91	D	Ansbach	34.3	36.0	102	34.2	104	29.7	96
91	D	Lörrach	34.3	36.0	102	34.2	104	29.7	96
93	D	Ludwigshafen	34.4	36.0	104	34.2	106	29.7	98
94	D	Ulm	34.4	36.0	105	34.2	107	29.7	99
95	F	Meuse	34.4	35.2	75	32.3	67	29.4	79
96	F	Haut-Rhin	34.4	35.3	76	32.3	68	29.4	80
97	F	Rhône	34.5	35.4	79	32.3	69	29.5	85
98	D	Traunstein	34.5	36.1	106	34.3	108	29.8	102
99	F	Doubs	34.5	35.4	78	32.3	70	29.5	91
100	D	Rastatt	34.6	36.2	108	34.4	109	29.9	104
101	F	Bas-Rhin	34.6	35.5	83	32.4	71	29.6	93
102	D	Passau	34.6	36.2	109	34.4	110	29.9	105
103	D	Bayreuth	34.6	36.2	110	34.4	111	29.9	106
104	D	Schweinfurt	34.6	36.2	111	34.5	112	30.0	107
105	D	Schwäbisch-Hall	34.7	36.3	113	34.6	113	30.0	108
106	F	Vosges	34.8	35.6	84	32.5	72	29.8	100
107	F	Loire	34.8	35.6	85	32.5	73	29.8	101
108	D	Freising	34.8	36.4	114	34.7	114	30.1	111
109	D	Heilbronn	34.8	36.5	115	34.7	115	30.2	112
110	D	Hof	34.8	36.5	116	34.7	116	30.2	113
111	D	Offenburg	34.8	36.5	117	34.7	117	30.2	114
111	D	Pforzheim	34.8	36.5	117	34.7	117	30.2	114
113	F	Haute-Savoie	34.9	35.7	86	32.6	74	29.9	103
114	D	Aschaffenburg	34.9	36.6	119	34.8	119	30.2	117
115	F	Ardèche	35.0	35.8	96	32.6	75	30.0	109
116	F	Savoie	35.0	35.8	97	32.7	76	30.1	110
117	D	Bamberg	35.1	36.7	120	34.9	120	30.4	118
118	D	Heidelberg	35.1	36.7	121	34.9	121	30.4	119
119	F	Meurthe-et-Moselle	35.1	35.9	99	32.7	79	30.2	116
120	D	Ingolstadt	35.3	37.0	123	35.2	122	30.6	120
121	D	Landshut	35.3	37.0	124	35.2	123	30.6	121
122	D	Rosenheim	35.3	37.0	125	35.2	124	30.6	123
123	D	Freiburg	35.4	37.0	126	35.2	125	30.7	124
124	F	Territoire-de-Belfort	35.5	36.2	107	33.0	81	30.6	122
125	D	Karlsruhe	35.5	37.2	127	35.4	126	30.8	126
126	D	Mannheim	35.7	37.3	129	35.5	128	30.9	128

Table C.3. continued (3)

Rk		Region	EATR 20	Study '01	Rk	Service Sector	Rk	Real interest rate 10 %	Rk
127	D	Berlin	35.7	37.3	128	35.5	127	30.9	129
128	F	Isère	35.7	36.3	112	33.1	82	30.8	127
129	D	Landau	35.8	37.4	130	35.6	129	31.0	130
130	D	Würzburg	35.8	37.4	131	35.6	130	31.0	131
131	D	Stuttgart	35.8	37.5	132	35.7	131	31.0	132
132	D	Regensburg	35.9	37.6	133	35.7	132	31.1	133
133	US	Boston	36.0	36.9	122	37.1	141	30.7	125
134	D	Mainz	36.2	37.9	134	36.1	133	31.4	134
134	D	Offenbach	36.2	37.9	134	36.1	133	31.4	134
136	D	Augsburg	36.3	38.0	136	36.2	135	31.5	136
137	D	Nürnberg	36.4	38.1	137	36.3	136	31.6	137
138	D	Köln	36.5	38.2	138	36.4	137	31.7	138
139	D	Düsseldorf	36.6	38.3	139	36.5	138	31.8	139
140	D	Hamburg	36.9	38.6	140	36.8	139	32.1	140
141	D	Essen	36.9	38.6	141	36.8	140	32.1	141
142	D	München	37.3	39.1	142	37.2	142	32.4	142
143	D	Frankfurt	37.3	39.1	143	37.2	143	32.4	143

Remarks:

EATR 20 EATR calculated at a pre-tax rate of return of 20 per cent
Study '01 Application of weights used by Gutekunst and Schwager (2002)
Service Sector Application of service sector weights

C.2 Ranking Figures

Fig. C.1. International variation of EATRs, 2001

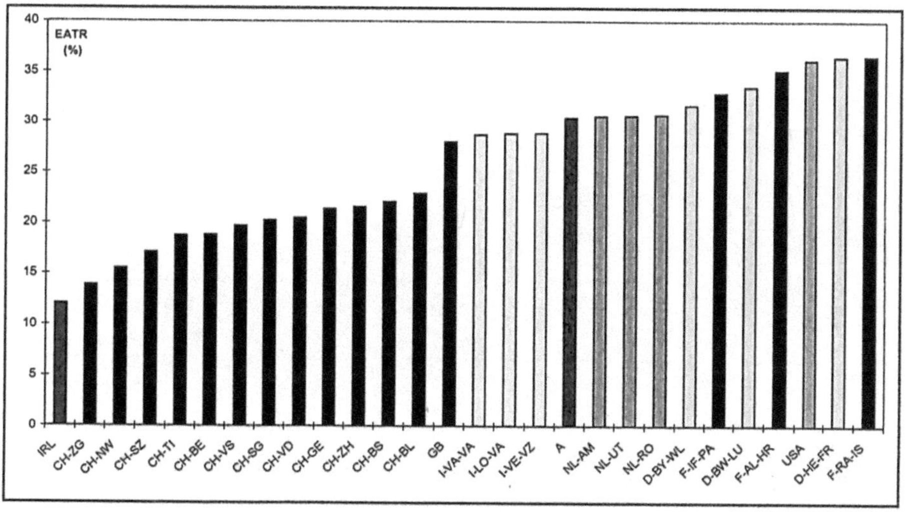

Fig. C.2. International variation of EMTRs, 2001

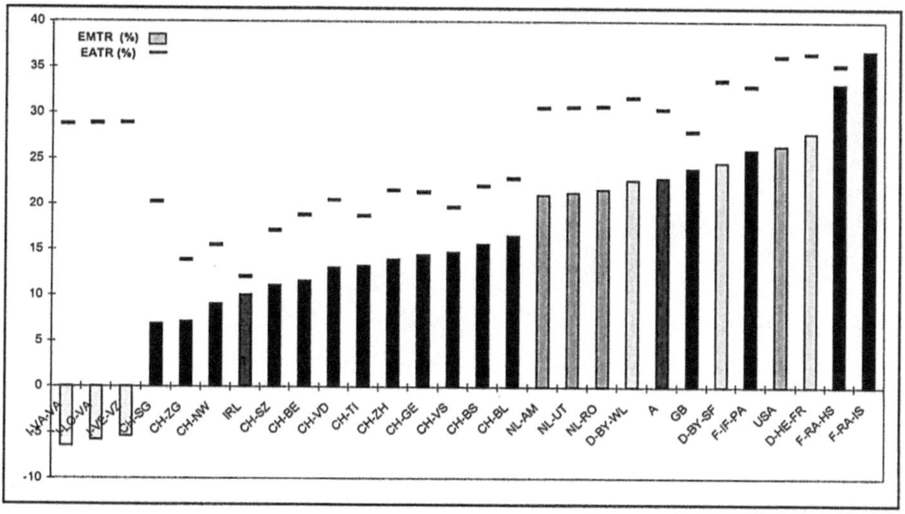

Fig. C.3. International variation of EATRs, 2002

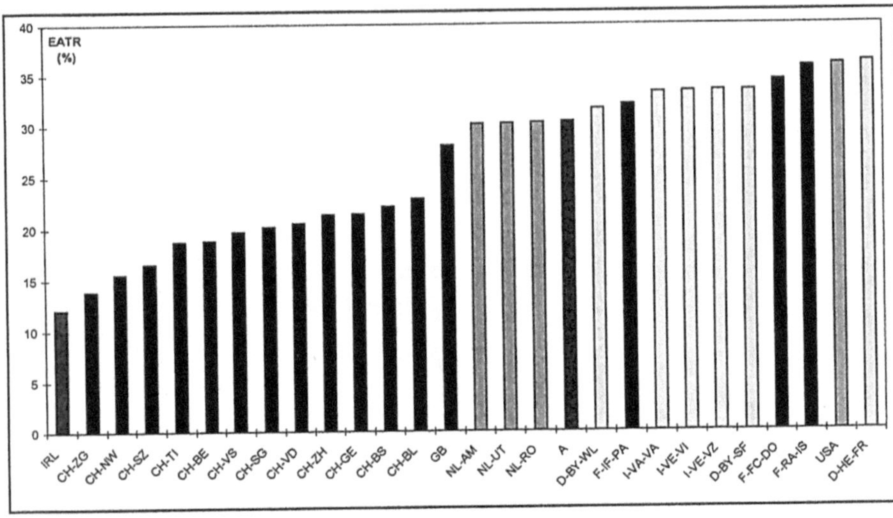

Fig. C.4. International variation of EMTRs, 2002

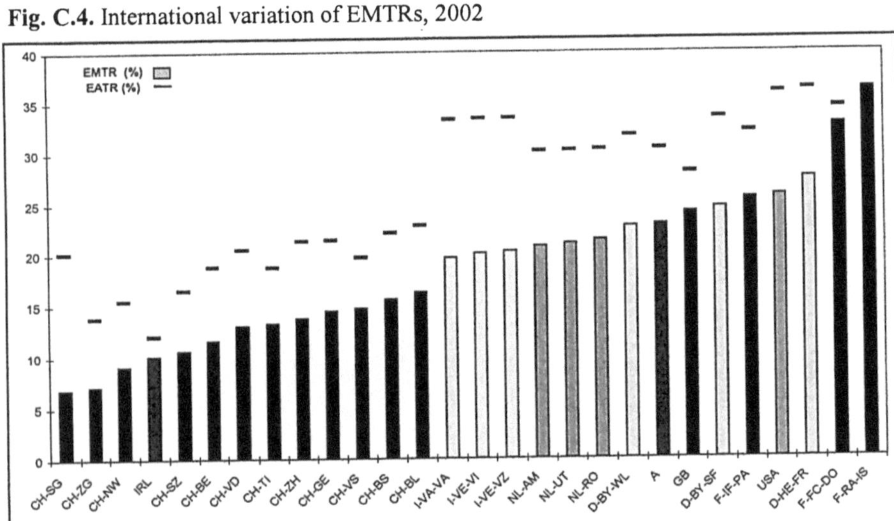

App. D Detailed Results

D.1 Time Series 2001–2003

D.1.1 Austria

Standard Case	Overall	Assets					Sources of finance		
		Intangibles	Industrial buildings	Machinery	Financial assets	Inventories	Retained earnings	New equity	Debt
Burgenland									
Cost of capital 2001	6.5	6.4	6.5	5.9	7.3	6.3	7.7	7.7	4.2
2002	6.5	6.4	6.5	5.9	7.3	6.3	7.7	7.7	4.2
2003	6.5	6.4	6.5	5.9	7.3	6.3	7.7	7.7	4.2
EMTR 2001	22.9	22.1	23.0	14.9	31.8	20.9	35.2	35.2	-19.1
2002	22.9	22.1	23.0	14.9	31.8	20.9	35.2	35.2	-19.1
2003	22.9	22.1	23.0	14.9	31.8	20.9	35.2	35.2	-19.1
EATR 2001	30.4	30.2	30.4	28.4	33.2	29.9	34.5	34.5	22.9
2002	30.4	30.2	30.4	28.4	33.2	29.9	34.5	34.5	22.9
2003	30.4	30.2	30.4	28.4	33.2	29.9	34.5	34.5	22.9
Kärnten									
Cost of capital 2001	6.5	6.4	6.5	5.9	7.3	6.3	7.7	7.7	4.2
2002	6.5	6.4	6.5	5.9	7.3	6.3	7.7	7.7	4.2
2003	6.5	6.4	6.5	5.9	7.3	6.3	7.7	7.7	4.2
EMTR 2001	22.9	22.1	23.0	14.9	31.8	20.9	35.2	35.2	-19.1
2002	22.9	22.1	23.0	14.9	31.8	20.9	35.2	35.2	-19.1
2003	22.9	22.1	23.0	14.9	31.8	20.9	35.2	35.2	-19.1
EATR 2001	30.4	30.2	30.4	28.4	33.2	29.9	34.5	34.5	22.9
2002	30.4	30.2	30.4	28.4	33.2	29.9	34.5	34.5	22.9
2003	30.4	30.2	30.4	28.4	33.2	29.9	34.5	34.5	22.9
Niederösterreich									
Cost of capital 2001	6.5	6.4	6.5	5.9	7.3	6.3	7.7	7.7	4.2
2002	6.5	6.4	6.5	5.9	7.3	6.3	7.7	7.7	4.2
2003	6.5	6.4	6.5	5.9	7.3	6.3	7.7	7.7	4.2
EMTR 2001	22.9	22.1	23.0	14.9	31.8	20.9	35.2	35.2	-19.1
2002	22.9	22.1	23.0	14.9	31.8	20.9	35.2	35.2	-19.1
2003	22.9	22.1	23.0	14.9	31.8	20.9	35.2	35.2	-19.1
EATR 2001	30.4	30.2	30.4	28.4	33.2	29.9	34.5	34.5	22.9
2002	30.4	30.2	30.4	28.4	33.2	29.9	34.5	34.5	22.9
2003	30.4	30.2	30.4	28.4	33.2	29.9	34.5	34.5	22.9

Standard Case	Overall	Assets: Intangibles	Industrial buildings	Machinery	Financial assets	Inventories	Sources of finance: Retained earnings	New equity	Debt
Oberösterreich									
Cost of capital 2001	6.5	6.4	6.5	5.9	7.3	6.3	7.7	7.7	4.2
2002	6.5	6.4	6.5	5.9	7.3	6.3	7.7	7.7	4.2
2003	6.5	6.4	6.5	5.9	7.3	6.3	7.7	7.7	4.2
EMTR 2001	22.9	22.1	23.0	14.9	31.8	20.9	35.2	35.2	-19.1
2002	22.9	22.1	23.0	14.9	31.8	20.9	35.2	35.2	-19.1
2003	22.9	22.1	23.0	14.9	31.8	20.9	35.2	35.2	-19.1
EATR 2001	30.4	30.2	30.4	28.4	33.2	29.9	34.5	34.5	22.9
2002	30.4	30.2	30.4	28.4	33.2	29.9	34.5	34.5	22.9
2003	30.4	30.2	30.4	28.4	33.2	29.9	34.5	34.5	22.9
Salzburg									
Cost of capital 2001	6.5	6.4	6.5	5.9	7.3	6.3	7.7	7.7	4.2
2002	6.5	6.4	6.5	5.9	7.3	6.3	7.7	7.7	4.2
2003	6.5	6.4	6.5	5.9	7.3	6.3	7.7	7.7	4.2
EMTR 2001	22.9	22.1	23.0	14.9	31.8	20.9	35.2	35.2	-19.1
2002	22.9	22.1	23.0	14.9	31.8	20.9	35.2	35.2	-19.1
2003	22.9	22.1	23.0	14.9	31.8	20.9	35.2	35.2	-19.1
EATR 2001	30.4	30.2	30.4	28.4	33.2	29.9	34.5	34.5	22.9
2002	30.4	30.2	30.4	28.4	33.2	29.9	34.5	34.5	22.9
2003	30.4	30.2	30.4	28.4	33.2	29.9	34.5	34.5	22.9
Steiermark									
Cost of capital 2001	6.5	6.4	6.5	5.9	7.3	6.3	7.7	7.7	4.2
2002	6.5	6.4	6.5	5.9	7.3	6.3	7.7	7.7	4.2
2003	6.5	6.4	6.5	5.9	7.3	6.3	7.7	7.7	4.2
EMTR 2001	22.9	22.1	23.0	14.9	31.8	20.9	35.2	35.2	-19.1
2002	22.9	22.1	23.0	14.9	31.8	20.9	35.2	35.2	-19.1
2003	22.9	22.1	23.0	14.9	31.8	20.9	35.2	35.2	-19.1
EATR 2001	30.4	30.2	30.4	28.4	33.2	29.9	34.5	34.5	22.9
2002	30.4	30.2	30.4	28.4	33.2	29.9	34.5	34.5	22.9
2003	30.4	30.2	30.4	28.4	33.2	29.9	34.5	34.5	22.9

Standard Case	Overall	Assets					Sources of finance		
		Intangibles	Industrial buildings	Machinery	Financial assets	Inventories	Retained earnings	New equity	Debt
Tirol									
Cost of capital 2001	6.5	6.4	6.5	5.9	7.3	6.3	7.7	7.7	4.2
2002	6.5	6.4	6.5	5.9	7.3	6.3	7.7	7.7	4.2
2003	6.5	6.4	6.5	5.9	7.3	6.3	7.7	7.7	4.2
EMTR 2001	22.9	22.1	23.0	14.9	31.8	20.9	35.2	35.2	-19.1
2002	22.9	22.1	23.0	14.9	31.8	20.9	35.2	35.2	-19.1
2003	22.9	22.1	23.0	14.9	31.8	20.9	35.2	35.2	-19.1
EATR 2001	30.4	30.2	30.4	28.4	33.2	29.9	34.5	34.5	22.9
2002	30.4	30.2	30.4	28.4	33.2	29.9	34.5	34.5	22.9
2003	30.4	30.2	30.4	28.4	33.2	29.9	34.5	34.5	22.9
Vorarlberg									
Cost of capital 2001	6.5	6.4	6.5	5.9	7.3	6.3	7.7	7.7	4.2
2002	6.5	6.4	6.5	5.9	7.3	6.3	7.7	7.7	4.2
2003	6.5	6.4	6.5	5.9	7.3	6.3	7.7	7.7	4.2
EMTR 2001	22.9	22.1	23.0	14.9	31.8	20.9	35.2	35.2	-19.1
2002	22.9	22.1	23.0	14.9	31.8	20.9	35.2	35.2	-19.1
2003	22.9	22.1	23.0	14.9	31.8	20.9	35.2	35.2	-19.1
EATR 2001	30.4	30.2	30.4	28.4	33.2	29.9	34.5	34.5	22.9
2002	30.4	30.2	30.4	28.4	33.2	29.9	34.5	34.5	22.9
2003	30.4	30.2	30.4	28.4	33.2	29.9	34.5	34.5	22.9
Wien									
Cost of capital 2001	6.5	6.4	6.5	5.9	7.3	6.3	7.7	7.7	4.2
2002	6.5	6.4	6.5	5.9	7.3	6.3	7.7	7.7	4.2
2003	6.5	6.4	6.5	5.9	7.3	6.3	7.7	7.7	4.2
EMTR 2001	22.9	22.1	23.0	14.9	31.8	20.9	35.2	35.2	-19.1
2002	22.9	22.1	23.0	14.9	31.8	20.9	35.2	35.2	-19.1
2003	22.9	22.1	23.0	14.9	31.8	20.9	35.2	35.2	-19.1
EATR 2001	30.4	30.2	30.4	28.4	33.2	29.9	34.5	34.5	22.9
2002	30.4	30.2	30.4	28.4	33.2	29.9	34.5	34.5	22.9
2003	30.4	30.2	30.4	28.4	33.2	29.9	34.5	34.5	22.9

Incentives Case (all locations)	Overall	Assets					Sources of finance		
		Intangibles	Industrial buildings	Machinery	Financial assets	Inventories	Retained earnings	New equity	Debt
Dual income tax only (2001–2003)									
Cost of capital	5.8	5.8	5.8	5.2	6.6	5.6	6.7	6.7	4.2
EMTR	14.0	13.2	14.0	4.2	24.7	11.3	25.2	25.2	-19.1
EATR	28.2	28.0	28.2	26.2	30.9	27.6	31.1	31.1	22.9
Incremental investment tax credit only (2002–2003)									
Cost of capital	5.8	6.4	6.5	2.6	7.3	6.3	7.0	7.0	3.6
EMTR	14.3	22.1	23.0	-93.1	31.8	20.9	29.0	29.0	-39.3
EATR	28.2	30.2	30.4	17.5	33.2	29.9	32.2	32.2	20.8
Both measures (2002–2003)									
Cost of capital	5.2	5.8	5.8	2.0	6.6	5.6	6.0	6.0	3.6
EMTR	3.3	13.2	14.0	-149.4	24.7	11.3	17.0	17.0	-39.3
EATR	26.1	28.0	28.2	15.6	30.9	27.6	28.9	28.9	20.8

D.1.2 France

	Overall	Assets					Sources of finance		
		Intangibles	Industrial buildings	Machinery	Financial assets	Inventories	Retained earnings	New equity	Debt
Bas-Rhin									
Cost of capital 2001	7.5	5.2	8.7	9.1	7.6	7.0	8.9	8.9	5.0
2002	7.5	5.1	8.6	9.1	7.5	6.9	8.8	8.8	5.1
2003	7.5	5.1	8.7	9.2	7.5	6.9	8.8	8.8	5.1
EMTR 2001	33.4	3.0	42.3	45.1	34.2	28.9	43.6	43.6	0.1
2002	33.0	2.8	42.1	45.1	33.2	28.0	42.9	42.9	1.2
2003	33.2	2.8	42.4	45.4	33.2	28.0	43.0	43.0	1.5
EATR 2001	35.3	27.8	39.0	40.4	35.6	33.8	39.6	39.6	27.3
2002	34.5	27.0	38.3	39.9	34.6	32.9	38.7	38.7	26.8
2003	34.6	27.0	38.4	40.0	34.6	32.9	38.8	38.8	26.8
Haut-Rhin									
Cost of capital 2001	7.5	5.2	8.6	8.9	7.6	7.0	8.8	8.8	4.9
2002	7.4	5.1	8.6	8.8	7.5	6.9	8.7	8.7	5.0
2003	7.4	5.1	8.7	8.9	7.5	6.9	8.7	8.7	5.0
EMTR 2001	32.9	3.0	42.1	43.5	34.2	28.9	43.2	43.2	-1.0
2002	32.5	2.8	42.0	43.5	33.2	28.0	42.5	42.5	0.1
2003	32.7	2.8	42.3	43.8	33.2	28.0	42.7	42.7	0.5
EATR 2001	35.1	27.8	38.9	39.6	35.6	33.8	39.4	39.4	27.2
2002	34.3	27.0	38.3	39.0	34.6	32.9	38.5	38.5	26.6
2003	34.4	27.0	38.4	39.2	34.6	32.9	38.6	38.6	26.6
Doubs									
Cost of capital 2001	7.5	5.2	8.9	8.8	7.6	7.0	8.8	8.8	5.0
2002	7.4	5.1	8.8	8.8	7.5	6.9	8.7	8.7	5.0
2003	7.5	5.1	8.9	8.8	7.5	6.9	8.7	8.7	5.0
EMTR 2001	33.3	3.0	43.6	43.2	34.2	28.9	43.4	43.4	-0.3
2002	32.8	2.8	43.4	43.1	33.2	28.0	42.7	42.7	0.7
2003	32.9	2.8	43.7	43.2	33.2	28.0	42.8	42.8	0.9
EATR 2001	35.2	27.8	39.6	39.4	35.6	33.8	39.5	39.5	27.3
2002	34.4	27.0	39.0	38.8	34.6	32.9	38.6	38.6	26.7
2003	34.5	27.0	39.1	38.9	34.6	32.9	38.7	38.7	26.7

	Overall	Assets					Sources of finance		
		Intangibles	Industrial buildings	Machinery	Financial assets	Inventories	Retained earnings	New equity	Debt
Jura									
Cost of capital 2001	7.4	5.2	8.9	8.2	7.6	7.0	8.7	8.7	4.9
2002	7.3	5.1	8.9	8.2	7.5	6.9	8.6	8.6	4.9
2003	7.4	5.1	9.0	8.3	7.5	6.9	8.7	8.7	5.0
EMTR 2001	32.3	3.0	43.9	39.3	34.2	28.9	42.8	42.8	-2.4
2002	31.8	2.8	43.6	39.2	33.2	28.0	42.0	42.0	-1.4
2003	32.1	2.8	44.3	39.7	33.2	28.0	42.3	42.3	-0.7
EATR 2001	34.9	27.8	39.8	37.6	35.6	33.8	39.2	39.2	26.9
2002	34.1	27.0	39.1	37.0	34.6	32.9	38.3	38.3	26.3
2003	34.2	27.0	39.4	37.2	34.6	32.9	38.4	38.4	26.5
Haute-Saône									
Cost of capital 2001	7.4	5.2	8.9	8.3	7.6	7.0	8.7	8.7	4.9
2002	7.3	5.1	8.9	8.3	7.5	6.9	8.6	8.6	4.9
2003	7.4	5.1	9.0	8.3	7.5	6.9	8.7	8.7	5.0
EMTR 2001	32.3	3.0	43.8	39.5	34.2	28.9	42.8	42.8	-2.4
2002	31.9	2.8	43.8	39.6	33.2	28.0	42.1	42.1	-1.1
2003	32.2	2.8	44.2	40.1	33.2	28.0	42.3	42.3	-0.6
EATR 2001	34.9	27.8	39.7	37.7	35.6	33.8	39.2	39.2	27.0
2002	34.2	27.0	39.1	37.1	34.6	32.9	38.3	38.3	26.4
2003	34.2	27.0	39.4	37.4	34.6	32.9	38.4	38.4	26.5
Territoire-de-Belfort									
Cost of capital 2001	7.8	5.2	9.3	10.0	7.6	7.0	9.2	9.2	5.3
2002	7.7	5.1	9.2	9.9	7.5	6.9	9.0	9.0	5.3
2003	7.8	5.1	9.3	10.0	7.5	6.9	9.1	9.1	5.4
EMTR 2001	36.0	3.0	46.0	50.2	34.2	28.9	45.5	45.5	5.7
2002	35.4	2.8	45.7	49.7	33.2	28.0	44.7	44.7	6.3
2003	35.7	2.8	46.0	50.1	33.2	28.0	44.9	44.9	6.7
EATR 2001	36.3	27.8	40.9	43.3	35.6	33.8	40.6	40.6	28.3
2002	35.4	27.0	40.2	42.5	34.6	32.9	39.6	39.6	27.7
2003	35.5	27.0	40.3	42.8	34.6	32.9	39.7	39.7	27.7

	Overall	Assets					Sources of finance		
		Intangibles	Industrial buildings	Machinery	Financial assets	Inventories	Retained earnings	New equity	Debt
Paris									
Cost of capital 2001	6.8	5.2	6.9	7.1	7.6	7.0	8.1	8.1	4.3
2002	6.7	5.1	6.9	7.1	7.5	6.9	8.0	8.0	4.3
2003	6.7	5.1	6.9	7.1	7.5	6.9	8.0	8.0	4.3
EMTR 2001	26.0	3.0	27.8	29.6	34.2	28.9	38.3	38.3	-17.2
2002	25.5	2.8	27.5	29.5	33.2	28.0	37.5	37.5	-15.8
2003	25.5	2.8	27.5	29.5	33.2	28.0	37.5	37.5	-15.8
EATR 2001	32.9	27.8	33.4	34.0	35.6	33.8	37.2	37.2	25.0
2002	32.1	27.0	32.7	33.3	34.6	32.9	36.3	36.3	24.4
2003	32.1	27.0	32.7	33.3	34.6	32.9	36.3	36.3	24.4
Meurthe-et-Moselle									
Cost of capital 2001	7.7	5.2	9.2	9.8	7.6	7.0	9.1	9.1	5.2
2002	7.7	5.1	9.1	9.7	7.5	6.9	9.0	9.0	5.3
2003	7.7	5.1	9.1	9.6	7.5	6.9	8.9	8.9	5.2
EMTR 2001	35.4	3.0	45.4	48.9	34.2	28.9	45.0	45.0	4.5
2002	34.8	2.8	45.0	48.5	33.2	28.0	44.3	44.3	5.1
2003	34.7	2.8	44.8	48.1	33.2	28.0	44.1	44.1	4.7
EATR 2001	36.1	27.8	40.5	42.6	35.6	33.8	40.3	40.3	28.1
2002	35.2	27.0	39.8	41.8	34.6	32.9	39.4	39.4	27.4
2003	35.1	27.0	39.7	41.5	34.6	32.9	39.3	39.3	27.4
Meuse									
Cost of capital 2001	7.3	5.2	8.6	8.1	7.6	7.0	8.6	8.6	4.8
2002	7.2	5.1	8.6	8.0	7.5	6.9	8.5	8.5	4.8
2003	7.4	5.1	9.0	8.5	7.5	6.9	8.7	8.7	5.0
EMTR 2001	31.4	3.0	42.0	37.9	34.2	28.9	42.1	42.1	-4.4
2002	31.0	2.8	41.8	37.9	33.2	28.0	41.4	41.4	-3.3
2003	32.6	2.8	44.6	41.2	33.2	28.0	42.6	42.6	0.3
EATR 2001	34.6	27.8	38.8	37.0	35.6	33.8	38.9	38.9	26.6
2002	33.8	27.0	38.2	36.4	34.6	32.9	38.0	38.0	26.1
2003	34.4	27.0	39.6	37.9	34.6	32.9	38.6	38.6	26.6

	Overall	Assets					Sources of finance		
		Intangibles	Industrial buildings	Machinery	Financial assets	Inventories	Retained earnings	New equity	Debt
Moselle									
Cost of capital 2001	7.4	5.2	8.4	8.7	7.6	7.0	8.7	8.7	4.9
2002	7.3	5.1	8.4	8.7	7.5	6.9	8.6	8.6	4.9
2003	7.3	5.1	8.3	8.7	7.5	6.9	8.6	8.6	4.9
EMTR 2001	32.2	3.0	40.4	42.6	34.2	28.9	42.7	42.7	-2.6
2002	31.8	2.8	40.2	42.5	33.2	28.0	42.0	42.0	-1.5
2003	31.7	2.8	40.1	42.4	33.2	28.0	41.9	41.9	-1.7
EATR 2001	34.9	27.8	38.1	39.1	35.6	33.8	39.2	39.2	26.9
2002	34.1	27.0	37.4	38.5	34.6	32.9	38.3	38.3	26.3
2003	34.1	27.0	37.4	38.4	34.6	32.9	38.2	38.2	26.3
Vosges									
Cost of capital 2001	7.6	5.2	9.1	8.9	7.6	7.0	8.9	8.9	5.1
2002	7.5	5.1	9.1	8.9	7.5	6.9	8.8	8.8	5.1
2003	7.5	5.1	9.1	9.0	7.5	6.9	8.8	8.8	5.1
EMTR 2001	33.9	3.0	45.2	44.0	34.2	28.9	43.9	43.9	1.2
2002	33.5	2.8	45.0	44.0	33.2	28.0	43.3	43.3	2.2
2003	33.7	2.8	45.3	44.3	33.2	28.0	43.4	43.4	2.6
EATR 2001	35.5	27.8	40.4	39.8	35.6	33.8	39.8	39.8	27.5
2002	34.7	27.0	39.8	39.2	34.6	32.9	38.9	38.9	26.9
2003	34.8	27.0	39.9	39.4	34.6	32.9	38.9	38.9	27.0
Ain									
Cost of capital 2001	7.4	5.2	8.5	8.7	7.6	7.0	8.8	8.8	4.9
2002	7.3	5.1	8.5	8.7	7.5	6.9	8.6	8.6	4.9
2003	7.4	5.1	8.5	8.7	7.5	6.9	8.6	8.6	5.0
EMTR 2001	32.5	3.0	41.3	42.8	34.2	28.9	42.9	42.9	-2.0
2002	31.9	2.8	41.0	42.4	33.2	28.0	42.1	42.1	-1.1
2003	32.0	2.8	41.3	42.3	33.2	28.0	42.2	42.2	-1.0
EATR 2001	35.0	27.8	38.5	39.2	35.6	33.8	39.3	39.3	27.0
2002	34.1	27.0	37.8	38.5	34.6	32.9	38.3	38.3	26.4
2003	34.2	27.0	37.9	38.4	34.6	32.9	38.3	38.3	26.4

	Overall	Assets					Sources of finance		
		Intangibles	Industrial buildings	Machinery	Financial assets	Inventories	Retained earnings	New equity	Debt
Ardèche									
Cost of capital 2001	7.6	5.2	9.2	9.2	7.6	7.0	9.0	9.0	5.1
2002	7.6	5.1	9.2	9.2	7.5	6.9	8.9	8.9	5.2
2003	7.6	5.1	9.2	9.3	7.5	6.9	8.9	8.9	5.2
EMTR 2001	34.5	3.0	45.6	45.7	34.2	28.9	44.4	44.4	2.4
2002	34.1	2.8	45.4	45.6	33.2	28.0	43.7	43.7	3.5
2003	34.3	2.8	45.7	46.0	33.2	28.0	43.8	43.8	3.9
EATR 2001	35.7	27.8	40.6	40.7	35.6	33.8	40.0	40.0	27.7
2002	34.9	27.0	40.0	40.1	34.6	32.9	39.1	39.1	27.2
2003	35.0	27.0	40.2	40.3	34.6	32.9	39.2	39.2	27.2
Drôme									
Cost of capital 2001	7.4	5.2	8.7	8.5	7.6	7.0	8.8	8.8	4.9
2002	7.4	5.1	8.7	8.5	7.5	6.9	8.7	8.7	5.0
2003	7.4	5.1	8.8	8.6	7.5	6.9	8.7	8.7	5.0
EMTR 2001	32.5	3.0	42.7	41.4	34.2	28.9	42.9	42.9	-2.0
2002	32.1	2.8	42.6	41.4	33.2	28.0	42.2	42.2	-0.8
2003	32.3	2.8	42.9	41.8	33.2	28.0	42.4	42.4	-0.3
EATR 2001	35.0	27.8	39.2	38.6	35.6	33.8	39.3	39.3	27.0
2002	34.2	27.0	38.5	38.0	34.6	32.9	38.4	38.4	26.4
2003	34.3	27.0	38.7	38.2	34.6	32.9	38.5	38.5	26.5
Isère									
Cost of capital 2001	7.9	5.2	9.9	9.9	7.6	7.0	9.3	9.3	5.4
2002	7.9	5.1	9.8	9.9	7.5	6.9	9.2	9.2	5.4
2003	7.8	5.1	9.8	9.8	7.5	6.9	9.1	9.1	5.4
EMTR 2001	36.8	3.0	49.4	49.5	34.2	28.9	46.0	46.0	7.4
2002	36.3	2.8	49.2	49.3	33.2	28.0	45.4	45.4	8.2
2003	36.2	2.8	49.1	49.1	33.2	28.0	45.3	45.3	7.9
EATR 2001	36.6	27.8	42.8	42.9	35.6	33.8	40.9	40.9	28.6
2002	35.8	27.0	42.2	42.3	34.6	32.9	40.0	40.0	28.0
2003	35.7	27.0	42.1	42.1	34.6	32.9	39.9	39.9	28.0

	Overall	Assets					Sources of finance		
		Intangibles	Industrial buildings	Machinery	Financial assets	Inventories	Retained earnings	New equity	Debt
Loire									
Cost of capital 2001	7.6	5.2	9.0	9.2	7.6	7.0	8.9	8.9	5.1
2002	7.5	5.1	8.9	9.1	7.5	6.9	8.8	8.8	5.1
2003	7.5	5.1	9.0	9.2	7.5	6.9	8.8	8.8	5.1
EMTR 2001	34.1	3.0	44.3	45.4	34.2	28.9	44.0	44.0	1.4
2002	33.6	2.8	44.0	45.3	33.2	28.0	43.3	43.3	2.4
2003	33.7	2.8	44.2	45.5	33.2	28.0	43.4	43.4	2.7
EATR 2001	35.5	27.8	40.0	40.5	35.6	33.8	39.8	39.8	27.6
2002	34.7	27.0	39.2	39.9	34.6	32.9	38.9	38.9	27.0
2003	34.8	27.0	39.4	40.0	34.6	32.9	39.0	39.0	27.0
Rhône									
Cost of capital 2001	7.4	5.2	8.4	8.8	7.6	7.0	8.7	8.7	4.9
2002	7.3	5.1	8.3	8.8	7.5	6.9	8.6	8.6	4.9
2003	7.4	5.1	8.5	9.1	7.5	6.9	8.7	8.7	5.0
EMTR 2001	32.4	3.0	40.2	43.4	34.2	28.9	42.8	42.8	-2.3
2002	31.9	2.8	40.0	43.4	33.2	28.0	42.1	42.1	-1.1
2003	32.8	2.8	41.4	45.1	33.2	28.0	42.8	42.8	0.8
EATR 2001	34.9	27.8	38.0	39.5	35.6	33.8	39.2	39.2	27.0
2002	34.2	27.0	37.3	39.0	34.6	32.9	38.3	38.3	26.4
2003	34.5	27.0	38.0	39.9	34.6	32.9	38.6	38.6	26.7
Savoie									
Cost of capital 2001	7.6	5.2	9.1	9.3	7.6	7.0	9.0	9.0	5.1
2002	7.6	5.1	9.1	9.3	7.5	6.9	8.9	8.9	5.2
2003	7.6	5.1	9.1	9.4	7.5	6.9	8.9	8.9	5.2
EMTR 2001	34.6	3.0	45.1	46.3	34.2	28.9	44.4	44.4	2.6
2002	34.1	2.8	44.9	46.1	33.2	28.0	43.7	43.7	3.5
2003	34.4	2.8	45.3	46.6	33.2	28.0	43.9	43.9	4.1
EATR 2001	35.7	27.8	40.4	41.0	35.6	33.8	40.0	40.0	27.7
2002	34.9	27.0	39.7	40.4	34.6	32.9	39.1	39.1	27.2
2003	35.0	27.0	40.0	40.7	34.6	32.9	39.2	39.2	27.3

	Overall	Assets					Sources of finance		
		Intangibles	Industrial buildings	Machinery	Financial assets	Inventories	Retained earnings	New equity	Debt
Haute-Savoie									
Cost of capital 2001	7.5	5.2	8.5	9.1	7.6	7.0	8.8	8.8	5.0
2002	7.5	5.1	8.6	9.3	7.5	6.9	8.8	8.8	5.1
2003	7.6	5.1	8.8	9.5	7.5	6.9	8.9	8.9	5.2
EMTR 2001	33.1	3.0	41.1	45.2	34.2	28.9	43.4	43.4	-0.6
2002	33.4	2.8	42.1	46.5	33.2	28.0	43.2	43.2	2.1
2003	33.9	2.8	43.2	47.1	33.2	28.0	43.6	43.6	3.1
EATR 2001	35.2	27.8	38.4	40.4	35.6	33.8	39.5	39.5	27.2
2002	34.7	27.0	38.3	40.6	34.6	32.9	38.9	38.9	26.9
2003	34.9	27.0	38.9	41.0	34.6	32.9	39.0	39.0	27.1

D.1.3 Germany

	Overall	Assets					Sources of finance		
		Intangibles	Industrial buildings	Machinery	Financial assets	Inventories	Retained earnings	New equity	Debt
Aalen									
Cost of capital 2001	6.6	5.4	6.8	6.0	7.9	6.7	7.8	7.8	4.3
2002	6.6	5.4	6.8	6.0	7.9	6.7	7.8	7.8	4.3
2003	6.7	5.4	6.9	6.1	8.1	6.8	7.9	7.9	4.3
EMTR 2001	24.0	6.7	26.9	17.0	36.8	25.8	35.7	35.7	-15.0
2002	24.0	6.7	26.9	17.0	36.8	25.8	35.7	35.7	-15.0
2003	24.9	6.9	28.0	17.7	38.0	26.8	37.0	37.0	-16.8
EATR 2001	32.9	29.1	33.8	31.2	37.1	33.5	36.7	36.7	26.0
2002	32.9	29.1	33.8	31.2	37.1	33.5	36.7	36.7	26.0
2003	34.1	30.2	35.0	32.3	38.4	34.6	38.0	38.0	26.8
Balingen									
Cost of capital 2001	6.6	5.4	6.8	6.0	7.9	6.7	7.7	7.7	4.3
2002	6.6	5.4	6.8	6.0	7.9	6.7	7.7	7.7	4.3
2003	6.6	5.4	6.9	6.1	8.0	6.8	7.9	7.9	4.3
EMTR 2001	23.7	6.6	26.8	16.8	36.5	25.6	35.5	35.5	-15.0
2002	23.7	6.6	26.8	16.8	36.5	25.6	35.5	35.5	-15.0
2003	24.7	6.8	27.7	17.5	37.7	26.5	36.8	36.8	-16.9
EATR 2001	32.7	28.9	33.6	31.0	36.8	33.2	36.4	36.4	25.8
2002	32.7	28.9	33.6	31.0	36.8	33.2	36.4	36.4	25.8
2003	33.9	29.9	34.7	32.1	38.1	34.4	37.8	37.8	26.6
Freiburg									
Cost of capital 2001	6.7	5.4	7.1	6.1	8.1	6.9	8.0	8.0	4.4
2002	6.7	5.4	7.1	6.1	8.1	6.9	8.0	8.0	4.4
2003	6.8	5.4	7.2	6.2	8.3	7.0	8.1	8.1	4.3
EMTR 2001	25.5	7.4	29.8	18.1	38.2	27.1	37.2	37.2	-13.7
2002	25.5	7.4	29.8	18.1	38.2	27.1	37.2	37.2	-13.7
2003	26.4	7.6	30.6	18.8	39.4	28.1	38.5	38.5	-15.6
EATR 2001	34.2	30.2	35.5	32.4	38.5	34.7	38.1	38.1	27.1
2002	34.2	30.2	35.5	32.4	38.5	34.7	38.1	38.1	27.1
2003	35.4	31.2	36.6	33.4	39.7	35.8	39.4	39.4	27.9

	Overall	Assets					Sources of finance		
		Intangibles	Industrial buildings	Machinery	Financial assets	Inventories	Retained earnings	New equity	Debt
Göppingen									
Cost of capital 2001	6.6	5.4	6.9	6.0	7.9	6.8	7.8	7.8	4.4
2002	6.6	5.4	6.9	6.0	7.9	6.8	7.8	7.8	4.4
2003	6.7	5.4	7.0	6.1	8.1	6.8	8.0	8.0	4.3
EMTR 2001	24.1	6.8	27.4	17.1	36.9	26.0	35.9	35.9	-14.8
2002	24.1	6.8	27.4	17.1	36.9	26.0	35.9	35.9	-14.8
2003	25.1	7.0	28.2	17.8	38.2	26.9	37.2	37.2	-16.7
EATR 2001	33.1	29.2	34.0	31.3	37.3	33.6	36.8	36.8	26.1
2002	33.1	29.2	34.0	31.3	37.3	33.6	36.8	36.8	26.1
2003	34.2	30.3	35.1	32.4	38.6	34.8	38.2	38.2	26.9
Heidelberg									
Cost of capital 2001	6.7	5.4	7.0	6.1	8.1	6.8	7.9	7.9	4.4
2002	6.7	5.4	7.0	6.1	8.1	6.8	7.9	7.9	4.4
2003	6.8	5.4	7.1	6.1	8.2	6.9	8.1	8.1	4.3
EMTR 2001	25.1	7.3	28.8	17.9	37.9	26.8	36.8	36.8	-14.2
2002	25.1	7.3	28.8	17.9	37.9	26.8	36.8	36.8	-14.2
2003	26.0	7.5	29.6	18.6	39.2	27.8	38.1	38.1	-16.1
EATR 2001	34.0	30.0	35.0	32.1	38.2	34.4	37.8	37.8	26.9
2002	34.0	30.0	35.0	32.1	38.2	34.4	37.8	37.8	26.9
2003	35.1	31.0	36.1	33.2	39.5	35.6	39.1	39.1	27.7
Heilbronn									
Cost of capital 2001	6.7	5.4	7.0	6.1	8.0	6.8	7.9	7.9	4.4
2002	6.7	5.4	7.0	6.1	8.0	6.8	7.9	7.9	4.4
2003	6.7	5.4	7.1	6.1	8.2	6.9	8.0	8.0	4.3
EMTR 2001	24.8	7.1	28.3	17.6	37.7	26.6	36.5	36.5	-14.4
2002	24.8	7.1	28.3	17.6	37.7	26.6	36.5	36.5	-14.4
2003	25.7	7.3	29.1	18.4	38.9	27.6	37.8	37.8	-16.3
EATR 2001	33.7	29.8	34.7	31.9	37.9	34.2	37.5	37.5	26.6
2002	33.7	29.8	34.7	31.9	37.9	34.2	37.5	37.5	26.6
2003	34.8	30.8	35.8	33.0	39.2	35.4	38.8	38.8	27.5

	Overall	Assets					Sources of finance		
		Intangibles	Industrial buildings	Machinery	Financial assets	Inventories	Retained earnings	New equity	Debt
Karlsruhe									
Cost of capital 2001	6.7	5.4	7.0	6.1	8.1	6.9	8.0	8.0	4.4
2002	6.7	5.4	7.0	6.1	8.1	6.9	8.0	8.0	4.4
2003	6.8	5.4	7.1	6.2	8.3	7.0	8.1	8.1	4.3
EMTR 2001	25.5	7.5	28.8	18.3	38.5	27.3	37.3	37.3	-14.3
2002	25.5	7.5	28.8	18.3	38.5	27.3	37.3	37.3	-14.3
2003	26.4	7.8	29.7	19.0	39.7	28.3	38.5	38.5	-16.2
EATR 2001	34.4	30.4	35.4	32.6	38.7	34.9	38.2	38.2	27.3
2002	34.4	30.4	35.4	32.6	38.7	34.9	38.2	38.2	27.3
2003	35.5	31.4	36.5	33.7	40.0	36.1	39.5	39.5	28.1
Konstanz									
Cost of capital 2001	6.6	5.4	6.9	6.0	7.9	6.8	7.8	7.8	4.4
2002	6.6	5.4	6.9	6.0	7.9	6.8	7.8	7.8	4.4
2003	6.7	5.4	7.0	6.1	8.1	6.9	8.0	8.0	4.3
EMTR 2001	24.2	6.8	27.2	17.2	37.1	26.1	35.9	35.9	-14.9
2002	24.2	6.8	27.2	17.2	37.1	26.1	35.9	35.9	-14.9
2003	25.1	7.1	28.1	17.9	38.3	27.1	37.2	37.2	-16.8
EATR 2001	33.2	29.3	34.0	31.4	37.4	33.7	37.0	37.0	26.2
2002	33.2	29.3	34.0	31.4	37.4	33.7	37.0	37.0	26.2
2003	34.3	30.4	35.2	32.5	38.7	34.9	38.3	38.3	27.0
Lörrach									
Cost of capital 2001	6.5	5.3	6.8	6.0	7.8	6.7	7.7	7.7	4.3
2002	6.6	5.4	6.9	6.0	7.9	6.8	7.8	7.8	4.4
2003	6.7	5.4	7.0	6.1	8.1	6.9	8.0	8.0	4.3
EMTR 2001	23.4	6.3	26.5	16.5	36.0	25.2	35.1	35.1	-15.1
2002	24.2	6.8	27.3	17.2	37.1	26.1	36.0	36.0	-14.9
2003	25.1	7.1	28.2	17.9	38.3	27.1	37.3	37.3	-16.8
EATR 2001	32.3	28.6	33.2	30.6	36.4	32.8	36.1	36.1	25.4
2002	33.2	29.3	34.1	31.4	37.4	33.7	37.0	37.0	26.2
2003	34.3	30.4	35.2	32.5	38.7	34.9	38.3	38.3	27.0

	Overall	Assets					Sources of finance		
		Intangibles	Industrial buildings	Machinery	Financial assets	Inventories	Retained earnings	New equity	Debt
Landkreis Mannheim									
Cost of capital 2001	6.5	5.3	6.7	6.0	7.8	6.7	7.7	7.7	4.3
2002	6.5	5.3	6.8	6.0	7.8	6.7	7.7	7.7	4.3
2003	6.6	5.4	6.8	6.0	8.0	6.8	7.9	7.9	4.3
EMTR 2001	23.0	6.3	25.4	16.3	35.9	25.0	34.8	34.8	-15.6
2002	23.4	6.4	25.9	16.6	36.2	25.3	35.1	35.1	-15.4
2003	24.3	6.6	26.8	17.3	37.4	26.3	36.4	36.4	-17.3
EATR 2001	32.1	28.5	32.8	30.5	36.3	32.7	35.9	35.9	25.3
2002	32.4	28.7	33.1	30.7	36.6	33.0	36.1	36.1	25.5
2003	33.6	29.7	34.3	31.9	37.9	34.1	37.5	37.5	26.3
Ludwigsburg									
Cost of capital 2001	6.6	5.4	6.9	6.1	8.0	6.8	7.8	7.8	4.4
2002	6.6	5.4	6.8	6.0	7.9	6.8	7.8	7.8	4.3
2003	6.7	5.4	6.9	6.1	8.1	6.9	8.0	8.0	4.3
EMTR 2001	24.5	7.0	27.3	17.5	37.5	26.5	36.3	36.3	-14.9
2002	24.1	6.8	26.9	17.2	37.1	26.1	35.9	35.9	-15.0
2003	25.1	7.1	27.8	17.9	38.3	27.1	37.2	37.2	-17.0
EATR 2001	33.5	29.7	34.3	31.8	37.8	34.1	37.3	37.3	26.5
2002	33.2	29.3	33.9	31.4	37.4	33.7	36.9	36.9	26.2
2003	34.3	30.4	35.1	32.5	38.7	34.9	38.3	38.3	27.0
Mannheim									
Cost of capital 2001	6.8	5.4	7.1	6.2	8.2	6.9	8.0	8.0	4.4
2002	6.7	5.4	7.1	6.1	8.1	6.9	8.0	8.0	4.4
2003	6.8	5.4	7.1	6.2	8.3	7.0	8.2	8.2	4.3
EMTR 2001	26.0	7.8	29.5	18.7	39.1	27.8	37.8	37.8	-14.0
2002	25.7	7.6	29.2	18.4	38.6	27.5	37.4	37.4	-14.1
2003	26.6	7.8	30.0	19.1	39.8	28.4	38.7	38.7	-16.0
EATR 2001	34.9	30.8	35.9	33.0	39.3	35.4	38.8	38.8	27.7
2002	34.5	30.5	35.5	32.7	38.9	35.0	38.4	38.4	27.4
2003	35.7	31.5	36.7	33.8	40.1	36.2	39.7	39.7	28.2

	Overall	Assets					Sources of finance		
		Intangibles	Industrial buildings	Machinery	Financial assets	Inventories	Retained earnings	New equity	Debt
Nagold									
Cost of capital 2001	6.6	5.4	6.9	6.0	7.9	6.7	7.8	7.8	4.4
2002	6.6	5.4	6.9	6.0	7.9	6.7	7.8	7.8	4.4
2003	6.7	5.4	7.0	6.1	8.1	6.8	7.9	7.9	4.3
EMTR 2001	24.0	6.7	27.4	17.0	36.8	25.8	35.8	35.8	-14.8
2002	24.0	6.7	27.4	17.0	36.8	25.8	35.8	35.8	-14.8
2003	25.0	6.9	28.2	17.7	38.0	26.8	37.1	37.1	-16.7
EATR 2001	33.0	29.1	33.9	31.2	37.1	33.5	36.7	36.7	26.0
2002	33.0	29.1	33.9	31.2	37.1	33.5	36.7	36.7	26.0
2003	34.1	30.2	35.0	32.3	38.4	34.6	38.0	38.0	26.8
Offenburg									
Cost of capital 2001	6.7	5.4	7.0	6.1	8.0	6.8	7.9	7.9	4.4
2002	6.7	5.4	7.0	6.1	8.0	6.8	7.9	7.9	4.4
2003	6.7	5.4	7.1	6.1	8.2	6.9	8.0	8.0	4.3
EMTR 2001	24.9	7.1	28.5	17.6	37.7	26.6	36.6	36.6	-14.3
2002	24.9	7.1	28.5	17.6	37.7	26.6	36.6	36.6	-14.3
2003	25.8	7.3	29.3	18.4	38.9	27.6	37.9	37.9	-16.2
EATR 2001	33.7	29.8	34.7	31.9	37.9	34.2	37.5	37.5	26.7
2002	33.7	29.8	34.7	31.9	37.9	34.2	37.5	37.5	26.7
2003	34.8	30.8	35.9	33.0	39.2	35.4	38.8	38.8	27.5
Pforzheim									
Cost of capital 2001	6.7	5.4	7.0	6.1	8.0	6.8	7.9	7.9	4.4
2002	6.7	5.4	7.0	6.1	8.0	6.8	7.9	7.9	4.4
2003	6.7	5.4	7.1	6.1	8.2	6.9	8.0	8.0	4.3
EMTR 2001	24.9	7.1	28.5	17.6	37.7	26.6	36.6	36.6	-14.3
2002	24.9	7.1	28.5	17.6	37.7	26.6	36.6	36.6	-14.3
2003	25.8	7.3	29.3	18.4	38.9	27.6	37.9	37.9	-16.2
EATR 2001	33.7	29.8	34.7	31.9	37.9	34.2	37.5	37.5	26.7
2002	33.7	29.8	34.7	31.9	37.9	34.2	37.5	37.5	26.7
2003	34.8	30.8	35.9	33.0	39.2	35.4	38.8	38.8	27.5

	Overall	Assets					Sources of finance		
		Intangibles	Industrial buildings	Machinery	Financial assets	Inventories	Retained earnings	New equity	Debt
Rastatt									
Cost of capital 2001	6.6	5.4	6.9	6.0	7.9	6.7	7.8	7.8	4.4
2002	6.6	5.4	6.9	6.1	8.0	6.8	7.8	7.8	4.4
2003	6.7	5.4	7.0	6.1	8.1	6.9	8.0	8.0	4.3
EMTR 2001	24.0	6.7	27.2	17.0	36.8	25.8	35.7	35.7	-14.9
2002	24.5	7.0	27.6	17.4	37.4	26.3	36.2	36.2	-14.7
2003	25.4	7.2	28.5	18.1	38.6	27.3	37.5	37.5	-16.7
EATR 2001	33.0	29.1	33.8	31.2	37.1	33.5	36.7	36.7	26.0
2002	33.4	29.6	34.3	31.7	37.7	34.0	37.2	37.2	26.4
2003	34.6	30.6	35.5	32.8	39.0	35.1	38.5	38.5	27.2
Ravensburg									
Cost of capital 2001	6.5	5.3	6.8	6.0	7.8	6.7	7.7	7.7	4.4
2002	6.5	5.3	6.8	6.0	7.8	6.7	7.7	7.7	4.4
2003	6.6	5.4	6.9	6.0	8.0	6.8	7.9	7.9	4.3
EMTR 2001	23.6	6.4	26.9	16.6	36.2	25.3	35.2	35.2	-14.9
2002	23.6	6.4	26.9	16.6	36.2	25.3	35.2	35.2	-14.9
2003	24.5	6.6	27.8	17.3	37.4	26.3	36.6	36.6	-16.8
EATR 2001	32.5	28.7	33.4	30.7	36.6	33.0	36.2	36.2	25.6
2002	32.5	28.7	33.4	30.7	36.6	33.0	36.2	36.2	25.6
2003	33.6	29.7	34.6	31.9	37.9	34.1	37.5	37.5	26.4
Reutlingen									
Cost of capital 2001	6.6	5.4	6.9	6.0	7.9	6.7	7.8	7.8	4.4
2002	6.6	5.4	6.9	6.0	7.9	6.7	7.8	7.8	4.4
2003	6.7	5.4	6.9	6.1	8.1	6.8	7.9	7.9	4.3
EMTR 2001	24.0	6.7	27.1	17.0	36.8	25.8	35.7	35.7	-14.9
2002	24.0	6.7	27.1	17.0	36.8	25.8	35.7	35.7	-14.9
2003	24.9	6.9	28.0	17.7	38.0	26.8	37.0	37.0	-16.8
EATR 2001	32.9	29.1	33.8	31.2	37.1	33.5	36.7	36.7	26.0
2002	32.9	29.1	33.8	31.2	37.1	33.5	36.7	36.7	26.0
2003	34.1	30.2	35.0	32.3	38.4	34.6	38.0	38.0	26.8

	Overall	Intangibles	Industrial buildings	Machinery	Financial assets	Inventories	Retained earnings	New equity	Debt
		Assets					Sources of finance		
Rottweil									
Cost of capital 2001	6.6	5.3	6.9	6.0	7.9	6.7	7.7	7.7	4.4
2002	6.6	5.3	6.9	6.0	7.9	6.7	7.7	7.7	4.4
2003	6.6	5.4	7.0	6.1	8.0	6.8	7.9	7.9	4.3
EMTR 2001	23.7	6.5	27.3	16.7	36.3	25.4	35.4	35.4	-14.7
2002	23.7	6.5	27.3	16.7	36.3	25.4	35.4	35.4	-14.7
2003	24.7	6.7	28.2	17.4	37.6	26.4	36.7	36.7	-16.6
EATR 2001	32.6	28.8	33.6	30.9	36.7	33.1	36.3	36.3	25.7
2002	32.6	28.8	33.6	30.9	36.7	33.1	36.3	36.3	25.7
2003	33.8	29.8	34.8	32.0	38.0	34.3	37.7	37.7	26.5
Schwäbisch-Hall									
Cost of capital 2001	6.6	5.4	6.9	6.1	8.0	6.8	7.9	7.9	4.4
2002	6.6	5.4	6.9	6.1	8.0	6.8	7.9	7.9	4.4
2003	6.7	5.4	7.0	6.1	8.2	6.9	8.0	8.0	4.3
EMTR 2001	24.6	7.0	27.9	17.5	37.5	26.5	36.4	36.4	-14.6
2002	24.6	7.0	27.9	17.5	37.5	26.5	36.4	36.4	-14.6
2003	25.6	7.3	28.8	18.3	38.7	27.4	37.7	37.7	-16.5
EATR 2001	33.6	29.7	34.5	31.8	37.8	34.1	37.4	37.4	26.5
2002	33.6	29.7	34.5	31.8	37.8	34.1	37.4	37.4	26.5
2003	34.7	30.7	35.6	32.9	39.1	35.2	38.7	38.7	27.3
Stuttgart									
Cost of capital 2001	6.7	5.4	7.1	6.1	8.2	6.9	8.0	8.0	4.4
2002	6.7	5.4	7.1	6.1	8.2	6.9	8.0	8.0	4.4
2003	6.8	5.4	7.2	6.2	8.3	7.0	8.2	8.2	4.3
EMTR 2001	25.9	7.7	29.7	18.5	38.8	27.6	37.6	37.6	-13.9
2002	25.8	7.7	29.5	18.5	38.8	27.6	37.6	37.6	-14.0
2003	26.7	7.9	30.3	19.2	40.0	28.6	38.8	38.8	-15.9
EATR 2001	34.7	30.6	35.8	32.8	39.0	35.2	38.5	38.5	27.5
2002	34.7	30.6	35.7	32.8	39.0	35.2	38.5	38.5	27.5
2003	35.8	31.6	36.8	33.9	40.3	36.3	39.8	39.8	28.3

		Assets					Sources of finance		
	Overall	Intangibles	Industrial buildings	Machinery	Financial assets	Inventories	Retained earnings	New equity	Debt
Tauberbischofs-heim									
Cost of capital 2001	6.5	5.3	6.8	6.0	7.8	6.7	7.7	7.7	4.3
2002	6.5	5.3	6.8	6.0	7.8	6.7	7.7	7.7	4.3
2003	6.6	5.4	6.9	6.0	8.0	6.8	7.9	7.9	4.3
EMTR 2001	23.4	6.4	26.2	16.6	36.2	25.3	35.1	35.1	-15.3
2002	23.4	6.4	26.2	16.6	36.2	25.3	35.1	35.1	-15.3
2003	24.3	6.6	27.1	17.3	37.4	26.3	36.4	36.4	-17.2
EATR 2001	32.4	28.7	33.2	30.7	36.6	33.0	36.2	36.2	25.5
2002	32.4	28.7	33.2	30.7	36.6	33.0	36.2	36.2	25.5
2003	33.6	29.7	34.4	31.9	37.9	34.1	37.5	37.5	26.4
Ulm									
Cost of capital 2001	6.6	5.4	6.9	6.0	7.9	6.8	7.8	7.8	4.4
2002	6.6	5.4	6.9	6.0	7.9	6.8	7.8	7.8	4.4
2003	6.7	5.4	7.0	6.1	8.1	6.9	8.0	8.0	4.3
EMTR 2001	24.3	6.8	27.8	17.2	37.1	26.1	36.0	36.0	-14.6
2002	24.3	6.8	27.8	17.2	37.1	26.1	36.0	36.0	-14.6
2003	25.2	7.1	28.7	17.9	38.3	27.1	37.3	37.3	-16.5
EATR 2001	33.2	29.3	34.2	31.4	37.4	33.7	37.0	37.0	26.2
2002	33.2	29.3	34.2	31.4	37.4	33.7	37.0	37.0	26.2
2003	34.4	30.4	35.3	32.5	38.7	34.9	38.3	38.3	27.0
Villingen-Schwenningen									
Cost of capital 2001	6.6	5.4	6.9	6.0	7.9	6.7	7.8	7.8	4.4
2002	6.6	5.4	6.9	6.0	7.9	6.7	7.8	7.8	4.4
2003	6.7	5.4	7.0	6.1	8.1	6.8	7.9	7.9	4.3
EMTR 2001	24.0	6.7	27.4	17.0	36.8	25.8	35.8	35.8	-14.8
2002	24.0	6.7	27.4	17.0	36.8	25.8	35.8	35.8	-14.8
2003	25.0	6.9	28.2	17.7	38.0	26.8	37.1	37.1	-16.7
EATR 2001	33.0	29.1	33.9	31.2	37.1	33.5	36.7	36.7	26.0
2002	33.0	29.1	33.9	31.2	37.1	33.5	36.7	36.7	26.0
2003	34.1	30.2	35.0	32.3	38.4	34.6	38.0	38.0	26.8

	Overall	Assets					Sources of finance		
		Intangibles	Industrial buildings	Machinery	Financial assets	Inventories	Retained earnings	New equity	Debt
Waiblingen									
Cost of capital 2001	6.6	5.4	6.8	6.0	7.9	6.7	7.8	7.8	4.3
2002	6.6	5.4	6.8	6.0	7.9	6.7	7.8	7.8	4.3
2003	6.7	5.4	6.9	6.1	8.1	6.8	7.9	7.9	4.3
EMTR 2001	23.9	6.7	26.8	17.0	36.8	25.8	35.7	35.7	-15.1
2002	23.9	6.7	26.8	17.0	36.8	25.8	35.7	35.7	-15.1
2003	24.8	6.9	27.7	17.7	38.0	26.8	37.0	37.0	-17.0
EATR 2001	32.9	29.1	33.7	31.2	37.1	33.5	36.7	36.7	26.0
2002	32.9	29.1	33.7	31.2	37.1	33.5	36.7	36.7	26.0
2003	34.1	30.2	34.9	32.3	38.4	34.6	38.0	38.0	26.8
Walldorf bei Heidelberg									
Cost of capital 2001	6.5	5.3	6.7	6.0	7.8	6.6	7.6	7.6	4.3
2002	6.5	5.3	6.7	6.0	7.8	6.6	7.6	7.6	4.3
2003	6.6	5.3	6.8	6.0	7.9	6.7	7.8	7.8	4.3
EMTR 2001	22.8	6.1	25.1	16.1	35.6	24.8	34.5	34.5	-15.7
2002	22.8	6.1	25.1	16.1	35.6	24.8	34.5	34.5	-15.7
2003	23.7	6.3	26.0	16.8	36.9	25.8	35.8	35.8	-17.6
EATR 2001	31.9	28.2	32.5	30.3	36.0	32.4	35.6	35.6	25.0
2002	31.9	28.2	32.5	30.3	36.0	32.4	35.6	35.6	25.0
2003	33.1	29.3	33.7	31.4	37.3	33.6	36.9	36.9	25.9
Ansbach									
Cost of capital 2001	6.6	5.4	6.9	6.0	7.9	6.8	7.8	7.8	4.4
2002	6.6	5.4	6.9	6.0	7.9	6.8	7.8	7.8	4.4
2003	6.7	5.4	7.0	6.1	8.1	6.9	8.0	8.0	4.3
EMTR 2001	24.2	6.8	27.3	17.2	37.1	26.1	36.0	36.0	-14.9
2002	24.2	6.8	27.3	17.2	37.1	26.1	36.0	36.0	-14.9
2003	25.1	7.1	28.2	17.9	38.3	27.1	37.3	37.3	-16.8
EATR 2001	33.2	29.3	34.1	31.4	37.4	33.7	37.0	37.0	26.2
2002	33.2	29.3	34.1	31.4	37.4	33.7	37.0	37.0	26.2
2003	34.3	30.4	35.2	32.5	38.7	34.9	38.3	38.3	27.0

	Overall	Assets					Sources of finance		
		Intangibles	Industrial buildings	Machinery	Financial assets	Inventories	Retained earnings	New equity	Debt
Aschaffenburg									
Cost of capital 2001	6.6	5.4	6.9	6.1	8.0	6.8	7.9	7.9	4.4
2002	6.6	5.4	6.9	6.1	8.0	6.8	7.9	7.9	4.4
2003	6.7	5.4	7.0	6.1	8.2	6.9	8.0	8.0	4.3
EMTR 2001	24.8	7.2	27.6	17.8	37.8	26.7	36.6	36.6	-14.8
2002	24.8	7.2	27.6	17.8	37.8	26.7	36.6	36.6	-14.8
2003	25.7	7.4	28.5	18.5	39.0	27.7	37.8	37.8	-16.7
EATR 2001	33.8	29.9	34.6	32.0	38.1	34.3	37.6	37.6	26.7
2002	33.8	29.9	34.6	32.0	38.1	34.3	37.6	37.6	26.7
2003	34.9	30.9	35.7	33.1	39.4	35.5	38.9	38.9	27.5
Augsburg									
Cost of capital 2001	6.7	5.4	7.1	6.1	8.2	6.9	8.0	8.0	4.4
2002	6.8	5.4	7.1	6.2	8.3	7.0	8.1	8.1	4.4
2003	6.9	5.5	7.2	6.2	8.4	7.1	8.2	8.2	4.3
EMTR 2001	25.8	7.7	29.2	18.5	38.8	27.6	37.5	37.5	-14.1
2002	26.4	8.0	29.7	19.0	39.5	28.2	38.1	38.1	-13.9
2003	27.2	8.3	30.5	19.7	40.6	29.2	39.4	39.4	-15.9
EATR 2001	34.6	30.6	35.6	32.8	39.0	35.2	38.5	38.5	27.5
2002	35.2	31.1	36.2	33.4	39.6	35.7	39.1	39.1	28.0
2003	36.3	32.1	37.3	34.4	40.9	36.9	40.4	40.4	28.8
Bamberg									
Cost of capital 2001	6.6	5.4	7.0	6.1	8.0	6.8	7.9	7.9	4.4
2002	6.7	5.4	7.0	6.1	8.1	6.8	7.9	7.9	4.4
2003	6.8	5.4	7.1	6.1	8.2	6.9	8.1	8.1	4.3
EMTR 2001	24.8	7.1	28.1	17.6	37.7	26.6	36.5	36.5	-14.5
2002	25.1	7.3	28.4	17.9	37.9	26.8	36.8	36.8	-14.4
2003	26.0	7.5	29.3	18.6	39.2	27.8	38.1	38.1	-16.3
EATR 2001	33.7	29.8	34.7	31.9	37.9	34.2	37.5	37.5	26.6
2002	33.9	30.0	34.9	32.1	38.2	34.4	37.8	37.8	26.9
2003	35.1	31.0	36.0	33.2	39.5	35.6	39.0	39.0	27.7

	Overall	Assets					Sources of finance		
		Intangibles	Industrial buildings	Machinery	Financial assets	Inventories	Retained earnings	New equity	Debt
Bayreuth									
Cost of capital 2001	6.6	5.4	6.9	6.1	8.0	6.8	7.8	7.8	4.4
2002	6.6	5.4	6.9	6.1	8.0	6.8	7.8	7.8	4.4
2003	6.7	5.4	7.0	6.1	8.1	6.9	8.0	8.0	4.3
EMTR 2001	24.5	7.0	27.9	17.4	37.4	26.3	36.3	36.3	-14.6
2002	24.5	7.0	27.9	17.4	37.4	26.3	36.3	36.3	-14.6
2003	25.5	7.2	28.7	18.1	38.6	27.3	37.6	37.6	-16.5
EATR 2001	33.5	29.6	34.4	31.7	37.7	34.0	37.2	37.2	26.4
2002	33.5	29.6	34.4	31.7	37.7	34.0	37.2	37.2	26.4
2003	34.6	30.6	35.5	32.8	39.0	35.1	38.5	38.5	27.2
Coburg									
Cost of capital 2001	6.6	5.4	6.9	6.0	7.9	6.8	7.8	7.8	4.4
2002	6.6	5.4	6.9	6.0	7.9	6.8	7.8	7.8	4.4
2003	6.6	5.3	6.8	6.0	7.9	6.7	7.8	7.8	4.3
EMTR 2001	24.2	6.8	27.3	17.2	37.1	26.1	36.0	36.0	-14.9
2002	24.2	6.8	27.3	17.2	37.1	26.1	36.0	36.0	-14.9
2003	23.7	6.2	26.9	16.6	36.6	25.5	35.7	35.7	-17.2
EATR 2001	33.2	29.3	34.1	31.4	37.4	33.7	37.0	37.0	26.2
2002	33.2	29.3	34.1	31.4	37.4	33.7	37.0	37.0	26.2
2003	32.9	29.1	33.8	31.1	37.0	33.4	36.7	36.7	25.7
Deggendorf									
Cost of capital 2001	6.5	5.3	6.8	6.0	7.8	6.7	7.7	7.7	4.3
2002	6.6	5.4	6.9	6.0	7.9	6.7	7.8	7.8	4.4
2003	6.7	5.4	6.9	6.1	8.1	6.8	7.9	7.9	4.3
EMTR 2001	23.3	6.3	26.5	16.3	35.9	25.0	35.0	35.0	-15.1
2002	24.0	6.7	27.2	17.0	36.8	25.8	35.7	35.7	-14.9
2003	24.9	6.9	28.0	17.7	38.0	26.8	37.0	37.0	-16.8
EATR 2001	32.2	28.5	33.1	30.5	36.3	32.7	35.9	35.9	25.3
2002	33.0	29.1	33.8	31.2	37.1	33.5	36.7	36.7	26.0
2003	34.1	30.2	35.0	32.3	38.4	34.6	38.0	38.0	26.8

	Overall	Intangibles	Industrial buildings	Machinery	Financial assets	Inventories	Retained earnings	New equity	Debt
		Assets					Sources of finance		
Donauwörth									
Cost of capital 2001	6.6	5.4	6.9	6.0	7.9	6.7	7.8	7.8	4.4
2002	6.6	5.4	6.9	6.0	7.9	6.7	7.8	7.8	4.4
2003	6.7	5.4	7.0	6.1	8.1	6.8	7.9	7.9	4.3
EMTR 2001	24.0	6.7	27.3	17.0	36.8	25.8	35.7	35.7	-14.8
2002	24.0	6.7	27.3	17.0	36.8	25.8	35.7	35.7	-14.8
2003	24.9	6.9	28.1	17.7	38.0	26.8	37.0	37.0	-16.7
EATR 2001	33.0	29.1	33.9	31.2	37.1	33.5	36.7	36.7	26.0
2002	33.0	29.1	33.9	31.2	37.1	33.5	36.7	36.7	26.0
2003	34.1	30.2	35.0	32.3	38.4	34.6	38.0	38.0	26.8
Freising									
Cost of capital 2001	6.6	5.4	6.9	6.1	8.0	6.8	7.9	7.9	4.4
2002	6.6	5.4	6.9	6.1	8.0	6.8	7.9	7.9	4.4
2003	6.7	5.4	7.0	6.1	8.2	6.9	8.0	8.0	4.3
EMTR 2001	24.7	7.1	27.5	17.6	37.7	26.6	36.4	36.4	-14.8
2002	24.7	7.1	27.5	17.6	37.7	26.6	36.4	36.4	-14.8
2003	25.6	7.3	28.4	18.4	38.9	27.6	37.7	37.7	-16.7
EATR 2001	33.7	29.8	34.5	31.9	37.9	34.2	37.5	37.5	26.6
2002	33.7	29.8	34.5	31.9	37.9	34.2	37.5	37.5	26.6
2003	34.8	30.8	35.6	33.0	39.2	35.4	38.8	38.8	27.4
Hof									
Cost of capital 2001	6.7	5.4	7.0	6.1	8.0	6.8	7.9	7.9	4.4
2002	6.7	5.4	7.0	6.1	8.0	6.8	7.9	7.9	4.4
2003	6.7	5.4	7.1	6.1	8.2	6.9	8.0	8.0	4.3
EMTR 2001	24.8	7.1	28.4	17.6	37.7	26.6	36.6	36.6	-14.4
2002	24.8	7.1	28.4	17.6	37.7	26.6	36.6	36.6	-14.4
2003	25.7	7.3	29.2	18.4	38.9	27.6	37.8	37.8	-16.3
EATR 2001	33.7	29.8	34.7	31.9	37.9	34.2	37.5	37.5	26.7
2002	33.7	29.8	34.7	31.9	37.9	34.2	37.5	37.5	26.7
2003	34.8	30.8	35.8	33.0	39.2	35.4	38.8	38.8	27.5

	Overall	Assets					Sources of finance		
		Intangibles	Industrial buildings	Machinery	Financial assets	Inventories	Retained earnings	New equity	Debt
Ingolstadt									
Cost of capital 2001	6.7	5.4	7.0	6.1	8.1	6.9	7.9	7.9	4.4
2002	6.7	5.4	7.0	6.1	8.1	6.9	7.9	7.9	4.4
2003	6.8	5.4	7.1	6.2	8.3	7.0	8.1	8.1	4.3
EMTR 2001	25.2	7.4	28.4	18.1	38.2	27.1	37.0	37.0	-14.4
2002	25.2	7.4	28.4	18.1	38.2	27.1	37.0	37.0	-14.4
2003	26.1	7.6	29.3	18.8	39.4	28.1	38.3	38.3	-16.4
EATR 2001	34.2	30.2	35.1	32.4	38.5	34.7	38.0	38.0	27.0
2002	34.2	30.2	35.1	32.4	38.5	34.7	38.0	38.0	27.0
2003	35.3	31.2	36.2	33.4	39.7	35.8	39.3	39.3	27.9
Kempten									
Cost of capital 2001	6.6	5.3	6.9	6.0	7.9	6.7	7.7	7.7	4.4
2002	6.6	5.3	6.9	6.0	7.9	6.7	7.7	7.7	4.4
2003	6.6	5.4	6.9	6.1	8.0	6.8	7.9	7.9	4.3
EMTR 2001	23.7	6.5	27.0	16.7	36.4	25.5	35.4	35.4	-14.9
2002	23.7	6.5	27.0	16.7	36.4	25.5	35.4	35.4	-14.9
2003	24.6	6.7	27.9	17.4	37.7	26.5	36.7	36.7	-16.8
EATR 2001	32.6	28.8	33.6	30.9	36.8	33.1	36.4	36.4	25.7
2002	32.6	28.8	33.6	30.9	36.8	33.1	36.4	36.4	25.7
2003	33.8	29.9	34.7	32.0	38.1	34.3	37.7	37.7	26.5
Landshut									
Cost of capital 2001	6.7	5.4	7.0	6.1	8.1	6.9	7.9	7.9	4.4
2002	6.7	5.4	7.0	6.1	8.1	6.9	7.9	7.9	4.4
2003	6.8	5.4	7.1	6.2	8.3	7.0	8.1	8.1	4.3
EMTR 2001	25.2	7.4	28.4	18.1	38.2	27.1	37.0	37.0	-14.4
2002	25.3	7.4	28.6	18.1	38.2	27.1	37.0	37.0	-14.3
2003	26.2	7.6	29.6	18.8	39.4	28.1	38.3	38.3	-16.2
EATR 2001	34.2	30.2	35.1	32.4	38.5	34.7	38.0	38.0	27.0
2002	34.2	30.2	35.1	32.4	38.5	34.7	38.0	38.0	27.1
2003	35.3	31.2	36.3	33.4	39.7	35.8	39.3	39.3	27.9

		Assets					Sources of finance		
	Overall	Intangibles	Industrial buildings	Machinery	Financial assets	Inventories	Retained earnings	New equity	Debt
Memmingen									
Cost of capital 2001	6.5	5.3	6.8	6.0	7.8	6.7	7.7	7.7	4.3
2002	6.5	5.3	6.8	6.0	7.8	6.7	7.7	7.7	4.3
2003	6.6	5.4	6.9	6.0	8.0	6.8	7.9	7.9	4.3
EMTR 2001	23.5	6.4	26.7	16.6	36.2	25.3	35.2	35.2	-15.0
2002	23.5	6.4	26.7	16.6	36.2	25.3	35.2	35.2	-15.0
2003	24.4	6.6	27.6	17.3	37.4	26.3	36.5	36.5	-16.9
EATR 2001	32.5	28.7	33.4	30.7	36.6	33.0	36.2	36.2	25.5
2002	32.5	28.7	33.4	30.7	36.6	33.0	36.2	36.2	25.5
2003	33.6	29.7	34.5	31.9	37.9	34.1	37.5	37.5	26.4
München									
Cost of capital 2001	6.9	5.5	7.2	6.2	8.4	7.1	8.2	8.2	4.4
2002	6.9	5.5	7.2	6.2	8.4	7.1	8.2	8.2	4.4
2003	7.0	5.5	7.3	6.3	8.6	7.2	8.4	8.4	4.3
EMTR 2001	27.4	8.6	30.7	19.9	40.7	29.3	39.2	39.2	-13.6
2002	27.4	8.6	30.7	19.9	40.7	29.3	39.2	39.2	-13.6
2003	28.3	8.9	31.5	20.6	41.8	30.2	40.4	40.4	-15.5
EATR 2001	36.2	32.0	37.2	34.3	40.8	36.8	40.2	40.2	28.9
2002	36.2	32.0	37.2	34.3	40.8	36.8	40.2	40.2	28.9
2003	37.3	33.0	38.3	35.4	42.0	37.9	41.4	41.4	29.7
Nürnberg									
Cost of capital 2001	6.8	5.4	7.1	6.2	8.3	7.0	8.1	8.1	4.4
2002	6.8	5.4	7.1	6.2	8.3	7.0	8.1	8.1	4.4
2003	6.9	5.5	7.2	6.2	8.4	7.1	8.3	8.3	4.3
EMTR 2001	26.4	8.1	29.9	19.1	39.5	28.3	38.2	38.2	-13.8
2002	26.4	8.1	29.9	19.1	39.5	28.3	38.2	38.2	-13.8
2003	27.3	8.3	30.8	19.8	40.7	29.2	39.5	39.5	-15.8
EATR 2001	35.3	31.2	36.3	33.4	39.7	35.8	39.2	39.2	28.0
2002	35.3	31.2	36.3	33.4	39.7	35.8	39.2	39.2	28.0
2003	36.4	32.2	37.4	34.5	40.9	36.9	40.4	40.4	28.8

	Overall	Assets					Sources of finance		
		Intangibles	Industrial buildings	Machinery	Financial assets	Inventories	Retained earnings	New equity	Debt
Passau									
Cost of capital 2001	6.6	5.4	6.9	6.1	8.0	6.8	7.8	7.8	4.4
2002	6.6	5.4	6.9	6.1	8.0	6.8	7.8	7.8	4.4
2003	6.7	5.4	7.0	6.1	8.1	6.9	8.0	8.0	4.3
EMTR 2001	24.5	7.0	27.8	17.4	37.4	26.3	36.3	36.3	-14.6
2002	24.5	7.0	27.8	17.4	37.4	26.3	36.3	36.3	-14.6
2003	25.4	7.2	28.7	18.1	38.6	27.3	37.5	37.5	-16.6
EATR 2001	33.4	29.6	34.4	31.7	37.7	34.0	37.2	37.2	26.4
2002	33.4	29.6	34.4	31.7	37.7	34.0	37.2	37.2	26.4
2003	34.6	30.6	35.5	32.8	39.0	35.1	38.5	38.5	27.2
Pfarrkirchen									
Cost of capital 2001	6.5	5.3	6.8	6.0	7.8	6.7	7.7	7.7	4.3
2002	6.5	5.3	6.8	6.0	7.8	6.7	7.7	7.7	4.3
2003	6.6	5.4	6.9	6.0	8.0	6.8	7.9	7.9	4.3
EMTR 2001	23.5	6.4	26.7	16.6	36.2	25.3	35.2	35.2	-15.0
2002	23.5	6.4	26.7	16.6	36.2	25.3	35.2	35.2	-15.0
2003	24.4	6.6	27.6	17.3	37.4	26.3	36.5	36.5	-16.9
EATR 2001	32.5	28.7	33.4	30.7	36.6	33.0	36.2	36.2	25.5
2002	32.5	28.7	33.4	30.7	36.6	33.0	36.2	36.2	25.5
2003	33.6	29.7	34.5	31.9	37.9	34.1	37.5	37.5	26.4
Regensburg									
Cost of capital 2001	6.7	5.4	7.1	6.1	8.2	6.9	8.0	8.0	4.4
2002	6.7	5.4	7.1	6.1	8.2	6.9	8.0	8.0	4.4
2003	6.8	5.4	7.1	6.2	8.3	7.0	8.2	8.2	4.3
EMTR 2001	25.9	7.7	29.1	18.6	38.9	27.7	37.6	37.6	-14.2
2002	25.9	7.7	29.1	18.6	38.9	27.7	37.6	37.6	-14.2
2003	26.7	8.0	30.0	19.3	40.1	28.7	38.9	38.9	-16.1
EATR 2001	34.8	30.7	35.7	32.9	39.1	35.3	38.6	38.6	27.6
2002	34.8	30.7	35.7	32.9	39.1	35.3	38.6	38.6	27.6
2003	35.9	31.7	36.8	34.0	40.4	36.4	39.9	39.9	28.4

	Overall	Assets					Sources of finance		
		Intangibles	Industrial buildings	Machinery	Financial assets	Inventories	Retained earnings	New equity	Debt
Rosenheim									
Cost of capital 2001	6.7	5.4	7.0	6.1	8.1	6.9	7.9	7.9	4.4
2002	6.7	5.4	7.0	6.1	8.1	6.9	7.9	7.9	4.4
2003	6.8	5.4	7.1	6.2	8.3	7.0	8.1	8.1	4.3
EMTR 2001	25.4	7.4	29.1	18.1	38.2	27.1	37.1	37.1	-14.1
2002	25.4	7.4	29.1	18.1	38.2	27.1	37.1	37.1	-14.1
2003	26.3	7.6	29.9	18.8	39.4	28.1	38.4	38.4	-16.0
EATR 2001	34.2	30.2	35.3	32.4	38.5	34.7	38.0	38.0	27.1
2002	34.2	30.2	35.3	32.4	38.5	34.7	38.0	38.0	27.1
2003	35.3	31.2	36.4	33.4	39.7	35.8	39.3	39.3	27.9
Schwandorf									
Cost of capital 2001	6.6	5.4	6.8	6.0	7.9	6.7	7.8	7.8	4.3
2002	6.6	5.4	6.8	6.0	7.9	6.7	7.8	7.8	4.3
2003	6.7	5.4	6.9	6.1	8.1	6.8	7.9	7.9	4.3
EMTR 2001	23.8	6.7	26.4	17.0	36.8	25.8	35.6	35.6	-15.3
2002	23.8	6.7	26.4	17.0	36.8	25.8	35.6	35.6	-15.3
2003	24.9	6.9	27.9	17.7	38.0	26.8	37.0	37.0	-16.9
EATR 2001	32.9	29.1	33.6	31.2	37.1	33.5	36.7	36.7	25.9
2002	32.9	29.1	33.6	31.2	37.1	33.5	36.7	36.7	25.9
2003	34.1	30.2	34.9	32.3	38.4	34.6	38.0	38.0	26.8
Schweinfurt									
Cost of capital 2001	6.6	5.4	7.0	6.1	8.0	6.8	7.9	7.9	4.4
2002	6.6	5.4	7.0	6.1	8.0	6.8	7.9	7.9	4.4
2003	6.7	5.4	7.0	6.1	8.1	6.9	8.0	8.0	4.3
EMTR 2001	24.6	7.0	28.1	17.4	37.4	26.3	36.3	36.3	-14.5
2002	24.6	7.0	28.1	17.4	37.4	26.3	36.3	36.3	-14.5
2003	25.5	7.2	29.0	18.1	38.6	27.3	37.6	37.6	-16.4
EATR 2001	33.5	29.6	34.5	31.7	37.7	34.0	37.3	37.3	26.4
2002	33.5	29.6	34.5	31.7	37.7	34.0	37.3	37.3	26.4
2003	34.6	30.6	35.6	32.8	39.0	35.1	38.6	38.6	27.3

	Overall	Assets					Sources of finance		
		Intangibles	Industrial buildings	Machinery	Financial assets	Inventories	Retained earnings	New equity	Debt
Traunstein									
Cost of capital 2001	6.6	5.4	6.9	6.0	8.0	6.8	7.8	7.8	4.4
2002	6.6	5.4	6.9	6.0	8.0	6.8	7.8	7.8	4.4
2003	6.7	5.4	7.0	6.1	8.1	6.9	8.0	8.0	4.3
EMTR 2001	24.4	6.9	27.8	17.3	37.2	26.2	36.2	36.2	-14.6
2002	24.4	6.9	27.8	17.3	37.2	26.2	36.2	36.2	-14.6
2003	25.3	7.1	28.7	18.0	38.5	27.2	37.4	37.4	-16.5
EATR 2001	33.3	29.5	34.3	31.6	37.5	33.8	37.1	37.1	26.3
2002	33.3	29.5	34.3	31.6	37.5	33.8	37.1	37.1	26.3
2003	34.5	30.5	35.4	32.7	38.8	35.0	38.4	38.4	27.1
Weiden									
Cost of capital 2001	6.6	5.4	6.9	6.1	8.0	6.8	7.8	7.8	4.4
2002	6.6	5.4	6.8	6.0	7.9	6.7	7.8	7.8	4.3
2003	6.7	5.4	6.9	6.1	8.1	6.8	7.9	7.9	4.3
EMTR 2001	24.4	6.9	27.3	17.4	37.3	26.3	36.1	36.1	-14.9
2002	23.9	6.7	26.9	17.0	36.8	25.8	35.7	35.7	-15.0
2003	24.9	6.9	27.8	17.7	38.0	26.8	37.0	37.0	-16.9
EATR 2001	33.4	29.5	34.2	31.6	37.6	33.9	37.1	37.1	26.3
2002	32.9	29.1	33.8	31.2	37.1	33.5	36.7	36.7	26.0
2003	34.1	30.2	34.9	32.3	38.4	34.6	38.0	38.0	26.8
Weilheim									
Cost of capital 2001	6.5	5.3	6.7	5.9	7.7	6.6	7.6	7.6	4.3
2002	6.5	5.3	6.7	5.9	7.7	6.6	7.6	7.6	4.3
2003	6.5	5.3	6.8	6.0	7.9	6.7	7.8	7.8	4.3
EMTR 2001	22.7	6.0	25.8	15.9	35.3	24.5	34.4	34.4	-15.4
2002	22.7	6.0	25.8	15.9	35.3	24.5	34.4	34.4	-15.4
2003	23.6	6.2	26.7	16.6	36.6	25.5	35.7	35.7	-17.3
EATR 2001	31.7	28.0	32.5	30.0	35.7	32.2	35.4	35.4	24.9
2002	31.7	28.0	32.5	30.0	35.7	32.2	35.4	35.4	24.9
2003	32.9	29.1	33.7	31.1	37.0	33.4	36.7	36.7	25.7

		Assets					Sources of finance		
	Overall	Intangibles	Industrial buildings	Machinery	Financial assets	Inventories	Retained earnings	New equity	Debt
Weißenburg i. Bayern									
Cost of capital 2001	6.6	5.4	6.9	6.0	7.9	6.7	7.8	7.8	4.4
2002	6.6	5.4	6.8	6.0	7.9	6.7	7.7	7.7	4.3
2003	6.6	5.4	6.9	6.1	8.0	6.8	7.9	7.9	4.3
EMTR 2001	23.9	6.6	27.7	16.8	36.5	25.6	35.6	35.6	-14.6
2002	23.8	6.6	26.9	16.8	36.5	25.6	35.5	35.5	-14.9
2003	24.7	6.8	27.8	17.5	37.7	26.5	36.8	36.8	-16.8
EATR 2001	32.8	28.9	33.8	31.0	36.8	33.2	36.5	36.5	25.8
2002	32.7	28.9	33.6	31.0	36.8	33.2	36.5	36.5	25.8
2003	33.9	29.9	34.8	32.1	38.1	34.4	37.8	37.8	26.6
Würzburg									
Cost of capital 2001	6.7	5.4	7.1	6.1	8.2	6.9	8.0	8.0	4.4
2002	6.7	5.4	7.1	6.1	8.2	6.9	8.0	8.0	4.4
2003	6.8	5.4	7.1	6.2	8.3	7.0	8.2	8.2	4.3
EMTR 2001	25.8	7.7	29.2	18.5	38.8	27.6	37.5	37.5	-14.1
2002	25.8	7.7	29.2	18.5	38.8	27.6	37.5	37.5	-14.1
2003	26.7	7.9	30.0	19.2	40.0	28.6	38.8	38.8	-16.0
EATR 2001	34.6	30.6	35.6	32.8	39.0	35.2	38.5	38.5	27.5
2002	34.6	30.6	35.6	32.8	39.0	35.2	38.5	38.5	27.5
2003	35.8	31.6	36.7	33.9	40.3	36.3	39.8	39.8	28.3
Berlin									
Cost of capital 2001	6.8	5.4	7.2	6.1	8.1	6.9	8.0	8.0	4.4
2002	6.8	5.4	7.2	6.1	8.1	6.9	8.0	8.0	4.4
2003	6.8	5.4	7.4	6.2	8.3	7.0	8.2	8.2	4.4
EMTR 2001	26.0	7.5	30.9	18.3	38.5	27.3	37.6	37.6	-13.2
2002	26.0	7.5	30.9	18.3	38.5	27.3	37.6	37.6	-13.2
2003	27.0	7.8	32.2	19.0	39.7	28.3	38.9	38.9	-14.8
EATR 2001	34.5	30.4	36.0	32.6	38.7	34.9	38.4	38.4	27.4
2002	34.5	30.4	36.0	32.6	38.7	34.9	38.4	38.4	27.4
2003	35.7	31.4	37.3	33.7	40.0	36.1	39.7	39.7	28.2

		Assets					Sources of finance		
	Overall	Intangibles	Industrial buildings	Machinery	Financial assets	Inventories	Retained earnings	New equity	Debt
Hamburg									
Cost of capital 2001	6.9	5.5	7.3	6.2	8.4	7.0	8.2	8.2	4.4
2002	6.9	5.5	7.3	6.2	8.4	7.0	8.2	8.2	4.4
2003	6.9	5.5	7.3	6.3	8.5	7.1	8.3	8.3	4.3
EMTR 2001	27.1	8.4	31.1	19.5	40.1	28.8	38.9	38.9	-13.3
2002	27.1	8.4	31.1	19.5	40.1	28.8	38.9	38.9	-13.3
2003	28.0	8.6	31.9	20.2	41.3	29.8	40.1	40.1	-15.2
EATR 2001	35.8	31.6	37.0	33.9	40.3	36.3	39.8	39.8	28.5
2002	35.8	31.6	37.0	33.9	40.3	36.3	39.8	39.8	28.5
2003	36.9	32.6	38.1	35.0	41.5	37.4	41.0	41.0	29.3
Frankfurt									
Cost of capital 2001	6.9	5.5	7.3	6.3	8.5	7.1	8.3	8.3	4.4
2002	6.9	5.5	7.3	6.2	8.4	7.1	8.2	8.2	4.4
2003	7.0	5.5	7.4	6.3	8.6	7.2	8.4	8.4	4.3
EMTR 2001	27.8	8.8	31.8	20.1	40.9	29.5	39.6	39.6	-13.0
2002	27.5	8.6	31.2	19.9	40.7	29.3	39.3	39.3	-13.3
2003	28.4	8.9	32.0	20.6	41.8	30.2	40.5	40.5	-15.2
EATR 2001	36.5	32.2	37.7	34.5	41.0	37.0	40.5	40.5	29.1
2002	36.3	32.0	37.3	34.3	40.8	36.8	40.2	40.2	28.9
2003	37.3	33.0	38.4	35.4	42.0	37.9	41.4	41.4	29.7
Offenbach									
Cost of capital 2001	6.8	5.4	7.1	6.2	8.2	7.0	8.1	8.1	4.4
2002	6.8	5.4	7.1	6.2	8.2	7.0	8.1	8.1	4.4
2003	6.9	5.4	7.2	6.2	8.4	7.0	8.2	8.2	4.3
EMTR 2001	26.3	8.0	29.7	18.9	39.3	28.1	38.0	38.0	-13.9
2002	26.3	8.0	29.7	18.9	39.3	28.1	38.0	38.0	-13.9
2003	27.1	8.2	30.5	19.6	40.5	29.0	39.3	39.3	-15.9
EATR 2001	35.1	31.0	36.1	33.3	39.5	35.6	39.0	39.0	27.9
2002	35.1	31.0	36.1	33.3	39.5	35.6	39.0	39.0	27.9
2003	36.2	32.0	37.2	34.3	40.8	36.8	40.3	40.3	28.7

	Overall	Intangibles	Industrial buildings	Machinery	Financial assets	Inventories	Retained earnings	New equity	Debt
		Assets					Sources of finance		
Düsseldorf									
Cost of capital 2001	6.8	5.4	7.2	6.2	8.3	7.0	8.1	8.1	4.4
2002	6.8	5.4	7.2	6.2	8.3	7.0	8.1	8.1	4.4
2003	6.9	5.5	7.3	6.2	8.5	7.1	8.3	8.3	4.3
EMTR 2001	26.9	8.2	30.9	19.3	39.9	28.6	38.6	38.6	-13.4
2002	26.8	8.2	30.7	19.2	39.7	28.4	38.5	38.5	-13.5
2003	27.6	8.4	31.5	19.9	40.9	29.4	39.7	39.7	-15.4
EATR 2001	35.6	31.4	36.8	33.7	40.0	36.1	39.5	39.5	28.3
2002	35.5	31.3	36.7	33.6	39.9	36.0	39.4	39.4	28.2
2003	36.6	32.3	37.7	34.6	41.1	37.1	40.7	40.7	29.0
Essen									
Cost of capital 2001	6.9	5.5	7.3	6.2	8.4	7.0	8.2	8.2	4.4
2002	6.9	5.5	7.3	6.2	8.4	7.0	8.2	8.2	4.4
2003	6.9	5.5	7.4	6.3	8.5	7.1	8.3	8.3	4.3
EMTR 2001	27.1	8.4	31.1	19.5	40.1	28.8	38.9	38.9	-13.3
2002	27.1	8.4	31.1	19.5	40.1	28.8	38.9	38.9	-13.3
2003	28.0	8.6	32.1	20.2	41.3	29.8	40.1	40.1	-15.1
EATR 2001	35.8	31.6	37.0	33.9	40.3	36.3	39.8	39.8	28.5
2002	35.8	31.6	37.0	33.9	40.3	36.3	39.8	39.8	28.5
2003	36.9	32.6	38.1	35.0	41.5	37.4	41.0	41.0	29.3
Köln									
Cost of capital 2001	6.8	5.4	7.2	6.2	8.3	7.0	8.1	8.1	4.4
2002	6.8	5.4	7.2	6.2	8.3	7.0	8.1	8.1	4.4
2003	6.9	5.5	7.3	6.2	8.4	7.1	8.3	8.3	4.3
EMTR 2001	26.7	8.1	30.8	19.1	39.6	28.3	38.4	38.4	-13.4
2002	26.7	8.1	30.8	19.1	39.6	28.3	38.4	38.4	-13.4
2003	27.6	8.3	31.6	19.8	40.8	29.3	39.6	39.6	-15.3
EATR 2001	35.4	31.2	36.6	33.5	39.8	35.9	39.3	39.3	28.1
2002	35.4	31.2	36.6	33.5	39.8	35.9	39.3	39.3	28.1
2003	36.5	32.2	37.7	34.5	41.0	37.0	40.6	40.6	28.9

	Overall	Assets					Sources of finance		
		Intangibles	Industrial buildings	Machinery	Financial assets	Inventories	Retained earnings	New equity	Debt
Landau									
Cost of capital 2001	6.7	5.4	7.0	6.1	8.2	6.9	8.0	8.0	4.4
2002	6.7	5.4	7.0	6.1	8.2	6.9	8.0	8.0	4.4
2003	6.8	5.4	7.1	6.2	8.3	7.0	8.2	8.2	4.3
EMTR 2001	25.7	7.7	29.0	18.5	38.8	27.6	37.5	37.5	-14.2
2002	25.7	7.7	29.0	18.5	38.8	27.6	37.5	37.5	-14.2
2003	26.6	7.9	29.9	19.2	40.0	28.6	38.8	38.8	-16.1
EATR 2001	34.6	30.6	35.6	32.8	39.0	35.2	38.5	38.5	27.5
2002	34.6	30.6	35.6	32.8	39.0	35.2	38.5	38.5	27.5
2003	35.8	31.6	36.7	33.9	40.3	36.3	39.8	39.8	28.3
Ludwigshafen									
Cost of capital 2001	6.7	5.4	7.0	6.1	8.1	6.8	7.9	7.9	4.4
2002	6.7	5.4	7.0	6.1	8.1	6.8	7.9	7.9	4.4
2003	6.7	5.4	7.0	6.1	8.1	6.9	8.0	8.0	4.3
EMTR 2001	25.0	7.3	28.4	17.9	37.9	26.8	36.8	36.8	-14.4
2002	25.0	7.3	28.4	17.9	37.9	26.8	36.8	36.8	-14.4
2003	25.2	7.1	28.6	17.9	38.3	27.1	37.3	37.3	-16.5
EATR 2001	33.9	30.0	34.9	32.1	38.2	34.4	37.8	37.8	26.9
2002	33.9	30.0	34.9	32.1	38.2	34.4	37.8	37.8	26.9
2003	34.4	30.4	35.3	32.5	38.7	34.9	38.3	38.3	27.0
Mainz									
Cost of capital 2001	6.8	5.4	7.1	6.2	8.2	7.0	8.1	8.1	4.4
2002	6.8	5.4	7.1	6.2	8.2	7.0	8.1	8.1	4.4
2003	6.9	5.4	7.2	6.2	8.4	7.0	8.2	8.2	4.3
EMTR 2001	26.3	8.0	29.7	18.9	39.3	28.1	38.0	38.0	-13.9
2002	26.3	8.0	29.7	18.9	39.3	28.1	38.0	38.0	-13.9
2003	27.1	8.2	30.5	19.6	40.5	29.0	39.3	39.3	-15.9
EATR 2001	35.1	31.0	36.1	33.3	39.5	35.6	39.0	39.0	27.9
2002	35.1	31.0	36.1	33.3	39.5	35.6	39.0	39.0	27.9
2003	36.2	32.0	37.2	34.3	40.8	36.8	40.3	40.3	28.7

D.1.4 Ireland

	Overall	Assets					Sources of finance		
		Intangibles	Industrial buildings	Machinery	Financial assets	Inventories	Retained earnings	New equity	Debt
Dublin									
Cost of capital 2001	5.6	5.3	5.5	5.0	6.5	5.4	5.9	5.9	4.9
2002	5.6	5.3	5.6	5.0	6.5	5.4	5.9	5.9	4.9
2003	5.7	5.4	5.6	5.3	6.5	5.5	6.1	6.1	4.9
EMTR 2001	10.1	5.7	9.9	0.9	23.2	7.3	15.8	15.8	-2.9
2002	10.1	5.7	10.3	0.9	23.2	7.3	15.8	15.8	-2.8
2003	11.9	7.2	11.5	5.9	23.2	9.2	18.2	18.2	-2.9
EATR 2001	12.0	8.9	10.0	7.7	24.4	9.3	13.6	13.6	9.1
2002	12.1	8.9	10.1	7.7	24.4	9.3	13.6	13.6	9.1
2003	14.0	11.1	12.2	10.7	24.4	11.6	15.8	15.8	10.6

D.1.5 Italy

Standard Case	Overall	Assets: Intangibles	Assets: Industrial buildings	Assets: Machinery	Assets: Financial assets	Assets: Inventories	Sources of finance: Retained earnings	Sources of finance: New equity	Sources of finance: Debt
Gorizia									
Cost of capital 2001	4.7	2.9	4.5	3.8	7.5	4.9	5.3	5.3	3.7
2002	6.3	4.6	6.5	5.7	7.5	6.9	7.6	7.6	3.7
2003	6.2	4.6	6.4	5.6	7.3	6.8	7.4	7.4	3.8
EMTR 2001	-5.7	-73.5	-10.4	-31.7	33.7	-2.1	5.6	5.6	-36.2
2002	20.0	-8.3	23.1	12.3	33.7	27.5	34.6	34.6	-36.2
2003	18.8	-7.6	22.1	11.5	31.8	26.0	32.7	32.7	-31.8
EATR 2001	28.8	23.9	28.8	26.6	35.1	29.9	30.6	30.6	25.6
2002	33.4	29.0	34.7	32.3	35.1	35.9	37.6	37.6	25.6
2003	31.7	27.6	33.1	30.7	33.2	34.1	35.7	35.7	24.3
Pordenone									
Cost of capital 2001	4.7	2.9	4.4	3.8	7.5	4.9	5.3	5.3	3.6
2002	6.2	4.6	6.5	5.7	7.5	6.9	7.6	7.6	3.7
2003	6.2	4.6	6.4	5.6	7.3	6.8	7.4	7.4	3.8
EMTR 2001	-6.3	-73.5	-13.5	-31.7	33.7	-2.1	5.2	5.2	-37.1
2002	19.9	-8.3	22.7	12.3	33.7	27.5	34.5	34.5	-36.5
2003	18.7	-7.6	21.6	11.5	31.8	26.0	32.7	32.7	-32.1
EATR 2001	28.8	23.9	28.4	26.6	35.1	29.9	30.5	30.5	25.5
2002	33.4	29.0	34.6	32.3	35.1	35.9	37.6	37.6	25.6
2003	31.7	27.6	32.9	30.7	33.2	34.1	35.7	35.7	24.3
Trieste									
Cost of capital 2001	4.7	2.9	4.5	3.8	7.5	4.9	5.3	5.3	3.7
2002	6.3	4.6	6.6	5.7	7.5	6.9	7.7	7.7	3.7
2003	6.2	4.6	6.5	5.6	7.3	6.8	7.4	7.4	3.8
EMTR 2001	-5.7	-73.5	-10.4	-31.7	33.7	-2.1	5.6	5.6	-36.2
2002	20.3	-8.3	24.1	12.3	33.7	27.5	34.7	34.7	-35.6
2003	19.0	-7.6	23.0	11.5	31.8	26.0	32.9	32.9	-31.2
EATR 2001	28.8	23.9	28.8	26.6	35.1	29.9	30.6	30.6	25.6
2002	33.5	29.0	34.9	32.3	35.1	35.9	37.7	37.7	25.6
2003	31.8	27.6	33.3	30.7	33.2	34.1	35.8	35.8	24.4

Standard Case	Overall	Assets					Sources of finance		
		Intangibles	Industrial buildings	Machinery	Financial assets	Inventories	Retained earnings	New equity	Debt
Udine									
Cost of capital 2001	4.7	2.9	4.4	3.8	7.5	4.9	5.3	5.3	3.7
2002	6.2	4.6	6.4	5.7	7.5	6.9	7.6	7.6	3.7
2003	6.1	4.6	6.3	5.6	7.3	6.8	7.4	7.4	3.8
EMTR 2001	-6.1	-73.5	-12.5	-31.7	33.7	-2.1	5.3	5.3	-36.8
2002	19.8	-8.3	22.2	12.3	33.7	27.5	34.4	34.4	-36.8
2003	18.6	-7.6	21.1	11.5	31.8	26.0	32.6	32.6	-32.3
EATR 2001	28.8	23.9	28.5	26.6	35.1	29.9	30.6	30.6	25.5
2002	33.4	29.0	34.4	32.3	35.1	35.9	37.6	37.6	25.5
2003	31.7	27.6	32.8	30.7	33.2	34.1	35.7	35.7	24.3
Bergamo									
Cost of capital 2001	4.7	2.9	4.5	3.8	7.5	4.9	5.3	5.3	3.7
2002	6.3	4.6	6.5	5.7	7.5	6.9	7.6	7.6	3.7
2003	6.2	4.6	6.4	5.6	7.3	6.8	7.4	7.4	3.8
EMTR 2001	-5.8	-73.5	-10.6	-31.7	33.7	-2.1	5.6	5.6	-36.2
2002	20.0	-8.3	23.1	12.3	33.7	27.5	34.6	34.6	-36.2
2003	18.8	-7.6	22.0	11.5	31.8	26.0	32.7	32.7	-31.8
EATR 2001	28.8	23.9	28.8	26.6	35.1	29.9	30.6	30.6	25.6
2002	33.4	29.0	34.7	32.3	35.1	35.9	37.6	37.6	25.6
2003	31.7	27.6	33.0	30.7	33.2	34.1	35.7	35.7	24.3
Brescia									
Cost of capital 2001	4.7	2.9	4.5	3.8	7.5	4.9	5.3	5.3	3.7
2002	6.3	4.6	6.5	5.7	7.5	6.9	7.6	7.6	3.7
2003	6.2	4.6	6.4	5.6	7.3	6.8	7.4	7.4	3.8
EMTR 2001	-5.8	-73.5	-10.8	-31.7	33.7	-2.1	5.6	5.6	-36.3
2002	20.0	-8.3	23.0	12.3	33.7	27.5	34.6	34.6	-36.3
2003	18.8	-7.6	21.9	11.5	31.8	26.0	32.7	32.7	-31.9
EATR 2001	28.8	23.9	28.7	26.6	35.1	29.9	30.6	30.6	25.6
2002	33.4	29.0	34.6	32.3	35.1	35.9	37.6	37.6	25.6
2003	31.7	27.6	33.0	30.7	33.2	34.1	35.7	35.7	24.3

Standard Case	Overall	Assets: Intangibles	Industrial buildings	Machinery	Financial assets	Inventories	Sources of finance: Retained earnings	New equity	Debt
Como									
Cost of capital 2001	4.7	2.9	4.5	3.8	7.5	4.9	5.3	5.3	3.7
2002	6.2	4.6	6.5	5.7	7.5	6.9	7.6	7.6	3.7
2003	6.2	4.6	6.5	5.6	7.3	6.8	7.4	7.4	3.8
EMTR 2001	-5.9	-73.5	-11.2	-31.7	33.7	-2.1	5.5	5.5	-36.4
2002	20.0	-8.3	22.8	12.3	33.7	27.5	34.5	34.5	-36.4
2003	19.0	-7.6	22.7	11.5	31.8	26.0	32.8	32.8	-31.5
EATR 2001	28.8	23.9	28.7	26.6	35.1	29.9	30.6	30.6	25.6
2002	33.4	29.0	34.6	32.3	35.1	35.9	37.6	37.6	25.6
2003	31.8	27.6	33.2	30.7	33.2	34.1	35.7	35.7	24.4
Cremona									
Cost of capital 2001	4.7	2.9	4.5	3.8	7.5	4.9	5.3	5.3	3.7
2002	6.3	4.6	6.5	5.7	7.5	6.9	7.7	7.7	3.7
2003	6.2	4.6	6.5	5.6	7.3	6.8	7.4	7.4	3.8
EMTR 2001	-5.9	-73.5	-11.1	-31.7	33.7	-2.1	5.5	5.5	-36.4
2002	20.2	-8.3	23.6	12.3	33.7	27.5	34.7	34.7	-35.9
2003	18.9	-7.6	22.6	11.5	31.8	26.0	32.8	32.8	-31.5
EATR 2001	28.8	23.9	28.7	26.6	35.1	29.9	30.6	30.6	25.6
2002	33.4	29.0	34.8	32.3	35.1	35.9	37.6	37.6	25.6
2003	31.8	27.6	33.2	30.7	33.2	34.1	35.7	35.7	24.4
Lecco									
Cost of capital 2001	4.7	2.9	4.5	3.8	7.5	4.9	5.3	5.3	3.7
2002	6.3	4.6	6.5	5.7	7.5	6.9	7.6	7.6	3.7
2003	6.2	4.6	6.5	5.6	7.3	6.8	7.4	7.4	3.8
EMTR 2001	-5.8	-73.5	-10.6	-31.7	33.7	-2.1	5.6	5.6	-36.2
2002	20.0	-8.3	23.1	12.3	33.7	27.5	34.6	34.6	-36.2
2003	19.0	-7.6	22.9	11.5	31.8	26.0	32.9	32.9	-31.3
EATR 2001	28.8	23.9	28.8	26.6	35.1	29.9	30.6	30.6	25.6
2002	33.4	29.0	34.7	32.3	35.1	35.9	37.6	37.6	25.6
2003	31.8	27.6	33.3	30.7	33.2	34.1	35.8	35.8	24.4

Standard Case	Overall	Assets: Intangibles	Assets: Industrial buildings	Assets: Machinery	Assets: Financial assets	Assets: Inventories	Sources of finance: Retained earnings	Sources of finance: New equity	Sources of finance: Debt
Lodi									
Cost of capital 2001	4.7	2.9	4.6	3.8	7.5	4.9	5.3	5.3	3.7
2002	6.3	4.6	6.5	5.7	7.5	6.9	7.7	7.7	3.7
2003	6.2	4.6	6.5	5.6	7.3	6.8	7.4	7.4	3.8
EMTR 2001	-5.5	-73.5	-9.4	-31.7	33.7	-2.1	5.8	5.8	-35.9
2002	20.2	-8.3	23.6	12.3	33.7	27.5	34.7	34.7	-35.9
2003	18.9	-7.6	22.6	11.5	31.8	26.0	32.8	32.8	-31.5
EATR 2001	28.9	23.9	28.9	26.6	35.1	29.9	30.6	30.6	25.6
2002	33.4	29.0	34.8	32.3	35.1	35.9	37.6	37.6	25.6
2003	31.8	27.6	33.2	30.7	33.2	34.1	35.7	35.7	24.4
Mantova									
Cost of capital 2001	4.7	2.9	4.6	3.8	7.5	4.9	5.3	5.3	3.7
2002	6.3	4.6	6.6	5.7	7.5	6.9	7.7	7.7	3.7
2003	6.2	4.6	6.5	5.6	7.3	6.8	7.4	7.4	3.8
EMTR 2001	-5.4	-73.5	-8.5	-31.7	33.7	-2.1	5.9	5.9	-35.6
2002	20.3	-8.3	24.1	12.3	33.7	27.5	34.7	34.7	-35.6
2003	19.0	-7.6	23.0	11.5	31.8	26.0	32.9	32.9	-31.2
EATR 2001	28.9	23.9	29.0	26.6	35.1	29.9	30.7	30.7	25.6
2002	33.5	29.0	34.9	32.3	35.1	35.9	37.7	37.7	25.6
2003	31.8	27.6	33.3	30.7	33.2	34.1	35.8	35.8	24.4
Milano									
Cost of capital 2001	4.7	2.9	4.4	3.8	7.5	4.9	5.3	5.3	3.7
2002	6.2	4.6	6.4	5.7	7.5	6.9	7.6	7.6	3.7
2003	6.1	4.6	6.3	5.6	7.3	6.8	7.4	7.4	3.8
EMTR 2001	-6.1	-73.5	-12.5	-31.7	33.7	-2.1	5.3	5.3	-36.8
2002	19.8	-8.3	22.2	12.3	33.7	27.5	34.4	34.4	-36.8
2003	18.6	-7.6	21.1	11.5	31.8	26.0	32.6	32.6	-32.3
EATR 2001	28.8	23.9	28.5	26.6	35.1	29.9	30.6	30.6	25.5
2002	33.4	29.0	34.4	32.3	35.1	35.9	37.6	37.6	25.5
2003	31.7	27.6	32.8	30.7	33.2	34.1	35.7	35.7	24.3

Standard Case	Overall	Assets: Intangibles	Industrial buildings	Machinery	Financial assets	Inventories	Sources of finance: Retained earnings	New equity	Debt
Pavia									
Cost of capital 2001	4.7	2.9	4.6	3.8	7.5	4.9	5.3	5.3	3.7
2002	6.3	4.6	6.5	5.7	7.5	6.9	7.7	7.7	3.7
2003	6.2	4.6	6.5	5.6	7.3	6.8	7.4	7.4	3.8
EMTR 2001	-5.5	-73.5	-9.4	-31.7	33.7	-2.1	5.8	5.8	-35.9
2002	20.2	-8.3	23.6	12.3	33.7	27.5	34.7	34.7	-35.9
2003	18.9	-7.6	22.6	11.5	31.8	26.0	32.8	32.8	-31.5
EATR 2001	28.9	23.9	28.9	26.6	35.1	29.9	30.6	30.6	25.6
2002	33.4	29.0	34.8	32.3	35.1	35.9	37.6	37.6	25.6
2003	31.8	27.6	33.2	30.7	33.2	34.1	35.7	35.7	24.4
Sondrio									
Cost of capital 2001	4.7	2.9	4.5	3.8	7.5	4.9	5.3	5.3	3.7
2002	6.3	4.6	6.5	5.7	7.5	6.9	7.6	7.6	3.7
2003	6.2	4.6	6.4	5.6	7.3	6.8	7.4	7.4	3.8
EMTR 2001	-5.8	-73.5	-10.8	-31.7	33.7	-2.1	5.6	5.6	-36.3
2002	20.0	-8.3	23.0	12.3	33.7	27.5	34.6	34.6	-36.3
2003	18.8	-7.6	21.9	11.5	31.8	26.0	32.7	32.7	-31.9
EATR 2001	28.8	23.9	28.7	26.6	35.1	29.9	30.6	30.6	25.6
2002	33.4	29.0	34.6	32.3	35.1	35.9	37.6	37.6	25.6
2003	31.7	27.6	33.0	30.7	33.2	34.1	35.7	35.7	24.3
Varese									
Cost of capital 2001	4.7	2.9	4.5	3.8	7.5	4.9	5.3	5.3	3.7
2002	6.3	4.6	6.5	5.7	7.5	6.9	7.6	7.6	3.7
2003	6.2	4.6	6.4	5.6	7.3	6.8	7.4	7.4	3.8
EMTR 2001	-5.8	-73.5	-10.6	-31.7	33.7	-2.1	5.6	5.6	-36.2
2002	20.0	-8.3	23.1	12.3	33.7	27.5	34.6	34.6	-36.2
2003	18.8	-7.6	22.0	11.5	31.8	26.0	32.7	32.7	-31.8
EATR 2001	28.8	23.9	28.8	26.6	35.1	29.9	30.6	30.6	25.6
2002	33.4	29.0	34.7	32.3	35.1	35.9	37.6	37.6	25.6
2003	31.7	27.6	33.0	30.7	33.2	34.1	35.7	35.7	24.3

Standard Case	Overall	Assets					Sources of finance		
		Intangibles	Industrial buildings	Machinery	Financial assets	Inventories	Retained earnings	New equity	Debt
Alessandria									
Cost of capital 2001	4.7	2.9	4.6	3.8	7.5	4.9	5.3	5.3	3.7
2002	6.3	4.6	6.6	5.7	7.5	6.9	7.7	7.7	3.7
2003	6.2	4.6	6.5	5.6	7.3	6.8	7.4	7.4	3.8
EMTR 2001	-5.5	-73.5	-9.4	-31.7	33.7	-2.1	5.8	5.8	-35.9
2002	20.3	-8.3	24.1	12.3	33.7	27.5	34.7	34.7	-35.6
2003	19.0	-7.6	23.0	11.5	31.8	26.0	32.9	32.9	-31.2
EATR 2001	28.9	23.9	28.9	26.6	35.1	29.9	30.6	30.6	25.6
2002	33.5	29.0	34.9	32.3	35.1	35.9	37.7	37.7	25.6
2003	31.8	27.6	33.3	30.7	33.2	34.1	35.8	35.8	24.4
Asti									
Cost of capital 2001	4.7	2.9	4.6	3.8	7.5	4.9	5.3	5.3	3.7
2002	6.3	4.6	6.5	5.7	7.5	6.9	7.7	7.7	3.7
2003	6.2	4.6	6.5	5.6	7.3	6.8	7.4	7.4	3.8
EMTR 2001	-5.5	-73.5	-9.4	-31.7	33.7	-2.1	5.8	5.8	-35.9
2002	20.2	-8.3	23.6	12.3	33.7	27.5	34.7	34.7	-35.9
2003	19.0	-7.6	23.0	11.5	31.8	26.0	32.9	32.9	-31.2
EATR 2001	28.9	23.9	28.9	26.6	35.1	29.9	30.6	30.6	25.6
2002	33.4	29.0	34.8	32.3	35.1	35.9	37.6	37.6	25.6
2003	31.8	27.6	33.3	30.7	33.2	34.1	35.8	35.8	24.4
Biella									
Cost of capital 2001	4.7	2.9	4.5	3.8	7.5	4.9	5.3	5.3	3.7
2002	6.3	4.6	6.5	5.7	7.5	6.9	7.6	7.6	3.7
2003	6.2	4.6	6.4	5.6	7.3	6.8	7.4	7.4	3.8
EMTR 2001	-5.6	-73.5	-9.9	-31.7	33.7	-2.1	5.7	5.7	-36.0
2002	20.1	-8.3	23.4	12.3	33.7	27.5	34.6	34.6	-36.0
2003	18.9	-7.6	22.3	11.5	31.8	26.0	32.8	32.8	-31.6
EATR 2001	28.9	23.9	28.8	26.6	35.1	29.9	30.6	30.6	25.6
2002	33.4	29.0	34.7	32.3	35.1	35.9	37.6	37.6	25.6
2003	31.7	27.6	33.1	30.7	33.2	34.1	35.7	35.7	24.3

Standard Case	Overall	Assets					Sources of finance		
		Intangibles	Industrial buildings	Machinery	Financial assets	Inventories	Retained earnings	New equity	Debt
Cuneo									
Cost of capital 2001	4.7	2.9	4.6	3.8	7.5	4.9	5.3	5.3	3.7
2002	6.3	4.6	6.5	5.7	7.5	6.9	7.7	7.7	3.7
2003	6.2	4.6	6.5	5.6	7.3	6.8	7.4	7.4	3.8
EMTR 2001	-5.5	-73.5	-9.4	-31.7	33.7	-2.1	5.8	5.8	-35.9
2002	20.2	-8.3	23.6	12.3	33.7	27.5	34.7	34.7	-35.9
2003	18.9	-7.6	22.6	11.5	31.8	26.0	32.8	32.8	-31.5
EATR 2001	28.9	23.9	28.9	26.6	35.1	29.9	30.6	30.6	25.6
2002	33.4	29.0	34.8	32.3	35.1	35.9	37.6	37.6	25.6
2003	31.8	27.6	33.2	30.7	33.2	34.1	35.7	35.7	24.4
Novara									
Cost of capital 2001	4.7	2.9	4.5	3.8	7.5	4.9	5.3	5.3	3.7
2002	6.3	4.6	6.6	5.7	7.5	6.9	7.7	7.7	3.7
2003	6.2	4.6	6.5	5.6	7.3	6.8	7.4	7.4	3.8
EMTR 2001	-5.8	-73.5	-10.8	-31.7	33.7	-2.1	5.6	5.6	-36.3
2002	20.2	-8.3	23.9	12.3	33.7	27.5	34.7	34.7	-35.7
2003	19.0	-7.6	22.9	11.5	31.8	26.0	32.9	32.9	-31.3
EATR 2001	28.8	23.9	28.7	26.6	35.1	29.9	30.6	30.6	25.6
2002	33.4	29.0	34.9	32.3	35.1	35.9	37.7	37.7	25.6
2003	31.8	27.6	33.3	30.7	33.2	34.1	35.8	35.8	24.4
Torino									
Cost of capital 2001	4.7	2.9	4.5	3.8	7.5	4.9	5.3	5.3	3.7
2002	6.3	4.6	6.5	5.7	7.5	6.9	7.7	7.7	3.7
2003	6.2	4.6	6.5	5.6	7.3	6.8	7.4	7.4	3.8
EMTR 2001	-5.7	-73.5	-10.4	-31.7	33.7	-2.1	5.6	5.6	-36.2
2002	20.2	-8.3	23.6	12.3	33.7	27.5	34.7	34.7	-35.9
2003	18.9	-7.6	22.6	11.5	31.8	26.0	32.8	32.8	-31.5
EATR 2001	28.8	23.9	28.8	26.6	35.1	29.9	30.6	30.6	25.6
2002	33.4	29.0	34.8	32.3	35.1	35.9	37.6	37.6	25.6
2003	31.8	27.6	33.2	30.7	33.2	34.1	35.7	35.7	24.4

Standard Case	Overall	Assets: Intangibles	Assets: Industrial buildings	Assets: Machinery	Assets: Financial assets	Assets: Inventories	Sources of finance: Retained earnings	Sources of finance: New equity	Sources of finance: Debt
Verbano-Cusio-Ossola									
Cost of capital 2001	4.7	2.9	4.5	3.8	7.5	4.9	5.3	5.3	3.7
2002	6.2	4.6	6.5	5.7	7.5	6.9	7.6	7.6	3.7
2003	6.2	4.6	6.4	5.6	7.3	6.8	7.4	7.4	3.8
EMTR 2001	-5.9	-73.5	-11.5	-31.7	33.7	-2.1	5.5	5.5	-36.5
2002	19.9	-8.3	22.7	12.3	33.7	27.5	34.5	34.5	-36.5
2003	18.7	-7.6	21.6	11.5	31.8	26.0	32.7	32.7	-32.1
EATR 2001	28.8	23.9	28.7	26.6	35.1	29.9	30.6	30.6	25.6
2002	33.4	29.0	34.6	32.3	35.1	35.9	37.6	37.6	25.6
2003	31.7	27.6	32.9	30.7	33.2	34.1	35.7	35.7	24.3
Vercelli									
Cost of capital 2001	4.7	2.9	4.4	3.8	7.5	4.9	5.3	5.3	3.7
2002	6.3	4.6	6.5	5.7	7.5	6.9	7.6	7.6	3.7
2003	6.2	4.6	6.4	5.6	7.3	6.8	7.4	7.4	3.8
EMTR 2001	-6.1	-73.5	-12.5	-31.7	33.7	-2.1	5.3	5.3	-36.8
2002	20.0	-8.3	23.1	12.3	33.7	27.5	34.6	34.6	-36.2
2003	18.8	-7.6	22.1	11.5	31.8	26.0	32.7	32.7	-31.8
EATR 2001	28.8	23.9	28.5	26.6	35.1	29.9	30.6	30.6	25.5
2002	33.4	29.0	34.7	32.3	35.1	35.9	37.6	37.6	25.6
2003	31.7	27.6	33.1	30.7	33.2	34.1	35.7	35.7	24.3
Bolzano									
Cost of capital 2001	4.7	2.9	4.5	3.8	7.5	4.9	5.3	5.3	3.7
2002	6.3	4.6	6.5	5.7	7.5	6.9	7.6	7.6	3.7
2003	6.2	4.6	6.4	5.6	7.3	6.8	7.4	7.4	3.8
EMTR 2001	-5.7	-73.5	-10.4	-31.7	33.7	-2.1	5.6	5.6	-36.2
2002	20.0	-8.3	23.1	12.3	33.7	27.5	34.6	34.6	-36.2
2003	18.8	-7.6	22.1	11.5	31.8	26.0	32.7	32.7	-31.8
EATR 2001	28.8	23.9	28.8	26.6	35.1	29.9	30.6	30.6	25.6
2002	33.4	29.0	34.7	32.3	35.1	35.9	37.6	37.6	25.6
2003	31.7	27.6	33.1	30.7	33.2	34.1	35.7	35.7	24.3

Standard Case	Overall	Assets: Intangibles	Assets: Industrial buildings	Assets: Machinery	Assets: Financial assets	Assets: Inventories	Sources of finance: Retained earnings	Sources of finance: New equity	Sources of finance: Debt
Trento									
Cost of capital 2001	4.7	2.9	4.4	3.8	7.5	4.9	5.3	5.3	3.7
2002	6.3	4.6	6.5	5.7	7.5	6.9	7.6	7.6	3.7
2003	6.2	4.6	6.4	5.6	7.3	6.8	7.4	7.4	3.8
EMTR 2001	-6.1	-73.5	-12.5	-31.7	33.7	-2.1	5.3	5.3	-36.8
2002	20.0	-8.3	23.1	12.3	33.7	27.5	34.6	34.6	-36.2
2003	18.8	-7.6	22.1	11.5	31.8	26.0	32.7	32.7	-31.8
EATR 2001	28.8	23.9	28.5	26.6	35.1	29.9	30.6	30.6	25.5
2002	33.4	29.0	34.7	32.3	35.1	35.9	37.6	37.6	25.6
2003	31.7	27.6	33.1	30.7	33.2	34.1	35.7	35.7	24.3
Valle d'Aosta									
Cost of capital 2001	4.7	2.9	4.4	3.8	7.5	4.9	5.3	5.3	3.6
2002	6.2	4.6	6.3	5.7	7.5	6.9	7.6	7.6	3.6
2003	6.1	4.6	6.3	5.6	7.3	6.8	7.4	7.4	3.8
EMTR 2001	-6.5	-73.5	-14.6	-31.7	33.7	-2.1	5.0	5.0	-37.4
2002	19.6	-8.3	21.1	12.3	33.7	27.5	34.3	34.3	-37.4
2003	18.4	-7.6	20.1	11.5	31.8	26.0	32.4	32.4	-32.9
EATR 2001	28.7	23.9	28.3	26.6	35.1	29.9	30.5	30.5	25.5
2002	33.3	29.0	34.2	32.3	35.1	35.9	37.5	37.5	25.5
2003	31.6	27.6	32.6	30.7	33.2	34.1	35.6	35.6	24.2
Belluno									
Cost of capital 2001	4.7	2.9	4.6	3.8	7.5	4.9	5.3	5.3	3.7
2002	6.3	4.6	6.6	5.7	7.5	6.9	7.7	7.7	3.7
2003	6.2	4.6	6.5	5.6	7.3	6.8	7.4	7.4	3.8
EMTR 2001	-5.4	-73.5	-8.5	-31.7	33.7	-2.1	5.9	5.9	-35.6
2002	20.3	-8.3	24.1	12.3	33.7	27.5	34.7	34.7	-35.6
2003	19.0	-7.6	23.0	11.5	31.8	26.0	32.9	32.9	-31.2
EATR 2001	28.9	23.9	29.0	26.6	35.1	29.9	30.7	30.7	25.6
2002	33.5	29.0	34.9	32.3	35.1	35.9	37.7	37.7	25.6
2003	31.8	27.6	33.3	30.7	33.2	34.1	35.8	35.8	24.4

Standard Case	Overall	Assets					Sources of finance		
		Intangibles	Industrial buildings	Machinery	Financial assets	Inventories	Retained earnings	New equity	Debt
Padova									
Cost of capital 2001	4.7	2.9	4.5	3.8	7.5	4.9	5.3	5.3	3.7
2002	6.3	4.6	6.5	5.7	7.5	6.9	7.6	7.6	3.7
2003	6.2	4.6	6.4	5.6	7.3	6.8	7.4	7.4	3.8
EMTR 2001	-5.9	-73.5	-11.5	-31.7	33.7	-2.1	5.5	5.5	-36.5
2002	20.1	-8.3	23.3	12.3	33.7	27.5	34.6	34.6	-36.1
2003	18.9	-7.6	22.3	11.5	31.8	26.0	32.8	32.8	-31.7
EATR 2001	28.8	23.9	28.7	26.6	35.1	29.9	30.6	30.6	25.6
2002	33.4	29.0	34.7	32.3	35.1	35.9	37.6	37.6	25.6
2003	31.7	27.6	33.1	30.7	33.2	34.1	35.7	35.7	24.3
Rovigo									
Cost of capital 2001	4.7	2.9	4.6	3.8	7.5	4.9	5.3	5.3	3.7
2002	6.3	4.6	6.6	5.7	7.5	6.9	7.7	7.7	3.7
2003	6.2	4.6	6.5	5.6	7.3	6.8	7.4	7.4	3.8
EMTR 2001	-5.4	-73.5	-8.5	-31.7	33.7	-2.1	5.9	5.9	-35.6
2002	20.3	-8.3	24.1	12.3	33.7	27.5	34.7	34.7	-35.6
2003	19.0	-7.6	23.0	11.5	31.8	26.0	32.9	32.9	-31.2
EATR 2001	28.9	23.9	29.0	26.6	35.1	29.9	30.7	30.7	25.6
2002	33.5	29.0	34.9	32.3	35.1	35.9	37.7	37.7	25.6
2003	31.8	27.6	33.3	30.7	33.2	34.1	35.8	35.8	24.4
Treviso									
Cost of capital 2001	4.7	2.9	4.6	3.8	7.5	4.9	5.3	5.3	3.7
2002	6.3	4.6	6.5	5.7	7.5	6.9	7.7	7.7	3.7
2003	6.2	4.6	6.5	5.6	7.3	6.8	7.4	7.4	3.8
EMTR 2001	-5.5	-73.5	-9.4	-31.7	33.7	-2.1	5.8	5.8	-35.9
2002	20.2	-8.3	23.6	12.3	33.7	27.5	34.7	34.7	-35.9
2003	18.9	-7.6	22.6	11.5	31.8	26.0	32.8	32.8	-31.5
EATR 2001	28.9	23.9	28.9	26.6	35.1	29.9	30.6	30.6	25.6
2002	33.4	29.0	34.8	32.3	35.1	35.9	37.6	37.6	25.6
2003	31.8	27.6	33.2	30.7	33.2	34.1	35.7	35.7	24.4

Standard Case	Overall	Assets					Sources of finance		
		Intangibles	Industrial buildings	Machinery	Financial assets	Inventories	Retained earnings	New equity	Debt
Venezia									
Cost of capital 2001	4.7	2.9	4.6	3.8	7.5	4.9	5.3	5.3	3.7
2002	6.3	4.6	6.6	5.7	7.5	6.9	7.7	7.7	3.7
2003	6.2	4.6	6.5	5.6	7.3	6.8	7.4	7.4	3.8
EMTR 2001	-5.4	-73.5	-8.5	-31.7	33.7	-2.1	5.9	5.9	-35.6
2002	20.3	-8.3	24.1	12.3	33.7	27.5	34.7	34.7	-35.6
2003	19.0	-7.6	23.0	11.5	31.8	26.0	32.9	32.9	-31.2
EATR 2001	28.9	23.9	29.0	26.6	35.1	29.9	30.7	30.7	25.6
2002	33.5	29.0	34.9	32.3	35.1	35.9	37.7	37.7	25.6
2003	31.8	27.6	33.3	30.7	33.2	34.1	35.8	35.8	24.4
Verona									
Cost of capital 2001	4.7	2.9	4.5	3.8	7.5	4.9	5.3	5.3	3.7
2002	6.2	4.6	6.5	5.7	7.5	6.9	7.6	7.6	3.7
2003	6.2	4.6	6.5	5.6	7.3	6.8	7.4	7.4	3.8
EMTR 2001	-5.9	-73.5	-11.5	-31.7	33.7	-2.1	5.5	5.5	-36.5
2002	19.9	-8.3	22.7	12.3	33.7	27.5	34.5	34.5	-36.5
2003	19.0	-7.6	22.9	11.5	31.8	26.0	32.9	32.9	-31.3
EATR 2001	28.8	23.9	28.7	26.6	35.1	29.9	30.6	30.6	25.6
2002	33.4	29.0	34.6	32.3	35.1	35.9	37.6	37.6	25.6
2003	31.8	27.6	33.3	30.7	33.2	34.1	35.8	35.8	24.4
Vicenza									
Cost of capital 2001	4.7	2.9	4.5	3.8	7.5	4.9	5.3	5.3	3.7
2002	6.3	4.6	6.5	5.7	7.5	6.9	7.6	7.6	3.7
2003	6.2	4.6	6.4	5.6	7.3	6.8	7.4	7.4	3.8
EMTR 2001	-5.7	-73.5	-10.4	-31.7	33.7	-2.1	5.6	5.6	-36.2
2002	20.0	-8.3	23.1	12.3	33.7	27.5	34.6	34.6	-36.2
2003	18.8	-7.6	22.1	11.5	31.8	26.0	32.7	32.7	-31.8
EATR 2001	28.8	23.9	28.8	26.6	35.1	29.9	30.6	30.6	25.6
2002	33.4	29.0	34.7	32.3	35.1	35.9	37.6	37.6	25.6
2003	31.7	27.6	33.1	30.7	33.2	34.1	35.7	35.7	24.3

Incentives Case	Overall	Assets					Sources of finance		
		Intangibles	Industrial buildings	Machinery	Financial assets	Inventories	Retained earnings	New equity	Debt
Minimum									
Cost of capital 2001	3.3	-1.2	4.2	-0.8	7.5	6.9	4.5	4.5	1.0
2002	3.3	-1.2	4.2	-0.8	7.5	6.9	4.5	4.5	1.0
EMTR 2001	-51.1	*>100*	-20.1	*>100*	33.7	27.5	-10.1	-10.1	-389.2
2002	-51.1	*>100*	-20.1	*>100*	33.7	27.5	-10.1	-10.1	-389.2
EATR 2001	24.6	11.5	27.7	12.8	35.1	35.9	28.3	28.3	17.7
2002	24.6	11.5	27.7	12.8	35.1	35.9	28.3	28.3	17.7
Median									
Cost of capital 2001	3.3	-1.2	4.3	-0.8	7.5	6.9	4.6	4.6	1.1
2002	3.3	-1.2	4.3	-0.8	7.5	6.9	4.6	4.6	1.1
EMTR 2001	-49.7	*>100*	-15.7	*>100*	33.7	27.5	-9.3	-9.3	-374.7
2002	-49.6	*>100*	-15.5	*>100*	33.7	27.5	-9.3	-9.3	-373.9
EATR 2001	24.7	11.5	28.2	12.8	35.1	35.9	28.4	28.4	17.8
2002	24.7	11.5	28.2	12.8	35.1	35.9	28.4	28.4	17.8
Maximum									
Cost of capital 2001	3.4	-1.2	4.4	-0.8	7.5	6.9	4.6	4.6	1.1
2002	3.4	-1.2	4.4	-0.8	7.5	6.9	4.6	4.6	1.1
EMTR 2001	-48.8	*>100*	-13.3	*>100*	33.7	27.5	-8.9	-8.9	-366.7
2002	-48.8	*>100*	-13.3	*>100*	33.7	27.5	-8.9	-8.9	-366.7
EATR 2001	24.8	11.5	28.4	12.8	35.1	35.9	28.5	28.5	17.8
2002	24.8	11.5	28.4	12.8	35.1	35.9	28.5	28.5	17.8

Remark: EMTR values above 100 per cent have not been stated explicitly as they are difficult to understand and might be misleading; see section 2.1.3 or further information.

D.1.6 The Netherlands

	Overall	Assets					Sources of finance		
		Intangibles	Industrial buildings	Machinery	Financial assets	Inventories	Retained earnings	New equity	Debt
Amsterdam									
Cost of capital 2001	6.3	5.1	6.8	5.9	7.4	6.4	7.6	7.6	4.0
2002	6.3	5.1	6.8	5.9	7.4	6.4	7.6	7.6	4.0
2003	6.3	5.1	6.8	5.9	7.4	6.4	7.6	7.6	4.0
EMTR 2001	21.1	2.7	26.6	15.5	32.8	21.6	34.3	34.3	-26.2
2002	20.7	2.6	26.2	15.2	32.3	21.3	33.9	33.9	-25.5
2003	20.8	2.6	26.4	15.2	32.3	21.3	33.9	33.9	-25.4
EATR 2001	30.6	26.7	32.1	29.2	34.2	30.7	34.7	34.7	22.9
2002	30.2	26.3	31.7	28.8	33.7	30.3	34.3	34.3	22.5
2003	30.2	26.3	31.7	28.8	33.7	30.3	34.3	34.3	22.6
Den Haag									
Cost of capital 2001	6.4	5.1	7.0	5.9	7.4	6.4	7.6	7.6	4.0
2002	6.3	5.1	6.9	5.9	7.4	6.4	7.6	7.6	4.0
2003	6.3	5.1	6.9	5.9	7.4	6.4	7.6	7.6	4.0
EMTR 2001	21.5	2.7	28.3	15.5	32.8	21.6	34.6	34.6	-25.2
2002	21.1	2.6	27.8	15.2	32.3	21.3	34.1	34.1	-24.6
2003	21.1	2.6	27.8	15.2	32.3	21.3	34.1	34.1	-24.6
EATR 2001	30.7	26.7	32.7	29.2	34.2	30.7	34.9	34.9	23.0
2002	30.3	26.3	32.2	28.8	33.7	30.3	34.4	34.4	22.6
2003	30.3	26.3	32.2	28.8	33.7	30.3	34.4	34.4	22.6
Rotterdam									
Cost of capital 2001	6.4	5.1	7.0	5.9	7.4	6.4	7.7	7.7	4.0
2002	6.4	5.1	7.0	5.9	7.4	6.4	7.6	7.6	4.0
2003	6.4	5.1	7.1	5.9	7.4	6.4	7.6	7.6	4.0
EMTR 2001	21.7	2.7	29.0	15.5	32.8	21.6	34.7	34.7	-24.8
2002	21.4	2.6	28.9	15.2	32.3	21.3	34.3	34.3	-23.9
2003	21.4	2.6	29.2	15.2	32.3	21.3	34.3	34.3	-23.8
EATR 2001	30.7	26.7	32.9	29.2	34.2	30.7	34.9	34.9	23.0
2002	30.3	26.3	32.5	28.8	33.7	30.3	34.4	34.4	22.7
2003	30.3	26.3	32.6	28.8	33.7	30.3	34.4	34.4	22.7

	Overall	Assets: Intangibles	Assets: Industrial buildings	Assets: Machinery	Assets: Financial assets	Assets: Inventories	Sources of finance: Retained earnings	Sources of finance: New equity	Sources of finance: Debt
Utrecht									
Cost of capital 2001	6.4	5.1	6.9	5.9	7.4	6.4	7.6	7.6	4.0
2002	6.3	5.1	6.9	5.9	7.4	6.4	7.6	7.6	4.0
2003	6.3	5.1	6.9	5.9	7.4	6.4	7.6	7.6	4.0
EMTR 2001	21.3	2.7	27.6	15.5	32.8	21.6	34.5	34.5	-25.6
2002	21.0	2.6	27.4	15.2	32.3	21.3	34.0	34.0	-24.8
2003	21.1	2.6	27.6	15.2	32.3	21.3	34.1	34.1	-24.7
EATR 2001	30.7	26.7	32.5	29.2	34.2	30.7	34.8	34.8	22.9
2002	30.2	26.3	32.1	28.8	33.7	30.3	34.3	34.3	22.6
2003	30.2	26.3	32.1	28.8	33.7	30.3	34.3	34.3	22.6

D.1.7 Switzerland

	Overall	Assets					Sources of finance		
		Intangibles	Industrial buildings	Machinery	Financial assets	Inventories	Retained earnings	New equity	Debt
Basel-Landschaft									
Cost of capital 2001	6.0	5.3	5.8	5.7	7.0	6.3	7.0	7.0	4.1
2002	6.0	5.3	5.8	5.6	6.9	6.3	7.0	7.0	4.1
2003	6.0	5.3	5.8	5.6	6.9	6.3	7.0	7.0	4.1
EMTR 2001	16.6	5.3	13.5	11.7	28.1	20.4	28.7	28.7	-22.0
2002	16.3	4.9	13.3	11.4	27.9	20.2	28.4	28.4	-22.1
2003	16.3	4.9	13.2	11.3	27.9	20.1	28.4	28.4	-22.1
EATR 2001	22.9	20.3	22.1	21.7	26.5	24.0	26.7	26.7	15.9
2002	22.9	20.2	22.1	21.6	26.4	23.9	26.6	26.6	15.9
2003	22.8	20.2	22.1	21.6	26.4	23.9	26.6	26.6	15.9
Basel-Stadt									
Cost of capital 2001	5.9	5.2	5.7	5.6	6.9	6.2	6.9	6.9	4.1
2002	5.9	5.2	5.7	5.6	6.9	6.2	6.9	6.9	4.1
2003	5.9	5.2	5.7	5.6	6.9	6.2	6.9	6.9	4.1
EMTR 2001	15.6	4.6	12.7	10.9	27.0	19.4	27.5	27.5	-21.0
2002	15.6	4.6	12.7	10.9	27.0	19.4	27.5	27.5	-21.0
2003	15.6	4.6	12.7	10.9	27.0	19.4	27.5	27.5	-21.0
EATR 2001	22.1	19.5	21.3	20.9	25.6	23.1	25.7	25.7	15.3
2002	22.1	19.5	21.3	20.9	25.6	23.1	25.7	25.7	15.3
2003	22.1	19.5	21.3	20.9	25.6	23.1	25.7	25.7	15.3
Bern									
Cost of capital 2001	5.7	5.1	5.6	5.4	6.4	5.9	6.4	6.4	4.3
2002	5.7	5.1	5.6	5.4	6.4	5.9	6.4	6.4	4.3
2003	5.6	5.0	5.5	5.3	6.3	5.8	6.3	6.3	4.3
EMTR 2001	11.6	1.1	10.4	6.8	22.0	14.8	21.8	21.8	-16.6
2002	11.6	1.1	10.4	6.8	22.0	14.8	21.8	21.8	-16.6
2003	10.6	-0.2	9.3	5.7	21.2	13.9	20.6	20.6	-16.6
EATR 2001	18.8	16.5	18.5	17.7	21.8	19.6	21.7	21.7	13.4
2002	18.8	16.5	18.5	17.7	21.8	19.6	21.7	21.7	13.4
2003	18.6	16.2	18.2	17.4	21.5	19.4	21.3	21.3	13.4

	Overall	Intangibles	Industrial buildings	Machinery	Financial assets	Inventories	Retained earnings	New equity	Debt
		Assets					Sources of finance		
Genève									
Cost of capital 2001	5.8	5.2	5.7	5.5	6.7	6.1	6.7	6.7	4.2
2002	5.8	5.2	5.7	5.5	6.7	6.1	6.7	6.7	4.2
2003	5.8	5.2	5.7	5.5	6.7	6.1	6.7	6.7	4.2
EMTR 2001	14.5	3.1	12.8	9.4	25.6	18.0	25.9	25.9	-19.7
2002	14.5	3.1	12.8	9.4	25.6	18.0	25.9	25.9	-19.7
2003	14.5	3.1	12.8	9.4	25.6	18.0	25.9	25.9	-19.7
EATR 2001	21.4	18.8	21.0	20.2	24.7	22.3	24.8	24.8	15.1
2002	21.4	18.8	21.0	20.2	24.7	22.3	24.8	24.8	15.1
2003	21.4	18.8	21.0	20.2	24.7	22.3	24.8	24.8	15.1
Nidwalden									
Cost of capital 2001	5.5	5.0	5.4	5.3	6.1	5.7	6.1	6.1	4.4
2002	5.5	5.0	5.4	5.3	6.1	5.7	6.1	6.1	4.4
2003	5.5	5.0	5.4	5.3	6.1	5.7	6.1	6.1	4.4
EMTR 2001	9.1	0.7	6.9	5.4	18.3	12.1	17.8	17.8	-13.4
2002	9.1	0.7	6.9	5.4	18.3	12.1	17.8	17.8	-13.4
2003	9.0	0.7	6.8	5.3	18.1	12.0	17.7	17.7	-13.3
EATR 2001	15.5	13.6	15.0	14.6	18.0	16.3	17.9	17.9	11.0
2002	15.5	13.6	15.0	14.6	18.0	16.3	17.9	17.9	11.0
2003	15.4	13.5	14.9	14.5	17.9	16.2	17.8	17.8	11.0
Schwyz									
Cost of capital 2001	5.6	5.1	5.5	5.4	6.3	5.8	6.3	6.3	4.4
2002	5.6	5.1	5.5	5.4	6.2	5.8	6.3	6.3	4.4
2003	5.6	5.1	5.5	5.4	6.2	5.8	6.2	6.2	4.4
EMTR 2001	11.1	2.3	8.8	7.2	20.7	14.3	20.8	20.8	-14.9
2002	10.6	2.1	8.4	6.8	20.0	13.7	20.0	20.0	-14.3
2003	10.6	2.0	8.3	6.8	20.0	13.7	20.0	20.0	-14.2
EATR 2001	17.1	15.1	16.5	16.2	19.9	18.0	19.9	19.9	12.0
2002	16.5	14.5	16.0	15.6	19.2	17.3	19.2	19.2	11.6
2003	16.5	14.5	15.9	15.6	19.2	17.3	19.2	19.2	11.6

	Overall	Assets					Sources of finance		
		Intangibles	Industrial buildings	Machinery	Financial assets	Inventories	Retained earnings	New equity	Debt
St. Gallen									
Cost of capital 2001	5.4	4.7	5.2	5.0	6.3	5.6	6.0	6.0	4.1
2002	5.4	4.7	5.2	5.0	6.3	5.6	6.0	6.0	4.1
2003	5.4	4.7	5.2	5.0	6.3	5.6	6.0	6.0	4.1
EMTR 2001	6.9	-7.0	4.6	0.7	20.4	11.0	17.1	17.1	-20.8
2002	6.8	-7.0	4.6	0.7	20.3	11.0	17.0	17.0	-20.7
2003	6.9	-7.0	4.6	0.7	20.4	11.0	17.1	17.1	-20.8
EATR 2001	20.3	17.6	19.8	19.0	23.7	21.2	22.7	22.7	15.6
2002	20.2	17.6	19.7	18.9	23.5	21.1	22.6	22.6	15.6
2003	20.3	17.6	19.8	19.0	23.7	21.2	22.7	22.7	15.6
Ticino									
Cost of capital 2001	5.8	5.2	5.8	5.5	6.5	6.0	6.5	6.5	4.3
2002	5.8	5.2	5.8	5.5	6.5	6.0	6.5	6.5	4.3
2003	5.7	5.1	5.7	5.4	6.4	5.9	6.4	6.4	4.3
EMTR 2001	13.3	3.3	13.4	8.5	22.7	16.0	23.5	23.5	-15.4
2002	13.3	3.3	13.4	8.5	22.7	16.0	23.5	23.5	-15.4
2003	12.2	2.0	12.3	7.4	21.9	15.0	22.3	22.3	-15.4
EATR 2001	18.7	16.4	18.8	17.6	21.5	19.5	21.8	21.8	13.1
2002	18.7	16.4	18.8	17.6	21.5	19.5	21.8	21.8	13.1
2003	18.5	16.1	18.5	17.3	21.3	19.2	21.4	21.4	13.1
Vaud									
Cost of capital 2001	5.8	5.1	5.7	5.4	6.6	6.0	6.6	6.6	4.2
2002	5.8	5.1	5.7	5.4	6.6	6.0	6.6	6.6	4.2
2003	5.8	5.1	5.7	5.4	6.6	6.0	6.6	6.6	4.2
EMTR 2001	13.1	1.6	12.1	7.8	24.0	16.4	24.0	24.0	-18.5
2002	13.1	1.6	12.1	7.8	24.0	16.4	24.0	24.0	-18.5
2003	13.1	1.6	12.1	7.8	24.0	16.4	24.0	24.0	-18.5
EATR 2001	20.5	17.9	20.3	19.2	23.7	21.4	23.7	23.7	14.6
2002	20.5	17.9	20.3	19.2	23.7	21.4	23.7	23.7	14.6
2003	20.5	17.9	20.3	19.2	23.7	21.4	23.7	23.7	14.6

	Overall	Assets					Sources of finance		
		Intangibles	Industrial buildings	Machinery	Financial assets	Inventories	Retained earnings	New equity	Debt
Valais									
Cost of capital 2001	5.9	5.2	5.8	5.7	6.6	6.1	6.7	6.7	4.3
2002	5.9	5.2	5.8	5.7	6.6	6.1	6.7	6.7	4.3
2003	5.9	5.2	5.8	5.7	6.6	6.1	6.7	6.7	4.3
EMTR 2001	14.7	4.6	13.3	11.6	24.3	17.5	25.4	25.4	-16.2
2002	14.7	4.6	13.3	11.6	24.3	17.5	25.4	25.4	-16.2
2003	14.7	4.6	13.3	11.6	24.3	17.5	25.4	25.4	-16.2
EATR 2001	19.7	17.2	19.3	18.9	22.6	20.5	23.0	23.0	13.6
2002	19.7	17.2	19.3	18.9	22.6	20.5	23.0	23.0	13.6
2003	19.7	17.2	19.3	18.9	22.6	20.5	23.0	23.0	13.6
Zug									
Cost of capital 2001	5.4	5.0	5.3	5.2	5.9	5.6	5.9	5.9	4.5
2002	5.4	5.0	5.3	5.2	5.9	5.6	5.9	5.9	4.5
2003	5.4	5.0	5.3	5.2	5.9	5.6	5.9	5.9	4.5
EMTR 2001	7.1	-0.6	5.1	3.7	15.8	10.0	14.9	14.9	-11.9
2002	7.1	-0.6	5.1	3.7	15.8	10.0	14.9	14.9	-11.9
2003	7.1	-0.6	5.1	3.6	15.7	9.9	14.8	14.8	-11.8
EATR 2001	13.8	12.1	13.4	13.0	16.2	14.6	15.9	15.9	10.0
2002	13.8	12.1	13.4	13.0	16.1	14.5	15.9	15.9	10.0
2003	13.8	12.1	13.3	13.0	16.1	14.5	15.9	15.9	10.0
Zürich									
Cost of capital 2001	5.8	5.1	5.6	5.5	6.7	6.1	6.7	6.7	4.1
2002	5.8	5.1	5.6	5.5	6.7	6.1	6.7	6.7	4.1
2003	5.8	5.1	5.6	5.5	6.7	6.1	6.7	6.7	4.2
EMTR 2001	14.0	2.6	10.9	9.1	25.7	17.9	25.5	25.5	-20.8
2002	13.8	2.5	10.8	8.9	25.4	17.7	25.2	25.2	-20.5
2003	13.6	2.4	10.6	8.7	25.1	17.4	24.9	24.9	-20.1
EATR 2001	21.6	19.0	20.8	20.4	25.0	22.6	25.0	25.0	15.3
2002	21.3	18.8	20.6	20.2	24.8	22.4	24.7	24.7	15.1
2003	21.0	18.5	20.3	19.9	24.4	22.1	24.4	24.4	14.9

D.1.8 United Kingdom

		Assets					Sources of finance		
	Overall	Intangibles	Industrial buildings	Machinery	Financial assets	Inventories	Retained earnings	New equity	Debt
London									
Cost of capital 2001	6.6	5.5	7.9	5.6	6.9	6.9	7.6	7.6	4.7
2002	6.6	5.5	8.0	5.6	6.9	6.9	7.6	7.6	4.7
2003	6.6	5.5	8.0	5.6	6.9	6.9	7.6	7.6	4.7
EMTR 2001	24.0	8.8	36.6	11.3	27.9	27.9	34.1	34.1	-6.5
2002	24.1	8.8	37.2	11.3	27.9	27.9	34.3	34.3	-6.2
2003	24.2	8.8	37.5	11.3	27.9	27.9	34.3	34.3	-6.0
EATR 2001	28.0	24.2	32.6	24.7	29.3	29.3	31.6	31.6	21.4
2002	28.1	24.2	32.9	24.7	29.3	29.3	31.6	31.6	21.5
2003	28.1	24.2	33.0	24.7	29.3	29.3	31.6	31.6	21.5

D.1.9 United States

	Overall	Assets					Sources of finance		
		Intangibles	Industrial buildings	Machinery	Financial assets	Inventories	Retained earnings	New equity	Debt
Boston									
Cost of capital 2001	6.8	6.9	7.0	4.8	8.2	7.1	8.4	8.4	3.7
2002	6.7	6.9	7.0	4.5	8.2	7.1	8.4	8.4	3.7
2003	6.7	6.9	7.0	4.5	8.2	7.1	8.4	8.4	3.7
EMTR 2001	26.5	28.0	28.7	-4.6	38.8	29.5	40.8	40.8	-33.8
2002	25.8	28.0	28.7	-11.8	38.8	29.5	40.2	40.2	-34.1
2003	25.8	28.0	28.7	-11.8	38.8	29.5	40.2	40.2	-34.1
EATR 2001	36.2	36.6	36.8	30.2	40.2	37.0	41.0	41.0	27.2
2002	36.0	36.6	36.8	29.3	40.2	37.0	40.8	40.8	27.1
2003	36.0	36.6	36.8	29.3	40.2	37.0	40.8	40.8	27.1

D.2 Sensitivity Analyses

D.2.1 Austria

	2001			2002			2003		
	Cost of capital	EMTR	EATR	Cost of capital	EMTR	EATR	Cost of capital	EMTR	EATR
Burgenland									
Basic weights	6.5	22.9	30.4	6.5	22.9	30.4	6.5	22.9	30.4
Level of profitability: 40%	6.5	22.9	32.2	6.5	22.9	32.2	6.5	22.9	32.2
Real interest rate: 10%	12.9	22.7	26.7	12.9	22.7	26.7	12.9	22.7	26.7
Weights '01	6.7	25.1	31.0	6.7	25.1	31.0	6.7	25.1	31.0
Service sector weights	6.1	17.9	29.1	6.1	17.9	29.1	6.1	17.9	29.1
Kärnten									
Basic weights	6.5	22.9	30.4	6.5	22.9	30.4	6.5	22.9	30.4
Level of profitability: 40%	6.5	22.9	32.2	6.5	22.9	32.2	6.5	22.9	32.2
Real interest rate: 10%	12.9	22.7	26.7	12.9	22.7	26.7	12.9	22.7	26.7
Weights '01	6.7	25.1	31.0	6.7	25.1	31.0	6.7	25.1	31.0
Service sector weights	6.1	17.9	29.1	6.1	17.9	29.1	6.1	17.9	29.1
Niederösterreich									
Basic weights	6.5	22.9	30.4	6.5	22.9	30.4	6.5	22.9	30.4
Level of profitability: 40%	6.5	22.9	32.2	6.5	22.9	32.2	6.5	22.9	32.2
Real interest rate: 10%	12.9	22.7	26.7	12.9	22.7	26.7	12.9	22.7	26.7
Weights '01	6.7	25.1	31.0	6.7	25.1	31.0	6.7	25.1	31.0
Service sector weights	6.1	17.9	29.1	6.1	17.9	29.1	6.1	17.9	29.1
Oberösterreich									
Basic weights	6.5	22.9	30.4	6.5	22.9	30.4	6.5	22.9	30.4
Level of profitability: 40%	6.5	22.9	32.2	6.5	22.9	32.2	6.5	22.9	32.2
Real interest rate: 10%	12.9	22.7	26.7	12.9	22.7	26.7	12.9	22.7	26.7
Weights '01	6.7	25.1	31.0	6.7	25.1	31.0	6.7	25.1	31.0
Service sector weights	6.1	17.9	29.1	6.1	17.9	29.1	6.1	17.9	29.1
Salzburg									
Basic weights	6.5	22.9	30.4	6.5	22.9	30.4	6.5	22.9	30.4
Level of profitability: 40%	6.5	22.9	32.2	6.5	22.9	32.2	6.5	22.9	32.2
Real interest rate: 10%	12.9	22.7	26.7	12.9	22.7	26.7	12.9	22.7	26.7
Weights '01	6.7	25.1	31.0	6.7	25.1	31.0	6.7	25.1	31.0
Service sector weights	6.1	17.9	29.1	6.1	17.9	29.1	6.1	17.9	29.1

	2001			2002			2003		
	Cost of capital	EMTR	EATR	Cost of capital	EMTR	EATR	Cost of capital	EMTR	EATR
Steiermark									
Basic weights	6.5	22.9	30.4	6.5	22.9	30.4	6.5	22.9	30.4
Level of profitability: 40%	6.5	22.9	32.2	6.5	22.9	32.2	6.5	22.9	32.2
Real interest rate: 10%	12.9	22.7	26.7	12.9	22.7	26.7	12.9	22.7	26.7
Weights '01	6.7	25.1	31.0	6.7	25.1	31.0	6.7	25.1	31.0
Service sector weights	6.1	17.9	29.1	6.1	17.9	29.1	6.1	17.9	29.1
Tirol									
Basic weights	6.5	22.9	30.4	6.5	22.9	30.4	6.5	22.9	30.4
Level of profitability: 40%	6.5	22.9	32.2	6.5	22.9	32.2	6.5	22.9	32.2
Real interest rate: 10%	12.9	22.7	26.7	12.9	22.7	26.7	12.9	22.7	26.7
Weights '01	6.7	25.1	31.0	6.7	25.1	31.0	6.7	25.1	31.0
Service sector weights	6.1	17.9	29.1	6.1	17.9	29.1	6.1	17.9	29.1
Vorarlberg									
Basic weights	6.5	22.9	30.4	6.5	22.9	30.4	6.5	22.9	30.4
Level of profitability: 40%	6.5	22.9	32.2	6.5	22.9	32.2	6.5	22.9	32.2
Real interest rate: 10%	12.9	22.7	26.7	12.9	22.7	26.7	12.9	22.7	26.7
Weights '01	6.7	25.1	31.0	6.7	25.1	31.0	6.7	25.1	31.0
Service sector weights	6.1	17.9	29.1	6.1	17.9	29.1	6.1	17.9	29.1
Wien									
Basic weights	6.5	22.9	30.4	6.5	22.9	30.4	6.5	22.9	30.4
Level of profitability: 40%	6.5	22.9	32.2	6.5	22.9	32.2	6.5	22.9	32.2
Real interest rate: 10%	12.9	22.7	26.7	12.9	22.7	26.7	12.9	22.7	26.7
Weights '01	6.7	25.1	31.0	6.7	25.1	31.0	6.7	25.1	31.0
Service sector weights	6.1	17.9	29.1	6.1	17.9	29.1	6.1	17.9	29.1

D.2.2 France

	2001			2002			2003		
	Cost of capital	EMTR	EATR	Cost of capital	EMTR	EATR	Cost of capital	EMTR	EATR
Bas-Rhin									
Basic weights	7.5	33.4	35.3	7.5	33.0	34.5	7.5	33.2	34.6
Level of profitability: 40%	7.5	33.4	35.9	7.5	33.0	35.0	7.5	33.2	35.0
Real interest rate: 10%	13.8	27.4	30.2	13.7	26.8	29.6	13.7	26.9	29.6
Weights '01	7.8	36.0	36.3	7.7	35.4	35.4	7.8	35.5	35.5
Service sector weights	6.8	26.9	33.2	6.8	26.4	32.4	6.8	26.5	32.4
Haut-Rhin									
Basic weights	7.5	32.9	35.1	7.4	32.5	34.3	7.4	32.7	34.4
Level of profitability: 40%	7.5	32.9	35.8	7.4	32.5	34.9	7.4	32.7	34.9
Real interest rate: 10%	13.7	27.1	30.0	13.6	26.5	29.4	13.6	26.6	29.4
Weights '01	7.8	35.6	36.1	7.7	35.0	35.3	7.7	35.1	35.3
Service sector weights	6.8	26.5	33.1	6.8	26.0	32.3	6.8	26.2	32.3
Doubs									
Basic weights	7.5	33.3	35.2	7.4	32.8	34.4	7.5	32.9	34.5
Level of profitability: 40%	7.5	33.3	35.8	7.4	32.8	34.9	7.5	32.9	35.0
Real interest rate: 10%	13.7	27.3	30.1	13.6	26.7	29.5	13.7	26.8	29.5
Weights '01	7.8	35.8	36.2	7.7	35.2	35.3	7.7	35.2	35.4
Service sector weights	6.8	26.7	33.1	6.8	26.3	32.3	6.8	26.3	32.3
Jura									
Basic weights	7.4	32.3	34.9	7.3	31.8	34.1	7.4	32.1	34.2
Level of profitability: 40%	7.4	32.3	35.7	7.3	31.8	34.8	7.4	32.1	34.8
Real interest rate: 10%	13.6	26.7	29.8	13.5	26.1	29.1	13.6	26.3	29.2
Weights '01	7.7	35.0	35.9	7.6	34.4	35.0	7.6	34.6	35.1
Service sector weights	6.8	26.1	32.9	6.7	25.6	32.1	6.7	25.8	32.2
Haute-Saône									
Basic weights	7.4	32.3	34.9	7.3	31.9	34.2	7.4	32.2	34.2
Level of profitability: 40%	7.4	32.3	35.7	7.3	31.9	34.8	7.4	32.2	34.8
Real interest rate: 10%	13.6	26.7	29.8	13.5	26.2	29.2	13.6	26.3	29.3
Weights '01	7.7	35.1	35.9	7.6	34.5	35.1	7.7	34.6	35.1
Service sector weights	6.8	26.1	32.9	6.7	25.7	32.1	6.7	25.8	32.2

	2001			2002			2003		
	Cost of capital	EMTR	EATR	Cost of capital	EMTR	EATR	Cost of capital	EMTR	EATR
Territoire-de-Belfort									
Basic weights	7.8	36.0	36.3	7.7	35.4	35.4	7.8	35.7	35.5
Level of profitability: 40%	7.8	36.0	36.4	7.7	35.4	35.4	7.8	35.7	35.5
Real interest rate: 10%	14.1	29.0	31.2	14.0	28.4	30.5	14.0	28.5	30.6
Weights '01	8.1	37.9	37.0	8.0	37.2	36.1	8.0	37.4	36.2
Service sector weights	7.0	28.8	33.7	7.0	28.2	32.9	7.0	28.3	33.0
Paris									
Basic weights	6.8	26.0	32.9	6.7	25.5	32.1	6.7	25.5	32.1
Level of profitability: 40%	6.8	26.0	34.7	6.7	25.5	33.8	6.7	25.5	33.8
Real interest rate: 10%	13.0	23.0	27.7	12.9	22.4	27.0	12.9	22.4	27.0
Weights '01	7.2	30.9	34.4	7.2	30.2	33.6	7.2	30.2	33.6
Service sector weights	6.4	21.7	31.7	6.3	21.2	30.9	6.3	21.2	30.9
Meurthe-et-Moselle									
Basic weights	7.7	35.4	36.1	7.7	34.8	35.2	7.7	34.7	35.1
Level of profitability: 40%	7.7	35.4	36.2	7.7	34.8	35.3	7.7	34.7	35.3
Real interest rate: 10%	14.0	28.6	31.0	13.9	28.0	30.3	13.9	27.9	30.2
Weights '01	8.0	37.5	36.9	7.9	36.8	36.0	7.9	36.6	35.9
Service sector weights	7.0	28.3	33.6	6.9	27.7	32.8	6.9	27.6	32.7
Meuse									
Basic weights	7.3	31.4	34.6	7.2	31.0	33.8	7.4	32.6	34.4
Level of profitability: 40%	7.3	31.4	35.5	7.2	31.0	34.6	7.4	32.6	34.9
Real interest rate: 10%	13.5	26.1	29.5	13.4	25.6	28.8	13.6	26.6	29.4
Weights '01	7.6	34.4	35.7	7.6	33.8	34.8	7.7	35.0	35.2
Service sector weights	6.7	25.4	32.7	6.7	25.0	31.9	6.8	26.1	32.3
Moselle									
Basic weights	7.4	32.2	34.9	7.3	31.8	34.1	7.3	31.7	34.1
Level of profitability: 40%	7.4	32.2	35.7	7.3	31.8	34.8	7.3	31.7	34.7
Real interest rate: 10%	13.6	26.6	29.7	13.5	26.1	29.1	13.5	26.0	29.1
Weights '01	7.7	35.2	35.9	7.6	34.5	35.1	7.6	34.5	35.1
Service sector weights	6.8	26.0	32.9	6.7	25.5	32.1	6.7	25.4	32.1

	2001			2002			2003		
	Cost of capital	EMTR	EATR	Cost of capital	EMTR	EATR	Cost of capital	EMTR	EATR
Vosges									
Basic weights	7.6	33.9	35.5	7.5	33.5	34.7	7.5	33.7	34.8
Level of profitability: 40%	7.6	33.9	36.0	7.5	33.5	35.1	7.5	33.7	35.1
Real interest rate: 10%	13.8	27.7	30.4	13.7	27.1	29.7	13.7	27.2	29.8
Weights '01	7.8	36.3	36.4	7.8	35.7	35.5	7.8	35.8	35.6
Service sector weights	6.9	27.2	33.3	6.8	26.8	32.5	6.8	26.9	32.5
Ain									
Basic weights	7.4	32.5	35.0	7.3	31.9	34.1	7.4	32.0	34.2
Level of profitability: 40%	7.4	32.5	35.7	7.3	31.9	34.8	7.4	32.0	34.8
Real interest rate: 10%	13.7	26.8	29.8	13.5	26.2	29.2	13.6	26.2	29.2
Weights '01	7.7	35.3	36.0	7.6	34.6	35.1	7.7	34.7	35.1
Service sector weights	6.8	26.2	33.0	6.7	25.6	32.1	6.7	25.7	32.2
Ardèche									
Basic weights	7.6	34.5	35.7	7.6	34.1	34.9	7.6	34.3	35.0
Level of profitability: 40%	7.6	34.5	36.1	7.6	34.1	35.2	7.6	34.3	35.2
Real interest rate: 10%	13.9	28.0	30.6	13.8	27.5	30.0	13.8	27.6	30.0
Weights '01	7.9	36.7	36.5	7.8	36.1	35.7	7.8	36.3	35.8
Service sector weights	6.9	27.7	33.4	6.9	27.2	32.6	6.9	27.3	32.6
Drôme									
Basic weights	7.4	32.5	35.0	7.4	32.1	34.2	7.4	32.3	34.3
Level of profitability: 40%	7.4	32.5	35.7	7.4	32.1	34.8	7.4	32.3	34.9
Real interest rate: 10%	13.7	26.8	29.9	13.6	26.3	29.2	13.6	26.4	29.3
Weights '01	7.7	35.3	36.0	7.7	34.6	35.1	7.7	34.8	35.2
Service sector weights	6.8	26.2	33.0	6.7	25.7	32.2	6.7	25.9	32.2
Isère									
Basic weights	7.9	36.8	36.6	7.9	36.3	35.8	7.8	36.2	35.7
Level of profitability: 40%	7.9	36.8	36.5	7.9	36.3	35.6	7.8	36.2	35.6
Real interest rate: 10%	14.2	29.5	31.5	14.1	28.9	30.9	14.1	28.9	30.8
Weights '01	8.1	38.4	37.2	8.0	37.7	36.4	8.0	37.7	36.3
Service sector weights	7.1	29.4	33.9	7.0	28.9	33.1	7.0	28.8	33.1

	2001			2002			2003		
	Cost of capital	EMTR	EATR	Cost of capital	EMTR	EATR	Cost of capital	EMTR	EATR
Loire									
Basic weights	7.6	34.1	35.5	7.5	33.6	34.7	7.5	33.7	34.8
Level of profitability: 40%	7.6	34.1	36.0	7.5	33.6	35.1	7.5	33.7	35.1
Real interest rate: 10%	13.8	27.7	30.4	13.7	27.2	29.8	13.7	27.3	29.8
Weights '01	7.9	36.4	36.4	7.8	35.8	35.6	7.8	35.9	35.6
Service sector weights	6.9	27.3	33.3	6.8	26.8	32.5	6.8	26.9	32.5
Rhône									
Basic weights	7.4	32.4	34.9	7.3	31.9	34.2	7.4	32.8	34.5
Level of profitability: 40%	7.4	32.4	35.7	7.3	31.9	34.8	7.4	32.8	34.9
Real interest rate: 10%	13.6	26.7	29.8	13.5	26.2	29.2	13.6	26.7	29.5
Weights '01	7.7	35.3	36.0	7.7	34.7	35.1	7.7	35.3	35.4
Service sector weights	6.8	26.1	32.9	6.7	25.6	32.1	6.8	26.3	32.3
Savoie									
Basic weights	7.6	34.6	35.7	7.6	34.1	34.9	7.6	34.4	35.0
Level of profitability: 40%	7.6	34.6	36.1	7.6	34.1	35.2	7.6	34.4	35.2
Real interest rate: 10%	13.9	28.1	30.6	13.8	27.5	30.0	13.8	27.7	30.1
Weights '01	7.9	36.8	36.6	7.8	36.1	35.7	7.9	36.4	35.8
Service sector weights	6.9	27.7	33.4	6.9	27.2	32.6	6.9	27.4	32.7
Haute-Savoie									
Basic weights	7.5	33.1	35.2	7.5	33.4	34.7	7.6	33.9	34.9
Level of profitability: 40%	7.5	33.1	35.8	7.5	33.4	35.1	7.6	33.9	35.1
Real interest rate: 10%	13.7	27.2	30.1	13.7	27.1	29.7	13.8	27.4	29.9
Weights '01	7.8	35.9	36.2	7.8	35.8	35.6	7.8	36.1	35.7
Service sector weights	6.8	26.6	33.1	6.8	26.7	32.5	6.9	27.1	32.6

D.2.3 Germany

	2001			2002			2003		
	Cost of capital	EMTR	EATR	Cost of capital	EMTR	EATR	Cost of capital	EMTR	EATR
Aalen									
Basic weights	6.6	24.0	32.9	6.6	24.0	32.9	6.7	24.9	34.1
Level of profitability: 40%	6.6	24.0	35.1	6.6	24.0	35.1	6.7	24.9	36.4
Real interest rate: 10%	13.1	23.9	28.5	13.1	23.9	28.5	13.3	24.9	29.5
Weights '01	7.1	29.3	34.5	7.1	29.3	34.5	7.2	30.4	35.7
Service sector weights	6.5	23.5	32.8	6.5	23.5	32.8	6.6	24.3	33.9
Balingen									
Basic weights	6.6	23.7	32.7	6.6	23.7	32.7	6.6	24.7	33.9
Level of profitability: 40%	6.6	23.7	34.9	6.6	23.7	34.9	6.6	24.7	36.1
Real interest rate: 10%	13.1	23.7	28.3	13.1	23.7	28.3	13.3	24.6	29.3
Weights '01	7.0	29.1	34.3	7.0	29.1	34.3	7.2	30.1	35.5
Service sector weights	6.5	23.2	32.6	6.5	23.2	32.6	6.6	24.0	33.7
Freiburg									
Basic weights	6.7	25.5	34.2	6.7	25.5	34.2	6.8	26.4	35.4
Level of profitability: 40%	6.7	25.5	36.4	6.7	25.5	36.4	6.8	26.4	37.7
Real interest rate: 10%	13.4	25.3	29.7	13.4	25.3	29.7	13.6	26.2	30.7
Weights '01	7.2	30.9	35.8	7.2	30.9	35.8	7.3	31.9	37.0
Service sector weights	6.7	25.1	34.1	6.7	25.1	34.1	6.7	25.9	35.2
Göppingen									
Basic weights	6.6	24.1	33.1	6.6	24.1	33.1	6.7	25.1	34.2
Level of profitability: 40%	6.6	24.1	35.3	6.6	24.1	35.3	6.7	25.1	36.5
Real interest rate: 10%	13.2	24.1	28.6	13.2	24.1	28.6	13.3	25.0	29.6
Weights '01	7.1	29.5	34.6	7.1	29.5	34.6	7.2	30.6	35.8
Service sector weights	6.6	23.7	33.0	6.6	23.7	33.0	6.6	24.5	34.1
Heidelberg									
Basic weights	6.7	25.1	34.0	6.7	25.1	34.0	6.8	26.0	35.1
Level of profitability: 40%	6.7	25.1	36.2	6.7	25.1	36.2	6.8	26.0	37.4
Real interest rate: 10%	13.3	25.0	29.4	13.3	25.0	29.4	13.5	25.9	30.4
Weights '01	7.2	30.5	35.5	7.2	30.5	35.5	7.3	31.6	36.7
Service sector weights	6.6	24.7	33.8	6.6	24.7	33.8	6.7	25.5	34.9

	2001			2002			2003		
	Cost of capital	EMTR	EATR	Cost of capital	EMTR	EATR	Cost of capital	EMTR	EATR
Heilbronn									
Basic weights	6.7	24.8	33.7	6.7	24.8	33.7	6.7	25.7	34.8
Level of profitability: 40%	6.7	24.8	35.9	6.7	24.8	35.9	6.7	25.7	37.1
Real interest rate: 10%	13.3	24.7	29.2	13.3	24.7	29.2	13.4	25.6	30.2
Weights '01	7.2	30.2	35.3	7.2	30.2	35.3	7.3	31.3	36.5
Service sector weights	6.6	24.4	33.6	6.6	24.4	33.6	6.7	25.2	34.7
Karlsruhe									
Basic weights	6.7	25.5	34.4	6.7	25.5	34.4	6.8	26.4	35.5
Level of profitability: 40%	6.7	25.5	36.7	6.7	25.5	36.7	6.8	26.4	37.9
Real interest rate: 10%	13.4	25.4	29.8	13.4	25.4	29.8	13.6	26.3	30.8
Weights '01	7.2	31.0	36.0	7.2	31.0	36.0	7.4	32.0	37.2
Service sector weights	6.7	25.2	34.3	6.7	25.2	34.3	6.8	26.0	35.4
Konstanz									
Basic weights	6.6	24.2	33.2	6.6	24.2	33.2	6.7	25.1	34.3
Level of profitability: 40%	6.6	24.2	35.4	6.6	24.2	35.4	6.7	25.1	36.6
Real interest rate: 10%	13.2	24.2	28.7	13.2	24.2	28.7	13.3	25.1	29.7
Weights '01	7.1	29.6	34.8	7.1	29.6	34.8	7.2	30.7	36.0
Service sector weights	6.6	23.8	33.1	6.6	23.8	33.1	6.6	24.6	34.2
Lörrach									
Basic weights	6.5	23.4	32.3	6.6	24.2	33.2	6.7	25.1	34.3
Level of profitability: 40%	6.5	23.4	34.5	6.6	24.2	35.4	6.7	25.1	36.6
Real interest rate: 10%	13.0	23.3	28.0	13.2	24.2	28.7	13.4	25.1	29.7
Weights '01	7.0	28.7	33.9	7.1	29.6	34.8	7.2	30.7	36.0
Service sector weights	6.5	22.8	32.2	6.6	23.8	33.1	6.6	24.6	34.2
Landkreis Mannheim									
Basic weights	6.5	23.0	32.1	6.5	23.4	32.4	6.6	24.3	33.6
Level of profitability: 40%	6.5	23.0	34.3	6.5	23.4	34.6	6.6	24.3	35.9
Real interest rate: 10%	13.0	23.1	27.8	13.0	23.4	28.0	13.2	24.3	29.0
Weights '01	7.0	28.4	33.7	7.0	28.7	34.0	7.1	29.8	35.2
Service sector weights	6.5	22.6	32.0	6.5	22.9	32.3	6.6	23.7	33.4

	2001			2002			2003		
	Cost of capital	EMTR	EATR	Cost of capital	EMTR	EATR	Cost of capital	EMTR	EATR
Ludwigsburg									
Basic weights	6.6	24.5	33.5	6.6	24.1	33.2	6.7	25.1	34.3
Level of profitability: 40%	6.6	24.5	35.8	6.6	24.1	35.4	6.7	25.1	36.6
Real interest rate: 10%	13.2	24.5	29.1	13.2	24.1	28.7	13.3	25.1	29.7
Weights '01	7.1	30.0	35.1	7.1	29.6	34.7	7.2	30.6	35.9
Service sector weights	6.6	24.1	33.4	6.6	23.7	33.1	6.6	24.5	34.2
Mannheim									
Basic weights	6.8	26.0	34.9	6.7	25.7	34.5	6.8	26.6	35.7
Level of profitability: 40%	6.8	26.0	37.1	6.7	25.7	36.8	6.8	26.6	38.0
Real interest rate: 10%	13.5	25.9	30.3	13.4	25.5	30.0	13.6	26.5	30.9
Weights '01	7.3	31.5	36.5	7.3	31.1	36.2	7.4	32.2	37.3
Service sector weights	6.7	25.7	34.8	6.7	25.3	34.4	6.8	26.1	35.5
Nagold									
Basic weights	6.6	24.0	33.0	6.6	24.0	33.0	6.7	25.0	34.1
Level of profitability: 40%	6.6	24.0	35.2	6.6	24.0	35.2	6.7	25.0	36.4
Real interest rate: 10%	13.2	24.0	28.5	13.2	24.0	28.5	13.3	24.9	29.5
Weights '01	7.1	29.4	34.5	7.1	29.4	34.5	7.2	30.4	35.7
Service sector weights	6.5	23.6	32.8	6.5	23.6	32.8	6.6	24.3	33.9
Offenburg									
Basic weights	6.7	24.9	33.7	6.7	24.9	33.7	6.7	25.8	34.8
Level of profitability: 40%	6.7	24.9	35.9	6.7	24.9	35.9	6.7	25.8	37.2
Real interest rate: 10%	13.3	24.7	29.2	13.3	24.7	29.2	13.5	25.7	30.2
Weights '01	7.2	30.2	35.3	7.2	30.2	35.3	7.3	31.3	36.5
Service sector weights	6.6	24.4	33.6	6.6	24.4	33.6	6.7	25.2	34.7
Pforzheim									
Basic weights	6.7	24.9	33.7	6.7	24.9	33.7	6.7	25.8	34.8
Level of profitability: 40%	6.7	24.9	35.9	6.7	24.9	35.9	6.7	25.8	37.2
Real interest rate: 10%	13.3	24.7	29.2	13.3	24.7	29.2	13.5	25.7	30.2
Weights '01	7.2	30.2	35.3	7.2	30.2	35.3	7.3	31.3	36.5
Service sector weights	6.6	24.4	33.6	6.6	24.4	33.6	6.7	25.2	34.7

	2001			2002			2003		
	Cost of capital	EMTR	EATR	Cost of capital	EMTR	EATR	Cost of capital	EMTR	EATR
Rastatt									
Basic weights	6.6	24.0	33.0	6.6	24.5	33.4	6.7	25.4	34.6
Level of profitability: 40%	6.6	24.0	35.1	6.6	24.5	35.7	6.7	25.4	36.9
Real interest rate: 10%	13.1	23.9	28.5	13.2	24.4	29.0	13.4	25.3	29.9
Weights '01	7.1	29.4	34.5	7.1	29.9	35.0	7.2	30.9	36.2
Service sector weights	6.5	23.5	32.8	6.6	24.1	33.3	6.7	24.9	34.4
Ravensburg									
Basic weights	6.5	23.6	32.5	6.5	23.6	32.5	6.6	24.5	33.6
Level of profitability: 40%	6.5	23.6	34.6	6.5	23.6	34.6	6.6	24.5	35.9
Real interest rate: 10%	13.1	23.5	28.1	13.1	23.5	28.1	13.2	24.4	29.1
Weights '01	7.0	28.8	34.0	7.0	28.8	34.0	7.1	29.9	35.2
Service sector weights	6.5	23.0	32.3	6.5	23.0	32.3	6.6	23.8	33.5
Reutlingen									
Basic weights	6.6	24.0	32.9	6.6	24.0	32.9	6.7	24.9	34.1
Level of profitability: 40%	6.6	24.0	35.1	6.6	24.0	35.1	6.7	24.9	36.4
Real interest rate: 10%	13.1	23.9	28.5	13.1	23.9	28.5	13.3	24.9	29.5
Weights '01	7.1	29.3	34.5	7.1	29.3	34.5	7.2	30.4	35.7
Service sector weights	6.5	23.5	32.8	6.5	23.5	32.8	6.6	24.3	33.9
Rottweil									
Basic weights	6.6	23.7	32.6	6.6	23.7	32.6	6.6	24.7	33.8
Level of profitability: 40%	6.6	23.7	34.8	6.6	23.7	34.8	6.6	24.7	36.0
Real interest rate: 10%	13.1	23.6	28.2	13.1	23.6	28.2	13.3	24.6	29.2
Weights '01	7.0	29.0	34.1	7.0	29.0	34.1	7.2	30.1	35.4
Service sector weights	6.5	23.2	32.5	6.5	23.2	32.5	6.6	24.0	33.6
Schwäbisch-Hall									
Basic weights	6.6	24.6	33.6	6.6	24.6	33.6	6.7	25.6	34.7
Level of profitability: 40%	6.6	24.6	35.8	6.6	24.6	35.8	6.7	25.6	37.0
Real interest rate: 10%	13.3	24.6	29.1	13.3	24.6	29.1	13.4	25.5	30.0
Weights '01	7.1	30.0	35.2	7.1	30.0	35.2	7.3	31.1	36.3
Service sector weights	6.6	24.2	33.5	6.6	24.2	33.5	6.7	25.0	34.6

	2001			2002			2003		
	Cost of capital	EMTR	EATR	Cost of capital	EMTR	EATR	Cost of capital	EMTR	EATR
Stuttgart									
Basic weights	6.7	25.9	34.7	6.7	25.8	34.7	6.8	26.7	35.8
Level of profitability: 40%	6.7	25.9	36.9	6.7	25.8	36.9	6.8	26.7	38.1
Real interest rate: 10%	13.5	25.7	30.1	13.5	25.7	30.1	13.6	26.6	31.0
Weights '01	7.3	31.3	36.3	7.3	31.3	36.3	7.4	32.3	37.5
Service sector weights	6.7	25.5	34.6	6.7	25.5	34.6	6.8	26.3	35.7
Tauberbischofsheim									
Basic weights	6.5	23.4	32.4	6.5	23.4	32.4	6.6	24.3	33.6
Level of profitability: 40%	6.5	23.4	34.6	6.5	23.4	34.6	6.6	24.3	35.9
Real interest rate: 10%	13.1	23.4	28.1	13.1	23.4	28.1	13.2	24.3	29.0
Weights '01	7.0	28.8	34.0	7.0	28.8	34.0	7.1	29.8	35.2
Service sector weights	6.5	22.9	32.3	6.5	22.9	32.3	6.6	23.7	33.4
Ulm									
Basic weights	6.6	24.3	33.2	6.6	24.3	33.2	6.7	25.2	34.4
Level of profitability: 40%	6.6	24.3	35.4	6.6	24.3	35.4	6.7	25.2	36.7
Real interest rate: 10%	13.2	24.2	28.8	13.2	24.2	28.8	13.4	25.2	29.7
Weights '01	7.1	29.7	34.8	7.1	29.7	34.8	7.2	30.7	36.0
Service sector weights	6.6	23.9	33.1	6.6	23.9	33.1	6.6	24.6	34.2
Villingen-Schwenningen									
Basic weights	6.6	24.0	33.0	6.6	24.0	33.0	6.7	25.0	34.1
Level of profitability: 40%	6.6	24.0	35.2	6.6	24.0	35.2	6.7	25.0	36.4
Real interest rate: 10%	13.2	24.0	28.5	13.2	24.0	28.5	13.3	24.9	29.5
Weights '01	7.1	29.4	34.5	7.1	29.4	34.5	7.2	30.4	35.7
Service sector weights	6.5	23.6	32.8	6.5	23.6	32.8	6.6	24.3	33.9
Waiblingen									
Basic weights	6.6	23.9	32.9	6.6	23.9	32.9	6.7	24.8	34.1
Level of profitability: 40%	6.6	23.9	35.1	6.6	23.9	35.1	6.7	24.8	36.4
Real interest rate: 10%	13.1	23.9	28.5	13.1	23.9	28.5	13.3	24.8	29.5
Weights '01	7.1	29.3	34.5	7.1	29.3	34.5	7.2	30.4	35.7
Service sector weights	6.5	23.5	32.8	6.5	23.5	32.8	6.6	24.3	33.9

	2001			2002			2003		
	Cost of capital	EMTR	EATR	Cost of capital	EMTR	EATR	Cost of capital	EMTR	EATR
Walldorf bei Heidelberg									
Basic weights	6.5	22.8	31.9	6.5	22.8	31.9	6.6	23.7	33.1
Level of profitability: 40%	6.5	22.8	34.1	6.5	22.8	34.1	6.6	23.7	35.3
Real interest rate: 10%	13.0	22.8	27.6	13.0	22.8	27.6	13.1	23.8	28.5
Weights '01	7.0	28.1	33.4	7.0	28.1	33.4	7.1	29.2	34.7
Service sector weights	6.4	22.3	31.8	6.4	22.3	31.8	6.5	23.1	32.9
Ansbach									
Basic weights	6.6	24.2	33.2	6.6	24.2	33.2	6.7	25.1	34.3
Level of profitability: 40%	6.6	24.2	35.4	6.6	24.2	35.4	6.7	25.1	36.6
Real interest rate: 10%	13.2	24.2	28.7	13.2	24.2	28.7	13.4	25.1	29.7
Weights '01	7.1	29.6	34.8	7.1	29.6	34.8	7.2	30.7	36.0
Service sector weights	6.6	23.8	33.1	6.6	23.8	33.1	6.6	24.6	34.2
Aschaffenburg									
Basic weights	6.6	24.8	33.8	6.6	24.8	33.8	6.7	25.7	34.9
Level of profitability: 40%	6.6	24.8	36.0	6.6	24.8	36.0	6.7	25.7	37.2
Real interest rate: 10%	13.3	24.7	29.3	13.3	24.7	29.3	13.5	25.7	30.2
Weights '01	7.2	30.2	35.4	7.2	30.2	35.4	7.3	31.3	36.6
Service sector weights	6.6	24.4	33.7	6.6	24.4	33.7	6.7	25.2	34.8
Augsburg									
Basic weights	6.7	25.8	34.6	6.8	26.4	35.2	6.9	27.2	36.3
Level of profitability: 40%	6.7	25.8	36.9	6.8	26.4	37.5	6.9	27.2	38.7
Real interest rate: 10%	13.4	25.6	30.1	13.6	26.2	30.6	13.7	27.1	31.5
Weights '01	7.3	31.2	36.3	7.3	31.9	36.9	7.5	32.9	38.0
Service sector weights	6.7	25.5	34.6	6.8	26.1	35.1	6.8	26.9	36.2
Bamberg									
Basic weights	6.6	24.8	33.7	6.7	25.1	33.9	6.8	26.0	35.1
Level of profitability: 40%	6.6	24.8	35.9	6.7	25.1	36.2	6.8	26.0	37.4
Real interest rate: 10%	13.3	24.7	29.2	13.3	24.9	29.4	13.5	25.9	30.4
Weights '01	7.2	30.2	35.3	7.2	30.5	35.5	7.3	31.5	36.7
Service sector weights	6.6	24.4	33.6	6.6	24.7	33.8	6.7	25.4	34.9

	2001			2002			2003		
	Cost of capital	EMTR	EATR	Cost of capital	EMTR	EATR	Cost of capital	EMTR	EATR
Bayreuth									
Basic weights	6.6	24.5	33.5	6.6	24.5	33.5	6.7	25.5	34.6
Level of profitability: 40%	6.6	24.5	35.7	6.6	24.5	35.7	6.7	25.5	36.9
Real interest rate: 10%	13.2	24.4	29.0	13.2	24.4	29.0	13.4	25.4	29.9
Weights '01	7.1	29.9	35.0	7.1	29.9	35.0	7.2	31.0	36.2
Service sector weights	6.6	24.1	33.3	6.6	24.1	33.3	6.7	24.9	34.4
Coburg									
Basic weights	6.6	24.2	33.2	6.6	24.2	33.2	6.6	23.7	32.9
Level of profitability: 40%	6.6	24.2	35.4	6.6	24.2	35.4	6.6	23.7	35.1
Real interest rate: 10%	13.2	24.2	28.7	13.2	24.2	28.7	13.1	23.7	28.4
Weights '01	7.1	29.6	34.8	7.1	29.6	34.8	7.0	29.1	34.4
Service sector weights	6.6	23.8	33.1	6.6	23.8	33.1	6.5	22.9	32.7
Deggendorf									
Basic weights	6.5	23.3	32.2	6.6	24.0	33.0	6.7	24.9	34.1
Level of profitability: 40%	6.5	23.3	34.4	6.6	24.0	35.1	6.7	24.9	36.4
Real interest rate: 10%	13.0	23.2	27.9	13.1	23.9	28.5	13.3	24.9	29.5
Weights '01	7.0	28.5	33.7	7.1	29.4	34.5	7.2	30.4	35.7
Service sector weights	6.5	22.7	32.1	6.5	23.5	32.8	6.6	24.3	33.9
Donauwörth									
Basic weights	6.6	24.0	33.0	6.6	24.0	33.0	6.7	24.9	34.1
Level of profitability: 40%	6.6	24.0	35.2	6.6	24.0	35.2	6.7	24.9	36.4
Real interest rate: 10%	13.1	23.9	28.5	13.1	23.9	28.5	13.3	24.9	29.5
Weights '01	7.1	29.4	34.5	7.1	29.4	34.5	7.2	30.4	35.7
Service sector weights	6.5	23.5	32.8	6.5	23.5	32.8	6.6	24.3	33.9
Freising									
Basic weights	6.6	24.7	33.7	6.6	24.7	33.7	6.7	25.6	34.8
Level of profitability: 40%	6.6	24.7	35.9	6.6	24.7	35.9	6.7	25.6	37.1
Real interest rate: 10%	13.3	24.6	29.2	13.3	24.6	29.2	13.4	25.5	30.1
Weights '01	7.2	30.1	35.3	7.2	30.1	35.3	7.3	31.2	36.4
Service sector weights	6.6	24.3	33.6	6.6	24.3	33.6	6.7	25.1	34.7

	2001			2002			2003		
	Cost of capital	EMTR	EATR	Cost of capital	EMTR	EATR	Cost of capital	EMTR	EATR
Hof									
Basic weights	6.7	24.8	33.7	6.7	24.8	33.7	6.7	25.7	34.8
Level of profitability: 40%	6.7	24.8	35.9	6.7	24.8	35.9	6.7	25.7	37.2
Real interest rate: 10%	13.3	24.7	29.2	13.3	24.7	29.2	13.4	25.6	30.2
Weights '01	7.2	30.2	35.3	7.2	30.2	35.3	7.3	31.3	36.5
Service sector weights	6.6	24.4	33.6	6.6	24.4	33.6	6.7	25.2	34.7
Ingolstadt									
Basic weights	6.7	25.2	34.2	6.7	25.2	34.2	6.8	26.1	35.3
Level of profitability: 40%	6.7	25.2	36.4	6.7	25.2	36.4	6.8	26.1	37.6
Real interest rate: 10%	13.4	25.1	29.6	13.4	25.1	29.6	13.5	26.1	30.6
Weights '01	7.2	30.7	35.8	7.2	30.7	35.8	7.3	31.7	37.0
Service sector weights	6.7	24.9	34.1	6.7	24.9	34.1	6.7	25.7	35.2
Kempten									
Basic weights	6.6	23.7	32.6	6.6	23.7	32.6	6.6	24.6	33.8
Level of profitability: 40%	6.6	23.7	34.8	6.6	23.7	34.8	6.6	24.6	36.1
Real interest rate: 10%	13.1	23.6	28.2	13.1	23.6	28.2	13.3	24.6	29.2
Weights '01	7.0	29.0	34.2	7.0	29.0	34.2	7.2	30.1	35.4
Service sector weights	6.5	23.2	32.5	6.5	23.2	32.5	6.6	24.0	33.6
Landshut									
Basic weights	6.7	25.2	34.2	6.7	25.3	34.2	6.8	26.2	35.3
Level of profitability: 40%	6.7	25.2	36.4	6.7	25.3	36.4	6.8	26.2	37.6
Real interest rate: 10%	13.4	25.1	29.6	13.4	25.2	29.6	13.5	26.1	30.6
Weights '01	7.2	30.7	35.8	7.2	30.7	35.8	7.3	31.8	37.0
Service sector weights	6.7	24.9	34.1	6.7	24.9	34.1	6.7	25.7	35.2
Memmingen									
Basic weights	6.5	23.5	32.5	6.5	23.5	32.5	6.6	24.4	33.6
Level of profitability: 40%	6.5	23.5	34.6	6.5	23.5	34.6	6.6	24.4	35.9
Real interest rate: 10%	13.1	23.5	28.1	13.1	23.5	28.1	13.2	24.4	29.1
Weights '01	7.0	28.8	34.0	7.0	28.8	34.0	7.1	29.9	35.2
Service sector weights	6.5	23.0	32.3	6.5	23.0	32.3	6.6	23.8	33.4

	2001			2002			2003		
	Cost of capital	EMTR	EATR	Cost of capital	EMTR	EATR	Cost of capital	EMTR	EATR
München									
Basic weights	6.9	27.4	36.2	6.9	27.4	36.2	7.0	28.3	37.3
Level of profitability: 40%	6.9	27.4	38.5	6.9	27.4	38.5	7.0	28.3	39.7
Real interest rate: 10%	13.7	27.2	31.5	13.7	27.2	31.5	13.9	28.1	32.4
Weights '01	7.5	33.0	37.9	7.5	33.0	37.9	7.6	34.0	39.1
Service sector weights	6.9	27.2	36.2	6.9	27.2	36.2	6.9	28.0	37.2
Nürnberg									
Basic weights	6.8	26.4	35.3	6.8	26.4	35.3	6.9	27.3	36.4
Level of profitability: 40%	6.8	26.4	37.5	6.8	26.4	37.5	6.9	27.3	38.7
Real interest rate: 10%	13.6	26.3	30.6	13.6	26.3	30.6	13.7	27.2	31.6
Weights '01	7.3	31.9	36.9	7.3	31.9	36.9	7.5	33.0	38.1
Service sector weights	6.8	26.2	35.2	6.8	26.2	35.2	6.8	26.9	36.3
Passau									
Basic weights	6.6	24.5	33.4	6.6	24.5	33.4	6.7	25.4	34.6
Level of profitability: 40%	6.6	24.5	35.7	6.6	24.5	35.7	6.7	25.4	36.9
Real interest rate: 10%	13.2	24.4	29.0	13.2	24.4	29.0	13.4	25.4	29.9
Weights '01	7.1	29.9	35.0	7.1	29.9	35.0	7.2	31.0	36.2
Service sector weights	6.6	24.1	33.3	6.6	24.1	33.3	6.7	24.9	34.4
Pfarrkirchen									
Basic weights	6.5	23.5	32.5	6.5	23.5	32.5	6.6	24.4	33.6
Level of profitability: 40%	6.5	23.5	34.6	6.5	23.5	34.6	6.6	24.4	35.9
Real interest rate: 10%	13.1	23.5	28.1	13.1	23.5	28.1	13.2	24.4	29.1
Weights '01	7.0	28.8	34.0	7.0	28.8	34.0	7.1	29.9	35.2
Service sector weights	6.5	23.0	32.3	6.5	23.0	32.3	6.6	23.8	33.4
Regensburg									
Basic weights	6.7	25.9	34.8	6.7	25.9	34.8	6.8	26.7	35.9
Level of profitability: 40%	6.7	25.9	37.0	6.7	25.9	37.0	6.8	26.7	38.2
Real interest rate: 10%	13.5	25.7	30.2	13.5	25.7	30.2	13.6	26.7	31.1
Weights '01	7.3	31.3	36.4	7.3	31.3	36.4	7.4	32.4	37.6
Service sector weights	6.7	25.6	34.7	6.7	25.6	34.7	6.8	26.3	35.7

	2001			2002			2003		
	Cost of capital	EMTR	EATR	Cost of capital	EMTR	EATR	Cost of capital	EMTR	EATR
Rosenheim									
Basic weights	6.7	25.4	34.2	6.7	25.4	34.2	6.8	26.3	35.3
Level of profitability: 40%	6.7	25.4	36.4	6.7	25.4	36.4	6.8	26.3	37.6
Real interest rate: 10%	13.4	25.2	29.7	13.4	25.2	29.7	13.5	26.1	30.6
Weights '01	7.2	30.8	35.8	7.2	30.8	35.8	7.3	31.8	37.0
Service sector weights	6.7	25.0	34.1	6.7	25.0	34.1	6.7	25.8	35.2
Schwandorf									
Basic weights	6.6	23.8	32.9	6.6	23.8	32.9	6.7	24.9	34.1
Level of profitability: 40%	6.6	23.8	35.1	6.6	23.8	35.1	6.7	24.9	36.4
Real interest rate: 10%	13.1	23.8	28.5	13.1	23.8	28.5	13.3	24.9	29.5
Weights '01	7.1	29.3	34.5	7.1	29.3	34.5	7.2	30.4	35.7
Service sector weights	6.5	23.4	32.8	6.5	23.4	32.8	6.6	24.3	33.9
Schweinfurt									
Basic weights	6.6	24.6	33.5	6.6	24.6	33.5	6.7	25.5	34.6
Level of profitability: 40%	6.6	24.6	35.7	6.6	24.6	35.7	6.7	25.5	36.9
Real interest rate: 10%	13.2	24.5	29.0	13.2	24.5	29.0	13.4	25.4	30.0
Weights '01	7.1	29.9	35.0	7.1	29.9	35.0	7.2	31.0	36.2
Service sector weights	6.6	24.1	33.3	6.6	24.1	33.3	6.7	24.9	34.5
Traunstein									
Basic weights	6.6	24.4	33.3	6.6	24.4	33.3	6.7	25.3	34.5
Level of profitability: 40%	6.6	24.4	35.5	6.6	24.4	35.5	6.7	25.3	36.8
Real interest rate: 10%	13.2	24.3	28.9	13.2	24.3	28.9	13.4	25.3	29.8
Weights '01	7.1	29.8	34.9	7.1	29.8	34.9	7.2	30.9	36.1
Service sector weights	6.6	24.0	33.2	6.6	24.0	33.2	6.6	24.8	34.3
Weiden									
Basic weights	6.6	24.4	33.4	6.6	23.9	32.9	6.7	24.9	34.1
Level of profitability: 40%	6.6	24.4	35.6	6.6	23.9	35.1	6.7	24.9	36.4
Real interest rate: 10%	13.2	24.3	28.9	13.1	23.9	28.5	13.3	24.8	29.5
Weights '01	7.1	29.8	34.9	7.1	29.3	34.5	7.2	30.4	35.7
Service sector weights	6.6	24.0	33.2	6.5	23.5	32.8	6.6	24.3	33.9

	2001			2002			2003		
	Cost of capital	EMTR	EATR	Cost of capital	EMTR	EATR	Cost of capital	EMTR	EATR
Weilheim									
Basic weights	6.5	22.7	31.7	6.5	22.7	31.7	6.5	23.6	32.9
Level of profitability: 40%	6.5	22.7	33.8	6.5	22.7	33.8	6.5	23.6	35.1
Real interest rate: 10%	12.9	22.7	27.4	12.9	22.7	27.4	13.1	23.6	28.4
Weights '01	6.9	28.0	33.2	6.9	28.0	33.2	7.0	29.0	34.4
Service sector weights	6.4	22.1	31.5	6.4	22.1	31.5	6.5	22.9	32.7
Weißenburg i. Bayern									
Basic weights	6.6	23.9	32.8	6.6	23.8	32.7	6.6	24.7	33.9
Level of profitability: 40%	6.6	23.9	34.9	6.6	23.8	34.9	6.6	24.7	36.1
Real interest rate: 10%	13.1	23.8	28.4	13.1	23.7	28.3	13.3	24.6	29.3
Weights '01	7.1	29.2	34.3	7.1	29.1	34.3	7.2	30.2	35.5
Service sector weights	6.5	23.4	32.6	6.5	23.3	32.6	6.6	24.1	33.7
Würzburg									
Basic weights	6.7	25.8	34.6	6.7	25.8	34.6	6.8	26.7	35.8
Level of profitability: 40%	6.7	25.8	36.9	6.7	25.8	36.9	6.8	26.7	38.1
Real interest rate: 10%	13.4	25.6	30.1	13.4	25.6	30.1	13.6	26.6	31.0
Weights '01	7.3	31.2	36.3	7.3	31.2	36.3	7.4	32.3	37.4
Service sector weights	6.7	25.5	34.6	6.7	25.5	34.6	6.8	26.2	35.6
Berlin									
Basic weights	6.8	26.0	34.5	6.8	26.0	34.5	6.8	27.0	35.7
Level of profitability: 40%	6.8	26.0	36.7	6.8	26.0	36.7	6.8	27.0	37.9
Real interest rate: 10%	13.4	25.6	30.0	13.4	25.6	30.0	13.6	26.6	30.9
Weights '01	7.3	31.2	36.1	7.3	31.2	36.1	7.4	32.3	37.3
Service sector weights	6.7	25.5	34.4	6.7	25.5	34.4	6.8	26.3	35.5
Hamburg									
Basic weights	6.9	27.1	35.8	6.9	27.1	35.8	6.9	28.0	36.9
Level of profitability: 40%	6.9	27.1	38.1	6.9	27.1	38.1	6.9	28.0	39.3
Real interest rate: 10%	13.7	26.9	31.1	13.7	26.9	31.1	13.8	27.8	32.1
Weights '01	7.4	32.6	37.5	7.4	32.6	37.5	7.5	33.6	38.6
Service sector weights	6.8	26.8	35.8	6.8	26.8	35.8	6.9	27.6	36.8

	2001			2002			2003		
	Cost of capital	EMTR	EATR	Cost of capital	EMTR	EATR	Cost of capital	EMTR	EATR
Frankfurt									
Basic weights	6.9	27.8	36.5	6.9	27.5	36.3	7.0	28.4	37.3
Level of profitability: 40%	6.9	27.8	38.8	6.9	27.5	38.6	7.0	28.4	39.7
Real interest rate: 10%	13.8	27.6	31.8	13.8	27.3	31.5	13.9	28.2	32.4
Weights '01	7.5	33.3	38.2	7.5	33.0	37.9	7.6	34.1	39.1
Service sector weights	6.9	27.6	36.4	6.9	27.3	36.2	7.0	28.1	37.2
Offenbach									
Basic weights	6.8	26.3	35.1	6.8	26.3	35.1	6.9	27.1	36.2
Level of profitability: 40%	6.8	26.3	37.4	6.8	26.3	37.4	6.9	27.1	38.6
Real interest rate: 10%	13.5	26.1	30.5	13.5	26.1	30.5	13.7	27.0	31.4
Weights '01	7.3	31.8	36.8	7.3	31.8	36.8	7.4	32.8	37.9
Service sector weights	6.8	26.0	35.0	6.8	26.0	35.0	6.8	26.8	36.1
Düsseldorf									
Basic weights	6.8	26.9	35.6	6.8	26.8	35.5	6.9	27.6	36.6
Level of profitability: 40%	6.8	26.9	37.9	6.8	26.8	37.8	6.9	27.6	38.9
Real interest rate: 10%	13.6	26.7	30.9	13.6	26.5	30.8	13.8	27.4	31.8
Weights '01	7.4	32.3	37.3	7.4	32.2	37.1	7.5	33.2	38.3
Service sector weights	6.8	26.6	35.5	6.8	26.5	35.4	6.9	27.2	36.5
Essen									
Basic weights	6.9	27.1	35.8	6.9	27.1	35.8	6.9	28.0	36.9
Level of profitability: 40%	6.9	27.1	38.1	6.9	27.1	38.1	6.9	28.0	39.3
Real interest rate: 10%	13.7	26.9	31.1	13.7	26.9	31.1	13.9	27.8	32.1
Weights '01	7.4	32.6	37.5	7.4	32.6	37.5	7.5	33.6	38.6
Service sector weights	6.8	26.8	35.8	6.8	26.8	35.8	6.9	27.6	36.8
Köln									
Basic weights	6.8	26.7	35.4	6.8	26.7	35.4	6.9	27.6	36.5
Level of profitability: 40%	6.8	26.7	37.6	6.8	26.7	37.6	6.9	27.6	38.8
Real interest rate: 10%	13.6	26.4	30.7	13.6	26.4	30.7	13.8	27.4	31.7
Weights '01	7.4	32.1	37.0	7.4	32.1	37.0	7.5	33.1	38.2
Service sector weights	6.8	26.4	35.3	6.8	26.4	35.3	6.9	27.1	36.4

	2001			2002			2003		
	Cost of capital	EMTR	EATR	Cost of capital	EMTR	EATR	Cost of capital	EMTR	EATR
Landau									
Basic weights	6.7	25.7	34.6	6.7	25.7	34.6	6.8	26.6	35.8
Level of profitability: 40%	6.7	25.7	36.9	6.7	25.7	36.9	6.8	26.6	38.1
Real interest rate: 10%	13.4	25.6	30.1	13.4	25.6	30.1	13.6	26.6	31.0
Weights '01	7.3	31.2	36.3	7.3	31.2	36.3	7.4	32.3	37.4
Service sector weights	6.7	25.4	34.6	6.7	25.4	34.6	6.8	26.2	35.6
Ludwigshafen									
Basic weights	6.7	25.0	33.9	6.7	25.0	33.9	6.7	25.2	34.4
Level of profitability: 40%	6.7	25.0	36.2	6.7	25.0	36.2	6.7	25.2	36.7
Real interest rate: 10%	13.3	24.9	29.4	13.3	24.9	29.4	13.4	25.2	29.7
Weights '01	7.2	30.4	35.5	7.2	30.4	35.5	7.2	30.7	36.0
Service sector weights	6.6	24.6	33.8	6.6	24.6	33.8	6.6	24.6	34.2
Mainz									
Basic weights	6.8	26.3	35.1	6.8	26.3	35.1	6.9	27.1	36.2
Level of profitability: 40%	6.8	26.3	37.4	6.8	26.3	37.4	6.9	27.1	38.6
Real interest rate: 10%	13.5	26.1	30.5	13.5	26.1	30.5	13.7	27.0	31.4
Weights '01	7.3	31.8	36.8	7.3	31.8	36.8	7.4	32.8	37.9
Service sector weights	6.8	26.0	35.0	6.8	26.0	35.0	6.8	26.8	36.1

D.2.4 Ireland

	2001			2002			2003		
	Cost of capital	EMTR	EATR	Cost of capital	EMTR	EATR	Cost of capital	EMTR	EATR
Dublin									
Basic weights	5.6	10.1	12.0	5.6	10.1	12.1	5.7	11.9	14.0
Level of profitability: 40%	5.6	10.1	12.5	5.6	10.1	12.5	5.7	11.9	14.5
Real interest rate: 10%	11.0	9.0	10.6	11.0	9.0	10.6	11.2	10.7	12.4
Weights '01	5.8	13.6	14.9	5.8	13.6	14.9	5.9	15.0	16.4
Service sector weights	5.7	11.8	19.9	5.7	11.8	18.9	5.7	12.2	18.1

D.2.5 Italy

	2001			2002			2003		
	Cost of capital	EMTR	EATR	Cost of capital	EMTR	EATR	Cost of capital	EMTR	EATR
Gorizia									
Basic weights	4.7	-5.7	28.8	6.3	20.0	33.4	6.2	18.8	31.7
Level of profitability: 40%	4.7	-5.7	34.1	6.3	20.0	36.4	6.2	18.8	34.6
Real interest rate: 10%	10.1	1.0	20.2	12.6	20.7	27.7	12.4	19.4	26.3
Weights '01	5.7	11.5	31.1	6.9	27.3	34.8	6.7	25.7	33.0
Service sector weights	5.7	11.7	30.3	6.1	18.0	31.6	6.0	16.8	30.0
Pordenone									
Basic weights	4.7	-6.3	28.8	6.2	19.9	33.4	6.2	18.7	31.7
Level of profitability: 40%	4.7	-6.3	34.1	6.2	19.9	36.4	6.2	18.7	34.6
Real interest rate: 10%	10.1	0.7	20.1	12.6	20.6	27.7	12.4	19.4	26.3
Weights '01	5.6	11.3	31.1	6.9	27.2	34.8	6.7	25.6	33.0
Service sector weights	5.6	11.4	30.3	6.1	17.9	31.6	6.0	16.8	30.0
Trieste									
Basic weights	4.7	-5.7	28.8	6.3	20.3	33.5	6.2	19.0	31.8
Level of profitability: 40%	4.7	-5.7	34.1	6.3	20.3	36.4	6.2	19.0	34.6
Real interest rate: 10%	10.1	1.0	20.2	12.6	20.8	27.7	12.4	19.5	26.4
Weights '01	5.7	11.5	31.1	6.9	27.4	34.8	6.7	25.8	33.0
Service sector weights	5.7	11.7	30.3	6.1	18.1	31.7	6.0	17.0	30.0
Udine									
Basic weights	4.7	-6.1	28.8	6.2	19.8	33.4	6.1	18.6	31.7
Level of profitability: 40%	4.7	-6.1	34.1	6.2	19.8	36.4	6.1	18.6	34.5
Real interest rate: 10%	10.1	0.8	20.1	12.6	20.6	27.6	12.4	19.3	26.3
Weights '01	5.6	11.4	31.1	6.9	27.2	34.7	6.7	25.6	33.0
Service sector weights	5.7	11.5	30.3	6.1	17.9	31.6	6.0	16.7	29.9
Bergamo									
Basic weights	4.7	-5.8	28.8	6.3	20.0	33.4	6.2	18.8	31.7
Level of profitability: 40%	4.7	-5.8	34.1	6.3	20.0	36.4	6.2	18.8	34.6
Real interest rate: 10%	10.1	1.0	20.2	12.6	20.7	27.7	12.4	19.4	26.3
Weights '01	5.7	11.5	31.1	6.9	27.3	34.8	6.7	25.7	33.0
Service sector weights	5.7	11.7	30.3	6.1	18.0	31.6	6.0	16.8	30.0

	2001			2002			2003		
	Cost of capital	EMTR	EATR	Cost of capital	EMTR	EATR	Cost of capital	EMTR	EATR
Brescia									
Basic weights	4.7	-5.8	28.8	6.3	20.0	33.4	6.2	18.8	31.7
Level of profitability: 40%	4.7	-5.8	34.1	6.3	20.0	36.4	6.2	18.8	34.6
Real interest rate: 10%	10.1	1.0	20.2	12.6	20.7	27.7	12.4	19.4	26.3
Weights '01	5.6	11.5	31.1	6.9	27.2	34.8	6.7	25.7	33.0
Service sector weights	5.7	11.6	30.3	6.1	18.0	31.6	6.0	16.8	30.0
Como									
Basic weights	4.7	-5.9	28.8	6.2	20.0	33.4	6.2	19.0	31.8
Level of profitability: 40%	4.7	-5.9	34.1	6.2	20.0	36.4	6.2	19.0	34.6
Real interest rate: 10%	10.1	0.9	20.2	12.6	20.7	27.7	12.4	19.5	26.3
Weights '01	5.6	11.5	31.1	6.9	27.2	34.8	6.7	25.7	33.0
Service sector weights	5.7	11.6	30.3	6.1	18.0	31.6	6.0	16.9	30.0
Cremona									
Basic weights	4.7	-5.9	28.8	6.3	20.2	33.4	6.2	18.9	31.8
Level of profitability: 40%	4.7	-5.9	34.1	6.3	20.2	36.4	6.2	18.9	34.6
Real interest rate: 10%	10.1	0.9	20.2	12.6	20.8	27.7	12.4	19.5	26.3
Weights '01	5.6	11.5	31.1	6.9	27.3	34.8	6.7	25.7	33.0
Service sector weights	5.7	11.6	30.3	6.1	18.1	31.7	6.0	16.9	30.0
Lecco									
Basic weights	4.7	-5.8	28.8	6.3	20.0	33.4	6.2	19.0	31.8
Level of profitability: 40%	4.7	-5.8	34.1	6.3	20.0	36.4	6.2	19.0	34.6
Real interest rate: 10%	10.1	1.0	20.2	12.6	20.7	27.7	12.4	19.5	26.4
Weights '01	5.7	11.5	31.1	6.9	27.3	34.8	6.7	25.8	33.0
Service sector weights	5.7	11.7	30.3	6.1	18.0	31.6	6.0	17.0	30.0
Lodi									
Basic weights	4.7	-5.5	28.9	6.3	20.2	33.4	6.2	18.9	31.8
Level of profitability: 40%	4.7	-5.5	34.1	6.3	20.2	36.4	6.2	18.9	34.6
Real interest rate: 10%	10.1	1.1	20.2	12.6	20.8	27.7	12.4	19.5	26.3
Weights '01	5.7	11.6	31.1	6.9	27.3	34.8	6.7	25.7	33.0
Service sector weights	5.7	11.7	30.3	6.1	18.1	31.7	6.0	16.9	30.0

	2001			2002			2003		
	Cost of capital	EMTR	EATR	Cost of capital	EMTR	EATR	Cost of capital	EMTR	EATR
Mantova									
Basic weights	4.7	-5.4	28.9	6.3	20.3	33.5	6.2	19.0	31.8
Level of profitability: 40%	4.7	-5.4	34.1	6.3	20.3	36.4	6.2	19.0	34.6
Real interest rate: 10%	10.1	1.2	20.2	12.6	20.8	27.7	12.4	19.5	26.4
Weights '01	5.7	11.7	31.2	6.9	27.4	34.8	6.7	25.8	33.0
Service sector weights	5.7	11.8	30.4	6.1	18.1	31.7	6.0	17.0	30.0
Milano									
Basic weights	4.7	-6.1	28.8	6.2	19.8	33.4	6.1	18.6	31.7
Level of profitability: 40%	4.7	-6.1	34.1	6.2	19.8	36.4	6.1	18.6	34.5
Real interest rate: 10%	10.1	0.8	20.1	12.6	20.6	27.6	12.4	19.3	26.3
Weights '01	5.6	11.4	31.1	6.9	27.2	34.7	6.7	25.6	33.0
Service sector weights	5.7	11.5	30.3	6.1	17.9	31.6	6.0	16.7	29.9
Pavia									
Basic weights	4.7	-5.5	28.9	6.3	20.2	33.4	6.2	18.9	31.8
Level of profitability: 40%	4.7	-5.5	34.1	6.3	20.2	36.4	6.2	18.9	34.6
Real interest rate: 10%	10.1	1.1	20.2	12.6	20.8	27.7	12.4	19.5	26.3
Weights '01	5.7	11.6	31.1	6.9	27.3	34.8	6.7	25.7	33.0
Service sector weights	5.7	11.7	30.3	6.1	18.1	31.7	6.0	16.9	30.0
Sondrio									
Basic weights	4.7	-5.8	28.8	6.3	20.0	33.4	6.2	18.8	31.7
Level of profitability: 40%	4.7	-5.8	34.1	6.3	20.0	36.4	6.2	18.8	34.6
Real interest rate: 10%	10.1	1.0	20.2	12.6	20.7	27.7	12.4	19.4	26.3
Weights '01	5.6	11.5	31.1	6.9	27.2	34.8	6.7	25.7	33.0
Service sector weights	5.7	11.6	30.3	6.1	18.0	31.6	6.0	16.8	30.0
Varese									
Basic weights	4.7	-5.8	28.8	6.3	20.0	33.4	6.2	18.8	31.7
Level of profitability: 40%	4.7	-5.8	34.1	6.3	20.0	36.4	6.2	18.8	34.6
Real interest rate: 10%	10.1	1.0	20.2	12.6	20.7	27.7	12.4	19.4	26.3
Weights '01	5.7	11.5	31.1	6.9	27.3	34.8	6.7	25.7	33.0
Service sector weights	5.7	11.7	30.3	6.1	18.0	31.6	6.0	16.8	30.0

	2001			2002			2003		
	Cost of capital	EMTR	EATR	Cost of capital	EMTR	EATR	Cost of capital	EMTR	EATR
Alessandria									
Basic weights	4.7	-5.5	28.9	6.3	20.3	33.5	6.2	19.0	31.8
Level of profitability: 40%	4.7	-5.5	34.1	6.3	20.3	36.4	6.2	19.0	34.6
Real interest rate: 10%	10.1	1.1	20.2	12.6	20.8	27.7	12.4	19.5	26.4
Weights '01	5.7	11.6	31.1	6.9	27.4	34.8	6.7	25.8	33.0
Service sector weights	5.7	11.7	30.3	6.1	18.1	31.7	6.0	17.0	30.0
Asti									
Basic weights	4.7	-5.5	28.9	6.3	20.2	33.4	6.2	19.0	31.8
Level of profitability: 40%	4.7	-5.5	34.1	6.3	20.2	36.4	6.2	19.0	34.6
Real interest rate: 10%	10.1	1.1	20.2	12.6	20.8	27.7	12.4	19.5	26.4
Weights '01	5.7	11.6	31.1	6.9	27.3	34.8	6.7	25.8	33.0
Service sector weights	5.7	11.7	30.3	6.1	18.1	31.7	6.0	17.0	30.0
Biella									
Basic weights	4.7	-5.6	28.9	6.3	20.1	33.4	6.2	18.9	31.7
Level of profitability: 40%	4.7	-5.6	34.1	6.3	20.1	36.4	6.2	18.9	34.6
Real interest rate: 10%	10.1	1.0	20.2	12.6	20.7	27.7	12.4	19.4	26.3
Weights '01	5.7	11.6	31.1	6.9	27.3	34.8	6.7	25.7	33.0
Service sector weights	5.7	11.7	30.3	6.1	18.0	31.6	6.0	16.9	30.0
Cuneo									
Basic weights	4.7	-5.5	28.9	6.3	20.2	33.4	6.2	18.9	31.8
Level of profitability: 40%	4.7	-5.5	34.1	6.3	20.2	36.4	6.2	18.9	34.6
Real interest rate: 10%	10.1	1.1	20.2	12.6	20.8	27.7	12.4	19.5	26.3
Weights '01	5.7	11.6	31.1	6.9	27.3	34.8	6.7	25.7	33.0
Service sector weights	5.7	11.7	30.3	6.1	18.1	31.7	6.0	16.9	30.0
Novara									
Basic weights	4.7	-5.8	28.8	6.3	20.2	33.4	6.2	19.0	31.8
Level of profitability: 40%	4.7	-5.8	34.1	6.3	20.2	36.4	6.2	19.0	34.6
Real interest rate: 10%	10.1	1.0	20.2	12.6	20.8	27.7	12.4	19.5	26.3
Weights '01	5.6	11.5	31.1	6.9	27.4	34.8	6.7	25.8	33.0
Service sector weights	5.7	11.6	30.3	6.1	18.1	31.7	6.0	16.9	30.0

	2001			2002			2003		
	Cost of capital	EMTR	EATR	Cost of capital	EMTR	EATR	Cost of capital	EMTR	EATR
Torino									
Basic weights	4.7	-5.7	28.8	6.3	20.2	33.4	6.2	18.9	31.8
Level of profitability: 40%	4.7	-5.7	34.1	6.3	20.2	36.4	6.2	18.9	34.6
Real interest rate: 10%	10.1	1.0	20.2	12.6	20.8	27.7	12.4	19.5	26.3
Weights '01	5.7	11.5	31.1	6.9	27.3	34.8	6.7	25.7	33.0
Service sector weights	5.7	11.7	30.3	6.1	18.1	31.7	6.0	16.9	30.0
Verbano-Cusio-Ossola									
Basic weights	4.7	-5.9	28.8	6.2	19.9	33.4	6.2	18.7	31.7
Level of profitability: 40%	4.7	-5.9	34.1	6.2	19.9	36.4	6.2	18.7	34.6
Real interest rate: 10%	10.1	0.9	20.2	12.6	20.6	27.7	12.4	19.4	26.3
Weights '01	5.6	11.4	31.1	6.9	27.2	34.8	6.7	25.6	33.0
Service sector weights	5.7	11.6	30.3	6.1	17.9	31.6	6.0	16.8	30.0
Vercelli									
Basic weights	4.7	-6.1	28.8	6.3	20.0	33.4	6.2	18.8	31.7
Level of profitability: 40%	4.7	-6.1	34.1	6.3	20.0	36.4	6.2	18.8	34.6
Real interest rate: 10%	10.1	0.8	20.1	12.6	20.7	27.7	12.4	19.4	26.3
Weights '01	5.6	11.4	31.1	6.9	27.3	34.8	6.7	25.7	33.0
Service sector weights	5.7	11.5	30.3	6.1	18.0	31.6	6.0	16.8	30.0
Bolzano									
Basic weights	4.7	-5.7	28.8	6.3	20.0	33.4	6.2	18.8	31.7
Level of profitability: 40%	4.7	-5.7	34.1	6.3	20.0	36.4	6.2	18.8	34.6
Real interest rate: 10%	10.1	1.0	20.2	12.6	20.7	27.7	12.4	19.4	26.3
Weights '01	5.7	11.5	31.1	6.9	27.3	34.8	6.7	25.7	33.0
Service sector weights	5.7	11.7	30.3	6.1	18.0	31.6	6.0	16.8	30.0
Trento									
Basic weights	4.7	-6.1	28.8	6.3	20.0	33.4	6.2	18.8	31.7
Level of profitability: 40%	4.7	-6.1	34.1	6.3	20.0	36.4	6.2	18.8	34.6
Real interest rate: 10%	10.1	0.8	20.1	12.6	20.7	27.7	12.4	19.4	26.3
Weights '01	5.6	11.4	31.1	6.9	27.3	34.8	6.7	25.7	33.0
Service sector weights	5.7	11.5	30.3	6.1	18.0	31.6	6.0	16.8	30.0

	2001			2002			2003		
	Cost of capital	EMTR	EATR	Cost of capital	EMTR	EATR	Cost of capital	EMTR	EATR
Valle d'Aosta									
Basic weights	4.7	-6.5	28.7	6.2	19.6	33.3	6.1	18.4	31.6
Level of profitability: 40%	4.7	-6.5	34.1	6.2	19.6	36.4	6.1	18.4	34.5
Real interest rate: 10%	10.1	0.7	20.1	12.6	20.5	27.6	12.4	19.2	26.2
Weights '01	5.6	11.2	31.1	6.9	27.0	34.7	6.7	25.4	32.9
Service sector weights	5.6	11.4	30.3	6.1	17.7	31.6	6.0	16.6	29.9
Belluno									
Basic weights	4.7	-5.4	28.9	6.3	20.3	33.5	6.2	19.0	31.8
Level of profitability: 40%	4.7	-5.4	34.1	6.3	20.3	36.4	6.2	19.0	34.6
Real interest rate: 10%	10.1	1.2	20.2	12.6	20.8	27.7	12.4	19.5	26.4
Weights '01	5.7	11.7	31.2	6.9	27.4	34.8	6.7	25.8	33.0
Service sector weights	5.7	11.8	30.4	6.1	18.1	31.7	6.0	17.0	30.0
Padova									
Basic weights	4.7	-5.9	28.8	6.3	20.1	33.4	6.2	18.9	31.7
Level of profitability: 40%	4.7	-5.9	34.1	6.3	20.1	36.4	6.2	18.9	34.6
Real interest rate: 10%	10.1	0.9	20.2	12.6	20.7	27.7	12.4	19.4	26.3
Weights '01	5.6	11.4	31.1	6.9	27.3	34.8	6.7	25.7	33.0
Service sector weights	5.7	11.6	30.3	6.1	18.0	31.6	6.0	16.9	30.0
Rovigo									
Basic weights	4.7	-5.4	28.9	6.3	20.3	33.5	6.2	19.0	31.8
Level of profitability: 40%	4.7	-5.4	34.1	6.3	20.3	36.4	6.2	19.0	34.6
Real interest rate: 10%	10.1	1.2	20.2	12.6	20.8	27.7	12.4	19.5	26.4
Weights '01	5.7	11.7	31.2	6.9	27.4	34.8	6.7	25.8	33.0
Service sector weights	5.7	11.8	30.4	6.1	18.1	31.7	6.0	17.0	30.0
Treviso									
Basic weights	4.7	-5.5	28.9	6.3	20.2	33.4	6.2	18.9	31.8
Level of profitability: 40%	4.7	-5.5	34.1	6.3	20.2	36.4	6.2	18.9	34.6
Real interest rate: 10%	10.1	1.1	20.2	12.6	20.8	27.7	12.4	19.5	26.3
Weights '01	5.7	11.6	31.1	6.9	27.3	34.8	6.7	25.7	33.0
Service sector weights	5.7	11.7	30.3	6.1	18.1	31.7	6.0	16.9	30.0

	2001			2002			2003		
	Cost of capital	EMTR	EATR	Cost of capital	EMTR	EATR	Cost of capital	EMTR	EATR
Venezia									
Basic weights	4.7	-5.4	28.9	6.3	20.3	33.5	6.2	19.0	31.8
Level of profitability: 40%	4.7	-5.4	34.1	6.3	20.3	36.4	6.2	19.0	34.6
Real interest rate: 10%	10.1	1.2	20.2	12.6	20.8	27.7	12.4	19.5	26.4
Weights '01	5.7	11.7	31.2	6.9	27.4	34.8	6.7	25.8	33.0
Service sector weights	5.7	11.8	30.4	6.1	18.1	31.7	6.0	17.0	30.0
Verona									
Basic weights	4.7	-5.9	28.8	6.2	19.9	33.4	6.2	19.0	31.8
Level of profitability: 40%	4.7	-5.9	34.1	6.2	19.9	36.4	6.2	19.0	34.6
Real interest rate: 10%	10.1	0.9	20.2	12.6	20.6	27.7	12.4	19.5	26.3
Weights '01	5.6	11.4	31.1	6.9	27.2	34.8	6.7	25.8	33.0
Service sector weights	5.7	11.6	30.3	6.1	17.9	31.6	6.0	16.9	30.0
Vicenza									
Basic weights	4.7	-5.7	28.8	6.3	20.0	33.4	6.2	18.8	31.7
Level of profitability: 40%	4.7	-5.7	34.1	6.3	20.0	36.4	6.2	18.8	34.6
Real interest rate: 10%	10.1	1.0	20.2	12.6	20.7	27.7	12.4	19.4	26.3
Weights '01	5.7	11.5	31.1	6.9	27.3	34.8	6.7	25.7	33.0
Service sector weights	5.7	11.7	30.3	6.1	18.0	31.6	6.0	16.8	30.0

D.2.6 The Netherlands

	2001			2002			2003		
	Cost of capital	EMTR	EATR	Cost of capital	EMTR	EATR	Cost of capital	EMTR	EATR
Amsterdam									
Basic weights	6.3	21.1	30.6	6.3	20.7	30.2	6.3	20.8	30.2
Level of profitability: 40%	6.3	21.1	32.8	6.3	20.7	32.3	6.3	20.8	32.3
Real interest rate: 10%	12.7	21.0	26.1	12.6	20.6	25.8	12.6	20.7	25.8
Weights '01	6.8	26.0	32.0	6.7	25.6	31.5	6.7	25.6	31.5
Service sector weights	6.1	18.4	29.9	6.1	18.0	29.5	6.1	18.1	29.5
Den Haag									
Basic weights	6.4	21.5	30.7	6.3	21.1	30.3	6.3	21.1	30.3
Level of profitability: 40%	6.4	21.5	32.8	6.3	21.1	32.4	6.3	21.1	32.4
Real interest rate: 10%	12.7	21.2	26.3	12.6	20.8	25.9	12.6	20.8	25.9
Weights '01	6.8	26.3	32.0	6.7	25.8	31.6	6.7	25.8	31.6
Service sector weights	6.1	18.6	30.0	6.1	18.3	29.5	6.1	18.3	29.5
Rotterdam									
Basic weights	6.4	21.7	30.7	6.4	21.4	30.3	6.4	21.4	30.3
Level of profitability: 40%	6.4	21.7	32.9	6.4	21.4	32.4	6.4	21.4	32.4
Real interest rate: 10%	12.7	21.3	26.3	12.7	21.0	25.9	12.7	21.0	26.0
Weights '01	6.8	26.4	32.1	6.8	26.0	31.6	6.8	26.0	31.6
Service sector weights	6.2	18.7	30.0	6.1	18.5	29.6	6.1	18.5	29.6
Utrecht									
Basic weights	6.4	21.3	30.7	6.3	21.0	30.2	6.3	21.1	30.2
Level of profitability: 40%	6.4	21.3	32.8	6.3	21.0	32.4	6.3	21.1	32.4
Real interest rate: 10%	12.7	21.1	26.2	12.6	20.8	25.8	12.6	20.8	25.9
Weights '01	6.8	26.2	32.0	6.7	25.8	31.6	6.7	25.8	31.6
Service sector weights	6.1	18.5	29.9	6.1	18.2	29.5	6.1	18.3	29.5

D.2.7 Switzerland

	2001			2002			2003		
	Cost of capital	EMTR	EATR	Cost of capital	EMTR	EATR	Cost of capital	EMTR	EATR
Basel-Landschaft									
Basic weights	6.0	16.6	22.9	6.0	16.3	22.9	6.0	16.3	22.8
Level of profitability: 40%	6.0	16.6	24.3	6.0	16.3	24.3	6.0	16.3	24.2
Real interest rate: 10%	11.7	14.4	19.0	11.7	14.2	19.0	11.7	14.2	19.0
Weights '01	6.4	21.5	24.3	6.3	21.3	24.3	6.3	21.2	24.2
Service sector weights	5.8	14.3	22.3	5.8	14.1	22.3	5.8	14.1	22.3
Basel-Stadt									
Basic weights	5.9	15.6	22.1	5.9	15.6	22.1	5.9	15.6	22.1
Level of profitability: 40%	5.9	15.6	23.5	5.9	15.6	23.5	5.9	15.6	23.5
Real interest rate: 10%	11.6	13.6	18.3	11.6	13.6	18.3	11.6	13.6	18.3
Weights '01	6.3	20.5	23.4	6.3	20.5	23.4	6.3	20.5	23.4
Service sector weights	5.8	13.6	21.6	5.8	13.6	21.6	5.8	13.6	21.6
Bern									
Basic weights	5.7	11.6	18.8	5.7	11.6	18.8	5.6	10.6	18.6
Level of profitability: 40%	5.7	11.6	20.2	5.7	11.6	20.2	5.6	10.6	20.1
Real interest rate: 10%	11.2	10.7	15.5	11.2	10.7	15.5	11.1	10.1	15.2
Weights '01	6.0	16.0	20.0	6.0	16.0	20.0	5.9	15.1	19.7
Service sector weights	5.6	10.4	18.5	5.6	10.4	18.5	5.5	9.7	18.3
Genève									
Basic weights	5.8	14.5	21.4	5.8	14.5	21.4	5.8	14.5	21.4
Level of profitability: 40%	5.8	14.5	22.8	5.8	14.5	22.8	5.8	14.5	22.8
Real interest rate: 10%	11.5	12.9	17.7	11.5	12.9	17.7	11.5	12.9	17.7
Weights '01	6.2	19.2	22.7	6.2	19.2	22.7	6.2	19.2	22.7
Service sector weights	5.7	12.7	20.9	5.7	12.7	20.9	5.7	12.7	20.9
Nidwalden									
Basic weights	5.5	9.1	15.5	5.5	9.1	15.5	5.5	9.0	15.4
Level of profitability: 40%	5.5	9.1	16.7	5.5	9.1	16.7	5.5	9.0	16.6
Real interest rate: 10%	10.9	8.4	12.8	10.9	8.4	12.8	10.9	8.4	12.7
Weights '01	5.7	12.9	16.5	5.7	12.9	16.5	5.7	12.8	16.4
Service sector weights	5.4	8.2	15.3	5.4	8.2	15.3	5.4	8.1	15.2

	2001			2002			2003		
	Cost of capital	EMTR	EATR	Cost of capital	EMTR	EATR	Cost of capital	EMTR	EATR
Schwyz									
Basic weights	5.6	11.1	17.1	5.6	10.6	16.5	5.6	10.6	16.5
Level of profitability: 40%	5.6	11.1	18.3	5.6	10.6	17.7	5.6	10.6	17.6
Real interest rate: 10%	11.1	9.9	14.2	11.0	9.5	13.7	11.0	9.5	13.6
Weights '01	5.9	15.1	18.2	5.8	14.5	17.6	5.8	14.5	17.5
Service sector weights	5.5	9.8	16.8	5.5	9.3	16.2	5.5	9.3	16.2
St. Gallen									
Basic weights	5.4	6.9	20.3	5.4	6.8	20.2	5.4	6.9	20.3
Level of profitability: 40%	5.4	6.9	22.7	5.4	6.8	22.6	5.4	6.9	22.7
Real interest rate: 10%	11.0	9.3	16.4	11.0	9.2	16.3	11.0	9.3	16.4
Weights '01	5.7	12.6	21.6	5.7	12.5	21.5	5.7	12.6	21.6
Service sector weights	5.4	7.9	20.5	5.4	7.9	20.4	5.4	7.9	20.5
Ticino									
Basic weights	5.8	13.3	18.7	5.8	13.3	18.7	5.7	12.2	18.5
Level of profitability: 40%	5.8	13.3	19.8	5.8	13.3	19.8	5.7	12.2	19.7
Real interest rate: 10%	11.3	11.4	15.6	11.3	11.4	15.6	11.2	10.8	15.3
Weights '01	6.0	17.3	19.8	6.0	17.3	19.8	6.0	16.3	19.6
Service sector weights	5.6	11.4	18.3	5.6	11.4	18.3	5.6	10.7	18.1
Vaud									
Basic weights	5.8	13.1	20.5	5.8	13.1	20.5	5.8	13.1	20.5
Level of profitability: 40%	5.8	13.1	22.0	5.8	13.1	22.0	5.8	13.1	22.0
Real interest rate: 10%	11.4	11.9	16.9	11.4	11.9	16.9	11.4	11.9	16.9
Weights '01	6.1	17.7	21.7	6.1	17.7	21.7	6.1	17.7	21.7
Service sector weights	5.7	11.6	20.1	5.7	11.6	20.1	5.7	11.6	20.1
Valais									
Basic weights	5.9	14.7	19.7	5.9	14.7	19.7	5.9	14.7	19.7
Level of profitability: 40%	5.9	14.7	20.7	5.9	14.7	20.7	5.9	14.7	20.7
Real interest rate: 10%	11.4	12.4	16.4	11.4	12.4	16.4	11.4	12.4	16.4
Weights '01	6.2	18.8	20.8	6.2	18.8	20.8	6.2	18.8	20.8
Service sector weights	5.7	12.5	19.1	5.7	12.5	19.1	5.7	12.5	19.1

	2001			2002			2003		
	Cost of capital	EMTR	EATR	Cost of capital	EMTR	EATR	Cost of capital	EMTR	EATR
Zug									
Basic weights	5.4	7.1	13.8	5.4	7.1	13.8	5.4	7.1	13.8
Level of profitability: 40%	5.4	7.1	15.1	5.4	7.1	15.1	5.4	7.1	15.0
Real interest rate: 10%	10.8	7.0	11.3	10.8	7.0	11.3	10.8	7.0	11.3
Weights '01	5.6	10.7	14.7	5.6	10.7	14.7	5.6	10.7	14.7
Service sector weights	5.4	6.7	13.7	5.4	6.7	13.7	5.4	6.7	13.7
Zürich									
Basic weights	5.8	14.0	21.6	5.8	13.8	21.3	5.8	13.6	21.0
Level of profitability: 40%	5.8	14.0	23.1	5.8	13.8	22.9	5.8	13.6	22.6
Real interest rate: 10%	11.5	12.7	17.8	11.4	12.5	17.6	11.4	12.3	17.4
Weights '01	6.2	19.0	22.9	6.2	18.7	22.7	6.1	18.4	22.4
Service sector weights	5.7	12.5	21.2	5.7	12.3	21.0	5.7	12.1	20.7

D.2.8 United Kingdom

	2001			2002			2003		
	Cost of capital	EMTR	EATR	Cost of capital	EMTR	EATR	Cost of capital	EMTR	EATR
London									
Basic weights	6.6	24.0	28.0	6.6	24.1	28.1	6.6	24.2	28.1
Level of profitability: 40%	6.6	24.0	29.0	6.6	24.1	29.0	6.6	24.2	29.0
Real interest rate: 10%	12.6	20.7	24.1	12.6	20.8	24.2	12.6	20.9	24.2
Weights '01	6.8	26.8	28.9	6.8	26.9	28.9	6.8	26.9	29.0
Service sector weights	6.1	18.6	26.5	6.2	18.8	26.5	6.2	18.8	26.6

D.2.9 United States

	2001			2002			2003		
	Cost of capital	EMTR	EATR	Cost of capital	EMTR	EATR	Cost of capital	EMTR	EATR
Boston									
Basic weights	6.8	26.5	36.2	6.7	25.8	36.0	6.7	25.8	36.0
Level of profitability: 40%	6.8	26.5	38.7	6.7	25.8	38.6	6.7	25.8	38.6
Real interest rate: 10%	13.6	26.3	31.1	13.4	25.6	30.7	13.4	25.6	30.7
Weights '01	7.1	29.7	37.1	7.1	29.2	36.9	7.1	29.2	36.9
Service sector weights	7.1	29.7	37.1	7.1	29.4	37.0	7.1	29.7	37.1

D.3 The Impact of Personal Taxation

D.3.1 Austria

Austria – all regions	Overall	Assets					Sources of finance		
		Intangibles	Industrial buildings	Machinery	Financial assets	Inventories	Retained earnings	New equity	Debt
Zero-rate sh.									
Cost of capital 2001	6.5	6.4	6.5	5.9	7.3	6.3	7.7	7.7	4.2
2002	6.5	6.4	6.5	5.9	7.3	6.3	7.7	7.7	4.2
2003	6.5	6.4	6.5	5.9	7.3	6.3	7.7	7.7	4.2
EMTR 2001	22.9	22.1	23.0	14.9	31.8	20.9	35.2	35.2	-19.1
2002	22.9	22.1	23.0	14.9	31.8	20.9	35.2	35.2	-19.1
2003	22.9	22.1	23.0	14.9	31.8	20.9	35.2	35.2	-19.1
Top-rate non-q. sh.									
Cost of capital 2001	5.1	5.1	5.1	4.7	5.9	4.9	5.2	7.8	4.3
2002	5.1	5.1	5.1	4.7	5.9	4.9	5.2	7.8	4.3
2003	5.1	5.1	5.1	4.7	5.9	4.9	5.2	7.8	4.3
EMTR 2001	36.5	36.1	36.4	30.4	44.6	33.1	37.3	58.2	23.6
2002	36.5	36.1	36.4	30.4	44.6	33.1	37.3	58.2	23.6
2003	36.5	36.1	36.4	30.4	44.6	33.1	37.3	58.2	23.6
Top-rate q. sh.									
Cost of capital 2001	5.9	5.9	5.9	5.4	6.7	5.7	6.7	7.7	4.2
2002	5.9	5.9	5.9	5.4	6.7	5.7	6.7	7.7	4.2
2003	5.9	5.9	5.9	5.4	6.7	5.7	6.7	7.7	4.2
EMTR 2001	45.0	44.5	44.9	39.4	51.6	43.0	51.1	57.9	22.9
2002	45.0	44.5	44.9	39.4	51.6	43.0	51.1	57.9	22.9
2003	45.0	44.5	44.9	39.4	51.6	43.0	51.1	57.9	22.9
Mean (sh. mix)									
Cost of capital 2001	5.8	5.8	5.8	5.3	6.6	5.6	6.5	7.8	4.2
2002	5.8	5.8	5.8	5.3	6.6	5.6	6.5	7.8	4.2
2003	5.8	5.8	5.8	5.3	6.6	5.6	6.5	7.8	4.2
EMTR 2001	34.3	33.8	34.3	27.7	42.2	31.9	41.2	50.5	9.3
2002	34.3	33.8	34.3	27.7	42.2	31.9	41.2	50.5	9.3
2003	34.3	33.8	34.3	27.7	42.2	31.9	41.2	50.5	9.3

D.3.2 France

France – minimum	Overall	Assets: Intangibles	Assets: Industrial buildings	Assets: Machinery	Assets: Financial assets	Assets: Inventories	Sources of finance: Retained earnings	Sources of finance: New equity	Sources of finance: Debt
Zero-rate sh.									
Cost of capital 2001	6.4	4.8	6.6	6.8	7.2	6.7	8.1	4.6	4.3
2002	6.4	4.8	6.5	6.8	7.1	6.6	8.0	4.5	4.3
2003	6.4	4.8	6.5	6.8	7.1	6.6	8.0	4.5	4.3
EMTR 2001	22.0	-3.9	23.8	26.2	30.8	25.0	38.3	-8.9	-17.2
2002	21.4	-4.0	23.6	26.1	29.8	24.1	37.5	-10.2	-15.8
2003	21.4	-4.0	23.6	26.1	29.8	24.1	37.5	-10.2	-15.8
Top-rate non-q. sh.									
Cost of capital 2001	6.5	5.0	6.7	6.9	7.3	6.7	7.1	10.9	4.3
2002	6.4	4.9	6.6	6.8	7.1	6.6	7.1	9.9	4.4
2003	6.4	4.9	6.6	6.8	7.1	6.6	7.1	9.8	4.4
EMTR 2001	77.7	70.9	78.2	78.9	80.0	78.3	79.6	86.6	66.3
2002	77.2	70.4	77.9	78.7	79.5	77.8	79.3	85.3	66.7
2003	77.2	70.3	77.8	78.6	79.4	77.7	79.3	85.1	66.7
Top-rate q. sh.									
Cost of capital 2001	4.6	3.4	4.8	5.3	5.1	4.5	4.3	6.6	4.5
2002	4.6	3.4	4.8	5.2	5.0	4.4	4.3	6.0	4.6
2003	4.5	3.4	4.8	5.2	5.0	4.4	4.3	5.9	4.6
EMTR 2001	68.5	57.4	69.9	72.3	71.3	67.7	66.3	77.9	67.9
2002	68.0	56.7	69.5	72.1	70.6	67.0	65.8	75.7	68.2
2003	67.9	56.6	69.5	72.0	70.5	66.9	65.8	75.3	68.2
Mean (sh. mix)									
Cost of capital 2001	5.9	4.4	6.0	6.3	6.5	6.0	6.5	7.4	4.4
2002	5.8	4.4	6.0	6.3	6.4	5.9	6.4	6.8	4.4
2003	5.8	4.4	6.0	6.3	6.4	5.9	6.4	6.7	4.4
EMTR 2001	54.9	40.2	56.3	58.3	59.6	55.8	59.6	64.1	39.7
2002	54.3	39.6	55.8	58.0	58.7	54.9	59.0	61.3	40.4
2003	54.2	39.5	55.8	57.9	58.7	54.9	59.0	60.9	40.4

France – median	Overall	Assets					Sources of finance		
		Intangibles	Industrial buildings	Machinery	Financial assets	Inventories	Retained earnings	New equity	Debt
Zero-rate sh.									
Cost of capital 2001	7.1	4.8	8.1	8.8	7.2	6.7	8.8	5.3	5.0
2002	7.1	4.8	8.5	8.5	7.1	6.6	8.7	5.3	5.0
2003	7.1	4.8	8.5	8.5	7.1	6.6	8.7	5.3	5.0
EMTR 2001	29.8	-3.9	38.5	43.1	30.8	25.0	43.4	5.7	-0.6
2002	29.5	-4.0	41.0	40.9	29.8	24.1	42.7	4.9	0.7
2003	29.6	-4.0	41.3	41.0	29.8	24.1	42.8	5.1	0.9
Top-rate non-q. sh.									
Cost of capital 2001	7.3	5.0	8.3	8.9	7.3	6.7	7.9	11.6	5.0
2002	7.1	4.9	8.5	8.5	7.1	6.6	7.8	10.7	5.1
2003	7.1	4.9	8.6	8.5	7.1	6.6	7.8	10.6	5.1
EMTR 2001	79.9	70.9	82.3	83.7	80.0	78.3	81.4	87.4	71.0
2002	79.5	70.4	82.9	82.9	79.5	77.8	81.2	86.3	71.4
2003	79.5	70.3	83.0	82.9	79.4	77.7	81.3	86.2	71.4
Top-rate q. sh.									
Cost of capital 2001	5.3	3.4	6.4	7.3	5.1	4.5	5.0	7.3	5.3
2002	5.3	3.4	6.7	6.9	5.0	4.4	5.0	6.7	5.3
2003	5.3	3.4	6.7	6.9	5.0	4.4	5.0	6.6	5.3
EMTR 2001	72.7	57.4	77.2	79.9	71.3	67.7	71.0	80.1	72.2
2002	72.3	56.7	78.2	78.8	70.6	67.0	70.7	78.3	72.5
2003	72.3	56.6	78.3	78.9	70.5	66.9	70.8	78.0	72.6
Mean (sh. mix)									
Cost of capital 2001	6.6	4.4	7.6	8.3	6.5	6.0	7.2	8.1	5.1
2002	6.5	4.4	7.9	8.0	6.4	5.9	7.2	7.6	5.1
2003	6.5	4.4	7.9	8.0	6.4	5.9	7.2	7.5	5.2
EMTR 2001	59.8	40.2	65.2	68.3	59.6	55.8	63.6	67.3	48.1
2002	59.4	39.6	66.6	66.9	58.7	54.9	63.2	65.1	48.7
2003	59.4	39.5	66.7	66.9	58.7	54.9	63.2	64.7	48.8

France – maximum	Overall	Assets					Sources of finance		
		Intangibles	Industrial buildings	Machinery	Financial assets	Inventories	Retained earnings	New equity	Debt
Zero-rate sh.									
Cost of capital 2001	7.6	4.8	9.5	9.6	7.2	6.7	9.3	5.7	5.4
2002	7.5	4.8	9.5	9.5	7.1	6.6	9.2	5.7	5.4
2003	7.5	4.8	9.5	9.5	7.1	6.6	9.1	5.7	5.4
EMTR 2001	33.8	-3.9	47.4	47.8	30.8	25.0	46.0	12.7	7.4
2002	33.4	-4.0	47.2	47.5	29.8	24.1	45.4	11.7	8.2
2003	33.3	-4.0	47.1	47.3	29.8	24.1	45.3	11.5	7.9
Top-rate non-q. sh.									
Cost of capital 2001	7.7	5.0	9.7	9.7	7.3	6.7	8.3	12.0	5.5
2002	7.5	4.9	9.5	9.6	7.1	6.6	8.2	11.1	5.5
2003	7.5	4.9	9.5	9.5	7.1	6.6	8.2	10.9	5.5
EMTR 2001	81.0	70.9	84.9	85.0	80.0	78.3	82.4	87.9	73.3
2002	80.7	70.4	84.7	84.8	79.5	77.8	82.2	86.9	73.5
2003	80.6	70.3	84.6	84.7	79.4	77.7	82.2	86.7	73.4
Top-rate q. sh.									
Cost of capital 2001	5.8	3.4	7.8	8.0	5.1	4.5	5.5	7.8	5.7
2002	5.7	3.4	7.7	8.0	5.0	4.4	5.4	7.1	5.7
2003	5.7	3.4	7.7	7.9	5.0	4.4	5.4	7.0	5.7
EMTR 2001	74.7	57.4	81.2	81.8	71.3	67.7	73.3	81.2	74.3
2002	74.3	56.7	81.0	81.7	70.6	67.0	72.9	79.6	74.5
2003	74.2	56.6	80.9	81.5	70.5	66.9	72.9	79.2	74.4
Mean (sh. mix)									
Cost of capital 2001	7.0	4.4	9.0	9.1	6.5	6.0	7.7	8.5	5.5
2002	6.9	4.4	8.9	9.0	6.4	5.9	7.6	8.0	5.6
2003	6.9	4.4	8.9	9.0	6.4	5.9	7.6	7.9	5.5
EMTR 2001	62.3	40.2	70.6	71.0	59.6	55.8	65.6	69.0	52.1
2002	61.8	39.6	70.3	70.8	58.7	54.9	65.2	66.9	52.5
2003	61.7	39.5	70.2	70.6	58.7	54.9	65.1	66.5	52.4

D.3.3 Germany

Germany – minimum	Overall	Assets					Sources of finance		
		Intangibles	Industrial buildings	Machinery	Financial assets	Inventories	Retained earnings	New equity	Debt
Zero-rate sh.									
Cost of capital 2001	6.5	5.3	6.7	5.9	7.7	6.6	7.6	7.6	4.3
2002	6.5	5.3	6.7	5.9	7.7	6.6	7.6	7.6	4.3
2003	6.5	5.3	6.8	6.0	7.9	6.7	7.8	7.8	4.3
EMTR 2001	22.7	6.0	25.8	15.9	35.3	24.5	34.4	34.4	-15.4
2002	22.7	6.0	25.8	15.9	35.3	24.5	34.4	34.4	-15.4
2003	23.6	6.2	26.7	16.6	36.6	25.5	35.7	35.7	-17.3
Top-rate non-q. sh.									
Cost of capital 2001	3.4	2.9	3.6	3.2	4.3	3.2	2.5	4.3	4.6
2002	3.4	2.9	3.6	3.2	4.3	3.2	2.5	4.3	4.6
2003	3.5	2.9	3.6	3.3	4.4	3.2	2.6	4.4	4.6
EMTR 2001	58.2	50.8	59.8	55.5	66.5	54.9	43.1	66.5	69.0
2002	58.2	50.8	59.8	55.5	66.5	54.9	43.1	66.5	69.0
2003	58.6	50.8	60.0	55.8	67.1	55.1	44.5	67.3	68.6
Top-rate q. sh.									
Cost of capital 2001	4.0	3.4	4.2	3.7	5.0	3.9	3.7	4.2	4.6
2002	4.0	3.4	4.2	3.7	5.0	3.9	3.7	4.2	4.6
2003	4.1	3.4	4.2	3.8	5.1	3.9	3.7	4.3	4.5
EMTR 2001	64.3	57.3	65.5	61.6	71.1	62.9	60.7	65.9	68.4
2002	64.3	57.3	65.5	61.6	71.1	62.9	60.7	65.9	68.4
2003	64.6	57.3	65.8	61.9	71.6	63.1	61.5	66.7	68.0
Mean (sh. mix)									
Cost of capital 2001	4.6	3.9	4.8	4.3	5.7	4.6	4.6	5.4	4.5
2002	4.6	3.9	4.8	4.3	5.7	4.6	4.6	5.4	4.5
2003	4.7	3.9	4.9	4.3	5.8	4.6	4.7	5.5	4.4
EMTR 2001	43.5	32.2	45.6	39.1	53.6	42.5	42.9	51.2	41.8
2002	43.5	32.2	45.6	39.1	53.6	42.5	42.9	51.2	41.8
2003	44.1	32.3	46.1	39.5	54.5	43.0	44.2	52.2	41.0

Germany – median	Overall	Assets: Intangibles	Assets: Industrial buildings	Assets: Machinery	Assets: Financial assets	Assets: Inventories	Sources of finance: Retained earnings	Sources of finance: New equity	Sources of finance: Debt
Zero-rate sh.									
Cost of capital 2001	6.6	5.4	7.0	6.1	8.0	6.8	7.9	7.9	4.4
2002	6.6	5.4	7.0	6.1	8.0	6.8	7.9	7.9	4.4
2003	6.7	5.4	7.0	6.1	8.1	6.9	8.0	8.0	4.3
EMTR 2001	24.6	7.0	28.1	17.4	37.4	26.3	36.3	36.3	-14.5
2002	24.6	7.0	28.1	17.4	37.4	26.3	36.3	36.3	-14.5
2003	25.5	7.2	28.7	18.1	38.6	27.3	37.6	37.6	-16.5
Top-rate non-q. sh.									
Cost of capital 2001	3.5	3.0	3.7	3.3	4.4	3.2	2.6	4.4	4.7
2002	3.5	3.0	3.7	3.3	4.4	3.2	2.6	4.4	4.7
2003	3.6	3.0	3.7	3.3	4.5	3.3	2.7	4.5	4.6
EMTR 2001	59.3	51.5	61.3	56.4	67.6	55.7	45.3	67.7	69.4
2002	59.3	51.5	61.3	56.4	67.6	55.7	45.3	67.7	69.4
2003	59.6	51.5	61.3	56.7	68.2	55.9	46.6	68.4	69.0
Top-rate q. sh.									
Cost of capital 2001	4.1	3.4	4.3	3.8	5.2	4.0	3.8	4.4	4.6
2002	4.1	3.4	4.3	3.8	5.2	4.0	3.8	4.4	4.6
2003	4.2	3.4	4.3	3.8	5.2	4.0	3.9	4.5	4.5
EMTR 2001	65.2	57.8	66.7	62.4	72.1	63.6	62.0	67.0	68.8
2002	65.2	57.8	66.7	62.4	72.1	63.6	62.0	67.0	68.8
2003	65.5	57.8	66.8	62.6	72.6	63.9	62.8	67.7	68.4
Mean (sh. mix)									
Cost of capital 2001	4.8	3.9	5.0	4.4	5.9	4.7	4.8	5.6	4.6
2002	4.8	3.9	5.0	4.4	5.9	4.7	4.8	5.6	4.6
2003	4.8	3.9	5.0	4.4	6.0	4.7	4.9	5.7	4.5
EMTR 2001	44.9	33.0	47.4	40.2	55.2	43.7	44.8	52.7	42.4
2002	44.9	33.0	47.4	40.2	55.2	43.7	44.8	52.7	42.4
2003	45.4	33.1	47.7	40.7	56.0	44.2	45.9	53.7	41.5

Germany – maximum	Overall	Assets: Intangibles	Assets: Industrial buildings	Assets: Machinery	Assets: Financial assets	Assets: Inventories	Sources of finance: Retained earnings	Sources of finance: New equity	Sources of finance: Debt
Zero-rate sh.									
Cost of capital 2001	6.9	5.5	7.3	6.3	8.5	7.1	8.3	8.3	4.4
2002	6.9	5.5	7.3	6.2	8.4	7.1	8.2	8.2	4.4
2003	7.0	5.5	7.4	6.3	8.6	7.2	8.4	8.4	4.3
EMTR 2001	27.8	8.8	31.8	20.1	40.9	29.5	39.6	39.6	-13.0
2002	27.5	8.6	31.2	19.9	40.7	29.3	39.3	39.3	-13.3
2003	28.4	8.9	32.0	20.6	41.8	30.2	40.5	40.5	-15.2
Top-rate non-q. sh.									
Cost of capital 2001	3.7	3.0	3.9	3.4	4.7	3.4	2.8	4.7	4.8
2002	3.7	3.0	3.9	3.4	4.7	3.4	2.8	4.7	4.8
2003	3.7	3.0	3.9	3.4	4.8	3.4	2.9	4.8	4.7
EMTR 2001	61.1	52.7	63.5	58.0	69.6	57.2	48.8	69.6	70.0
2002	60.9	52.6	63.0	57.9	69.4	57.1	48.4	69.4	69.9
2003	61.2	52.6	63.2	58.1	70.0	57.3	49.7	70.1	69.6
Top-rate q. sh.									
Cost of capital 2001	4.3	3.5	4.6	4.0	5.5	4.1	4.0	4.6	4.7
2002	4.3	3.5	4.5	3.9	5.4	4.1	4.0	4.6	4.7
2003	4.3	3.5	4.5	4.0	5.6	4.1	4.1	4.7	4.6
EMTR 2001	66.7	58.8	68.5	63.7	73.7	65.0	64.2	68.9	69.4
2002	66.5	58.7	68.1	63.6	73.6	64.9	64.0	68.7	69.3
2003	66.8	58.7	68.4	63.8	74.1	65.1	64.8	69.4	68.9
Mean (sh. mix)									
Cost of capital 2001	5.0	4.0	5.3	4.5	6.2	4.9	5.0	5.9	4.6
2002	5.0	4.0	5.2	4.5	6.2	4.8	5.0	5.8	4.6
2003	5.0	4.0	5.3	4.6	6.3	4.9	5.1	6.0	4.6
EMTR 2001	47.3	34.4	50.3	42.3	57.8	45.9	47.8	55.3	43.4
2002	47.0	34.3	49.7	42.1	57.6	45.7	47.5	55.1	43.3
2003	47.6	34.4	50.2	42.5	58.4	46.3	48.7	56.0	42.5

D.3.4 Ireland

Ireland – Dublin	Overall	Assets: Intangibles	Assets: Industrial buildings	Assets: Machinery	Assets: Financial assets	Assets: Inventories	Sources of finance: Retained earnings	Sources of finance: New equity	Sources of finance: Debt
Zero-rate sh.									
Cost of capital 2001	4.4	4.2	4.5	4.0	5.2	4.3	4.2	4.2	4.9
2002	4.5	4.3	4.6	4.1	5.3	4.4	4.4	4.4	4.9
2003	4.6	4.4	4.6	4.3	5.3	4.5	4.5	4.5	4.9
EMTR 2001	21.8	17.8	22.4	13.7	33.1	19.1	17.4	17.4	28.9
2002	20.6	16.5	21.4	12.3	31.9	17.8	17.2	17.2	26.1
2003	22.0	17.7	22.4	16.6	31.9	19.3	19.7	19.7	26.0
Top-rate non-q. sh.									
Cost of capital 2001	5.4	5.2	5.4	4.9	6.3	5.3	5.1	9.1	4.9
2002	5.5	5.2	5.5	5.0	6.4	5.3	5.3	9.0	4.9
2003	5.6	5.3	5.6	5.3	6.4	5.4	5.4	9.2	4.9
EMTR 2001	36.0	32.9	36.0	29.7	45.3	34.0	32.1	61.8	28.7
2002	34.5	31.2	34.6	28.0	43.9	32.4	31.7	59.8	25.9
2003	35.7	32.3	35.6	31.4	43.9	33.7	33.7	60.9	25.8
Top-rate q. sh.									
Cost of capital 2001	5.4	5.2	5.4	4.9	6.3	5.3	5.1	9.1	4.9
2002	5.5	5.2	5.5	5.0	6.4	5.3	5.3	9.0	4.9
2003	5.6	5.3	5.6	5.3	6.4	5.4	5.4	9.2	4.9
EMTR 2001	36.0	32.9	36.0	29.7	45.3	34.0	32.1	61.8	28.7
2002	34.5	31.2	34.6	28.0	43.9	32.4	31.7	59.8	25.9
2003	35.7	32.3	35.6	31.4	43.9	33.7	33.7	60.9	25.8
Mean (sh. mix)									
Cost of capital 2001	5.1	4.9	5.1	4.6	6.0	4.9	4.8	7.5	4.9
2002	5.2	4.9	5.2	4.7	6.1	5.0	5.0	7.4	4.9
2003	5.3	5.0	5.3	4.9	6.1	5.1	5.1	7.6	4.9
EMTR 2001	31.9	28.5	32.0	25.1	41.7	29.7	27.8	53.5	28.8
2002	30.4	26.9	30.8	23.4	40.4	28.1	27.5	51.5	26.0
2003	31.7	28.1	31.7	27.1	40.4	29.5	29.6	52.8	25.9

D.3.5 Italy

Italy – minimum	Overall	Assets					Sources of finance		
		Intangibles	Industrial buildings	Machinery	Financial assets	Inventories	Retained earnings	New equity	Debt
Zero-rate sh.									
Cost of capital 2001	3.9	2.3	3.6	3.1	6.7	3.9	4.0	4.0	3.8
2002	5.4	4.1	5.5	5.0	6.7	6.0	6.4	6.4	3.8
2003	5.4	4.1	5.5	5.0	6.5	5.8	6.2	6.2	3.9
EMTR 2001	-5.4	-78.3	-16.1	-32.9	38.0	-4.6	-3.1	-3.1	-9.9
2002	24.1	-1.9	25.4	17.6	38.0	30.6	35.0	35.0	-9.9
2003	23.1	-1.2	24.5	16.9	36.2	29.3	33.1	33.1	-6.7
Top-rate non-q. sh.									
Cost of capital 2001	4.4	2.7	4.1	3.6	7.2	4.6	4.7	5.3	3.7
2002	6.0	4.4	6.1	5.5	7.2	6.6	7.1	7.7	3.7
2003	5.9	4.5	6.0	5.4	7.0	6.4	6.9	7.4	3.8
EMTR 2001	6.8	-53.0	-1.1	-15.8	42.9	9.5	12.9	22.3	-12.0
2002	30.6	6.9	31.9	24.5	42.9	37.1	41.7	46.1	-12.0
2003	29.6	7.5	31.0	23.8	41.3	35.8	40.1	44.5	-8.5
Top-rate q. sh.									
Cost of capital 2001	5.0	3.1	4.7	4.1	7.9	5.3	5.8	5.6	3.6
2002	6.5	4.8	6.7	6.0	7.9	7.3	8.1	8.0	3.6
2003	6.5	4.9	6.6	5.9	7.7	7.1	7.9	8.1	3.7
EMTR 2001	17.3	-33.3	11.7	-1.7	47.6	21.5	28.4	26.9	-14.9
2002	36.7	14.6	37.9	30.8	47.6	43.2	49.1	48.3	-14.9
2003	36.0	15.6	37.4	30.5	46.3	42.2	47.7	49.2	-11.0
Mean (sh. mix)									
Cost of capital 2001	4.4	2.7	4.1	3.6	7.3	4.6	4.8	5.0	3.7
2002	6.0	4.4	6.1	5.5	7.3	6.6	7.2	7.3	3.7
2003	5.9	4.5	6.0	5.4	7.1	6.5	7.0	7.2	3.8
EMTR 2001	7.2	-52.7	-0.6	-15.4	43.1	10.0	14.6	17.2	-12.2
2002	30.9	7.0	32.1	24.7	43.1	37.4	42.5	43.7	-12.2
2003	30.0	7.8	31.4	24.2	41.6	36.2	40.9	43.0	-8.7

Italy – median	Overall	Assets: Intangibles	Assets: Industrial buildings	Assets: Machinery	Assets: Financial assets	Assets: Inventories	Sources of finance: Retained earnings	Sources of finance: New equity	Sources of finance: Debt
Zero-rate sh.									
Cost of capital 2001	3.9	2.3	3.7	3.1	6.7	3.9	4.0	4.0	3.8
2002	5.5	4.1	5.7	5.0	6.7	6.0	6.4	6.4	3.8
2003	5.4	4.1	5.7	5.0	6.5	5.8	6.2	6.2	3.9
EMTR 2001	-4.6	-78.3	-11.2	-32.9	38.0	-4.6	-2.3	-2.3	-9.0
2002	24.6	-1.9	27.6	17.6	38.0	30.6	35.3	35.3	-8.9
2003	23.6	-1.2	27.2	16.9	36.2	29.3	33.5	33.5	-5.6
Top-rate non-q. sh.									
Cost of capital 2001	4.5	2.7	4.2	3.6	7.2	4.6	4.8	5.3	3.7
2002	6.0	4.4	6.2	5.5	7.2	6.6	7.1	7.7	3.7
2003	5.9	4.5	6.2	5.4	7.0	6.4	6.9	7.5	3.8
EMTR 2001	7.4	-53.0	2.6	-15.8	42.9	9.5	13.5	22.7	-11.1
2002	31.0	6.9	33.7	24.5	42.9	37.1	42.0	46.3	-11.0
2003	30.1	7.5	33.2	23.8	41.3	35.8	40.4	44.8	-7.4
Top-rate q. sh.									
Cost of capital 2001	5.0	3.1	4.8	4.1	7.9	5.3	5.8	5.7	3.6
2002	6.6	4.8	6.8	6.0	7.9	7.3	8.1	8.0	3.6
2003	6.5	4.9	6.8	5.9	7.7	7.1	7.9	8.2	3.8
EMTR 2001	17.8	-33.3	14.5	-1.7	47.6	21.5	28.8	27.3	-13.9
2002	37.0	14.6	39.4	30.8	47.6	43.2	49.3	48.6	-13.9
2003	36.4	15.6	39.3	30.5	46.3	42.2	47.9	49.4	-9.8
Mean (sh. mix)									
Cost of capital 2001	4.5	2.7	4.3	3.6	7.3	4.6	4.9	5.0	3.7
2002	6.0	4.4	6.3	5.5	7.3	6.6	7.2	7.4	3.7
2003	5.9	4.5	6.2	5.4	7.1	6.5	7.0	7.3	3.8
EMTR 2001	7.8	-52.7	3.1	-15.4	43.1	10.0	15.2	17.7	-11.3
2002	31.2	7.0	33.9	24.7	43.1	37.4	42.8	44.0	-11.2
2003	30.4	7.8	33.6	24.2	41.6	36.2	41.2	43.3	-7.6

Italy – maximum	Overall	Assets: Intangibles	Industrial buildings	Machinery	Financial assets	Inventories	Sources of finance: Retained earnings	New equity	Debt
Zero-rate sh.									
Cost of capital 2001	4.0	2.3	3.8	3.1	6.7	3.9	4.1	4.1	3.8
2002	5.5	4.1	5.8	5.0	6.7	6.0	6.4	6.4	3.8
2003	5.4	4.1	5.7	5.0	6.5	5.8	6.2	6.2	3.9
EMTR 2001	-4.1	-78.3	-8.6	-32.9	38.0	-4.6	-1.9	-1.9	-8.5
2002	24.8	-1.9	28.6	17.6	38.0	30.6	35.5	35.5	-8.5
2003	23.7	-1.2	27.7	16.9	36.2	29.3	33.6	33.6	-5.4
Top-rate non-q. sh.									
Cost of capital 2001	4.5	2.7	4.3	3.6	7.2	4.6	4.8	5.4	3.7
2002	6.0	4.4	6.3	5.5	7.2	6.6	7.1	7.7	3.7
2003	5.9	4.5	6.2	5.4	7.0	6.4	6.9	7.5	3.9
EMTR 2001	7.8	-53.0	4.7	-15.8	42.9	9.5	13.8	23.0	-10.5
2002	31.2	6.9	34.6	24.5	42.9	37.1	42.1	46.4	-10.5
2003	30.2	7.5	33.7	23.8	41.3	35.8	40.5	44.9	-7.1
Top-rate q. sh.									
Cost of capital 2001	5.0	3.1	4.9	4.1	7.9	5.3	5.8	5.7	3.6
2002	6.6	4.8	6.9	6.0	7.9	7.3	8.2	8.0	3.6
2003	6.5	4.9	6.8	5.9	7.7	7.1	7.9	8.2	3.8
EMTR 2001	18.1	-33.3	16.1	-1.7	47.6	21.5	29.0	27.5	-13.4
2002	37.1	14.6	40.2	30.8	47.6	43.2	49.4	48.7	-13.4
2003	36.5	15.6	39.6	30.5	46.3	42.2	48.0	49.5	-9.6
Mean (sh. mix)									
Cost of capital 2001	4.5	2.7	4.4	3.6	7.3	4.6	4.9	5.0	3.7
2002	6.0	4.4	6.3	5.5	7.3	6.6	7.2	7.4	3.7
2003	5.9	4.5	6.3	5.4	7.1	6.5	7.0	7.3	3.8
EMTR 2001	8.2	-52.7	5.1	-15.4	43.1	10.0	15.5	18.0	-10.8
2002	31.4	7.0	34.8	24.7	43.1	37.4	42.9	44.1	-10.8
2003	30.5	7.8	34.0	24.2	41.6	36.2	41.3	43.4	-7.3

D.3.6 The Netherlands

The Netherlands – median	Overall	Assets: Intangibles	Assets: Industrial buildings	Assets: Machinery	Assets: Financial assets	Assets: Inventories	Sources of finance: Retained earnings	Sources of finance: New equity	Sources of finance: Debt
Zero-rate sh.									
Cost of capital 2001	6.4	5.1	6.9	5.9	7.4	6.4	7.6	7.6	4.0
2002	6.3	5.1	6.9	5.9	7.4	6.4	7.6	7.6	4.0
2003	6.3	5.1	6.9	5.9	7.4	6.4	7.6	7.6	4.0
EMTR 2001	21.3	2.7	27.6	15.5	32.8	21.6	34.5	34.5	-25.6
2002	21.0	2.6	27.4	15.2	32.3	21.3	34.0	34.0	-24.8
2003	21.1	2.6	27.6	15.2	32.3	21.3	34.1	34.1	-24.7
Top-rate non-q. sh.									
Cost of capital 2001	6.4	5.1	6.9	5.9	7.4	6.4	7.6	7.6	4.0
2002	6.3	5.1	6.9	5.9	7.4	6.4	7.6	7.6	4.0
2003	6.3	5.1	6.9	5.9	7.4	6.4	7.6	7.6	4.0
EMTR 2001	40.2	26.1	45.0	35.7	48.9	40.4	50.2	50.2	4.6
2002	40.0	26.0	44.8	35.5	48.5	40.2	49.9	49.9	5.1
2003	40.0	26.0	45.0	35.5	48.5	40.2	49.9	49.9	5.2
Top-rate q. sh.									
Cost of capital 2001	6.4	5.2	6.9	6.0	7.5	6.4	7.5	8.8	4.0
2002	6.4	5.2	6.9	5.9	7.4	6.4	7.4	8.7	4.0
2003	6.4	5.2	6.9	5.9	7.4	6.4	7.4	8.7	4.0
EMTR 2001	40.6	26.8	45.3	36.2	49.1	40.8	49.3	56.7	4.7
2002	40.3	26.7	45.1	36.0	48.8	40.5	48.9	56.4	5.3
2003	40.4	26.7	45.3	36.0	48.8	40.5	49.0	56.4	5.4
Mean (sh. mix)									
Cost of capital 2001	6.4	5.2	6.9	5.9	7.4	6.4	7.6	8.0	4.0
2002	6.3	5.2	6.9	5.9	7.4	6.4	7.5	8.0	4.0
2003	6.3	5.2	6.9	5.9	7.4	6.4	7.5	8.0	4.0
EMTR 2001	34.1	18.5	39.3	29.2	43.6	34.3	44.6	47.6	-5.4
2002	33.8	18.5	39.1	28.9	43.2	34.0	44.3	47.2	-4.8
2003	33.8	18.5	39.3	28.9	43.2	34.0	44.3	47.2	-4.7

D.3.7 Switzerland

Switzerland – Basel-Landschaft	Overall	Assets: Intangibles	Assets: Industrial buildings	Assets: Machinery	Assets: Financial assets	Assets: Inventories	Sources of finance: Retained earnings	Sources of finance: New equity	Sources of finance: Debt
Zero-rate sh.									
Cost of capital 2001	6.0	5.3	5.8	5.7	7.0	6.3	7.0	7.0	4.1
2002	6.0	5.3	5.8	5.6	6.9	6.3	7.0	7.0	4.1
2003	6.0	5.3	5.8	5.6	6.9	6.3	7.0	7.0	4.1
EMTR 2001	16.6	5.3	13.5	11.7	28.1	20.4	28.7	28.7	-22.0
2002	16.3	4.9	13.3	11.4	27.9	20.2	28.4	28.4	-22.1
2003	16.3	4.9	13.2	11.3	27.9	20.1	28.4	28.4	-22.1
Top-rate non-q. sh.									
Cost of capital 2001	4.0	3.6	3.9	3.9	4.8	4.1	3.3	7.2	4.3
2002	4.0	3.6	3.9	3.8	4.7	4.1	3.3	7.2	4.3
2003	4.0	3.6	3.9	3.8	4.7	4.1	3.3	7.1	4.3
EMTR 2001	68.8	65.0	67.7	67.4	73.4	69.0	62.1	82.4	70.4
2002	68.5	64.7	67.4	67.1	73.3	68.8	61.7	82.3	70.3
2003	68.5	64.7	67.4	67.1	73.2	68.8	61.6	82.3	70.3
Top-rate q. sh.									
Cost of capital 2001	4.0	3.6	3.9	3.9	4.8	4.1	3.3	7.2	4.3
2002	4.0	3.6	3.9	3.8	4.7	4.1	3.3	7.2	4.3
2003	4.0	3.6	3.9	3.8	4.7	4.1	3.3	7.1	4.3
EMTR 2001	68.8	65.0	67.7	67.4	73.4	69.0	62.1	82.4	70.4
2002	68.5	64.7	67.4	67.1	73.3	68.8	61.7	82.3	70.3
2003	68.5	64.7	67.4	67.1	73.2	68.8	61.6	82.3	70.3
Mean (sh. mix)									
Cost of capital 2001	4.7	4.2	4.5	4.5	5.5	4.8	4.6	7.1	4.2
2002	4.7	4.1	4.5	4.4	5.5	4.8	4.5	7.1	4.2
2003	4.7	4.1	4.5	4.4	5.5	4.8	4.5	7.1	4.2
EMTR 2001	46.6	39.8	44.7	43.8	54.3	47.9	45.0	64.8	40.4
2002	46.3	39.5	44.4	43.5	54.1	47.6	44.6	64.6	40.3
2003	46.2	39.4	44.3	43.5	54.1	47.6	44.5	64.6	40.3

Switzerland – Basel-Stadt	Overall	Assets: Intangibles	Assets: Industrial buildings	Assets: Machinery	Assets: Financial assets	Assets: Inventories	Sources of finance: Retained earnings	Sources of finance: New equity	Sources of finance: Debt
Zero-rate sh.									
Cost of capital 2001	5.9	5.2	5.7	5.6	6.9	6.2	6.9	6.9	4.1
2002	5.9	5.2	5.7	5.6	6.9	6.2	6.9	6.9	4.1
2003	5.9	5.2	5.7	5.6	6.9	6.2	6.9	6.9	4.1
EMTR 2001	15.6	4.6	12.7	10.9	27.0	19.4	27.5	27.5	-21.0
2002	15.6	4.6	12.7	10.9	27.0	19.4	27.5	27.5	-21.0
2003	15.6	4.6	12.7	10.9	27.0	19.4	27.5	27.5	-21.0
Top-rate non-q. sh.									
Cost of capital 2001	4.1	3.7	4.0	3.9	4.8	4.1	3.4	7.0	4.3
2002	4.1	3.7	4.0	3.9	4.8	4.1	3.4	7.0	4.3
2003	4.1	3.7	4.0	3.9	4.8	4.2	3.5	7.0	4.3
EMTR 2001	68.7	65.0	67.6	67.2	73.2	69.0	62.6	81.8	70.1
2002	68.7	65.0	67.6	67.2	73.2	69.0	62.6	81.8	70.1
2003	65.1	61.0	63.9	63.5	70.1	65.5	58.8	79.5	66.3
Top-rate q. sh.									
Cost of capital 2001	4.1	3.7	4.0	3.9	4.8	4.1	3.4	7.0	4.3
2002	4.1	3.7	4.0	3.9	4.8	4.1	3.4	7.0	4.3
2003	4.1	3.7	4.0	3.9	4.8	4.2	3.5	7.0	4.3
EMTR 2001	68.7	65.0	67.6	67.2	73.2	69.0	62.6	81.8	70.1
2002	68.7	65.0	67.6	67.2	73.2	69.0	62.6	81.8	70.1
2003	65.1	61.0	63.9	63.5	70.1	65.5	58.8	79.5	66.3
Mean (sh. mix)									
Cost of capital 2001	4.7	4.2	4.5	4.5	5.5	4.8	4.6	7.0	4.2
2002	4.7	4.2	4.5	4.5	5.5	4.8	4.6	7.0	4.2
2003	4.7	4.2	4.6	4.5	5.5	4.9	4.6	7.0	4.2
EMTR 2001	46.4	39.8	44.5	43.7	53.9	47.8	45.0	64.0	40.5
2002	46.4	39.8	44.5	43.7	53.9	47.8	45.0	64.0	40.5
2003	44.4	37.6	42.5	41.6	52.2	45.9	43.2	62.4	37.9

Switzerland – Bern	Overall	Assets: Intangibles	Assets: Industrial buildings	Assets: Machinery	Assets: Financial assets	Assets: Inventories	Sources of finance: Retained earnings	Sources of finance: New equity	Sources of finance: Debt
Zero-rate sh.									
Cost of capital 2001	5.7	5.1	5.6	5.4	6.4	5.9	6.4	6.4	4.3
2002	5.7	5.1	5.6	5.4	6.4	5.9	6.4	6.4	4.3
2003	5.6	5.0	5.5	5.3	6.3	5.8	6.3	6.3	4.3
EMTR 2001	11.6	1.1	10.4	6.8	22.0	14.8	21.8	21.8	-16.6
2002	11.6	1.1	10.4	6.8	22.0	14.8	21.8	21.8	-16.6
2003	10.6	-0.2	9.3	5.7	21.2	13.9	20.6	20.6	-16.6
Top-rate non-q. sh.									
Cost of capital 2001	3.8	3.4	3.8	3.7	4.4	3.8	3.0	6.5	4.4
2002	3.8	3.4	3.8	3.7	4.4	3.8	3.0	6.5	4.4
2003	3.8	3.4	3.7	3.6	4.3	3.8	2.9	6.4	4.4
EMTR 2001	63.3	59.2	63.1	61.6	68.0	63.5	52.6	78.5	68.2
2002	63.3	59.2	63.1	61.6	68.0	63.5	52.6	78.5	68.2
2003	62.7	58.5	62.4	60.9	67.5	62.8	51.0	78.1	68.2
Top-rate q. sh.									
Cost of capital 2001	3.8	3.4	3.8	3.7	4.4	3.8	3.0	6.5	4.4
2002	3.8	3.4	3.8	3.7	4.4	3.8	3.0	6.5	4.4
2003	3.8	3.4	3.7	3.6	4.3	3.8	2.9	6.4	4.4
EMTR 2001	63.3	59.2	63.1	61.6	68.0	63.5	52.6	78.5	68.2
2002	63.3	59.2	63.1	61.6	68.0	63.5	52.6	78.5	68.2
2003	62.7	58.5	62.4	60.9	67.5	62.8	51.0	78.1	68.2
Mean (sh. mix)									
Cost of capital 2001	4.4	4.0	4.4	4.2	5.1	4.5	4.1	6.5	4.4
2002	4.4	4.0	4.4	4.2	5.1	4.5	4.1	6.5	4.4
2003	4.4	3.9	4.3	4.2	5.0	4.5	4.0	6.4	4.4
EMTR 2001	41.3	34.7	40.8	38.4	48.6	42.4	36.6	59.8	40.5
2002	41.3	34.7	40.8	38.4	48.6	42.4	36.6	59.8	40.5
2003	40.5	33.6	39.9	37.5	47.9	41.6	35.1	59.2	40.5

Switzerland – Genève	Overall	Assets					Sources of finance		
		Intangibles	Industrial buildings	Machinery	Financial assets	Inventories	Retained earnings	New equity	Debt
Zero-rate sh.									
Cost of capital 2001	5.8	5.2	5.7	5.5	6.7	6.1	6.7	6.7	4.2
2002	5.8	5.2	5.7	5.5	6.7	6.1	6.7	6.7	4.2
2003	5.8	5.2	5.7	5.5	6.7	6.1	6.7	6.7	4.2
EMTR 2001	14.5	3.1	12.8	9.4	25.6	18.0	25.9	25.9	-19.7
2002	14.5	3.1	12.8	9.4	25.6	18.0	25.9	25.9	-19.7
2003	14.5	3.1	12.8	9.4	25.6	18.0	25.9	25.9	-19.7
Top-rate non-q. sh.									
Cost of capital 2001	3.8	3.4	3.8	3.6	4.4	3.8	2.9	6.9	4.3
2002	3.8	3.4	3.8	3.6	4.4	3.8	2.9	6.9	4.3
2003	3.8	3.4	3.8	3.6	4.4	3.8	2.9	6.9	4.3
EMTR 2001	77.5	74.8	77.2	76.4	80.6	77.5	70.5	87.6	80.2
2002	77.5	74.8	77.2	76.4	80.6	77.5	70.5	87.6	80.2
2003	77.5	74.8	77.2	76.4	80.6	77.5	70.5	87.6	80.2
Top-rate q. sh.									
Cost of capital 2001	3.8	3.4	3.8	3.6	4.4	3.8	2.9	6.9	4.3
2002	3.8	3.4	3.8	3.6	4.4	3.8	2.9	6.9	4.3
2003	3.8	3.4	3.8	3.6	4.4	3.8	2.9	6.9	4.3
EMTR 2001	77.5	74.8	77.2	76.4	80.6	77.5	70.5	87.6	80.2
2002	77.5	74.8	77.2	76.4	80.6	77.5	70.5	87.6	80.2
2003	77.5	74.8	77.2	76.4	80.6	77.5	70.5	87.6	80.2
Mean (sh. mix)									
Cost of capital 2001	4.5	4.0	4.4	4.3	5.2	4.6	4.2	6.9	4.3
2002	4.5	4.0	4.4	4.3	5.2	4.6	4.2	6.9	4.3
2003	4.5	4.0	4.4	4.3	5.2	4.6	4.2	6.9	4.3
EMTR 2001	50.1	43.9	49.5	47.5	57.0	51.0	46.6	67.3	47.8
2002	50.1	43.9	49.5	47.5	57.0	51.0	46.6	67.3	47.8
2003	50.1	43.9	49.5	47.5	57.0	51.0	46.6	67.3	47.8

Switzerland – Nidwalden	Overall	Assets: Intangibles	Assets: Industrial buildings	Assets: Machinery	Assets: Financial assets	Assets: Inventories	Sources of finance: Retained earnings	Sources of finance: New equity	Sources of finance: Debt
Zero-rate sh.									
Cost of capital 2001	5.5	5.0	5.4	5.3	6.1	5.7	6.1	6.1	4.4
2002	5.5	5.0	5.4	5.3	6.1	5.7	6.1	6.1	4.4
2003	5.5	5.0	5.4	5.3	6.1	5.7	6.1	6.1	4.4
EMTR 2001	9.1	0.7	6.9	5.4	18.3	12.1	17.8	17.8	-13.4
2002	9.1	0.7	6.9	5.4	18.3	12.1	17.8	17.8	-13.4
2003	9.0	0.7	6.8	5.3	18.1	12.0	17.7	17.7	-13.3
Top-rate non-q. sh.									
Cost of capital 2001	4.4	4.0	4.2	4.2	4.9	4.4	3.9	6.1	4.5
2002	4.4	4.0	4.2	4.2	4.9	4.4	3.9	6.1	4.5
2003	4.4	4.0	4.2	4.2	4.9	4.4	4.0	6.1	4.5
EMTR 2001	31.8	25.8	30.1	29.3	39.1	33.2	24.8	51.7	33.6
2002	31.8	25.8	30.1	29.3	39.1	33.2	24.8	51.7	33.6
2003	31.5	25.5	29.8	29.0	38.8	32.9	24.6	51.4	33.3
Top-rate q. sh.									
Cost of capital 2001	4.2	3.9	4.1	4.1	4.7	4.3	3.9	5.3	4.5
2002	4.2	3.9	4.1	4.1	4.7	4.3	3.9	5.3	4.5
2003	4.2	3.9	4.1	4.1	4.7	4.3	3.9	5.3	4.5
EMTR 2001	29.6	23.4	27.8	27.0	37.3	31.0	23.1	43.7	33.7
2002	29.6	23.4	27.8	27.0	37.3	31.0	23.1	43.7	33.7
2003	29.3	23.1	27.5	26.8	37.0	30.7	22.9	43.4	33.3
Mean (sh. mix)									
Cost of capital 2001	4.7	4.3	4.6	4.5	5.2	4.8	4.6	5.8	4.5
2002	4.7	4.3	4.6	4.5	5.2	4.8	4.6	5.8	4.5
2003	4.7	4.3	4.6	4.5	5.2	4.8	4.6	5.8	4.5
EMTR 2001	22.3	15.3	20.3	19.3	30.4	24.2	21.3	37.5	18.1
2002	22.3	15.3	20.3	19.3	30.4	24.2	21.3	37.5	18.1
2003	22.1	15.1	20.1	19.1	30.2	24.0	21.1	37.3	17.9

Switzerland – Schwyz	Overall	Assets					Sources of finance		
		Intangibles	Industrial buildings	Machinery	Financial assets	Inventories	Retained earnings	New equity	Debt
Zero-rate sh.									
Cost of capital 2001	5.6	5.1	5.5	5.4	6.3	5.8	6.3	6.3	4.4
2002	5.6	5.1	5.5	5.4	6.2	5.8	6.3	6.3	4.4
2003	5.6	5.1	5.5	5.4	6.2	5.8	6.2	6.2	4.4
EMTR 2001	11.1	2.3	8.8	7.2	20.7	14.3	20.8	20.8	-14.9
2002	10.6	2.1	8.4	6.8	20.0	13.7	20.0	20.0	-14.3
2003	10.6	2.0	8.3	6.8	20.0	13.7	20.0	20.0	-14.2
Top-rate non-q. sh.									
Cost of capital 2001	4.5	4.1	4.4	4.4	5.1	4.7	4.3	6.4	4.4
2002	4.6	4.2	4.4	4.4	5.1	4.7	4.3	6.3	4.4
2003	4.6	4.2	4.4	4.4	5.1	4.7	4.3	6.3	4.4
EMTR 2001	34.4	28.2	32.6	31.8	41.9	35.9	30.5	53.3	32.5
2002	32.8	26.6	31.0	30.2	40.2	34.3	29.0	51.4	30.9
2003	32.7	26.6	31.0	30.2	40.1	34.3	29.0	51.4	30.9
Top-rate q. sh.									
Cost of capital 2001	4.5	4.1	4.4	4.4	5.1	4.7	4.3	6.4	4.4
2002	4.6	4.2	4.4	4.4	5.1	4.7	4.3	6.3	4.4
2003	4.6	4.2	4.4	4.4	5.1	4.7	4.3	6.3	4.4
EMTR 2001	34.4	28.2	32.6	31.8	41.9	35.9	30.5	53.3	32.5
2002	32.8	26.6	31.0	30.2	40.2	34.3	29.0	51.4	30.9
2003	32.7	26.6	31.0	30.2	40.1	34.3	29.0	51.4	30.9
Mean (sh. mix)									
Cost of capital 2001	4.9	4.5	4.8	4.7	5.5	5.0	5.0	6.4	4.4
2002	4.9	4.5	4.8	4.7	5.5	5.0	5.0	6.3	4.4
2003	4.9	4.5	4.8	4.7	5.5	5.0	5.0	6.3	4.4
EMTR 2001	25.5	18.3	23.5	22.4	33.8	27.6	26.4	42.5	16.8
2002	24.3	17.3	22.4	21.3	32.5	26.4	25.2	41.0	16.0
2003	24.3	17.3	22.4	21.3	32.5	26.4	25.2	41.0	16.0

Switzerland – St. Gallen	Overall	Assets					Sources of finance		
		Intangibles	Industrial buildings	Machinery	Financial assets	Inventories	Retained earnings	New equity	Debt
Zero-rate sh.									
Cost of capital 2001	5.4	4.7	5.2	5.0	6.3	5.6	6.0	6.0	4.1
2002	5.4	4.7	5.2	5.0	6.3	5.6	6.0	6.0	4.1
2003	5.4	4.7	5.2	5.0	6.3	5.6	6.0	6.0	4.1
EMTR 2001	6.9	-7.0	4.6	0.7	20.4	11.0	17.1	17.1	-20.8
2002	6.8	-7.0	4.6	0.7	20.3	11.0	17.0	17.0	-20.7
2003	6.9	-7.0	4.6	0.7	20.4	11.0	17.1	17.1	-20.8
Top-rate non-q. sh.									
Cost of capital 2001	3.7	3.3	3.7	3.5	4.4	3.8	2.9	6.2	4.3
2002	3.7	3.3	3.7	3.5	4.4	3.8	3.0	6.2	4.3
2003	3.7	3.3	3.7	3.5	4.4	3.8	2.9	6.2	4.3
EMTR 2001	48.1	40.7	47.0	45.1	56.3	48.6	34.0	68.6	54.7
2002	47.6	40.1	46.5	44.5	55.8	48.2	33.7	68.2	54.2
2003	48.1	40.7	47.0	45.1	56.3	48.6	34.0	68.6	54.7
Top-rate q. sh.									
Cost of capital 2001	3.7	3.3	3.7	3.5	4.4	3.8	2.9	6.2	4.3
2002	3.7	3.3	3.7	3.5	4.4	3.8	3.0	6.2	4.3
2003	3.7	3.3	3.7	3.5	4.4	3.8	2.9	6.2	4.3
EMTR 2001	48.1	40.7	47.0	45.1	56.3	48.6	34.0	68.6	54.7
2002	47.6	40.1	46.5	44.5	55.8	48.2	33.7	68.2	54.2
2003	48.1	40.7	47.0	45.1	56.3	48.6	34.0	68.6	54.7
Mean (sh. mix)									
Cost of capital 2001	4.3	3.7	4.2	4.0	5.0	4.4	4.0	6.1	4.2
2002	4.3	3.7	4.2	4.0	5.0	4.4	4.0	6.1	4.2
2003	4.3	3.7	4.2	4.0	5.0	4.4	4.0	6.1	4.2
EMTR 2001	30.8	20.8	29.3	26.6	41.4	32.6	25.5	51.7	30.1
2002	30.6	20.5	29.1	26.3	41.1	32.3	25.3	51.4	29.8
2003	30.8	20.8	29.3	26.6	41.4	32.6	25.5	51.7	30.1

Switzerland – Ticino	Overall	Assets: Intangibles	Assets: Industrial buildings	Assets: Machinery	Assets: Financial assets	Assets: Inventories	Sources of finance: Retained earnings	Sources of finance: New equity	Sources of finance: Debt
Zero-rate sh.									
Cost of capital 2001	5.8	5.2	5.8	5.5	6.5	6.0	6.5	6.5	4.3
2002	5.8	5.2	5.8	5.5	6.5	6.0	6.5	6.5	4.3
2003	5.7	5.1	5.7	5.4	6.4	5.9	6.4	6.4	4.3
EMTR 2001	13.3	3.3	13.4	8.5	22.7	16.0	23.5	23.5	-15.4
2002	13.3	3.3	13.4	8.5	22.7	16.0	23.5	23.5	-15.4
2003	12.2	2.0	12.3	7.4	21.9	15.0	22.3	22.3	-15.4
Top-rate non-q. sh.									
Cost of capital 2001	3.8	3.5	3.9	3.7	4.3	3.8	2.9	6.7	4.5
2002	3.8	3.5	3.9	3.7	4.3	3.8	2.9	6.7	4.5
2003	3.9	3.5	3.9	3.7	4.4	3.9	3.0	6.6	4.5
EMTR 2001	67.4	63.9	67.9	65.8	71.2	67.3	57.2	81.2	72.0
2002	67.4	63.9	67.9	65.8	71.2	67.3	57.2	81.2	72.0
2003	63.8	59.8	64.3	62.0	68.0	63.7	53.3	78.6	68.6
Top-rate q. sh.									
Cost of capital 2001	3.8	3.5	3.9	3.7	4.3	3.8	2.9	6.7	4.5
2002	3.8	3.5	3.9	3.7	4.3	3.8	2.9	6.7	4.5
2003	3.9	3.5	3.9	3.7	4.4	3.9	3.0	6.6	4.5
EMTR 2001	67.4	63.9	67.9	65.8	71.2	67.3	57.2	81.2	72.0
2002	67.4	63.9	67.9	65.8	71.2	67.3	57.2	81.2	72.0
2003	63.8	59.8	64.3	62.0	68.0	63.7	53.3	78.6	68.6
Mean (sh. mix)									
Cost of capital 2001	4.5	4.0	4.5	4.3	5.1	4.5	4.1	6.6	4.4
2002	4.5	4.0	4.5	4.3	5.1	4.5	4.1	6.6	4.4
2003	4.5	4.0	4.5	4.3	5.1	4.5	4.1	6.5	4.4
EMTR 2001	44.2	38.0	44.7	41.3	50.5	44.8	39.4	62.3	43.4
2002	44.2	38.0	44.7	41.3	50.5	44.8	39.4	62.3	43.4
2003	41.9	35.3	42.4	38.9	48.6	42.7	37.3	60.1	41.1

Switzerland – Vaud	Overall	Assets: Intangibles	Assets: Industrial buildings	Assets: Machinery	Assets: Financial assets	Assets: Inventories	Sources of finance: Retained earnings	Sources of finance: New equity	Sources of finance: Debt
Zero-rate sh.									
Cost of capital 2001	5.8	5.1	5.7	5.4	6.6	6.0	6.6	6.6	4.2
2002	5.8	5.1	5.7	5.4	6.6	6.0	6.6	6.6	4.2
2003	5.8	5.1	5.7	5.4	6.6	6.0	6.6	6.6	4.2
EMTR 2001	13.1	1.6	12.1	7.8	24.0	16.4	24.0	24.0	-18.5
2002	13.1	1.6	12.1	7.8	24.0	16.4	24.0	24.0	-18.5
2003	13.1	1.6	12.1	7.8	24.0	16.4	24.0	24.0	-18.5
Top-rate non-q. sh.									
Cost of capital 2001	3.9	3.5	3.9	3.7	4.5	3.9	3.1	6.7	4.4
2002	3.9	3.5	3.9	3.7	4.5	3.9	3.1	6.7	4.4
2003	3.9	3.5	3.9	3.7	4.5	3.9	3.1	6.7	4.4
EMTR 2001	66.1	61.9	66.1	64.3	70.7	66.2	57.1	80.4	69.8
2002	66.1	61.9	66.1	64.3	70.7	66.2	57.1	80.4	69.8
2003	66.1	61.9	66.1	64.3	70.7	66.2	57.1	80.4	69.8
Top-rate q. sh.									
Cost of capital 2001	3.9	3.5	3.9	3.7	4.5	3.9	3.1	6.7	4.4
2002	3.9	3.5	3.9	3.7	4.5	3.9	3.1	6.7	4.4
2003	3.9	3.5	3.9	3.7	4.5	3.9	3.1	6.7	4.4
EMTR 2001	66.1	61.9	66.1	64.3	70.7	66.2	57.1	80.4	69.8
2002	66.1	61.9	66.1	64.3	70.7	66.2	57.1	80.4	69.8
2003	66.1	61.9	66.1	64.3	70.7	66.2	57.1	80.4	69.8
Mean (sh. mix)									
Cost of capital 2001	4.5	4.0	4.5	4.3	5.2	4.6	4.2	6.7	4.3
2002	4.5	4.0	4.5	4.3	5.2	4.6	4.2	6.7	4.3
2003	4.5	4.0	4.5	4.3	5.2	4.6	4.2	6.7	4.3
EMTR 2001	43.6	36.4	43.3	40.4	51.0	44.6	40.0	61.8	41.0
2002	43.6	36.4	43.3	40.4	51.0	44.6	40.0	61.8	41.0
2003	43.6	36.4	43.3	40.4	51.0	44.6	40.0	61.8	41.0

Switzerland – Valais	Overall	Assets					Sources of finance		
		Intangibles	Industrial buildings	Machinery	Financial assets	Inventories	Retained earnings	New equity	Debt
Zero-rate sh.									
Cost of capital 2001	5.9	5.2	5.8	5.7	6.6	6.1	6.7	6.7	4.3
2002	5.9	5.2	5.8	5.7	6.6	6.1	6.7	6.7	4.3
2003	5.9	5.2	5.8	5.7	6.6	6.1	6.7	6.7	4.3
EMTR 2001	14.7	4.6	13.3	11.6	24.3	17.5	25.4	25.4	-16.2
2002	14.7	4.6	13.3	11.6	24.3	17.5	25.4	25.4	-16.2
2003	14.7	4.6	13.3	11.6	24.3	17.5	25.4	25.4	-16.2
Top-rate non-q. sh.									
Cost of capital 2001	4.2	3.8	4.2	4.1	4.8	4.2	3.6	6.8	4.4
2002	4.2	3.8	4.2	4.1	4.8	4.2	3.6	6.8	4.4
2003	4.2	3.8	4.2	4.1	4.8	4.2	3.6	6.8	4.4
EMTR 2001	57.9	53.1	57.3	56.8	62.8	58.0	50.9	73.9	59.7
2002	57.9	53.1	57.3	56.8	62.8	58.0	50.9	73.9	59.7
2003	57.9	53.1	57.3	56.8	62.8	58.0	50.9	73.9	59.7
Top-rate q. sh.									
Cost of capital 2001	4.2	3.8	4.2	4.1	4.8	4.2	3.6	6.8	4.4
2002	4.2	3.8	4.2	4.1	4.8	4.2	3.6	6.8	4.4
2003	4.2	3.8	4.2	4.1	4.8	4.2	3.6	6.8	4.4
EMTR 2001	57.9	53.1	57.3	56.8	62.8	58.0	50.9	73.9	59.7
2002	57.9	53.1	57.3	56.8	62.8	58.0	50.9	73.9	59.7
2003	57.9	53.1	57.3	56.8	62.8	58.0	50.9	73.9	59.7
Mean (sh. mix)									
Cost of capital 2001	4.8	4.3	4.7	4.6	5.4	4.8	4.7	6.8	4.4
2002	4.8	4.3	4.7	4.6	5.4	4.8	4.7	6.8	4.4
2003	4.8	4.3	4.7	4.6	5.4	4.8	4.7	6.8	4.4
EMTR 2001	40.2	33.3	39.3	38.4	47.1	41.1	38.7	57.9	34.9
2002	40.2	33.3	39.3	38.4	47.1	41.1	38.7	57.9	34.9
2003	40.2	33.3	39.3	38.4	47.1	41.1	38.7	57.9	34.9

Switzerland – Zug	Overall	Assets					Sources of finance		
		Intangibles	Industrial buildings	Machinery	Financial assets	Inventories	Retained earnings	New equity	Debt
Zero-rate sh.									
Cost of capital 2001	5.4	5.0	5.3	5.2	5.9	5.6	5.9	5.9	4.5
2002	5.4	5.0	5.3	5.2	5.9	5.6	5.9	5.9	4.5
2003	5.4	5.0	5.3	5.2	5.9	5.6	5.9	5.9	4.5
EMTR 2001	7.1	-0.6	5.1	3.7	15.8	10.0	14.9	14.9	-11.9
2002	7.1	-0.6	5.1	3.7	15.8	10.0	14.9	14.9	-11.9
2003	7.1	-0.6	5.1	3.6	15.7	9.9	14.8	14.8	-11.8
Top-rate non-q. sh.									
Cost of capital 2001	4.4	4.1	4.3	4.2	4.9	4.5	4.0	5.9	4.5
2002	4.4	4.1	4.3	4.2	4.9	4.5	4.0	5.9	4.5
2003	4.4	4.1	4.3	4.2	4.9	4.5	4.0	5.9	4.5
EMTR 2001	31.7	26.2	30.1	29.3	38.4	33.1	25.5	49.4	33.7
2002	31.7	26.2	30.1	29.3	38.4	33.1	25.5	49.4	33.7
2003	31.7	26.2	30.1	29.3	38.3	33.1	25.5	49.4	33.7
Top-rate q. sh.									
Cost of capital 2001	4.4	4.1	4.3	4.2	4.9	4.5	4.0	5.9	4.5
2002	4.4	4.1	4.3	4.2	4.9	4.5	4.0	5.9	4.5
2003	4.4	4.1	4.3	4.2	4.9	4.5	4.0	5.9	4.5
EMTR 2001	31.7	26.2	30.1	29.3	38.4	33.1	25.5	49.4	33.7
2002	31.7	26.2	30.1	29.3	38.4	33.1	25.5	49.4	33.7
2003	31.7	26.2	30.1	29.3	38.3	33.1	25.5	49.4	33.7
Mean (sh. mix)									
Cost of capital 2001	4.7	4.4	4.6	4.6	5.2	4.8	4.6	5.9	4.5
2002	4.7	4.4	4.6	4.6	5.2	4.8	4.6	5.9	4.5
2003	4.7	4.4	4.6	4.6	5.2	4.8	4.6	5.9	4.5
EMTR 2001	22.3	16.0	20.6	19.6	29.8	24.3	21.0	38.0	18.6
2002	22.3	16.0	20.6	19.6	29.8	24.3	21.0	38.0	18.6
2003	22.3	16.0	20.6	19.6	29.8	24.2	21.0	37.9	18.6

Switzerland – Zürich	Overall	Assets					Sources of finance		
		Intangibles	Industrial buildings	Machinery	Financial assets	Inventories	Retained earnings	New equity	Debt
Zero-rate sh.									
Cost of capital 2001	5.8	5.1	5.6	5.5	6.7	6.1	6.7	6.7	4.1
2002	5.8	5.1	5.6	5.5	6.7	6.1	6.7	6.7	4.1
2003	5.8	5.1	5.6	5.5	6.7	6.1	6.7	6.7	4.2
EMTR 2001	14.0	2.6	10.9	9.1	25.7	17.9	25.5	25.5	-20.8
2002	13.8	2.5	10.8	8.9	25.4	17.7	25.2	25.2	-20.5
2003	13.6	2.4	10.6	8.7	25.1	17.4	24.9	24.9	-20.1
Top-rate non-q. sh.									
Cost of capital 2001	3.9	3.5	3.8	3.8	4.6	4.0	3.2	6.9	4.3
2002	3.9	3.5	3.8	3.8	4.6	4.0	3.2	6.8	4.3
2003	4.0	3.5	3.8	3.8	4.6	4.0	3.2	6.8	4.3
EMTR 2001	64.0	59.7	62.7	62.3	69.3	64.3	55.3	79.4	67.0
2002	62.9	58.5	61.6	61.2	68.3	63.3	54.2	78.6	65.9
2003	61.5	57.0	60.2	59.8	67.1	62.0	52.8	77.6	64.6
Top-rate q. sh.									
Cost of capital 2001	3.9	3.5	3.8	3.8	4.6	4.0	3.2	6.9	4.3
2002	3.9	3.5	3.8	3.8	4.6	4.0	3.2	6.8	4.3
2003	4.0	3.5	3.8	3.8	4.6	4.0	3.2	6.8	4.3
EMTR 2001	64.0	59.7	62.7	62.3	69.3	64.3	55.3	79.4	67.0
2002	62.9	58.5	61.6	61.2	68.3	63.3	54.2	78.6	65.9
2003	61.5	57.0	60.2	59.8	67.1	62.0	52.8	77.6	64.6
Mean (sh. mix)									
Cost of capital 2001	4.6	4.1	4.4	4.3	5.3	4.7	4.4	6.8	4.2
2002	4.6	4.1	4.4	4.3	5.3	4.7	4.4	6.8	4.2
2003	4.6	4.1	4.4	4.4	5.3	4.7	4.4	6.8	4.3
EMTR 2001	42.7	35.6	40.7	39.8	50.9	44.2	40.0	61.7	38.4
2002	42.1	34.9	40.1	39.2	50.3	43.6	39.4	61.1	37.8
2003	41.3	34.1	39.3	38.4	49.5	42.8	38.6	60.3	37.0

D.3.8 United Kingdom

United Kingdom – London	Overall	Assets: Intangibles	Assets: Industrial buildings	Assets: Machinery	Assets: Financial assets	Assets: Inventories	Sources of finance: Retained earnings	Sources of finance: New equity	Sources of finance: Debt
Zero-rate sh.									
Cost of capital 2001	6.6	5.5	7.9	5.6	6.9	6.9	7.6	7.6	4.7
2002	6.6	5.5	8.0	5.6	6.9	6.9	7.6	7.6	4.7
2003	6.6	5.5	8.0	5.6	6.9	6.9	7.6	7.6	4.7
EMTR 2001	24.0	8.8	36.6	11.3	27.9	27.9	34.1	34.1	-6.5
2002	24.1	8.8	37.2	11.3	27.9	27.9	34.3	34.3	-6.2
2003	24.2	8.8	37.5	11.3	27.9	27.9	34.3	34.3	-6.0
Top-rate non-q. sh.									
Cost of capital 2001	5.3	4.4	6.6	4.5	5.6	5.6	5.6	5.7	4.8
2002	5.4	4.4	6.7	4.5	5.6	5.6	5.7	5.7	4.8
2003	5.4	4.4	6.8	4.5	5.6	5.6	5.7	5.7	4.8
EMTR 2001	58.5	49.3	66.6	50.8	60.4	60.4	60.7	61.3	53.5
2002	58.6	49.3	67.0	50.8	60.4	60.4	60.8	61.4	53.6
2003	59.0	49.8	67.4	51.2	60.7	60.7	61.4	61.4	53.7
Top-rate q. sh.									
Cost of capital 2001	4.8	3.9	6.1	4.0	5.0	5.0	4.7	5.8	4.8
2002	4.9	3.9	6.2	4.0	5.0	5.0	4.7	5.8	4.8
2003	4.7	3.8	6.1	3.9	4.9	4.9	4.5	5.8	4.8
EMTR 2001	54.2	43.6	64.0	45.2	56.1	56.1	52.8	61.6	53.8
2002	54.4	43.6	64.4	45.2	56.1	56.1	53.0	61.7	54.0
2003	53.3	42.1	63.9	43.7	54.9	54.9	50.7	61.8	54.1
Mean (sh. mix)									
Cost of capital 2001	5.6	4.6	6.9	4.7	5.9	5.9	6.0	6.4	4.8
2002	5.6	4.6	7.0	4.7	5.9	5.9	6.0	6.4	4.8
2003	5.6	4.6	7.0	4.7	5.8	5.8	6.0	6.4	4.8
EMTR 2001	43.7	31.6	54.4	33.5	46.3	46.3	47.4	50.6	33.9
2002	43.9	31.6	54.9	33.5	46.3	46.3	47.5	50.7	34.1
2003	43.7	31.3	54.9	33.2	46.1	46.1	47.2	50.8	34.2

D.3.9 United States

United States – Boston	Overall	Assets					Sources of finance		
		Intangibles	Industrial buildings	Machinery	Financial assets	Inventories	Retained earnings	New equity	Debt
Zero-rate sh.									
Cost of capital 2001	6.8	6.9	7.0	4.8	8.2	7.1	8.4	8.4	3.7
2002	6.7	6.9	7.0	4.5	8.2	7.1	8.4	8.4	3.7
2003	6.7	6.9	7.0	4.5	8.2	7.1	8.4	8.4	3.7
EMTR 2001	26.5	28.0	28.7	-4.6	38.8	29.5	40.8	40.8	-33.8
2002	25.8	28.0	28.7	-11.8	38.8	29.5	40.2	40.2	-34.1
2003	25.8	28.0	28.7	-11.8	38.8	29.5	40.2	40.2	-34.1
Top-rate non-q. sh.									
Cost of capital 2001	5.0	5.1	5.1	3.5	6.1	5.0	5.0	8.6	3.9
2002	4.8	5.0	4.9	3.1	5.9	4.9	4.7	8.5	3.9
2003	4.8	5.0	4.9	3.1	6.0	4.9	5.2	5.7	3.9
EMTR 2001	59.7	60.8	60.5	43.2	67.1	60.1	59.8	76.7	48.6
2002	56.2	58.0	57.6	33.6	64.8	57.0	55.1	75.5	46.2
2003	51.3	53.3	52.9	24.9	61.0	52.5	55.1	59.4	39.7
Top-rate q. sh.									
Cost of capital 2001	5.0	5.1	5.1	3.5	6.1	5.0	5.0	8.6	3.9
2002	4.6	4.8	4.8	3.0	5.8	4.7	4.4	8.5	3.9
2003	4.8	5.0	4.9	3.1	6.0	4.9	5.2	5.7	3.9
EMTR 2001	59.7	60.8	60.5	43.2	67.1	60.1	59.8	76.7	48.6
2002	54.9	56.8	56.3	31.5	63.8	55.5	52.4	75.5	46.4
2003	51.3	53.3	52.9	24.9	61.0	52.5	55.1	59.4	39.7
Mean (sh. mix)									
Cost of capital 2001	5.6	5.7	5.7	3.9	6.8	5.7	6.1	8.6	3.8
2002	5.4	5.6	5.6	3.6	6.6	5.5	5.8	8.5	3.8
2003	5.4	5.6	5.6	3.6	6.7	5.6	6.2	6.6	3.8
EMTR 2001	46.2	47.6	47.5	23.9	55.8	47.5	51.1	64.9	21.9
2002	43.1	45.2	45.1	14.0	53.8	44.9	47.2	63.9	20.2
2003	40.7	42.9	42.8	9.5	52.0	42.8	48.5	51.3	15.7

List of Tables

List of Figures

References

Alworth, J., G. Arachi, R. Hamaui, and R. Violi (2001), *The Taxation of Income from Capital in Italy*, Mimeo.

Baker & McKenzie (Eds.) (1999), *Survey of the Effective Tax Burden in the European Union*, Amsterdam.

Baker & McKenzie (Eds.) (2001), *The Effective Tax Burden of Companies in the Member States of the EU – The Perspective of a Multinational Investor*, Amsterdam.

Bond, S. R. and L. Chennells, *Corporate Income Taxes and Investment: A Comparative Study*, London.

Bordignon, M., S. Giannini, and P. Panteghini (1999), Corporate Taxation in Italy: An Analysis of the 1998 Reform, *Finanzarchiv N. F.* 56, 335-362.

Devereux, M. P. (2003), *Measuring Taxes on Income from Capital*, CESifo Working Paper No. 962, Munich.

Devereux, M. P. and R. Griffith (1998), Taxes and the Location of Production: Evidence from a Panel of US Multinationals, *Journal of Public Economics* 68, 335-367.

Devereux, M. P. and R. Griffith (1999), *The Taxation of Discrete Investment Choices*, IFS Working Paper 98/16 (Revision 2), London.

Devereux, M. P. and R. Griffith (2003), Evaluating Tax Policy for Location Decisions, *International Tax and Public Finance* 10, 107-126.

Devereux, M. P., L. Lammersen, and C. Spengel (2000), *The Effective Levels of Company Taxation in the Member States of the EU*, Report Prepared for the Taxation and Customs Union Directorate General, Warwick.

Devereux, M. P., L. Lammersen, and C. Spengel (2001), *Changes in the Effective Levels of Company Taxation in the Member States of the EU: 1999 to 2001*, Supplementary Report Prepared for the Taxation and Customs Union Directorate General, Mannheim and Warwick.

Elschner, C. and R. Schwager (2004), *The Effective Tax Burden on Highly Qualified Employees: An International Comparison*, ZEW Economic Studies, Heidelberg, forthcoming.

European Commission (1992), *Report of the Committee of Independent Experts on Company Taxation*, Brussels.

European Commission (2002), *Company Taxation in the Internal Market*, Commission Staff Working Paper, COM (2001) 582 final, Luxembourg.

Gutekunst, G., R. Hermann, and L. Lammersen (2003), Deutschland ist kein Niedrigsteuerland, *Perspektiven der Wirtschaftspolitik* 4, 123-136.

Gutekunst, G. and R. Schwager (2001), *The Effective Tax Burden of Companies in Selected Regions of the Extended Alpine Space*, Executive Summary prepared for International Benchmark Forum of BAK Konjunkturforschung Basel AG, Mannheim.

Gutekunst, G. and R. Schwager (2002), *Steuerbelastung von Unternehmen im Alpenraum*, ZEW Wirtschaftsanalysen, Vol. 59, Baden-Baden.

Jacobs, O. H. and C. Spengel (2000), Measurement and Development of the Effective Tax Burden of Companies – An Overview and International Comparison, *Intertax* 28, 334-351.

Jacobs, O. H. and C. Spengel (2002), *Effective Tax Burden in Europe*, ZEW Economic Studies 15, Heidelberg.

Johansson, S.-E. (1961), *Skatt, investering, värdering*, Stockholm.

Johansson, S.-E. (1969), Income Taxes and Investment Decisions, *Swedish Journal of Economics* 71, 104-110.

King, M. A. and D. Fullerton (Eds.) (1984), *The Taxation of Income from Capital*, Chicago/London.

Knirsch, D. (2002), *Neutrality-Based Effective Tax Rates*, Tübinger Diskussionsbeiträge 249, Tübingen.

Lammersen, L. (1999), *Die zinsbereinigte Einkommen- und Gewinnsteuer – Ökonomische Analyse eines aktuellen Reformvorschlages*, Forum Finanzwissenschaft 16, Nürnberg.

Lammersen, L. (2002), *The Measurement of Effective Tax Rates: Common Themes in Business Management and Economics*, ZEW Discussion Paper No. 02-46, Mannheim.

Lammersen, L. (2003), Investitionsentscheidungen und Steueraufkommen bei zinsbereinigter Besteuerung, *Recht der Internationalen Wirtschaft* 49, 938-945.

OECD (1991), *Taxing Profits in a Global Economy: Domestic and International Issues*, Paris.

OECD (2001), *Tax Ratios: A Critical Survey*, OECD Tax Policy Studies No. 5, Paris.

Oldenburg, A. (1998), Zur Ermittlung effektiver Grenzsteuersätze vorteilhafter und unvorteilhafter Handlungsmöglichkeiten in Anknüpfung an den Ansatz von König, *Schmalenbachs Zeitschrift für betriebswirtschaftliche Forschung* 50, 41-48.

Richter, W. F., H. Seitz, and W. Wiegard (1996), Steuern und unternehmensbezogene Staatsausgaben als Standortfaktoren, in: Siebert, H. (Ed.), *Steuerpolitik und Standortqualität*, Tübingen, 13-47.

Ruf, M. (2002), *Extending King and Fullerton for Measuring EATR*, Working Paper, University of Mannheim, Mannheim.

Sachverständigenrat zur Begutachtung der gesamtwirtschaftlichen Entwicklung (Council of Economic Experts in Germany) (2001), *Für Stetigkeit – gegen Aktionismus*, Jahresgutachten 2001/02, Stuttgart.

Sachverständigenrat zur Begutachtung der gesamtwirtschaftlichen Entwicklung (Council of Economic Experts in Germany) (2003), *Staatsfinanzen konsolidieren – Steuersystem reformieren*, Jahresgutachten 2003/04, Wiesbaden.

Samuelson, P. A. (1964), Tax Deductibility of Economic Depreciation to Insure Invariant Valuations, *Journal of Political Economy* 72, 604-606.

Schneider, D. (1992), *Investition, Finanzierung und Besteuerung*, 7th edition, Wiesbaden.

Schreiber, U., C. Spengel, and L. Lammersen (2002), Measuring the Impact of Taxation on Investment and Financing Decisions, *Schmalenbach Business Review* 54, 2-23.

Sinn, H.-W. (1987), *Capital Income Taxation and Resource Allocation*, Studies in Mathematical and Managerial Economics 35, Amsterdam.

Sinn, H.-W. (1991), Taxation and the Cost of Capital: The 'Old' View, the 'New' View and Another View, in: Bradford, D. F. (Ed.), *Tax Policy and the Economy* 5, Cambridge, 25-54.

Sørensen, P. B. (1995), Changing Views of the Corporate Income Tax, *National Tax Journal* 48, 279-294.

Spengel, C. (2003), *Internationale Unternehmensbesteuerung in der Europäischen Union*, Düsseldorf.

Spengel, C. and L. Lammersen (2001), Methoden zur Messung und zum Vergleich von internationalen Steuerbelastungen, *Steuer und Wirtschaft* 78, 222-238.

Willenborg, F. (2003), La Taxe Professionelle *[sic!]* – Die französische Gewerbesteuer, *Internationale Wirtschaftsbriefe* 14.5.2003, Section 5/Group 2/1353-1358.

Winner, Hannes (2000), *Unternehmensbesteuerung in Europa*, Baden-Baden and Vienna.

Wurmsdobler, N. (2002), *Steuerreform und effektive Grenzsteuerbelastungen in Deutschland und Österreich*, Frankfurt.

Zodrow, G. R. (1991), On the 'Traditional' and 'New' Views of Dividend Taxation, *National Tax Journal* 44, 497-509.

MIX
Papier | Fördert gute Waldnutzung
FSC® C083411

Kolibri 360 GmbH
Ferdinand-Jühlke-Straße 7
99095 Erfurt, Deutschland
produktsicherheit@kolibri360.de